SOVEREIGNTY

BOOKS BY JEAN BETHKE ELSHTAIN

Public Man, Private Woman: Women in Social and Political Thought

Editor, The Family in Political Thought

Meditations on Modern Political Thought

Women and War

Co-Editor, Women, Militarism, and War

Editor, Just War Theory

Power Trips and Other Journeys

Coauthor, But Was It Just?: Reflections on the Persian Gulf War

Democracy on Trial

Coeditor, Politics and the Human Body

Real Politics: At the Center of Everyday Life

Augustine and the Limits of Politics

Who Are We?: Critical Reflections, Hopeful Possibilities

New Wine and Old Bottles: International Politics and Ethical Discourse

Coauthor, Religion and American Public Life

Jane Addams and the Dream of American Democracy

Editor, The Jane Addams Reader

Just War Against Terror

SOVEREIGNTY

GOD, STATE, AND SELF

The Gifford Lectures

Jean Bethke Elshtain

BASIC
BOOKS

A MEMBER OF THE PERSEUS BOOKS GROUP
NEW YORK

Copyright © 2008 by Jean Bethke Elshtain
Published by Basic Books,
A Member of the Perseus Books Group

Books published by Basic Books are available at special discounts for bulk purchases in the
United States by corporations, institutions, and other organizations. For more information,
please contact the Special Markets Department at the Perseus Books Group, 2300 Chestnut
Street, Suite 200, Philadelphia, PA 19103, or call (800) 810-4145, ext. 5000, or e-mail
special.markets@perseusbooks.com.

Designed by Timm Bryson
Set in 12-pt. BulmerMT

A CIP catalog record for this book is available from the Library of Congress.
ISBN–13: 978-0-465-03759-9
10 9 8 7 6 5 4 3 2 1

TO THE MEMORY OF MY PARENTS

Paul George Bethke and Helen Lind Bethke
and for
Dr. Harry Rosenberg,
who taught me to love the Middle Ages

We all carry within us our places of exile, our crimes and our ravages. But our task is not to unleash them on the world; it is to fight them in ourselves and others.

—Albert Camus

I knew, always, that I would be a worker in the vineyard, as are all men and women living at the same time, whether they are aware of it or not.

—Czeslaw Milosz

CONTENTS

PREFACE

The bulky envelope, forwarded to my Nashville, Tennessee, home from Chicago, bore the return address: University of Edinburgh. "Funny," I mused, "I don't think I know anyone at Edinburgh." I opened the letter and entered into that condition of happy shock known to every person invited to be a Gifford lecturer. Being a lecturer in this most distinguished series is an unstated yearning for laborers in the vineyards of moral philosophy, theology, and, though something of a stretch, political theory. As I am not officially a philosopher, nor can I claim a theology degree, a Gifford appointment seemed a bit out of reach. But . . . then . . . there was Gifford lecturer, Hannah Arendt, she who insisted she was a political *theorist*, not a political philosopher, and that a good bit hung on the difference. This was cold comfort, of course, as who among us—certainly not I—would put ourselves in the same camp as the learned and erudite Arendt. Thus I had resigned myself—as a hedge against disappointment, no doubt—that a Gifford appointment would likely pass me by.

My delight at being included in the table of worthies is felt keenly. To be sure, the emotion that follows close upon delight is fear and intimidation. So many years . . . so many great books. At one point these considerations must be put aside. One does what one does, for better or worse. What I do is political theory with ethics as the heart of the matter. I decided long ago that one could no more separate the study of politics from ethics than one could hold back the tides. Important, then, to bring the ethics embedded in one's political analysis to the fore as a constituent feature of what one has to say. I am enormously grateful to the Gifford selection committee for giving me the opportunity to explore in depth an issue that I have probed for over a decade now: sovereignty. How does one begin to take the measure of this protean topic? I begin here by reviewing my past work and noting the relevance of previous books to this study.

In my scholarly work and my life, I have learned that one cannot erect a bright line separating what we call public from what we call private. This was the subject of my first book. The issue of public in relation to private haunts me yet.[1] No matter what the topic at hand, one can refract it in such a way that the public and private, the political and the personal, come into play. This involves no identity between public and private; indeed, that particular claim intimated noxious outcomes that I assay in yet another book.[2] Public and private attaches itself to a third distinction—some insist a bright line—between what we call religion and what we call politics. It is this particular distinction, and its interweaving with public and private, that figures importantly in *Sovereignty: God, State, and Self.*

A bit of personal history will help the reader to appreciate the importance of this latter distinction to the book in hand. Let me take the reader back to a particular time, namely, the late 1960s. This was not a calm time culturally and politically speaking, as all Americans of a certain age well remember. The civil rights movement was in full swing. President Kennedy had been assassinated. Protest surrounding the war in Vietnam was heating up. The counterculture was preaching a "make love, not war" gospel. Some of us were struggling to understand what was going on and to sort out just where we "fit" in the overall scheme of things. Who were we anyway—as a people, as singular persons? I was at the time a graduate student in politics and, with a few rare exceptions, none of my graduate courses in political science touched on any of these matters. We were more or less obliged to leave such burning concerns off to one side when we entered the classroom.

The reigning epistemology was a variant on positivism called behaviorism. Its devotees proclaimed from the rooftops that the study of politics should be cleansed from the smudginess, messiness, and taint of "values." A chasm separated descriptive and evaluative statements, we were told. There were facts—a kind of translucent relationship between a "name" and its object was assumed—or there were "subjective" things like "values," "biases," "emotional preferences," none of which had any cognitive status. According to the critics, one wound up with a crummy deal: reductionistic "scientism" and subjectivistic emotionalism.

The upshot? Most of what people had to say politically, most of the emotions stirred up by politics, most of the language in and through which real politics was conducted, was consigned to a conceptual netherworld. No wonder I and so many of my classmates were vexed. We had entered graduate school on fire with ideas and passions, including political passions about creating a more fair, more free, more decent America, only to learn that these were "biases" that one could attach to the "facts" if one so desired. But such ideas and passions could never pass muster as a feature of the scientific study of politics.[3]

The hard version of the fact/value distinction made little sense to me. It made short shrift of concerns flowing from religion, or any other strong, normative commitments. In the narrow political science world, these were biases with no warrant for truth. Although my scholastic interests at the time did not touch on religion explicitly, they did revolve around consideration of the link between political inquiry and moral imperatives presupposed by classical theorists in the history of political thought. Political theory became a refuge for me precisely because I could take up the "big" questions—the nature of political order, justice, freedom, liberty, community—in the historic texts. Complex questions arose from the great tradition, and studying the canon drew me into a world of vital debates.

I observed, however, that something funny had happened on the road to canon creation in political theory: The "religious thinkers," with few exceptions, were missing in action. As well, the religious dimensions of those thinkers who were central to the canon were often ignored or diminished. For example, John Locke's scriptural references from his classic *Two Treatises on Government* were often eliminated from consideration, as if it was obligatory of Locke to toss that "stuff" in but one should attach little real meaning to it.[4] Locke's religion didn't figure, save to position him as someone doing the sensible and right thing in severing statescraft from soulcraft in his famous *Letter on Toleration*. The thinkers whose religious commitments couldn't be scraped off like so much stale icing from a two-day-old cake were admitted to the political theory world in excised form. Perhaps portions of St. Augustine's *City of God* were taken up but not, certainly, his *Confessions*.

As for explicitly theological titles like *On the Trinity* or Augustine's great arguments against the Manicheans and the Pelagians—that was the stuff of arcana, interesting only to that odd duck, the theologian. Perhaps a bit of St. Thomas Aquinas on the law from his *Summa Contra Gentiles*, but the reformers—Luther and Calvin—were nowhere to be seen. I recall to this day how transgressive I felt when I first began teaching Western political thought and assigned Martin Luther's classic essay *On the Freedom of the Christian* in the same section in which we read Machiavelli's *The Prince*, insisting, as I did so, that Luther's text was arguably more important over the long run of Western history as it presaged profound alterations in the structures of selfhood, understandings of freedom, views of everyday life, ideas of authority and rule, and on and on. That this was a "bold move" on my part brings a smile to my face from my perch decades later.

Working on my first book, I incorporated thinkers that were usually omitted from the study of political theory. I further determined that ethical matters would take center stage. As I wrote *Public Man, Private Woman*, my assessment of my own state of mind was that whatever religious belief clung to me was scarcely visible in an overt way. Looking back, I realize that my critique of various thinkers from the canon, as well as of certain schools, tendencies, and ideologies in feminism, often reflected, if in derivative form, religious (specifically Christian in origin) ideas and commitments I scarcely knew I held at the time. I refer to such weighty matters as ontological presuppositions, anthropological considerations, ideas of human purpose and dignity, birth and death, the moral development of the child, and "the ethical polity," as I called it. It took others to point out to me, often in the form of rather tart criticism that I had permitted too much "religious stuff" to creep into political theory. But the die was cast and I have, for thirty years now, worked to build bridges between religious and political concepts and understandings—more overtly so over the past fifteen years.

Being asked to join the University of Chicago Divinity School in 1995 gave me the opportunity to pursue with renewed vigor my effort to include the political dimensions in the texts of the great theologians and, in turn, the theological dimensions of the great political theorists in treatments of Western political thought. In other words, for the first time, I began working in reverse (so to speak) by bringing political theorists to bear on the indispensable works in theology. I mention "theology" with a certain trepidation. Although I have written an appreciative exegesis of St. Augustine's magisterial *De Trinitate*—as part of a rather modest book on Augustine—I remain an amateur in theological studies.[5] I say this not to be coy but, rather, from a profession of my own limits. Despite this I seem to venture onto theological turf with an alarming degree of regularity and thus far I have escaped the scholarly equivalent of being ridden out of town on a rail. This no doubt says more about the generosity of critics than it does of my own expertise. I am at it once again. One cannot write about sovereignty and God and escape theology. To the contrary, one is in the thick of it.

How come? Isn't sovereignty primarily a *political* concept after all? I had indeed once thought so. To be sure, I uttered, with all Protestants, a version of the Lord's Prayer that ends with these words: "For thine is the kingdom, and the power, and the glory. Amen." This would seem to locate sovereignty full square in, or as, divinity itself. Kingdom, power, and glory sum up much of what students of political history summon when they recall the glories and treacheries of classical sovereignty in the majesty of kings and kingdoms.

I had not really studied any history of sovereignty, or the nexus between God and kingdoms, as a young student of government—this was only just before the study of politics became "political science." As a student in several IR (international relations) courses as an undergraduate, I had, of course, learned that "sovereignty" is the *locus classicus* of the state, the *sine qua non* of political life. Sovereignty was the place from which one began. It was a concept to be accepted rather than explored—that had nigh ontological status. It was the membership card in the world of nation-states.

It occurred to me that this was a rather remarkable concept when I was working on my book *Women and War*.[6] It seemed astonishing that a notion linked to medieval *pro patria mori*—to die for the father or the feudal lord—had transmogrified over the centuries, becoming attached to love and affection for one's national home. The most common juridical or legitimate political configuration, the sovereign state, continued to underwrite the ideal (contested, to be sure) of dying for one's homeland.

This sent me to the early modern sovereigntists, foremost if not first among these the redoubtable Thomas Hobbes. With Hobbes one finds the pretensions of sovereignty majestically enshrined as he writes of the sovereign's awesome power; his terrible power; his not-to-be-trifled-with power that is subject to none save the sovereign God, although Hobbes's sovereign God seems not to play much of a role in chastening earthly sovereignty, one of the key attributes of God for medieval theologians—at least until the emergence and imperfect triumph of nominalism. For with nominalism—as we shall see—construal of the deity shifted away from the lushness of Augustine's trinitarianism with its heavy emphasis on the Mediator (the second person of the trinity); away from the elaborated and Aristotelianized trinitarianism of St. Thomas Aquinas, to a radical stress on God's absolute power and his willfulness. It further occurred to me that there was something of that absoluteness and willfulness in early modern (which is to say postmedieval) construal of political sovereignty.

It followed that perhaps—just perhaps—theological understandings had migrated into early modern political sovereigntism. The more I thought about this, the more sense it made, given Hobbes's nominalism and his ill-tempered but witty assaults on the "churchmen," the Scholastics and their theological and moral realism, as contrasted with nominalism. At least as interesting was the undeniable fact that the theological backdrop to political concepts had fallen away in the study of political thought; indeed, there were some editions of Hobbes's great work *Leviathan* that eliminated the entire second half on "A Christian Commonwealth" and "The Kingdom of Darkness." Hobbes's project was a political theology, but the theology fell out of the picture as the "canon" of Western political thought got "normalized."

Perchance, I mused, there was a connection between the God of Augustine and Thomas and the notions of political life that prevailed in the Middle Ages, recalling my master's degree in medieval history attained before the late 1960s hit and we all decided we had to study something "relevant." (For me this had meant political science.) I now consider myself fortunate for having studied medieval and early modern history as the medieval epoch displayed a bewildering variety of overlapping jurisdictions, none of which could claim de facto the kind of absolutism that sovereigns began to embrace from the sixteenth century or so on. I also speculated that the papal doctrine of *plenitudo potestatis*, or a plenitude of power proclaimed de jure, added to the revival of Roman law, served as underpinning for early modern notions of political sovereignty. All of this is explored in detail in the text through historic reconstruction and interpretive political theory.

To this already complicated picture, one additional piece had to be added to make the matter complete, namely, modern notions of self-sovereignty. I pondered whether there might be a connection between prior constructions of state sovereignty, with notions of a possessed and inviolable territory, a kind of autarchy, and the celebrations of self-sovereignty and triumph of the individual will to power in which we are currently awash. What was the philosophical backdrop to this astonishing notion of the self? For there are alternative ways of thinking about persons that are more modest concerning how much we define and control our very selves. How did all of these pieces go together? I followed my hunch that the modern sovereign self owes a good deal to the modern territorial state: It is as if that entity got parceled out to constitute so many mini-sovereignties—ontological individualisms—in much of modern theory. The cultural critique and constructive argumentation in the book's concluding chapters take up this challenge.

With these musings in mind, I began stalking sovereignty. In residence at the Library of Congress as the holder of the Maguire Chair of Ethics, fall of 2003, I decided to proceed "logically" by searching for titles under "sovereignty." This message came back: "Your search retrieved more records than can be displayed. Only the first 10,000 will be shown." Well, that was a relief! I gave up proceeding "logically" nearly as soon as I had embraced that strategy and decided to follow my hunches, in full awareness that I could but scratch the surface of this inexhaustible topic. These preliminary skirmishes led me to the rueful acknowledgment that my entry on sovereignty for the *Encyclopedia Americana*, 1997, limited as it was by space constraints, posited more than it proved. The Gifford lectures, and this follow-up volume, have given me the wonderful opportunity to make good on my preliminary musings and hunches. But it is a frustrating business withal knowing, as I do, that I am painting with broad strokes and that the devil is always in the details. Still . . . trying to bring some form to the canvas is the first step before one fills in the details.

A heads-up to readers: The discussion of God's sovereignty will likely have the strongest appeal to historians of theological and political thought. I rather unabashedly bring back the notion of the "history of ideas"—an approach that seems to have run afoul of criticism in recent decades. This is a pity as, well done, tracing the evolution and migration of ideas is an important, even exhilarating, enterprise. This means, among other things, that one cannot abstract ideas from the textures, the warp and woof, of history. There exists a huge gulf that separates abstract concepts that the political theorist cannot do without, from abstractedness, draining all the messy life out of one's subject matter. Without concrete history, political thought becomes a gnostic enterprise—all words, no flesh; all spirit, no-body. Then, disastrously, that disembodied enterprise invites schemes and ideologies that are imposed over the living, incarnate tissue of human life. One is left staring at the ruins wrought by this sort of arrogance when it is brought to bear on political and social life, even as one recognizes the palpable inadequacies of philosophies that are, quite literally, *nowhere.* The chapters on God's sovereignty are a complex bringing together of theological themes, teasing out their political implications. The chapters on political sovereignty that follow work, so to speak, in reverse, as I unpack the theological themes imbedded in political argumentation, offering as I move along interpretations of key political thinkers in the West. These chapters involve nothing less than a retelling of the story of Western political thought.[7]

The final chapters on self-sovereignty offer cultural criticisms and constructive alternatives. Readers devoted to contemporary cultural criticism may turn directly to the self-sovereignty chapters and begin reading; hopefully, this in turn will send them back to the earlier chapters in order to figure out "how come."

As I grow older and, hopefully, a bit wiser, I am ever mindful that St. Bernard of Clairvaux's observation that "we stand on the shoulders of giants" is a truth that engenders humility and an appropriate awareness of the finiteness of one's own enterprises. We are all laborers in the vineyard and, if we are lucky, we add just a bit to the storehouse of wisdom and knowledge that is our shared human inheritance. One of my persistent worries about our own time is that we may be squandering a good bit of that rich heritage through processes of organized "forgetting," a climate of opinion that encourages presentism rather than a historic perspective that reminds us that we are always boats moving against the current, "borne back ceaselessly into the past," in F. Scott Fitzgerald's memorable words from *The Great Gatsby*. This historic recognition should not occasion resentment or dour heaviness; rather, it should instill gratitude. As this book drew to a close, I realized that it was no culminating magnum opus—few books are—but, rather, a contribution to the shared memory of our time and place. And that is enough.

Jean Bethke Elshtain
Chicago, Illinois, and Nashville, Tennessee, fall 2006

1

SOVEREIGN GOD:
FROM LOGOS TO WILL

THAT GOD ALONE IS SOVEREIGN IN ALL THINGS, IMMUTABLE, THE FULLNESS OF truth, reason, and goodness was an article of faith—faith being the most perfect act of human reason—within the regnant Thomism of Europe's High Middle Ages. God's sovereignty over the human intellect held that human beings could come to God and discern his existence and divinity through the light of intellect and reason. Faith was not cast in opposition to reason, as many now have it, most often critics who seek to discredit faith as irrational emotionalism. Too, for our medieval forebears in the West, human law should aspire to emulate the laws of God. Should human law deny or transgress divine law, the lesser (human) law must give way before the greater. It followed that kings who became tyrants, hence lawless, were despots who might be removed from office, for they had defied its normative requirements.

But something happened to this cluster of imperatives as theological nominalism and voluntarism—to be explained in detail below—challenged the theological realism that held there was a moral order, discernable through reason and available to all. This chapter will be challenging for the reader—it was certainly challenging for the author—as we trace the movement from God as Logos to God as will on the level of thought *and* as proleptic to modern sovereign political configurations.

The central question and puzzlement is this: If God's power is absolute and immutable, is God in any way bound, or is, instead, God free to undo what he has already done, overturn the laws of nature, perhaps, or even bring creation to an end? At first blush, it isn't easy to discern what the political implications of these theological issues might be. That will be our task as we unpack construals of God's sovereignty and their possible implications for the earthly tasks of fashioning communities, kingdoms, principalities, laws, and justice.

There are at least three sets of considerations that confront us: (a) God's sovereignty as a theological proposition and the nature of that divine power and authority, (b) the relative positions of spiritual and secular authority on the level of thought once Christianity had introduced that distinction, and (c) the working out "on the ground" of these respective authorities, including whether either can be said to be sovereign and, if so, how.[1] Our task here is to describe a "moral concept" of sovereignty that can be distinguished from the later, territorial one with which we are all familiar: sovereignty as the *sine qua non* of states.

One begins with Sovereign God.[2] What does it mean to say "God the Father Almighty, Maker of Heaven and Earth"? This moral concept of sovereignty was *not* attached to a notion of territory but assigned as one of God's powers, the heart of God's authority over all of creation. Just how terrifying, comforting, or enduring a concept is this? God's sovereignty has passed the endurance test, although challenges have been mounted as to whether God is, in fact, sovereign and in what ways it might be said that he is. Throughout history Christians have been terrified and comforted by the idea. For this is a sovereign God who empties himself of his power and binds himself to human beings through the second person of the Trinity, Jesus the Christ, who is born, crucified, and risen again in Christian theology and doctrine.[3]

AUGUSTINE ON THE TRINITY

A place to begin "working" these questions is with St. Augustine and his magisterial treatment of the Christian doctrine of the triune God.[4]

Augustine understood that God's all-powerful immutability gives him dominion over all his creatures and, further, that God's power and glory is all-encompassing, so that not even a hair on a human head goes unnumbered. Human beings are subject to their creator. But how are we to "think" the question of God? Can we in any way rise to him? Does he in any way come down to us? The answer to each of these questions, for Augustine, is yes. To him it was clear that ever "since the Prologue to the Gospel of John, the concept of *logos* has been at the very center of our Christian faith in God," in the words of Pope Benedict XVI, who adds: "*Logos* signifies reason, meaning, or even 'word'—a meaning, therefore, that is Word, that is relationship, that is creative. The God who is *logos* guarantees the intelligibility of the world, the intelligibility of our existence, the aptitude of reason to know God . . . and the reasonableness of God . . . even though his understanding infinitely surpasses ours and to us may often appear to be darkness."[5] Christians proclaimed the word is love before the Beatles: "Say the word and you'll be free." Reason and love are not severed as both are embodied in a person (the second person of the Trinity) and that person is love incarnate. This person/love is accessible to human reason, if imperfectly: We are not struck dumb at the thought of the mystery. It is to this complex of notions, and the vision of God's power, justice, love, and mercy, that Christian thinkers attached the notion of the "good news" despite all the miseries of the world.[6]

Of the unity and equality of each person of the Trinity, Augustine has no doubt. But there are tricky and insistent matters that nag. One of these has to do with God the Father Almighty linked as he was to visions of power and sovereignty, and how it is possible that he is not superior to God as incarnate, a human person. How can they be coequal if one "gives" the other to us?[7] If we cast this query through the prism of sovereignty: How can God's sovereignty be divided? Augustine responds: To the form of God, the son is equal; in the form of man born of woman, under the law, he is a servant who came that "he might redeem those who were under the law."[8] For example, we say of human beings that they are both body and soul—ensouled bodies—but we don't for a moment believe that each person appears in the world as body with a "soulful" sovereign self attached as a kind of permanent shadow to the lesser corporeal self, reminiscent of Robert Louis Stevenson's "My Shadow," a poem for children that begins "I have a little shadow that goes in and out with me,/And what can be the use of him is more than I can see."[9] So God is both father and son—and the one is not a pale shadow of the other.[10]

For Augustine, a creative intelligence lies behind this world and the beings that call it home. Human beings, created in God's image (*imago Dei*) participate in God's creativity. But it is pride and folly to pretend one can emulate God directly.[11] There are *limits*—intrinsic, not accidental or contingent—to our capacity to understand fully, to divine (if you will) the Divine person(s). Touch sets a limit; sight sets a limit; speech sets a limit. Augustine is especially brilliant on speech and language, those imperfect ways human beings attest to what they have experienced, contemplated, or come to understand.

A Dog Really Is Man's Best Friend

Most famous among Augustine's musings on speech is the way sentient creatures are divided by linguistic difference. In the famous Book XIX, chapter 7, of *The City of God,* he concludes that most human beings "would be more cheerful with [his] dog for company than with a foreigner."[12] Why is that? Because of the difficulties, at times the seeming impossibilities, of communication if two people speak different languages. Even with members of one's own speech community, including one's family and friends, full transparency of understanding is never possible.[13] That said, Augustine is *primus inter pares* of those who have, through the centuries, reminded us of the murkiness and impenetrability of speech.[14]

Rue the inadequacies of our terms of understanding as we will, we have no choice but to follow the conventions of human language. We cannot leap out of the world and attain an Archimedean point or devise a meta-language purged of earthly usage by fallible creatures. It follows that human beings possess only a "creature's knowledge" that comes in "faded colours, compared with the knowledge that comes when it is known in the Wisdom of God." Godlike wisdom is not attainable on this earth.[15] Reason "of itself could never directly reach the truth; it acted in the light of faith; and was essentially an accompaniment to man in his transitory state as voyager in this world."[16]

Why belabor these matters? For two reasons. First, because what Augustine is about in *The Trinity* is to offer thoughts that were taken up by those among the faithful who "think what they are doing," in Hannah Arendt's famous phrase. Second, because articulation of *limits* intrinsic to sovereignty, whether limits God has freely imposed on himself, limits to earthly rule, or limits to human self-governance, are central to this study and conspicuous, at times, by their absence in human history and thought. Where sovereign God is concerned, Augustine's teaching stresses just how shocking the incarnation was to classical philosophy and anthropology and, further, how one must have humility to see this truth. Christ, he tells us, taught a fisherman's wisdom, not a philosophy available only to an elite few.[17] The concept of the Trinity redeems human reason and willing, thus dignifying the person as a whole.

Despite the intricacies Augustine puts before us, there is something beautifully stark about the triune God's nature.[18] God is "good without quality . . . great without quantity . . . the Creator who lacks nothing, who rules but from no position, and who contains all things without an external form, as being whole everywhere without limitation of space, as eternal without time, as making mutable things without any change in Himself, and as a Being without passion."[19]

Augustine reminds us that human beings are earthy, fallible, and unable to sustain perfectly certain abstract truths, especially philosophic understanding that omits grace and love.[20] Claiming otherwise is epistemic presumptiveness, a flawed embrace of the "Selfsame," Augustine's word for the immutability that is God's alone. Apparently far removed from the political issues taken up in any discussion of sovereignty, this point will be vital. Human finiteness is the grounding of any form of human life, including political life. Our finiteness prompted many antique philosophers to downgrade that which is mutable and decays—the body, in the overall scheme of things—having seen in knowledge that comes through the body only detritus that the real "knower" must slough off.[21]

We come to know and to love God through our ensouled bodies. As subjects or citizens, we find ourselves in political formations that culminate—at least since the late Middle Ages—in structures we define as sovereign.[22] Because trinity can be represented, in language, law, philosophy, story, and art, it takes on a worldly character. We come to see and to know trinity through understanding, imagining, naming, willing, and love.[23] Augustine offers an ingenious probing of the dynamics of the mind in a world of bodies, a world in which bodies confine us and free us at one and the same time. If one forgets that he or she is not God, one forgets the neighbor, and solipsism takes over, for human beings can never be three in one—they can only "imitate" the God they believe is all-powerful, a solipsistic God, not the trinitarian God of Augustinian Christianity.[24] It is easier to imagine a solipsistic God isolated in transcendent splendor if one plucks the self out of the web of entanglements that are the stuff of a human life.[25] This Augustine never did.

It is the God of a purely contemplative philosophy that is "essentially self-centered: thought contemplating itself. The God of faith is basically defined by the category of relationship."[26] This God comes down to us through the son so that we might rise to him: The relational dimension is never severed. There is much more that might be said, but this must suffice for now: God is the apogee of knowledge and of love. Even as one believes in order to understand (the famous *credo ut intelligam*), so God passes our understanding. We know him through his deeds and a love that gave his "only begotten Son" that we might be redeemed.[27] Augustine reminds his readers that the Christ now "preached throughout the world is not a Christ who is adorned with an earthly kingdom, nor a Christ rich in earthly possessions, nor a Christ shining with any earthly splendour, but Christ crucified."[28]

GOD'S SOVEREIGNTY AND HUMAN SOCIAL LIFE IN THE EARTHLY CITY

An understanding as powerful as Augustine's was destined to have a profound and lasting impact in a society that defined itself as "Christian."

Augustinianism was the dominant way of thinking about God and earthly
matters until the triumph of St. Thomas Aquinas and Scholasticism.[29]
Medieval theology and philosophy is inseparable from the ways our
forebears from the late Antique World through the late Middle Ages
sorted out a tale of two kingdoms, or powers, laid down by Jesus when he
picked up the coin and stated tantalizingly: "Render unto Caesar that
which is Caesar's and unto God that which is God's,"[30] vexing Christians—and more than Christians—ever since. Jesus' distinction invites
one to ask about the nature of the two sides of the coin. Is there a single
power or are there two? Or more?

My focus is the internal, or what we call domestic, model of human
social and political life. Is power divisible or is it singular and brooks no
competition? Do we face a monistic, plenipotentiary sovereign—or a
plurality of powers, multiple authoritative sites within a single body
politic? This is one way the sovereignty question is refracted on the
ground, not so much in a causal line from God's sovereignty but, rather,
as an emanation of theological contestation, as I hope to demonstrate.

Of course, Augustine was not primarily a political thinker. He cannot
be looked to as a systematizer of political ideas or categories; nevertheless, his thought is rich with implication and, at times, explicit commentary on earthly rule. Augustine's acerbic articulation of pridefulness in
politics and the manner in which pride spurs unjust dominion, retains
its resonance. Here Augustine on Rome: A city characterized by an
excess of pride is one "which holds nations in enslavement, but is itself
dominated by that very lust of domination."[31] Augustine offers an alternative to the received Ciceronian definition of a commonwealth in Book
II, chapter 21, of his *City of God*, namely, as a people united by a
common sense of interest. Augustine, by contrast, infuses peoplehood
with love and desire, to wit: "A people is the association of a multitude
of rational beings united by a common agreement on the objects of their
love." It follows "that to observe the character of a particular people we
must examine the objects of its love."[32]

The famous Book XIX of *The City of God* is often mined for precepts
about the interests government should serve, including Augustine's arguments against slavery "by nature," for he repudiates Aristotle's claim that

slavery exists "by nature." To the contrary, no one is "naturally" enslaved to another and no human being by nature enjoys absolute dominion over another life. Augustine's definition of a just commonwealth, the question of war, and his analogizing between the peace and the good of various layers, levels, and institutions found within the commonwealth—all can be brought to bear to challenge monistic and solipsistic understandings of God's sovereignty and, as well, the authority of bodies politic. For Augustine, there is a "darkness that attends the life of human society," and this holds within, and cuts across, all levels or circles of human existence, from the *domus*, or household; to the *civitas*, or city; from clans and tribes to great and terrible empires; on to the *orbis terrae*, or the earth; finally, the *cosmos*, or universe, the heaven and the earth.[33] Social life is full of ills and yet to be cherished. The Church could not have made "its first start . . . if the life of the saints were not social."[34]

As to how human beings should organize their earthly living together, Augustine begins with the human person. Whether Christian or not, each has access to a naturalistic morality.[35] For example, God's sentient creatures share deeply embedded strictures against wrongful death, or murder. That is why we recoil in horror at the willful murder of a human being. The family derives from nature and is an institution in which any hierarchy is based as service and crude domination has no legitimate space. Augustine departs from the classic Greek philosophers, however, in refusing to sever the household from the city or, as the Greeks would have it, the *oikos* from the *polis*. Instead, each feeds into the other. Augustine finds in the household "the beginning, or rather a small component part of the city, and every beginning is directed to some end of its own kind, and every component part contributes to the completeness of the whole of which it forms a part. The implication is that domestic peace contributes to the peace of the city, for an ordered harmony of those who live together in a house contributes to the ordered harmony concerning authority and obedience obtaining among citizens."[36]

In Augustine's earthly rule, each beginning carries within it a portion of the whole and the whole overlaps with, and is internally connected to, each part. The life of household, church, and city is a social life erected, initially, on the ground of a basic grammar of human actions and possibilities framed by finitude, by birth and by death. As to the rest, we owe the necessity for earthly rule to the fact of human fallenness. Tainted forever after by the legacy of "original sin," human beings must erect barriers to their worst tendencies even as they seek to realize their best. That is the only legitimate purpose of earthly dominion. Because no one can claim sovereignty in relation to another—authority is something very different—we are not denuded if we give of ourselves to others. Embracing *caritas*, love of the neighbor, or enslaved by *cupiditas*, a drive for more pleasure, more pelf, more power, human beings are caught within the workings-out of this dialectic in every sphere, from family to what we now call state.[37] And in those spheres, Christians share space with others who do not profess Christianity—yet this civil community makes legitimate claims on all, Christians and non-Christians alike.

POLITICS, LOVE, AND NECESSITY

Politics is erected on the altar of necessity, but not reducible to it. Unfortunately, politics offers a grand canvas on which those who prey on others can paint their gruesome pictures. The ruthless leader of the robber band and the avaricious emperor alike need other human beings to work on and to work over. The sin that mars the earthly city is the story of arbitrary power, or the ever-present possibility of such. Within this common mortal life, Augustine offers an understanding of earthly dominion into which love, *caritas*, enters. This does not solve the problems of politics but it offers intimations of a form of earthly rule not reducible to domination. Although Augustine does not speak in this way, it is surely the case that the pretensions of an absolutist notion of sovereignty aid and abet a lust to dominate and must be repudiated. Earthly institutions make legitimate claims on us but these can never be absolute and should not be divinized.[38] Within *each* earthly city, the saved and unsaved come together: That is a given. At the same time, one can distinguish between better and worse earthly cities.

How does one make such evaluations? Augustine asks us to reflect on the way a city is "turned." Does it live exclusively according to its own

designs? Do its rules reflect the goods of justice, civic peace, and fellowship? On this earth, there are two rules all can follow: "First, to do no
harm to anyone, and, secondly, to help everyone whenever possible."[39]
There must be compromises between conflicting human wills lest human social life be turned into the nightmare later dreamt by Thomas
Hobbes in chapter 13 of *The Leviathan*, a world in which all human beings prey on all others and life is nasty, brutish, and short. The heavenly
city—the society of the faithful on earthly pilgrimage—is not an earthly
city unto itself; rather, citizens of the city of God are sprinkled throughout multiple earthly cities within which they should be decent, obedient
citizens in full awareness that the earthly kingdom is, like the human beings that populate it, finite, partial, incomplete, estranged. But that does-
n't mean justice should be ignored or that love of neighbor doesn't
pertain. It also lifts up the possibility of a secular faith, appropriately relativized, that *all* citizens may share.

Justice, or giving to each his or her due, affords scope for earthly
righteousness and can be a form of love. Depredation, radical suffering,
arbitrariness imposed by earthly authority betrays a depraved love of
domination rather than a love of neighbor. Augustine doesn't give us the
complete architecture of the form of rule most compatible with his understandings of love and justice. It seems safe to say, however, that it would be
a type of governance that builds in barriers to cruel and capricious
behavior on the part of earthly rulers. Augustine knew only the experience
of the late empire but he was well aware that there were other possibilities,
including that of the patriarchs in the scriptural story of the people of Israel. No earthly city can exist without legitimate authority; nor can rule
proceed without a capacity for coercion, as wrongdoers must be brought
to heel lest they carry out a reign of terror unimpeded.[40]

Alas, with the Romans even "peace" was often more cruel than "war,"
Augustine opines. Plunder is not synonymous with politics, however,
and, as I already indicated, a decent order characterized by a measure of
justice is the heart of the matter. Augustine appreciates what today international relations thinkers call *the security dilemma*. People never possess a kingdom "so securely as not to fear subjugation by their enemies;
in fact, such is the instability of human affairs that no people has ever
been allowed such a degree of tranquility as to remove all dread of hos-

tile attacks on their life in this world."[41] For nearly all Christian thinkers, the Fall occasioned earthly rule and set the basis for reflections on it. Before the Fall, there was no need to adjudicate between "conflicting human wills" as there was no perverse willfulness. This shared backdrop did not lead to unanimity among Christian theologians on the nature, ends, and dignity of earthly rule, including whether it can be said to be "sovereign" and, if so, how and in what ways.

REGNUM AND SACERDOTIUM: COOPERATION AND CONFLICT

Augustine penned his great works before the articulation of the dominant theory of rule for a thousand years of Western Christian history: the so-called two swords doctrine. The two swords are *regnum* and *sacerdotium*, respectively, earthly and spiritual dominion, roughly. There was much that Augustine had not addressed and that required sorting out as Christianity rose to become the official religion of the empire. The Bishop of Rome emerged over time as the de facto if not de jure wielder of power and authority in the West (the deposition of the last Emperor in the West occurred in 476 AD). When the Western and Eastern halves of the Empire split, they went their respective ways and developed distinctive modes of political organization and theology. In the Eastern half of the Empire, or Byzantium, there emerged an amalgam of the forces of what we now call "church" and "state" that was given the name of "caesaro-papism."[42]

It was in the West that dominion took the form of clarifying the spiritual "sword" and the secular or earthly "sword," to use the metaphor made doctrine by Pope Gelasius I, and the authority and dominion of each.[43] Gelasius proffered a doctrine of imperial or secular rule (*regnum*) and spiritual or episcopal rule (*sacerdotium*) that laid the groundwork for subsequent thinking and controversy surrounding *ecclesia* and empires, and kingdoms and kingships. Although the disintegration of effective imperial authority in the West invited the Bishop of Rome to assume authority as a necessity, it was also the case that Roman pontiffs used the opportunity to define the nature of earthly and spiritual dominion, respectively.

The power of the Roman bishop rested, in the first instance, on the scriptural deeding to St. Peter by Christ articulated in Matthew 16:18-19 and interpreted to mean that the pope possessed the power to "bind and loose" on earth.[44] Assuming this authority, Pope Gelasius drew upon the history of Roman rule and law of which the successors of Peter were the direct heir and on whom they modeled their episcopal offices.[45] He insisted that pope and emperor (or earthly ruler, by extension) enjoyed their own spheres of *responsibility*, although the spiritual "sword" of authority possessed a higher dignity than could be claimed by imperial or royal power. The sacred and the political were *not* welded together into one sovereign, monistic structure—despite the misleading characterizations one hears frequently labeling the medieval period one of theocracy. Not so.[46]

As Augustine had insisted, earthly rule and dominion and spiritual offices had different ends and were directed toward distinctive purposes. The one, the spiritual, gestured toward the eschaton, that which was eternal. The other, the secular or temporal, was time-bound, a part of history that would come to an end. If Christ was King of Kings and Lord of Lords, no one else could make any such proclamation or claim any such identity on this earth save in utterances that bordered on blasphemy. Not being God incarnate, no one else could emulate this fully.[47] Political aims must never be cast in the language of ultimacy. They are, at best, penultimate as they cannot claim the entirety of human loyalty and hope, thought and action. Now, to be sure, some later medieval popes mounted claims of a breathtaking "plenitude" of papal power (of which more later), but the distinction itself, the "two swords," was never foresworn. Although there was no straightforward and simple identification of spiritual and temporal authority, there was overlap between the two that made conflict inevitable between competing jurisdictions. The saga of sorting this out gave the history of the Western half of Christendom a distinctive dynamic that channele cultural energy, conflict, and contestation.

An intriguing feature to Gelasius's articulation of the two swords theory, noted in his "Letter to the Emperor Anastasius," is the fact that the pontiff reserves *auctoritas,* or authority, to the papacy—this in part because the pope has no coercive power in and through which to back up his authoritative claims: He hasn't the means of force.[48] By contrast, the emperor or monarch, who possesses power, *potestas,* does have the means of force at his disposal. But *auctoritas* enjoys a higher dignity than *potestas.* This particular distinction is key to the perennial question of what made or makes rule, or power, legitimate and authoritative. For now, I will simply note the distinction—as it precludes any claim of overall and complete sovereignty in forms of rule: It assumes an antimonistic doctrine. The question of monism—and the totalistic temptation it trails in its wake—becomes ever more important as we proceed.

In his "Letter to the Emperor Anastasius" Gelasius writes, "Two there are . . . by which this world is ruled: the consecrated authority of priests and the royal power. Of these priests have the greater responsibility, in that they will have to give account before God's judgment seat for those who have been kings of men."[49] Each "sword" is wielded by respective office holders in a legitimate way only insofar as each observes their distinctive competence. No emperor can set himself above "the priesthood" in all things. Although there may be one Christian society, within this unity one finds a plurality or, minimally, a duality of powers. There is one body—to deploy the corporeal metaphor that infused medieval thought of a "body politic"—but two distinct and exalted persons within it. From these few words, centuries of thinking and strife. . . .

From *Jus Gentium* to the Thomistic Synthesis

Important as we go forward is the assumption of a *jus gentium,* or law of the peoples, on which both emperor and pope relied. A systematic articulation of such law was undertaken by one of the last emperors before the final breach between East and West, Justinian with his famous "code," the *Corpus Juris Civilis* in the sixth century. Because all subsequent thinking in the West, at least until the fracturing of Christendom in the sixteenth century, took the form of law-based argument, the importance of the Justinian synthesis of law in the sixth century can scarcely be overstated.[50]

The code proffered the prejudgments by now characteristic of Christian thinking, including the insistence that the subjection of man, and the rule of man by man, is *not* part of the natural order of things but is an inheritance of the Fall. It assumes further a single human nature—or theological anthropology—all are one in and through the faith, relying on St. Paul's *Letter to the Galatians*: "There is neither Jew nor Greek, there is neither bond nor free, there is neither male nor female: For ye are all one in Christ Jesus."[51] An assumption of a shared humanity is required if one is to articulate a *jus gentium*, or law of the peoples; indeed, some such notion is presumptive in current articulations of universal human rights.[52] Law is the expression of this universal community, "endorsed by the sovereign Lordship of God."[53] Central, too, is a *jus naturale*, or natural law, that is permanent and to which particular civil laws should conform.[54]

The seeds are sown for generative tension and conflict between the presumptions of a *jus gentium* and *jus naturale* and, by contrast, the multiple civil or positive laws of particular societies. The guiding assumption held that the foundation of law is accessible to all rational beings: Law is not part of revelation but a feature of the rational foundation of all things human having, therefore, an intrinsic value apart from the coercive or enforcement power of a polity.[55] The binding of the earthly power of sovereign kings or emperors proceeds apace, with the *Corpus Juris Civilis* in the background. So much is this the case that by the ninth century the insistence that earthly authority is limited by its end, namely, the establishment and maintenance of a measure of justice and, further, that this authority is also limited by natural law, God's authority, and the dignity and majesty of the Church, is well established.

As a member of the Church Universal, the earthly ruler is simply another believer, subject, like all Christians, to church governance—a point that was underscored dramatically when the fourth-century bishop Ambrose compelled the emperor Theodosius to perform public penance for the sin of a massacre by the army at Thessalonica that took place on his watch. St. Ambrose accepted that earthly rule was divinely ordained but, as a Christian, the emperor is within the Church and not above it.[56] Specifically, Ambrose excluded Theodosius from the eucharist until he repented of this sin. In his letter to Theodosius, Ambrose asserts "the principle that the Church exercises jurisdiction over all Christian believers, even the most exalted." Ambrose also maintains, with equal emphasis, the principle that in "religious matters the civil magistrate has no authority over ecclesiastics."[57] Because the emperor's power is of divine origin, he should be sensitive to avoid positioning himself against, or usurping, anything that belongs directly to God, including the priestly office and spiritual authority. This is *not* a form of theocratic absolutism but the use of a distinction based on the "twinned" identities of earthly rulers and the sacral office, respectively.

Summarizing briefly, one sees that the king or emperor is not free to do anything he wills, for that which runs counter to the law lacks legitimacy. Kings who would undo the law or who violate it systematically, putting themselves in place of the law, do not rule justly. The ruler who fails to fulfill his respective office with its distinctive and particular responsibilities, is a tyrant, not king. There is no proper rule in a state lacking justice. Because the legitimacy of earthly rule is laid out in its end, systematic violation of that end marks illegitimate rule.[58] These are remarkable ideas—incendiary even—for they suggest that, in forms both direct and indirect, legitimacy flows from two sources—God and a notion of "the people"—and, further, that legitimacy can be withdrawn under specific sets of circumstances.

This recognition is critical in subsequent political thought and law in the West, namely, the distinction between legitimate and illegitimate rule that can and, at times, must be made. St. Thomas Aquinas is the direct heir of the Roman-Gelasian system in and through which law binds earthly authorities and powers, and authority is stripped from kings turned tyrants. Such kings, so to speak, delegitimate themselves. Recognizing this fact, the king's subjects may (perhaps) seek some remedy. Thomas also inherits Augustine's rich notion of the person and the insistence that no political configuration enjoys ontological priority *over* the person. Thomas could never credit the person as having status, dignity, and meaning only because he or she is a portion or segment of a state.[59]

At this juncture let's take note of John of Salisbury's famous (or infamous) counsel of tyrannicide in his twelfth century *Policraticus*, a long exegesis on the body politic, in which John writes: "It is not only permitted, but it is also equitable and just to slay tyrants. For he who receives the sword deserves to perish by the sword."[60] The pope might, for example, command subjects to dispossess a tyrant. This ecclesiastical "right" did not sit well with strong and aspiring earthly rulers, of course, for the implication is that he who sits in judgment of the other is superior in authority if not the coercive power of enforcement.[61] The ruler never enjoys sovereignty in unchastened and willful splendor. No earthly ruler can claim an absolute, unconditional right to power. A king gone bad is a tyrant and, perforce, ceases to be a king: He is stripped of legitimacy. We see that the term *king* isn't simply descriptive but also normative—it embeds at its heart a concept of legitimacy or right to rule.[62] In the words of S. B. Chrimes: "The right of resistance against the king who violated the law was inherent in the ancient and prefeudal Germanic ideas, and was itself a universally recognized and well-established part of early medieval constitutional law."[63] It is out of this cluster of ideas, traditions, and laws that both absolutist and constitutional theories of rule eventually emerge.

The salient point for now is that magistracy was bound by an objective legal order that transcended the positive law of particular entities of rule. This order is part of God's creation, a manifestation of God's fullness of goodness, reason, and love. The king does not unite in his person the sacral and legal elements of authority; nor, for that matter, does the pope. Within this understanding *regnum* and *sacerdotium* are distinct but related in myriad ways. But there is a hitch: Does each—pope and emperor (or king)—possess the sword directly, via divine authority and command or, alternatively, does spiritual authority, superior in dignity to the earthly, hold both swords, one of which it gives to the emperor or king to wield rightly and at the sufferance of *sacerdotium?* Medieval rulers chafed at the claim that they owed their thrones and their legitimacy to the Bishop of Rome, one way or the other. It remains the case, whether handed to him by the pope or wielded by him directly, that the prince is "limited in the free exercise of his princely will, and obliged to respect legal limitations outside his own control."[64]

With the Thomistic synthesis, as it is called, one finds a fusion of the previous features of medieval thought—Gelasianism; Roman law; the

Justinian Code, with its insistence on natural law and a *jus gentium* by which, or under which, particular "positive laws" are assessed; canon law; and so-called Germanic ideas of law and kingship, yet to be discussed. A particular dynamic was at work that refracted the interplay of these elements in new ways given the singular importance of the recovery of Aristotle's *Politics* in the West as this text, unknown to St. Augustine, made its way into the West via Arabic translators. By the twelfth century, there was as yet no single entity in Western Christendom that claimed sovereign power over all others. Canon lawyers argued that divine or natural law was obligatory. It followed that earthly rulers were tethered to and by an objective legal order that existed outside the desires or designs of any particular ruler or kingdom. Subjects and kings alike were bound to this legal order. Should the king violate that order, remedies could be taken to chastise or, most dramatically, remove the king.

THOMISTIC LIMITS TO EARTHLY DOMINION

St. Thomas emphasized the human ability to attain knowledge of God through the use of reason, even though the Trinity exceeds our reasoning capacity. For Thomas, God as Logos means that God is not only knowable by his creatures but is himself the apogee of reason.[65] By definition, truth and reason cannot run contrary to the truths of the Christian faith. As well, God is the bearer of order in all things. In the second person of the Trinity, God magnifies the dignity of man "by directly assuming the nature of man"—here the relational dimension of the nexus between human and divine is intact and robust.[66] Given Thomas's devotion to analogical reasoning, he works out the nature of earthly kings and kingdoms within the framework of God as reason, as Logos, as the eternal and immutable good. One way Thomas diverges from Augustine lies in his insistence that the state is natural to human beings, an outgrowth of, and necessary to, our natures.[67] He agrees with Aristotle that man is not only a social animal but a political one.

Within political life, as one distinctive form of social life, no person is sufficient unto himself or herself in Thomism. There is no such thing as a sovereign self, for example. No single person on his or her own "can arrive at the knowledge of all [these] things through the use of his reason. Thus it is necessary for him to live in society so that one person can help another and different men can employ their reasons in different ways."[68] Nor can groups of persons, organized as kingdoms, be solipsistically sovereign and beholden to no one or nothing outside themselves.

Each kingdom is nestled within the body of a wider Christian society; each king is subject to the legal order; and, finally, although earthly rule has a newfound dignity and status in Thomas's writings, being natural to man rather than derived from the exigencies of his fallen condition, each ruler is but one among the universal community of believers, a communicant of a universal *oikumene,* and obligated thereby to do good and avoid evil.

The heart of Thomas's case for the good of earthly rule lies in his insistence that the only legitimate end of that rule is the common good, not the king's "private good," for "private concerns divide the community while the common good unites it."[69] The unjust ruler seeks his own advantage. If, therefore, "a government is under one man who seeks his own benefit and not the good of those subject to him, the ruler is called a tyrant. The word is derived from *tyro,* the Greek word for "strength," because he uses force to oppress the people instead of justice to rule."[70] The most important responsibility of the ruler is to achieve the peace of the community. This point is not open to negotiation.

The question is that of "appropriate means." The form of rule that best conforms to higher law and God's singular authority is monarchy understood through the lens of servanthood, not domination. A just ruler or monarch is the best form of government and his opposite—the tyrant—is the very worst. Tyranny is the "most unjust form of government." Tyrants sow discord and destroy community. Here one recalls Hannah Arendt's famous description of the "iron band of tyranny" that welds people together in a totalitarian system, these same people having already been driven into desperate isolation given the dynamics of totalitarian movements and rule. Because tyranny works to disintegrate, to isolate, a good king instead integrates and creates peaceful order within, while our natural sociality is made manifest through plural institutions under the canopy of law whose "first and foremost purpose" is "the ordering of the common good. To order something to the common good is the responsibility of the whole people, or of someone who represents the whole people."[71]

Aquinas is second to none in lifting up the majesty and dignity of law. But law, too, may run amuck if it pretends that some human beings can read into the hearts of others and that law should reach and control this interiority: a kind of moralistic omniscience. Chastening the overreach that turns the law into a tyranny over human beings requires that it acknowledge that it cannot eliminate or prohibit "every human action, because in trying to eliminate evils, it may also do away with many good things and the interest of the common good which is necessary for human society may be adversely affected."[72] Tyrannical law—which does not deserve the appellation "law" at all—is characterized by pretenses that are not in accord with reason and not ordered to the common good. The tyrant uses the "law" to make war on law understood as a rational order of sentient beings directed toward a common good.

A tyrant might, claiming Christian inspiration as he does so, seek to tear children from their families in order to compel Christian belief for those same children. This apparently "good end" is besmirched and destroyed by its means, for, in taking such a cruel liberty, the tyrant violates the natural order of things, namely, that natural justice that holds that children must not be removed from the care of their parents before the age of reason—age of consent, we would say nowadays.[73] The family has its own sphere of competence and responsibility: It is not brought into being by political regimes but predates them.

We can see the importance of avoiding any pretense of absolute power or control on the part of any authority within Christendom. If law is perverted to become impositional and all-knowing, backed up by force, it is no longer properly law but a distortion of it. All of this sounds very good—indeed it *is* very good. But we also recognize that "on the ground" things often played themselves out rather differently. There is that. There is also the worm in the apple, so to speak. For the same doctrine that lifted up the dignity of earthly rule—seeing government as a divine remedy for sin or as having a divinely created status—could become untethered to the whole, to the intricate interweaving of laws, principalities, institutions, overlapping jurisdictions, and, in its isolation, grow distorted as the divine right of kings cast in absolutist form.

At this point, the ruler presumes a sovereignty unknown to the Thomistic system. The puzzlement for our purposes is whether or not there were developments in understandings of God's authority and power that either helped to pave the way for absolutism in politics or were concomitant with its emergence. This is not such an easy thing to sort out and it cannot be done with absolute precision. Still, we must try.

GOD BOUND OR UNBOUND

Although I take up this matter in greater detail in subsequent chapters, note must be made of an important precursor of later developments. Even as the sacking of Rome by the Visigoths in 410 BC occasioned Augustine's masterwork, *The City of God,* so another giant of the early Church, St. Jerome, responded to this dreadful happening with deep personal sorrow. According to historian Francis Oakley, it was a famous letter of St. Jerome's, written with the Fall of Rome in mind, that prompted over time a fierce debate about God's sovereignty.[74] If God is sovereign, it seems reasonable to assume that he is all-powerful; and if he is all-powerful, he can do what he will. Contemporary conceits of self-sovereignty posit something for the individual very much along these lines: One does one's own thing, does it "my way," is more or less a law unto oneself.

Is God's a sovereignty of this sort? Is God a law unto himself such that he can make and unmake at will?[75] On this portentous matter theologians, canonists, legists, and philosophers from Augustine and Jerome to the early modern period were divided. I claimed earlier that an omnipotent deity who behaved capriciously and arbitrarily is a deity with whom the believer could have little or no relation: How does one engage with caprice on a grand scale? Submission would seem to be the only answer. Perhaps this puts the matter melodramatically. But the example Jerome adduces to illustrate God's sovereign power, and the implications he draws from it, are themselves rather dramatic.

Jerome lifts up the virtue of virginity before going on to concede that "although God can do all things, he cannot raise up a virgin after she has fallen."[76] A God who can do all things cannot change all things: His power encounters limits in the what-is-already-done. This insistence that God's power is bound—*potestas ordinata*—rather than unbound—*potestas absoluta*—drew fire from those theologians and publicists who held that God's absolute power meant that God can indeed "undo." In other words, theological debates about God's power incorporate a distinction between God's absolute power and God's ordained power.[77]

Let's clarify this distinction. God's absolute power refers to the sum total of possibilities available to God before he acts, limited only by contradiction. (That is, God cannot act in direct contradiction to himself.) Ordained power refers to what God does and the way God does it, which is reliable and regulated. Both notions of power presuppose that God is sovereign in the sense that God enjoys a plenitude of power not available to, or attainable by, mutable earthly powers of any kind. God's reason, including wisdom refracted through the Thomistic system, is fully compatible with Christian revelation. Divine reason enjoys a priority over divine will. We have access to God not only via revelation but via reason.[78] Our access to God through reason, superadded to the mediation of the second person of the Trinity, draws God nearer to humanity. This spurs one strand of concern: If we are so close to God or, rather, if God is so accessible to us, what happens to God's omnipotence, his awesome power that stuns us into wondering and worshipful silence?

Although the seeds are sown earlier, this debate flares up from the eleventh century on. Consider the views of the eleventh-century thinker, Peter Damiani, whose topic is the divine omnipotence. Argues Damiani, God "has no need of any creature and is judged by no necessity to create, out of that nothing into existence draws this natural world of ours, establish its order, imposing upon it its customary laws. Incapable in his omnipotence and in his eternal present of suffering any diminution or alteration of his creature power, that natural order *he could well replace, those laws at any moment change.*" Responding to St. Jerome, Damiani throws down the gauntlet: "How . . . dare we doubt that God can restore the virginity of a fallen woman?" For God "can undo the past—that is, so act that an actual historical event should not have occurred." [79]

Damiani's God is the possessor of an absolute power whose "essence . . . is to be self-sufficient perfection," with creation an arbitrary act.[80] God has no need of any creature. This chilly remoteness cannot help but color how one thinks about God's relation to the human person created in his image. As well, this is not the sort of God out of which pluralities are made. By contrast, the Thomistic God is the apogee of goodness, reason, and love, and the bringing into being of Creation is an act of love. Thomas retained the inner connection between God's reason, justice, and love, and the manner in which God wills. God's omnipotence remains but he is bound in ways accessible to human reason and through the workings of grace. God's will is just, insisted Aquinas. It follows that God can do nothing contrary to his nature and to what he has ordained. God's ordained power offers a world that is stable and knowable: God will not pull the rug out from under us.

THE PRINCE: BOUND OR UNBOUND

As we have already observed, there is a limit to the actualization of God's omnipotence, even as there is a limit to the rule of any prince in the Thomistic system. Although the Roman dictum that the prince is the sole legislator, this superiority is not of an arbitrary sort, for "the natural and rational order of justice . . . limits the sovereignty of particular states."[81] No single human legislator can compass the totality of things, spiritual and secular. There are multiple powers—and the power of each is ordained, not absolute. More of this political history pops up in subsequent chapters but, for the moment, it is important to take stock of the place markers that push away from God as the fullness of truth, reason, and goodness and towards God's power as absolute will. Cast so starkly, this account is subject to multiple criticisms, to be sure, but there is surely "something to it."[82]

Tracking sovereignty takes us in several directions with potentially explosive political implications: the first on the level of theory concerning the nature and limits of God's power, and the second on the level of practices, the playing-out of changing configurations of proclaimed power(s) in the late medieval world, the world that gave us political sovereignty. On the level of thought, we note that the distinction between absolute and ordained power emerges in the late Middle Ages as a way to help understand the freedom and omnipotence of God, while at the same time affirming the reliability of the orders of nature and grace.[83] These discussions began in earnest prior to St. Thomas's grand synthesis.[84] With thinkers in this legal tradition, the king's power derives from law. A king cannot do just anything he pleases; his power is ordained, hence limited: The king *must* "bridle himself to avoid *iniuria*. His functions as minister and vicar of God require him to act in accordance with law." [85] The king's status is not above or out-side the law, no more than God's power puts him in a realm altogether outside his creation. The king must be under the law. It follows that the king's "sovereignty . . . was essentially judicial and executive; he did not set the king above the law."[86]

For example, Henry Bracton, whose major work was completed between 1230 and 1250, limits the authority of the prince's *will*: The prince, like the sovereign God, is obliged to keep his promises and to govern in a way that is regular.[87] By introducing the Roman *lex regia* into the picture, Bracton opens up the possibility of a certain arbitrariness.[88] Be that as it may, the prince, he insists, cannot simply do what he likes. Even in lawmaking the prince is bound "to observe certain formal rules."[89]

Jousting between pope and Holy Roman Emperor peaked from the papal side with the extraordinary claims of Pope Boniface VIII in his 1302 bull, *Unam Sanctum*.[90] Boniface insisted that the pope enjoys a plenitude of power unavailable to, and unattainable by, any other power or authority in Christendom. The pope, perforce, could make and unmake kings, being the final word in all things. Although the theory of *plenitudo potestatis* had been deployed previously, the concept flour-ished as a staple of papal authority. It was interpreted so "as to give him [the Roman pontiff] a practically absolute position in Church govern-ment and even . . . in secular affairs also. The pope was thought by most decretalists to enjoy the same *absolute* sovereignty over the *Sacerdotium*" even as he granted power to the secular ruler. *Only* the divine and natural law could hold a pope in check.[91] Pope Innocent IV, for example, insisted that the papal plenitude of power was fully consistent with the role of cardinals and bishops in the overall body of the Church.[92] The doctrine of a papal plenitude of power pushed Church doctrines in a monistic direction: Is there to be but one and all others subordinate rather than the two of the Gelasian doctrine?[93] The monistic answer is yes.

Even as claims of papal power grew ever more grand, monarchical centralization proceeded apace, aided and abetted by the rediscovery of Roman law, including the *patria potestas*, the law of the family. The *lex regia*, the means by which the people of Rome had allegedly deeded authority to rulers through the centuries independent of the church, was plied by legists full of vim and vigor who thrived at young universities, such as the famous law school in Bologna. These legists offered secular rulers a plethora of arguments to justify and authorize secular power in its relation to the pope, some presenting a mirror image of papal *plenitudo potestatis* by insisting that such power was available to monarchs who were emperors within their respective kingdoms. It was legists in the pay of the centralizing French monarchy who first began to use the word *sovereignty* in the thirteenth century as a characterization of political rule, analogous to God's sovereignty.

Two features of the revived Roman law will be of continuing importance for this work: the role attributed to the *populus Romanus* in giving rise to and legitimating earthly rule, first, and second, Roman legal theories that held that *ownership must be singular and indivisible: There is one.*[94] Transferred to theories of earthly rule, the king is said to be a proprietor as "some writers . . . make the king the sole proprietor of his whole kingdom."[95] Contrast this sovereignty with the limitations to absoluteness in the thought of St. Thomas, namely, the existence of a "natural and rational order which limits the sovereignty of the particular state," or, one might add, a particular pope.[96] What is right is constrained by nature, God's rational order of things.

Sovereignty, the *Oxford English Dictionary* tells us, is spelled variously as *souerein, souereyn, sovereigne,* and in many other ways. The definition of *sovereignty* is "supremacy or preeminence in respect of excellence or efficacy, supremacy in respect of power, domination or rank; supreme dominion, authority, or rule." The term *supreme* appears repeatedly in various definitions of a sovereign as "supreme ruler or monarch . . . supreme controlling power . . . absolute and independent authority." This is no shy term hiding its candle under a bushel. Although de facto definitions of power and authority met the test of sovereignty before the twelfth and thirteenth centuries, it is in this time frame that the term enters into common usage.[97]

The die is here cast for a major break (according to some), or a wrinkle (according to others), with the emergence of the so-called nominalists, Duns Scotus and William of Ockham being two of its powerful representatives.[98] They relocate the gravamen of God's power and, in so doing, reframe and refract earthly rule in a direction that sounds eerily familiar to any student of absolute monarchy or, for that matter, any form, whether benign or perverse, of the operation of the *will* in politics.[99]

"THY WILL BE DONE": GOD'S WILL AND EARTHLY EMANATIONS

Once introduced, nominalism clings to all future projects in political thought and theology—whether as an unwelcome "hanger-on" or as a liberating note that breaks the chokehold of the established medieval realism and universalism. For some theologians, it was under the canopy of God's ordained powers that an account of God's power as absolute yet self-limiting was sheltered. God was limited by what he has done. But the intelligibility of the world is more difficult to assert if one associates God's absolute power with a notion of limitlessness: *absoluta* rather than *ordinata*. There are strong and weak versions of the thesis that holds that God's ordained order is contingent, as God saves and damns whomever he will.[100] The strong thesis is usually associated with nominalism as articulated, first, by Duns Scotus and then by William of Ockham.[101] A weak statement of the thesis sees more continuity than change and avers that Ockham and the nominalists were not all that different in their views of God's sovereignty than Aquinas. It would be a mistake to charge that with

Ockham God becomes an arbitrary sovereign whose will is not bound by either intellect or law—as if this settles the matter. And yet . . . there is a shift. [102]

This much can be safely said: With Duns Scotus, Ockham's peer, the will or *voluntas* moves to center stage. Free choice applies univocally to God and to man. God's absolute power is not in a "realm of possibility from which God created a physical and moral order; rather, it is the ability to act outside of an order that is *already established*," as one scholar puts it. [103] Ordinary citizens cannot act outside the established order. Sovereign powers, however, because they make the laws, can suspend them and create new laws. Similarly, God acts in accord with his ordained creation, but he also acts outside of this order as he exercises his absolute power.

By the early fourteenth century, it is common for theologians to maintain that the Father has a form of absolute power that is beyond the power of the Son or the Holy Spirit. [104] The equality of the three persons of the Trinity fades in this formulation in favor of the absolutism of God the Father. It is easy to see—though one shouldn't make it *too* easy—the ways in which the migration of such accounts into theories and laws of earthly dominion is fraught with possibilities, for good or ill.

That God's power is both contingent and omnipotent is deepened in the work of William of Ockham, at least on the strong statements of the thesis I noted above. The challenge arises in determining where Ockham's innovations lie. For theologians prior to Ockham had also insisted that God is able to do whatever can be done, whatever does not imply a contradiction. Ockham introduces a note of contingency into the picture; thus, for example, God can save a person lacking in charity and by his power two bodies can exist in the same place at the same time. [105] Created nature does not constrain the power of God fully, any more than an established system of laws constrains a truly sovereign ruler. [106] In the world of medieval realism, the freely willing human being was fundamentally rational and could be brought to will the good; after nominalism, holding this all together becomes more difficult. [107]

Once the structure of medieval Thomism starts to crack, God's omnipotence leaves human beings stewing in a kind of permanent impotence as their agency is swamped by God's arbitrary power or, alternatively, human free willing and capacity to "do" shrinks the realm of divine agency as sovereign selves go to work. The will of an all-powerful God is the ultimate cause of things and we cannot come to know this God with any degree of certainty. Nothing lies in between God's will and the countless individuals that exist in space and time. There is no intelligible world nor any free order in nature that we can discern.[108] Whatever Ockham and those who followed him believed they were doing in invoking such claims about God's absolute power—the motivation, according to some, was "the wish to vindicate the Old Testament vision of Yahweh as a personal God of power and might against the threat of philosophic determinism"—the political fallout is fraught.[109]

In Ockham's defense some insist that his "radically antinecessitarian" theology offers a God who can act apart from the laws he has decreed, but who freely binds himself through a covenant with human beings on whom he has mercy.[110] But, by analogy, who must the free, unbound king keep faith with, and how does one insure that the king binds himself? Suffice to say that with post-Ockham theology, God is less frequently represented as the fullness of reason and goodness than as the site of sovereign will. This latter vision came to dominate sovereignty talk and helped to lay the basis for the juristic conception of the state when man decided that he, too, could be sovereign in this way.

2

SOVEREIGN GOD:
BOUND OR UNBOUND

WHY DID THE STRUCTURE OF MEDIEVAL THOUGHT, WITH ITS ROMAN AND Germanic law, neo-Platonism and Aristotelianism, intertwined with Christian revelation, prove to be inherently unstable?[1] Conflicts over the nature of God's sovereignty and its earthly correlates is surely part of the answer. To explore how and why this is so one must look not only at the interplay of ideas but, as well, consider the ways of life to which Christianity gave rise and the practices that sustained medieval Christendom.[2] Turmoil over how the transcendent God's earthly embodiment transformed earthly rule and governance is one of the most striking features of Western history.[3]

I concluded the previous chapter on a note of conflict. This conflict must be unpacked further if we are to make sense of the shape political sovereignty took in the West. Recall, if you will, the classical Augustinian-Thomistic insistence that God is a God in relation to the only creature made in his image. God is logos, but dia-logos is central to this understanding. Within this medieval realism, the human ability to reason affords us a distinctive moral power: We can act from the law that we discern. We can do this because God committed himself to the integrity of the nature that is his creation, meaning that "natural law" is stabilized. God's sovereign powers are, therefore, limited by what God himself has brought into being; creation tells us what God actually chose to do and God will not, as I noted in the previous chapter, pull the rug out from under us.[4]

Medieval law is the way God's justice got transmitted to earthly institutions and actions. Political meanings were layered over potent images of the sacred; indeed, the OED reflects this by demonstrating that power, as a characteristic of political or national attributes, is a "late use" preceded by "a celestial or spiritual being having control or influence, a divinity." This gives one the sense of angels fluttering about, but one takes the point. Claims to earthly power or *potestas* as dominion, and *auctoritas*, or right authority, migrated over to politics from arguments about God's power and authority, in a word, God's sovereignty.

One needs to be cautious about making sweeping claims, but an overview is helpful given the intricacy of the material. As we reach the later Middle Ages, theological understandings of God's fullness of reason and goodness and his relational complexity are featured less prominently; instead, God, as the site of sovereign will, moves to the forefront of controversy and implication. For strong nominalists, God is not bound by anything other than his will. Does God's volitionality, then, trump other features medieval realists identified with God's powers? Certainly a monistic conception, i.e., a concentration on a singular, sovereign will, squeezes out more relational and dialogic understandings. God's power in this vision is not only absolute but arbitrary. God's rights are coterminous with his sovereign power, including rights of dominion, rule, possession: "all-pervasive and efficient . . . omnipotent and undefeatable."[5] This vision helped to lay the basis for the juristic conception of the strong sovereign state as a political entity. Writes the controversial German political theorist, Carl Schmitt: "All significant concepts were transferred from theology to the theory of the state, whereby, for example, the omnipotent God became the omnipotent lawgiver . . . the recognition of which is necessary for a sociological consideration of these concepts."[6]

PAPAL PLENITUDO

Let's take up the thread of argumentation with an uncontroversial claim, namely that, although the bishop of Rome assumed power and authority in light of the collapse of the Roman Empire in the West, over time papal power was elaborated and strengthened much beyond any act of necessity. For medieval pontiffs, law was an instrument of temporal and spiritual authority, carrying political and theological meaning; indeed, the Romanization of the Western Church—noted by Hannah Arendt in order to account for its durability—incorporated terms and notions from Roman jurists.[7]

One early occupant of the Petrine office, Pope Leo I (the Great), put forward an exposition of the monarchical function of the pope as the juristic successor to the powers and functions given by Christ to St. Peter.[8] His thesis held that Christ had established such authority in Matthew 16:18–19: "Thou art Peter and upon this rock I will build my church. . . . And I will give unto thee the keys of the kingdom of heaven; and whatsoever thou shalt bind on earth shall be bound in heaven; and whatsoever thou shalt loose on earth shall be loosed in heaven." Binding and loosing were interpreted as the power to make and break kings and emperors as one prerogative of the papal office.[9]

It takes little imagination to see how and why these claims would be contested by ambitious rulers. But, interestingly enough, they were not contested in a manner that aimed to eliminate claims of sovereignty; rather, they aimed to order it variously. There is no single text or author who makes this case: no medieval Machiavelli or Hobbes or Locke. Contestations over sovereignty emerge in practices. One must, therefore, look to theologians, popes, rulers, and legists to assay the playing-out on the ground of doctrines and claims. Who is making what sorts of claims depends very much on whether a particular political or pastoral need is being addressed or whether a theological argument is being advanced abstractly. One way or the other, it is clear that these debates migrated into discussions of politics.

God's Sovereignty Translated

As we have seen, vehement disagreements characterize medieval thought, none more vehement than parsing the connection between God's sovereignty and earthly dominion, whether spiritual or sacred. As

I noted in chapter 1, the official doctrine of the church was the so-called two swords doctrine: Both *regnum* and *sacerdotium* wielded the sword legitimately.[10] The theory was neat. The practice sowed the seeds of dissension: Did the pope hand over the "secular" sword to the emperor, in which case he held his power on sufferance? Or, was the emperor or king the wielder of the sword independently? It is important—to remind us once again—that all of these controversies take place within a single Christian society. No struggle involved faith versus unfaith or "secular" versus "religious." The way we think today makes no sense in the context we are exploring. It goes without saying that in order to have law you require a lawgiver. Who is that lawgiver? Where does law come from? St. Thomas had argued that law derives from God's providence, as an act of God's will, and the will of God is reasoned, not arbitrary; indeed, St. Anselm, preceding Aquinas, had argued that God had restricted his own sovereignty by giving human beings free will.[11] With that in mind, let's revisit the enormously important and rich controversy over God's powers, for this debate is fraught with implications for later concepts of political sovereignty. Medieval legists mined Justinian's famous sixth-century Code to put forward a case that the emperor's power is *not* altogether bound, no more than God's, for no code of law, however comprehensive, can "fully anticipate that emergencies may hereafter arise which are not enclosed in the bounds of legal rules. . . . The emperor is not bound by statutes."[12] This is the famous doctrine of what came to be called "the exception" or "prerogative" and is sometimes taken, mistakenly, as the innovation and contribution of the twentieth-century political theorist (and Nazi sympathizer) Schmitt. But the notion is venerable, trailing in its wake the dust of centuries.[13]

If we are to understand the direction Ockham and nominalism took things, it requires a deeper appreciation of the powers claimed by the medieval papacy—and these were considerable. Gratian's monumental *Decretum* was the great law book of the twelfth century and played a key role in the expansion of papal power. Various decretalists, or Decretists, as they were called, were experts at innovative interpretation. The three main schools of Decretist activity were Bologna, Paris, and Oxford, and "in studying the Decretist texts we can observe some of the best minds from every part of Christendom engaged in a systematic reflection on a thousand years of the experience of the church in the world."[14] The culmination of this experience led to the articulation of an ideal of papal supremacy that pertained spiritually *and* temporally. It followed that, were one to trace any legitimate exercise of authority, it would wend its way back to the papal office: All roads indeed led to Rome.

Emperors fought against this notion of delegation; popes battled back. The *pas de deux* between pope and emperor, pope and king, is a fascinating thing to watch, knowing, as we do from our vantage point, the monumental implications that turned on the outcome of these scrapes. One strain of contestation held that the emperor's "power of the sword and the imperial dignity" derived from "election by the princes and people . . . for there was an emperor before there was a pope, an empire before papacy."[15] The pope has jurisdiction over the emperor "in spiritual matters, so that he can bind and loose him . . . [but] by no means in temporal matters though the pope can judge him in temporal matters and depose him by the wish of the princes who elect him according to customary law."[16]

Still and all, it is the pope who hands over the sword, the Petrine doctrine insisted, with the apogee of this doctrine articulated by ambitious popes like Gregory VII, Boniface VIII, and Innocent III. Innocent, who assumed the papacy in 1198, insisted that the pope was granted supremacy not only in spiritual but in worldly affairs, for the spiritual sword is superior to the earthly in all things, not just in matters that touch on sin.[17] These debates inaugurate what scholars call a crisis in late medieval theology and law—a crisis that Ockham and nominalism deepened and extended and out of which early modern notions of political sovereignty emerged.

Leading into this crisis there were at least two notions of temporal rulership. One held that the ruler received his legitimate authority when the pope handed him the temporal sword. Another claimed that the ruler's legitimacy derived from election as the ancient *populus Romanus* had been translated—carried over—from Rome to the medieval world.

As well, competing accounts of papal authority filled the air, with one, as we have noted, insisting on a plenitude of power, and a second circumscribing that power in a variety of ways. And behind it all is God's sovereignty—whether God's powers are bound or unbound, or whether the fullness of reason and love are infused with the tincture of will whose colors grow bolder with the passage of time. It was never easy to draw a bright line between temporal and ecclesiastical jurisdiction. If popes meddled with emperors and kings, they returned the favor . . . and then some. No one doubted that papal authority held sway over any earthly power in matters of belief. But that is about it—everything else was up for grabs, sooner or later.

BINDING AND LOOSING: BOUND OR FREE

Here recall Peter Damiani's articulation of divine omnipotence. God is in no way capable of "suffering any diminution or alteration of his creative power" and "[the] natural order he could well replace," and this at a moment's notice.[18] God could do what science fiction and children's fantasy imagines—undo what has been done. One thinks here of the "time turner" in J. K. Rowling's Harry Potter series, the third volume, *Harry Potter and the Prisoner of Azkaban*, in which Buckbeak the hippogriff is beheaded—for allegedly attacking the nasty Draco Malfoy, Harry Potter's nemesis at Hogwarts School of Witchcraft and Wizardry. But, subsequently, Buckbeak is unbeheaded—thanks to the handy device that Professor Minerva McGonagal has handed Hermione Granger, one of Harry's best friends and a brilliant student, in order that she can be in two places at once, she being an indefatigable student and determined to take an overload of courses.[19]

The God who can undo is resonant in his self-same splendor, lacking "in his nature, any reason or desire to bring a universe of imperfect beings into existence," with the result that the creative act is "conceived to be entirely groundless and arbitrary in itself, and therefore in its inclusions and exclusions."[20] If Augustine fleshed out a notion of God's splendor, he also took great care, as we have seen, to stress the role of God-as-Mediator, the Lord who came down to us so that we might rise to him. This dialogic dimension of God's sovereign power fades in late medieval nominalist construal.[21]

Medieval thinkers troubled themselves over divine arbitrariness and divine obedience, paying attention to those divine and natural laws God had brought into being in the first place. For the medieval realists, God's goodness and rationality is a necessity—God has to act as he does. But how does one articulate or "clarify the relationship between God's power and his other attributes, notably his will"?[22] In other words, does one hold constant God's power in relation to his goodness, truth, and love? Or does God's will go on holiday, forge forth on its own accord? In the Thomistic formulation, God never acts in capricious ways. God is not primarily a *voluntarist* sovereign who can do what he pleases, but the good God of Augustine and Aquinas, motivated by a fullness of love.[23]

It is the stability of *ordo,* God's created order, on which the accent is placed in that formulation rather than on God as untrammeled will. In a God-drenched time, such haunting questions were unavoidable and very real. Has God done what he chose to do with creation and human beings, and for better or worse, must we just "live with it"? Or is God's will as a fashioning, ordering, and reordering power yet at work in the world, meaning that God can undo, can bind and loose, can reshape creation at his will? If we cast this latter formulation in the language of freedom, God is free to do anything, his will being unbound. One may believe God through the third person of the Trinity is at work within the world—but that is quite different from embracing a notion of God's absolute and arbitrary will.

The God of reason of Aquinas was a God that guaranteed the intelligibility of the world. The God that emerged out of the shadows into the full glare of day among the late medieval voluntarists was a God both omnipotent and free, with his will enjoying primacy. Medieval scholars argue that this idea exacted a severe cost, namely, that it diminished the intelligibility of the world and threw medieval thought and practice into a whirlwind of controversy from which it never recovered. For example, if God can act contrary to what we have come to understand as natural law, where does that leave earthly power and the understanding of selves?[24]

THE FRUITS OF NOMINALISM

Let us proceed with the thinkers and thought that serve as key markers on the pathway of this story. It is the fruit of the nominalist shift that moves the unwieldy structure in another direction. One might think of medieval thought, theory, law, and doctrine as a gerrymandered entity, delicately calibrated, each part grinding with, and against, the whole. No single part is absolute. The structure is kept intact, if precariously so. When the structure breaks apart, one is left with the parts. The whole is nowhere to be found, save in the dreams of past unities or wholenesses that are conspicuous by their absence in later epochs. It is fair to say that, with Ockham, pieces are hived off and magnified in isolation. One would be hard pressed to identify in Ockham any single proclamation of God's contingent and arbitrary power by contrast to his necessitarian and orderly power, but there are points scattered throughout his writing that signal a shift.

Ockham was exercised by claims of a papal plenitude of power. In countering those claims, he stresses God's radical omnipotence. It isn't necessary to unpack the entire structure of late medieval argumentation—something beyond my capabilities in any case—in order to take the measure of a "climate of opinion" that Ockham either solidified or deepened, if he did not inaugurate it.[25] Uncontroversially, it can be said that Ockham held to a very high notion of divine sovereignty that culminates in creation. Here things get murky. If natural law is central to St. Thomas's complex theology, a version of what exists by "nature" or is "natural" also figures in Ockham and for the nominalists generally. But one has a distinct sense that they are not talking about "the same thing."

Does law derive in the first instance from a creative act of God's reason and, given that God created human beings as rational beings in his image, is it thereby accessible to human ratiocination? Or, by contrast, does law derive from God's will and command, and what human beings must do is obey? This command-obedience theory bursts with implications. For now the point is that it seems reasonable to associate Ockham with an emphasis on God's willful command rather than in direct opposition to God's reason. If this is taken in the context of a nominalist philosophy that breaks things down into

particulars—what has been called a "radical individualist ontology"—
you can picture one piece of the rambling structure of medieval
thought listing dangerously and teetering if not collapsing.

Ockham insists that Caesar has legitimacy that predates papal
autonomy and religious institutions but, at the same time, he does not
relegate "religion to a realm of pure subjectivity or secular life to a
moral limbo of avarice and force."[26] Papal power, insisted Ockham,
cannot claim derivation from God alone but also from the concate-
nated activities of men over many years. But some Roman bishops
have "impermissibly and presumptuously" extended "to both divine
and human matters a wrongly usurped power so that their inexcusable
wickedness should be revealed," and such "supreme pontiffs . . . have
tried to rule like tyrants."[27] One might say that such pontiffs—and one
need not accept the particulars of Ockham's polemic to agree to this
point—ruled *monistically*, forsaking thereby the "two" of Gelasian
doctrine.

The papal position he opposes is the one that locates the pope above
both canon and civil law.[28] Ockham trounces the plenitude of power
proclaimed by the most ambitious popes of his era as a distortion of
Christ's law, turning it into a "most horrendous servitude," when he
insists Christians have been freed from the Old Law and should not be
placed in servitude to a new set of demands.[29] Ockham further presses
the analogy to other "offices," including the authority of the father in the
family where it is clear that the father does not have plenipotentiary power
"over his sons, because then fatherly rule would not differ from despotism
and the condition of sons would be indistinguishable from that of
slaves."[30] The freedom of the gospel precludes the pope from requiring
supererogatory burdens against the wills of those involved.[31]

GOD AS WILL AND COMMAND

I suspect that many readers find this sensible—so why not hail Ockham
rather than criticize him? To oversimplify, what came to be known as
Ockhamism marks the shift from God as love and reason to God as
command. Natural law, in the hands of Thomas and within orthodox

Thomism, appealed to reason, not primarily to authority. By driving things back to Biblical texts and stripping away authoritative interpretations, Ockham spurred a resort to revelation and authority, paradoxically enough, given that it is papal power and the presumption of monistic authority that he denounces! As many have avowed, Ockham reveres and lifts up God's sovereignty . . . but his version exacts a fairly substantial price. As God becomes more remote, it is more difficult for human beings to reason about God and to analogize aspects of their own experience—as Augustine had done so brilliantly—in order to reach conclusions about God's divinity.[32]

If creation is primarily an act of will rather than reason and love, the implication is that God's contingent will selected a particular course of action. This means that God may (or may not, depending on the thinker) have subjected himself to the laws he created. One way or the other, however, these are contingent laws.[33] God does everything through his infallible will. Matters get very dense at this point: What, then, is within the purview of a sovereign power? If God acts outside his laws, can an earthly sovereign act outside the established laws of a polity? Yes, say the nominalists, rulers may suspend the laws if the need arises.

This leads the great medievalist Etienne Gilson to lament that nominalism undermines the intelligibility of the world and offers a God who is cruel because he can, if he wills, damn the innocent and save the guilty.[34] This point is disputed insofar as Gilson attributes it to Ockham, but it can fairly be said that a version of "Ockhamism" comes to this conclusion.[35] Important for future consideration is the fact that analogies are drawn between divine power and human sovereignty. In the canon-law mode, absolute power is not thought of as a realm of sheer possibility but is construed as a sphere of action within an established order.[36] Ockham, however, insists that absolute and ordained powers are one. God can act to alter things and exercise thereby his absolute power. But God could as well do many things he doesn't wish to do—this is the contingent feature of the created order. Absolute power remains in the realm of possibility—haunting temptation if the analogy is drawn to earthly power.[37] The dialectic of *potentia absoluta* and *potentia ordinata* grows ever more important. *Potentia absoluta* is the domain of God's unlimited freedom abstracted, finally, from his commitment *de potentia ordinata*.[38] The rejection of realist metaphysics and ontology, though a seemingly arid and arcane debate, bore strange fruit over time. It also scared the wits out of lots of people, Martin Luther among them, as we shall see.

VOLUNTARISTIC GOD, VOLUNTARISTIC PRINCE

If God's sovereignty is cast voluntaristically, so, too, is political authority: A command-obedience theory of secular rule takes hold.[39] This involves a profound rearrangement of the furniture of moral and political argumentation. Ockham's individualist ontology, combined with the divine-command argument, expands and magnifies a vision of God's awesome power. But God's reason takes something of a nosedive. Here competing and contrasting views on nature and natural law are critical.[40] Aquinas, remember, holds that human beings possess a form of natural knowledge and can arrive at certain truths—natural laws— through the use of reason. This natural law involves the participation in eternal law by God's rational creatures.

Eternal law is not subject to the vagaries of time; rather, it refers to God's rational ordering of things. Looking ahead for a moment, what Thomas Hobbes, the greatest of the postmedieval nominalists, does with the *lex naturalis* is to set forth as primary a drive toward self-preservation that is essentially individualistic for we are all monads—so many billiard balls careening out of control—until such time as our lives are ordered by a masterful leviathan. Having rejected the Aristotelianized Christianity of Scholasticism, Hobbes goes for a nominalist construal with gusto. He is a canny reductionist, as we shall see. The point for now is that the use of the word *nature* or *natural* doesn't mean a thinker is using these terms in the same way as classical natural-law philosophers and theologians.[41]

When nominalists talk about natural law, they mean something different from the Thomists. Although Ockham may be no innovator where a distinction between absolute and ordained power is concerned, he is an innovator in breaking up unities that natural law and nature represented. When Ockham appeals to nature and natural law, he means a law imposed on human beings and the universe by divine fiat—an outside coercive and impositional command: the primacy of will over reason. This may overstate—still, it is difficult to see how one can affirm certain dictates—e.g., "Thou shalt not kill [commit murder]"—and make these intelligible to human beings save as an act of obedience if we see *only* individuals or particulars, i.e., a series, not a community and the moral norms necessary for a community to persist over time.

It becomes more difficult for us to link such dicta as "Thou shall not murder" to well-being of a wider human community, its animating reason having been downgraded in the overall scheme of things.[42] Medieval historian Oakley puts it thus: "The order of the created world (both the moral order governing human behavior and the natural order governing the behavior of irrational beings) came with the nominalists to be understood no longer as a participation in a divine reason that is in some measure transparent to human reason, but as the deliverance of an inscrutable divine will."[43] Suffice to say that with the consolidation of medieval nominalist theology, we are dealing with a *voluntarist God* who may bind his power via his will . . . or not, Ockham "being among the first that maintained . . . that there is no act evil but as it is prohibited by God, and which cannot be made good if it be commanded by God . . . this doctrine hath been since chiefly promoted and advanced by such as thinking nothing so essential to the Deity as uncontrollable power and arbitrary will," in the words of a Platonist alarmed by this direction of thought.[44]

EARTHLY DOMINION: WILL THE REAL SOVEREIGN PLEASE STAND UP?

I noted in the first chapter that Augustine cherishes "our business within this common mortal life" but is wary about conferring on earthly dominion a status that serves as a goad to the sin of pride. With the Thomistic synthesis, earthly rule acquires a new dignity and status. That's the easy part. More difficult by far is tracing the vagaries of justifications for, and understandings of, the purpose of earthy kingdoms and empires. Some years ago, political theorist and historian Walter Ullmann identified an "ascending" theory of political legitimation that traced back to the *populus Romanus*. In a God-drenched age, that alone would not suffice to structure rule, but does it come to be seen as necessary? Further, is the aim or end of earthly dominion primarily to prevent the worst from happening or, more grandly, to achieve positive goods?

The theological accounts thus far adumbrated are backdrop to competing accounts of the development of the state. One account—let's call it the standard account—emphasizes the idea of state sovereignty, even absolute sovereignty of the sort, "the king is emperor in his kingdom"—as a response to the chaos and fragmentation of medieval Europe and its competing powers—feudal principalities, Holy Roman Emperor, the papacy, ever-more-aggressive consolidators of centralized monarchies, and so on. For the medieval system was "a patchwork of overlapping and incomplete rights of government . . . inextricably superimposed and tangled" with different "juridical instances . . . geographically interwoven and stratified . . . plural allegiances, asymmetrical suzerainties and anomalous enclaves" abounding.[45] The state as a territorial entity possessing sovereignty is seen as a historic necessity given what is inevitably construed as the hopeless medieval mess.

But there is another story—not necessarily incompatible with the standard account but rather more interesting. In this account, the idea of the state develops out of the medieval incorporation of Roman law. Part of this has to do with the introduction of Roman private law into political theory in three ways: The state is conceived along the lines of private property, which is immune from public control; sovereignty is conceived along the lines of rule of a paterfamilias over the Roman *domus*—a form of dominion Augustine criticized; finally, sovereignty is conceived along the lines that the law (*jus*) has legal subjectivity because it is able to represent the Roman people as a unified subject.

In other words, the rediscovery "from Roman law of the concept of absolute private property and the simultaneous emergence of mutually exclusive territorial state formations" go together.[46] It took time for this redolent little seed to germinate meaningfully. This happened when legists, mostly French, crystallized the idea of state sovereignty with metahistorical justification drawn from Roman law and imperial practice. For example, consider this 1443 statement updating Roman law from Bologna University, famous for its law school, which claims, in part: "There is one judge from whom the final decision of cases comes, lest with many judges contending, and no one supreme, litigations would never be finished. Also, no family, no community, no kingdom can remain in its full *status*, unless it has one supreme ruler; because from the divisions of heads there easily arises division and schism among the members."[47] One might call this the law brief heard "round the world," or at least "round the West," and it is fraught with implications for political rule.[48]

Roman imperial doctrine was deployed strategically by national kings to fight for their autonomy and territorial centralization as against pope and Holy Roman Emperor. Papal doctrine, as Antony Black has shown, "supplied something of the more abstract . . . notion of sovereignty which was to be fully developed in the work of Bodin."[49] If the doctrine of papal supremacy figured in the emergence of the modern notion of state sovereignty, the richness and fullness of that doctrine is fully on view with Pope Gregory VII.[50]

Although there is a dispute concerning whether Gregory aimed knowingly at a "sovereign lawmaking power over the Church and a temporal supremacy over the Empire," his *plenitudo potestatis*, encompassing all of Christendom, is rather breathtaking—"one great universal state, with the Pope as its head."[51] Gregory's revival of Roman law as a weapon against Holy Roman Emperor Henry IV created the legal research equivalent of an arms race between emperor and pope: Both sides wanted to find in Roman law the principles that allowed it to be supreme to the other party.[52]

ON THE ROAD TO THE SOVEREIGN STATE

Sovereignty comes in many varieties but, sooner or later, sovereignty takes on a legal or legalistic form. Even the moral sovereignty of God got cast in terms of law, whether God-as-reason or God-as-will, depending on the accent placed by a particular commentator.[53] Sovereignty is identified with a right to govern—what we call legitimacy—and not simply or exclusively with might or force, with the power to coerce. Rome deeded not only an account of legislative power and authority, with the people cast as the source of political power but with notions of the prince as above the law. *If* the people are the final source of legitimate authority, the tacit implication is that this grant of authority is conditional. As John Locke would later argue, should government become destructive of the ends for which it was created, this grant could be withdrawn. If, however, the grant of authority is unconditional and government is understood as legal command-obedience backed up by coercive force, then the will of the prince or emperor takes primacy.[54] One can no more challenge the word of he who lays down the law than one could turn back the tides.

In these latter construals, the monarch is a lord who is always above; others always below. The site, or seat, of sovereignty must be an individual will: It must be *one, singular, monistic.*[55] A sovereign of this sort cannot be judged by anyone—save God—as there is none higher. Further, if all power is top-down, it follows that the power that flows from apex to periphery in no way diminishes the apex. This is the plenipotentiary idea of the state—or monarch—or pope.[56] Power here is a *totality*, something very different from classical medieval notions of a unity that relies upon particular overlapping parts that are by no means diminished by being forged into this unity.

I noted in the previous chapter that the word *sovereignty* was coined by French legists in the thirteenth century.[57] The French legists were keenly interested in proclaiming sovereignty for a king—their king. This points us in the direction of yet another conflict, that between king and emperor as well as king, emperor, and pope. If the Holy Roman Empire was a creature of the papacy, it, like Dr. Frankenstein's monster, went its own way. At the same time, centralizing monarchies slowly but surely drained off the power of independent feudal principalities to coalesce at the top. If feudal lords or barons at the apogee of the feudal system were so many mini-sovereigns, then the work of nationalizing monarchs was a work of centralization and simplification. The king shifts from *primus inter pares* among feudal rulers to holding primacy above all others. Whether this primacy is delegated from above or authorized from below, is it limited in any way and, if so, by whom? This became a central task posed centuries *before* sovereignty in our modern understanding was legally adopted.[58]

KINGS AND KINGDOMS: THE CENTRALIZING IMPERATIVE

Medieval kingships were not creatures of the papacy. The great medieval popes did assert authority, *auctoritas,* over each, however, particularly the French king, who was anointed with holy oil in a symbolic religious ceremony, a form of royal unction. The articulation of a plenitude of power advanced by medieval canonists was appropriated by legists in the service of ambitious earthly monarchs and turned against the papacy. The coalescence of power and authority in the papacy helped to spur the rise of claims to sovereign power among kings as the formula *rex et imperator in regno suo* got laid on.

Pope Boniface VIII, for example, had proclaimed de jure that both swords, spiritual and earthly, are in the hands of the Church and that kings hold their authority "at the will and sufferance of the priest. One sword . . . ought to be under the other, and the temporal authority is to be subjected to the spiritual. When the apostle says 'there is no power but of God, and the powers that are of God ordained,' it means that one sword, the lesser, is under the greater.[59] In this account, rulership is a *beneficium*, a kind of gift presented to the king from the pope. But the gift is given on sufferance. Rulership "is a favour" and cannot be "gained by man of his own volition." The king, therefore, "has no self-sufficiency, no independence of action, no existence at all, except in so far as the pope wills it."[60]

This account de jure was promulgated within the framework of the intricate structures of medieval canon law. Two points need to be made. Canon law was not the only legal system. The laws of emperors and kings existed alongside and frequently clashed with canon law that proclaimed papal jurisdiction over all of Christendom, not law for a narrowly circumscribed "church," as we would say today. Whatever the papacy's de jure claims, de facto the pope enjoyed nothing like this plenitude of power. The pope's power cast in legalistic and juridical terms might be supreme for the canonists, but this supremacy was tested over and over again. Law was the little engine that never rested, an animated soul that infused the corporate body of Christendom.[61]

Kneeling at Canossa

That said, there are a few highlights if you delight in the sight of kings humbled. One of the most familiar is the story of Henry IV at Canossa.[62] A second famous story, not about pope vs. an emperor but king vs. an archbishop, is the tale of Henry II and Becket, the stuff of legend, drama, and a movie starring Peter O'Toole and Richard Burton. (Hollywoodization aside, the serious issues come through, though in rather histrionic form.) The drama of King Henry and Pope Gregory pits two ardent articulators of "divine right" against one another. The background to the conflict was an episode in the long "investiture controversy" having to do with whether kings, emperors, or popes could appoint bishops who, at that time, exercised considerable sway of both a spiritual and temporal nature. For popes, the independence of the spiritual sword and its superior status over the temporal was at stake. For kings, trying to gain some control over independent sites of power within their kingdoms was the high-stakes game.

The humbling of Henry is our first tale, being undoubtedly the most dramatic although it is chronologically later than the conflict between Becket and Henry II. Pope Gregory threw down the gauntlet—the particulars that catalyzed this need not concern us at this juncture—proclaiming the pope's plenitude of power, his "binding and loosing" attributes. All kings are *bound*—neither their authority nor their power is unlimited—and one way this binding occurs is that they are obligated to obey relevant papal decrees, he insisted. King Henry—the German king and Holy Roman Emperor—called "his" bishops together to denounce Gregory as a usurper and tyrant. Henry's tone was not gentle. His salutation is a blast against the pope's assumption of authority: "Henry, King not by usurpation, but by the pious ordination of God, to Hildebrand, now not Pope, but false monk." Henry goes on to burnish his own kingship by the grace of God and to render nugatory the "sword" wielded by Pope Gregory. I, the King, he proclaims, can be "judged by God alone and am not to be deposed for any crime unless—may it never happen—I should deviate from the faith," concluding with a call to Gregory to abdicate: "Descend! Descend!"[63]

Gregory parried by hauling out one of the most formidable weapons in his arsenal—the pope had no regiments but he did have potent tools. He excommunicated Henry and stripped him of his royal prerogative—deposed him, in other words, claiming, as he did so, that this was well within the prerogatives of the papacy, the "binding and loosing" authority. Reaffirming that the pope's sovereign power derives directly from Almighty God, Gregory writes: "I deprive King Henry, son of the emperor Henry, who has rebelled against thy Church with unheard of audacity, of the government over the whole kingdom of Germany and Italy, and I release all Christian men from the allegiance which they may have sworn or may swear to him, and I forbid anyone to serve him as a king."[64] A shaken Henry fired off two ripostes reaffirming the fact that God had given him his office and he held it by divine right.[65] Henry called up the Gelasian two swords doctrine of kingship and priesthood. Does this not require "two," a duality? Does this not mean that a king holds his royal throne as a "representative of God"?[66]

To make the proverbial long story short, Henry capitulates in 1077 having wildly overstated his own authority and clout de facto. The moral effect of the ruling of excommunication was powerful. The bishops who had been loyal to Henry abandoned him.[67] So the hapless king trekked to a diet, or a council, to be held at Augsburg with nobles and bishops there gathered. The pope, traveling northward, would preside at this diet. Here things get juicy. The pope stopped at a castle, Canossa, on the Italian side of the Alps. High drama soon followed as Henry crossed the Alps with a few retainers and came before the pope as a penitent. He stood barefoot in the snow, waiting patiently at the entrance to the pope's castle. The pope kept the king lingering in this pitiful condition for three days before granting him absolution and lifting the deposition and excommunication. Over the long haul, the episode boomeranged on Gregory but it is a dramatic illustration of the highly personal and contentious ways struggles about authority and power worked themselves out.

About a century later the Holy Roman Emperor turned the tables on the papacy by citing the Justinian Code to the effect the "Emperor is not bound by statues," and that law, public and private, affirms this conclusion. Frederick Barbarossa claimed that imperial power enjoyed its own direct "divine right" and did not exist as a "gift" from the papacy, thus throwing down an important marker in the evolution of the full-blown divine right of kings.[68] The source of the king's power was twofold, argued Frederick. It derived directly from God and, via a "transfer" of sovereign authority from the *populus Romanus* of old to the people of the present moment, via a grant of power.[69]

How Far Does the King's Writ Run?

One of the most familiar episodes in twelfth-century political history is the struggle between Henry II and Archbishop Thomas Becket. The English monarch by the time of Henry II freely "bound" himself via a coronation oath.[70] The beginnings, or *a* beginning certainly, of constitutional sovereignty lay in the self-binding of medieval kings. Who judged whether the king had violated his oath is the million-dollar question. The long history of quarrels between English kings and the Church before the Becket affair had to do with the competing writs of canon law and the king's law. Does the king ever have a hand in "investing" Church officials with the temporal symbols of their offices as feudal lords who are themselves subject to the king in that capacity? And so on.

Henry was keen to arrest and to try clerics who committed crimes in the Royal Courts. A hornet's nest of complexities had been sorted out in the time of Henry I having to do with the nature of procedural appeals for criminous clerks, who answered in what court, what aspects were exclusively under the purview of canon law and what under the royal law. None of these "solutions" worked out smoothly as the claims of the Church—not only the papacy but the local churches that were, by the twelfth century, becoming "national" churches—often clashed with those of ambitious monarchs in a very real sense. The independent

power of the Church, whether under the banner of a superior authority
to that of earthly monarchs, or simply its own autonomy that could not
be meddled with by kings, was a barrier to the fullness of power sought
by national monarchs in the name of sovereignty. The particulars of
whether notorious crimes committed by clerics were treated too lightly
in Church courts, or whether a bishop could use his spiritual and moral
authority to excommunicate a feudal vassal in direct service to the king,
are rather less interesting than the grand theories backing up these particular cases.

Henry consolidated his sway against not only the Church but other
feudal lords, insisting that a church set against the monarch is a church
on a collision course out of which it will suffer a diminution of its
authority. His friend, Thomas Becket, had been Henry's Chancellor of
England. In order to try to control the Church, Henry appointed his
friend Becket archbishop only to find Becket doing a 180-degree turn
and becoming a tenacious prelate who proclaimed that the Church's
authority was coequal to the King's. At stake, Becket insisted, were the
rights of the Church and the rights of God against Caesar. Although
Becket, assassinated, became a martyr and rallying point, over the long
haul the English church split from Rome and became a territorial state
church. Henry may have lost the "PR battle," but he—or his urgent and
sweeping claims of royal authority—won the war.[71]

Who Is Subject? Who Rules?

Although Pope Innocent III is the first pope to embrace the notion of
"prerogative" as a characteristic of Church power, applying Jeremiah
1:10, "I have set thee over the nations and kingdoms," Innocent's declaration that he was "less than God but more than man," a grand
declaration of papal sovereignty and supremacy, meant the die had
been cast.[72] Innocent IV, in turn, proclaimed that the person of the
pope was a kind of corporate representative on earth of Jesus himself
and, it followed perforce, that all human beings and not only Christians "were subjects of the pope," de jure the universal monarch.[73]
Why belabor this point? Because the papal view—whatever the ex-

cesses of its most grandiose publicists—held that the human person was implicated in his and her totality by the faith. There was no "on the one hand" but then "on the other": for the body is one but has many members. As members of the one body, there must be a kind of sovereign to hold the body intact and give it direction. Because the spiritual sword is superior, that person is the pope.

As this claim was contested on many fronts, the battle lines were redrawn and eventually the Church wound up fighting defensively for her own relative autonomy and freedom from complete control by, or absorption within, nationalizing temporal powers. The spiritual sword weakened in relation to the temporal sword and, in some formulations, the sword was yanked from the hands of *ecclesia*, bishop, pope, and priest, as the two swords were wielded by the divine-right monarch, a step en route to the birth of the sovereign state.

Connections have often been drawn between the sovereign lordship of God and the person, or quasi-divine, status of the king.[74] Less frequently does one find mutually constitutive lines being drawn from sovereign God to sovereign state, perhaps because the governing notion of the state is legalistic, abstract, and impersonal, whereas medieval royal governance was highly personal and relied heavily on that "divinity that doth hedge a king."

ON THE ROAD TO THE SOVEREIGN STATE

With the shift to voluntarist understandings—law and rule as command—it is inevitable that wills should clash with the pope, jockeying for position and seeking supremacy over earthly principates, and vice versa. Setting wills in motion sooner or later triggers a "master-slave" scenario: Someone must dominate another as there is no room for a stable, coequal governance of mutually cooperative wills—save in utopian fantasies. Wills *must* compete if one defines the essence of something—whether the deity or the state—as a site of a unitary will. It is in the nature of wills that once one moves from the "free will" of the Christian believer to the commanding wills of rulers, the battle is joined. This no doubt proclaims a case yet to be made, so let's deepen our understanding of what is involved.

If there is a vital move in theology, law, and ethics with nominalism, it is this: An emphasis on the primacy of will over intellect is lodged as the gravamen of understandings of power and authority—a seismic shift from realist emphases. Within medieval realism, even as Jesus, the Mediator, helps us to "rise to him," as Augustine puts it, so an enduring fabric and structure of unchanging law forges a connection between God and human beings. Human reason has access to it and can come to know and to embrace law freely. The grounding of ethics lies in law. There is an element of predictability here: You can "take it to the bank," as we nowadays say.

By contrast, the rise of a command-obedience account of law, what in modernity came to be called legal positivism, turned, at least in its early formulations, on the theory of a willful supreme being who might as well have created things differently than he did—and might yet do so by undoing what has been done. We entered this territory earlier and we must forge into it again, although it is bumpy terrain. Tracking the sovereign God–sovereign state nexus doesn't require pegging every thinker, every school of thought, every pronouncement that, whether incorrectly or correctly interpreted, can be said to lead to an articulation of a triumph of the will, late medieval style. Yet we know such a voluntarist-nominalist philosophy took center stage, in part because we are familiar with later reactions against it.

Remaining on the trail of the will in theology and politics—the voluntarist tendency—earthly sovereignty is to social, political, and religious life as God's sovereignty is to the emergence of law and dominion in the first instance. In strong articulations of the voluntarist theory, God holds the potential power in reserve—power as *absoluta*—and possesses the latent power to alter prior revelations of divine law and natural law as reason-based in favor of an alternative command structure. In earthly affairs, law as an expression of will derives from several sources, whether the prince as a sole legislator, *legibus solutus*, or the "people," as the constitutive power of the *populus Romanus*, "translated" or transferred to the Western, Latin part of what had once been the great empire of Rome in imperial doctrine. The *populus Romanus* is always in session, and law is the expression of its collective will.

The "sovereign" or ruler, whether pontiff, emperor, or king, might be understood to be above the law and not beholden to it lest he choose to be so; or as a lawgiver who is himself bound by the law he gives (in which case a purely voluntarist structure does not pertain); or as a bit of both—possessing at times absolute power, the famous prerogative, but for the most part his power is ordained and bound. In this latter case, the ruler may bind himself by entering into contracts . . . but there was usually an escape clause of some sort.

The first and the third of these options can reasonably be called voluntarist: the first a strong statement of a voluntaristic thesis, the second a rather weaker formulation.[75] Everyone agreed that without rule or dominion of some kind, human beings would face a lawless existence. Only perfectionists and utopianists held that human beings, at least as far as politics was concerned, could free themselves entirely of rulers and could create and sustain orderly and peaceful communities more or less spontaneously. So the question was never between governance or no governance. The question was the why and how of governance, and with what justification.

A second characteristic of medieval rule and tradition held, as we have seen, that although there was one Christian society or civilization, there were distinctive "powers" within it: the famous "two swords." The fate of papal power in theory and practice is also a significant thread leading to the power and legal theory of the sovereign state. Each of the distinctive authorities in Christendom was divine in origin or legitimacy. Strong theories of papal supremacy and equally vehement proclamations of royal supremacy had this in common: Each pushed toward a unified or *monistic* structure in which the lines of power and authority were funneled in a singular way rather than being messily distinguished and entangled in a manner that invited the sorts of contestations I have already described between competing accounts of kingly and papal rule. In words drawn from a classical study of medieval thought:

> If we are to avoid falling into confusion, we must here be careful to make some distinctions. It might be asserted that one power was superior in intrinsic dignity, and important to

the other; or it might be meant that the nature of one power was so much superior to the other that, if any question arose between them, the judgment of the superior authority must prevail; or it might be meant that one of the two powers was the *source* of the authority of the other, and in principle to possess a superior authority over it even in its own sphere.[76]

The centralizing claims of the great medieval popes to the contrary notwithstanding, by the beginning of the fourteenth century this conflict was pretty well exhausted. The popes had fired their best shot, but the general trend was against the papacy, against the maintenance of the "two"—even if the most aggressive popes had insisted that the second existed at the sufferance of its superior. There are no doubt many reasons for this, none more important than the impatience of rowdy and often ruthless kings who wanted to exercise power and authority freed from the temporal authority of Rome. Never, however, in the long history of this elaborate drama, did a medieval pope proffer a command-obedience understanding of law. For law in the Thomistic structure, and law as the "good old" law of Germanic notions, had become *the* fabric of medieval life. Nor could rule ever be separated from *jus* or justice. Even for Ockham, the emperor, while above positive law and capable of making and unmaking it, was bound by the *jus gentium*, or law of the people.[77]

A WAY OF LIFE OR A PLAYGROUND OF WILLS

The recovery or rediscovery of "the will" in temporal, ethical, and legal affairs is a complex matter. In traditional medieval thought, as noted, there are "two" and there is law. Law is supreme, with positive law being as much an expression of custom as an explicit "act" on the part of anyone in authority.[78] The source for the new "willfulness" wasn't invented *de novo* but located in two possible places in the Roman heritage: in the power and authority of the prince as legislator, and in the "will" of the Roman people, the people being the source of political authority. Accounts of delegation imply some sort of ongoing relationship between delegator and delegated . . . unless one presumes that the grant is "once and for all." As with all the other complex developments we have discussed, it took centuries to sort this out. Debates about God's absolute or ordained power migrated over to politics. Those who emphasized that God is not bound by anything save his will followed one strand; those who argued that God, and the prince by analogy, were bound, followed another. That both should at one point redound on the singular point of *sovereignty* is a rather remarkable development.

Because the nation-state system in Europe took shape during and immediately after the period of absolute monarchs, we tend to forget that the absolute monarchy, was thought to be the most "modern" and developed form of government in its time, streamlining the raggedy multiple strands of medieval rule. Whether the literature compares what became the state or commonwealth to a single, corporate person with a common will, or a single will of a supreme ruler, singleness is a distinguishing feature: There is "one," not "two." With the appearance of divine-right monarchy in the fifteenth century, the Thomistic legacy fades or is ignored in part because it spoke of a right of resistance and conjured with the possibility of deposing an unjust ruler. Such notions become more alien as all roads now led, not to Rome, but to Paris—if we trust the early modern sovereigntists. (We might less provocatively say, to the royal palace—wherever it sits.) A dense structure of argument holds that the king or prince is a sole legislator; that the prince may act arbitrarily if he deems it necessary; and that there is no right to resist him, no matter how oppressed and injured a people might be.

The ordinary power of the prince is deemed absolute, limited only by binding agreements he might make, although even these can be overridden should he find it necessary. The strains of divine absolutism or divine right flow from secular kings and their busy legists and, as well, from papal theory turned *against* proclamations of papal power and authority. "Canonized" as the *point d'appui* of political theory, even as the "scientific" study of politics (with Machiavelli), political sovereignty magnifies itself. From the papal plenitude of power flowed the claim that the pontiff was a direct representative of God, his embodiment on earth, and he could not, thereby, be opposed.[79] From the centralizing monarchs comes the overthrow of the earlier notion of the medieval king as *primus inter pares* among multiple "authorities"—the nobles and feudal lords of a given territory or principality—to the king as singular, sole, absolute in his splendor.

Let's take up Jean Bodin, first as a publicist for the French king and, second, as the thinker who proclaimed himself originator of the full-blown doctrine of sovereignty.[80] There was nothing shy about Bodin's articulation. The king is a supreme force, the way in which God appears on earth.[81] Without him there can be no commonwealth. The options Bodin presents are stark: either monarchical supremacy, what Bodin calls *majestas*, or chaos. It is single or it is many and the many cannot and does not cohere without the animating force and will of the one. Such contrasts are often the way with strong sovereigntists who insist that sovereignty can neither be shared nor mixed. Breaking with the medieval tradition, Bodin locates the basis of earthly rule, or the state, in *force*, not justice. Citizens or, better, subjects, are subjected to the supreme authority—the will—of the patriarch prince. And, for Bodin, it is will, not reasonable and faithful adherence to the laws of God and nature, that counts preeminently.

The prince's power is double, with *majestas*, his absolute and unbound power, tethered to a legal, or bound authority. Law is the command of this sovereign. Somewhere in the state—as in all human institutions—there must be a supreme authority.[82] Bodin resurrects the claim that one man has power of life and death; this is his *majestas*. The source is surely the Roman law of *patria potestas*, the absolute father in the household who carries the power of life and death over members of that household. One might summarize in this way: The state is conceived along the lines of Roman private property, immune from public control; sovereignty is conceived along the lines of the rule of a paterfamilias over the Roman *domus*. And the idea that the law has legal subjectivity because it is able to represent the Roman people as a unified subject—all come into play and are fused into a monistic structure.

There is a conduit between patriarchal fathers and households and the patriarchal king with his divine right to demand unquestioning obedience. The lordly father and fatherly lord both hold their authority via a divine grant. The family, however, lacks the scope and telos of the state; therefore, the ruler of the family does not possess the perpetual and absolute sovereignty which is the king's alone. But the family is a kind of image of the state, "the right order in the commonwealth." To the father should be restored the power of the Roman paterfamilias. The power, authority, and command a husband exercises over his wife is "allowed by divine and positive law to be honorable and right" and he possesses a natural and divine right to command, for the father bears the image of God, the father of all things.[83]

The prince exists in his full *majestas* with the French monarchy. He commands and his commands bear the force of law: He wills and through willing, controls. Sovereignty is here to stay and it is a monistic command-obedience structure that the first full-blown theory of sovereignty takes. It is a pity that sovereignty veered in this absolutist direction as one reflects on the centuries of grief and conflict to come, much of it directed at taming sovereignty. The break-up of a single Christian society also meant that future debates and clashes begin to "look" more familiar to us. For now, let us remember that the more "liberal" features of the debate are the older, medieval ones deriving from the authority of law and its limits. (We would no doubt call this conservative now, as it embodied received tradition.) The "progressive" view of the time endorsed aggrandizing sovereign power proffered by monarchists, many of them armed with absolutist doctrine and justification.

3
WILL, POWER,
AND EARTHLY DOMINION

THE STAGE IS NOW SET FOR THE EMERGENCE OF THE SOVEREIGN STATE AS the key *dramatis personae* prepare to take the stage. And it is high-stakes drama. Let's summarize briefly in order to take our bearings for what is to follow. We have arrived at Jean Bodin[1] and the birth of sovereignty as a political concept in its recognizably modern form. The way the "story of the state" is usually told is that politics springs itself free from the deadening hand of clericalism and spiritual power, all "archaisms" and "irrationalisms."[2] In this account, the Reformation aided and abetted the emergence of the state as did other great moments and movements that followed—Enlightenment, constitutionalism—and voilà, we find ourselves in the world of modern secular states. With secular states comes the autonomy of selves that, having stumbled in the dark and under the thumb of powers dead set against human beings standing up for themselves, now can live in a way that isn't subservient and beholden.

No serious scholar accepts this simplistic version of events any longer, although many hard-core secularists—as distinguished from those who concur that we live in a secular world—do. But it remains the general frame within which the "story of the state" is told.[3] Several decades ago, I took exception to the received narrative in observing that this trajectory paid scant attention to the far different arc followed by "gender relations," public and private.[4] What I am up to here is a rethinking of the story of modernity and the manner in which it emerged when medieval structures swayed and finally toppled with sovereignty as the conceptual lever to pry open dense historic accounts.

WHAT HAPPENED TO *Plenitudo Potestatis*?

That earthly dominion is about *jus* or justice and governed by law is a primary inheritance of the Middle Ages, as is the conviction that, were a ruler to violate systematically the reasons for why we have earthly dominion in the first place, he would be a "tyrant" and his rule no longer legitimate. Various remedies were proffered should this sort of disaster occur. One might endure tyranny prayerfully, longing for release. Or, according to some theologians, legists, and philosophers, active remedies to remove the tyrant might be in order. Whatever the solution to tyranny, and these varied, all medieval thinkers were agreed that each particular regime needed to be evaluated with reference to the legitimate end of rule. No canopy of legitimacy was thrown over temporal rule *tout court*. Called the medieval "right of resistance," such concepts were to figure importantly in John Locke's "appeal to Heaven" and in constitutionalism, including the American founding, in the centuries to come—although the medieval contribution is frequently forgotten given general ignorance of, and disdain for, the so-called dark ages.

There were, to be sure, problematic features of the medieval inheritance as the accent shifted from sovereign God as the apogee of reason and love, a God bound to and by his loving creation, to God as force and will, a God less accessible to us and less trustworthy. In the Augustinian-Thomistic system, remember, persons have access to the transcendent God through that God made immanent in the second person of the trinity. Also important is the fact that society was construed as a whole—a *societas Christiana*—within which one identified two distinctive authorities and powers, each with its own legitimacy and rationale.[5]

This vision was *anti*-monistic insofar as it resisted two forms of fusion: (1) All power, sacred and secular, is fused into a single overarching structure, or, contrastingly, (2) "the people" are welded into an undifferentiated whole under the aegis of an omnicompetent state. For medieval political understanding was not, as is often argued, "organic" or undifferentiated. It was more supple and plural. The Thomistic notion of a "common good," for example, is not a monistic idea; rather, it emerges from the interaction of plural institutions in and through which human "wills" can be reconciled and the public good articulated. The Gelasian "two swords" doctrine is also anti-monistic insofar as the spiritual sword possesses autonomy and has say over the independence of its own law-governed structure, meaning, in practice, that kings and emperors had no authority over ecclesiastical persons.[6] When the delicate calibration of the medieval system teetered one way or another, the monistic temptation came into play, whether from the side of the papacy or from the side of increasingly aggressive Holy Roman Emperors and centralizing monarchs.

Within the monistic urgency, the so-called right of resistance fades as the claim triumphs that, because all authority is from God, no resistance can be legitimate. The seeds of absolutism are here sown. On the papal side, the slide toward absolutism fused the two swords into one held by the pope, who then delegated power as he saw fit. In this articulation, the pope could withdraw delegated power in the same way: as he saw fit. In the anti-monistic theory, by contrast, the two swords are at one and the same time independent in their own spheres, but dependent when operating in the sphere of the other. Ambitious popes and rulers chafed at this interdependency and strove to take over more and more of the terrain of the other—all in the interest of a monistic fusion of power, whether into a plenipotentiary state or a plenipotentiary spiritual earthly kingdom.

With Pope Gregory VII—he of the contretemps with Henry IV depicted in the previous chapter—the fullness of medieval *plenitudo potestatis* was articulated as a power that included a right to free all subjects, including a king or emperor's feudal retainers bound by a personal oath before God to their ruler, from obedience to that ruler. In other words, a temporal correlative of a spiritual power—the right to excommunicate in practice—was articulated de jure as the right to depose and to "free" subjects from bonds to ruler. By the thirteenth century the principle of a plenitude of papal power is fully articulated even as the actual power of the spiritual authority wanes. Historian Wilks reminds us of how "foreign" the notion of a plenitude of power sounds to the ears of us citizens of modern constitutional democracies. "It was," he writes, "sovereignty pure and simple, the power to do all things: 'Papa omnia potest,' and this must be the case . . . when all matters affecting a society which is the *corpus Christi* take on the aura of divine matters."[7] We associate such proclamations, with an analogy that obscures more than it reveals, to twentieth-century articulations of absolute political rule. There are many reasons to resist such an analogy, not least among them the fact that all power and its workings are *under* God for the medievals. That is one reason the nature of God is worth belaboring.

If one sees in the run-up to full-blown plenitude a preliminary articulation of divine right and power, it is clear that it helped to pave the way for secular raison d'état and the absolutist temptation.[8] The ideal of unity posed by the medieval Church touched on eternal, not simply earthly things, and that is why it has been called "perhaps the most majestic ever imagined and one of the most powerful sovereign weapons ever exercised. Extending from the Creation to the ultimate Judgment Day, the Christian Epic included in its panoply the heavens, the earth, each princeling, and every miserable serf through all eternity."[9]

Aggressive and aggrandizing rulers found a norm holding that earthly dominion was not self-sufficient—the ruler was not even master of his own domain—a burden to the sort of power they hoped to wield. "He [the ruler] has absolutely no rights of his own, and it is this which characterises the papal supremacy over the other members of Christian society," a doctrine of full sovereignty.[10] Innocent III[11] appends the notion of "prerogative" as one dimension of papal power; there is none on earth who is "above" and can "judge" a pope.[12]

THE KING TAKES THE STAGE

Articulations of the full-blown sovereignty of temporal power predated and anticipated the "real thing." Bodin offered a rationale for the centralizing monarchs, as we have seen, insisting that the king is absolute, *legibus solutus,* the supreme monistic power within the kingdom insofar as his *majestas* is concerned—with a "moment" of binding reserved in the exercise of his ordinary power, which is limited by divine and natural law. What triumphed was the insistence that there must be a supreme and absolute authority somewhere, a view that echoes through the centuries, even when absolute temporal rule is "long gone" politically. In the words of a legalist construction of sovereignty that came out of the law school at Bologna University in the fifteenth century: "There is one judge, from whom the final decision of cases comes, lest with many judges contending, and no one supreme, litigations would never be finished. Also, no family, no community, no kingdom can remain in its full *status,* unless it has one supreme ruler; because from division . . . there easily arises division and schism among members."[13]

This calls to mind a curious tidbit from the pen of the English utilitarian, Jeremy Bentham, with his plaintive insistence that husbands must have the "final say" in marriage. "The man would have the meat roasted, the woman boiled: shall they both fast till the judge comes in to dress it for them?"[14] Alas, poor roast, we knew it well! This is rather sad but Bentham claims that utilitarian logic requires a recognition of a de facto implicit law of the stronger to which statutory law may as well acquiesce de jure in the interest of civic peace, hoping that the legal vestment of power in the hands of the physically stronger will result in the "producing of a benefit to somebody." This curious argument, pronounced centuries after the events we are analyzing, demonstrates the persistence of the view that power must, in the end, be singular *somewhere*: monism simply cannot be done with.

Decisive conflicts in the thirteenth and fourteenth centuries are illustrative, showing the appropriation of a theory of sovereign power from papacy and applying it to centralizing monarchy. Jean Bodin, for example, cites the canonists and claims that popes best understood "the meaning of absolute power." The so-called "age of absolutism owed a

good deal to the papal notion of a 'fullness of power.'"[15] Another
important dimension of sovereigntist disputes was whether political
accounts are embodied or disembodied—incarnate or excarnate, in
philosopher Charles Taylor's felicitous term. The dynamic of embodiment or disembodiment begins with the nature of the king within the
purview of his kingdom. We underestimate at our peril the importance
of the papal person—the holder of the Petrine office—as an earthly
mediator to sovereign God, a mortal "stand-in" for the incarnate one.
Wilks writes, "We cannot overestimate the importance of the mediatory
role assigned to the pope in the religious and political thought of the
Middle Ages. He becomes the bridge between heaven and earth, and
this not only means that mankind cannot attain to God except through
the medium of the pope, but equally that divine wisdom as expressed in
the Christian faith is obtainable only through the same channel."[16]

John of Salisbury's political theory was based on an incarnate metaphor, a "body politic": The body is one but has many members—with
the head, or governing organ, represented by the king. It is he who gives
motion to the whole. The medieval era was one of "incorporated" understandings of power. This medieval corporatism should by no means
be understood in the sense later pushed by absolutists to mean one
seamless structure of power under a dictator. Medieval "corporatism"
relied on distinctive offices and statuses, but over it all, animating the
parts, stood the head playing a role analogous to that of the human head
in relation to the body.

This embodiment of thought located kings in two spheres: the divine
and the temporal, the metaphysical and the physical. There was that
majesty that doth hedge the king but there was also the king's "touch,"
said to enact miracles on earth, miracles of, and for, the body. The attri-
bution of healing powers to divinized figures is not altogether gone with
the wind, demolished by "the silent artillery of time."[17] At the height of
Beatlemania, for example, throngs of persons with crippling diseases,
thalidomide babies having no limbs and carried in baskets, spastics,
paraplegics, were brought to the Beatles in the hope that the sight or
touch of a Beatle might heal.[18] The belief that the touch of a divinized

object can heal divisions, estrangements, including the estrangement of the body from its wholeness, lingers.

Despite this lingering, to modern excarnation medieval incarnation seems the bizarre outcropping of musty irrationalism. But in a radically embodied faith, like Christianity, surely not. Indeed, the embodiment of political thought makes sense. We may find instances of its playing out in the temporal sphere. For the Lord comes to earth in the body of a new-born baby; he is crucified in the flesh; risen in the flesh. The earthiness of the "body politic" metaphor preserved an incarnated understanding. It followed that changes in and of the body signaled changes in the body politic. For the body, too, seeks "peace" within itself and this peace is possible only if there is a harmonious *ordo* or ordering of the parts.[19]

This personalization of earthly rule is documented masterfully in Ernst Kantorowicz's classic, *The King's Two Bodies*, as he unpacks the king's "twinned nature," embodied in mortal "natural" man and the office which perdures in perpetuity with another "body" holding that office when a previous fleshly monarch dies: The King is dead. Long live the King! The king comes to supplant the pope as the mediator between the earthly and the divine. Thus, in the embodied account, "the king appears the perfect *christomimētēs* . . . with regard to power, since his power is the same as that of Christ . . . the One who is God and Anointed by nature, acts through his royal vicar who is 'God and Christ by Grace.' "[20] The will of the ruler brings the body to life.[21] The head must "literally be an individual mind or will. Most clearly of all, supreme power cannot be except . . . in one," else it would not be supreme.[22] So potent was this embodied ideal that, as we move into ever more abstract and legalistic accounts of earthly dominion and sovereignty, there remains a residue of embodiment in the insistence that the prince must tend to the "needs" of the body politic for sustenance. And it is the mind—the prince—that offers the body politic what it requires for life to continue.

This trajectory shifts from embodied Church, represented as a mother to all the faithful, to embodied king to—eventually—disembodied state, without losing all quasi-mystical and divine elements. Even as the king cannot die—as king rather than personal holder of office—so the body politic or commonwealth does not die as it persists after particular kings and rulers have perished. Legal immortality is conferred, despite all sorts of changes; it follows that nations historically could disappear from the map, like Poland in 1772, 1790, and 1795, for example, and yet live on.[23]

A BRIEF (BUT NECESSARY) DIGRESSION

It is important not to mislead as one lays out the movement to sovereign state on the level of theory. By that I mean that it is easy to overlook the fact that the overwhelming bulk of medieval thought on spiritual and temporal matters consisted of *livres de circonstance*, written *in medias res*, in the very thick of things, and intending to achieve something concrete. Self-conscious political theory was rarer: John of Salisbury is an example, as is Jean Bodin, but in these two examples, as well, a specific, concrete political aim was in mind. In other words, political thought did not consist in abstract speculations about ideal worlds or what-ifs but was very much work cast within the repertoire of available concepts, aiming to stretch them this way or that.

I have already noted the highly personal nature of medieval rule, papal and kingly. It is unsurprising, therefore, that much of "political thought" was directed to the king, to the holder of that specific office, and got the name "mirror of princes" literature. What is a "true prince"? How should he behave? What attributes and virtues are, or ought to be, his? By lifting up the example of the "good Christian king" and proffering, as well, the story of a king gone bad, writers labored to sustain the essential dimension of earthly rule, namely, a commitment to *jus,* to justice and righteousness.

For example, one Jean de Joinville in the thirteenth century set forth the story of "our holy King Lewis . . . so that those who may be found here set in order for the edifying of those who shall hear thereof."[24] Good King Louis, for example, arranged matters that "every day he heard the hours sung, and a requiem mass without song; and then, if it was convenient, the mass of the day, or of the saint, with song."[25] He was kind and generous to a fault. He loved God and loved his mother and it grieved him when people behaved badly. He never cursed and he ruled with justice.

By contrast, Salibeme, writing in the thirteenth century as well, describes the various misfortunes and follies of the emperor Frederick II: "Of faith in God he had none. He was a crafty man, wily, avaricious, mistrustful, malicious, and wrathful."[26] To be sure, he possessed some good qualities but of his follies there were too many. Indeed, the second folly Salibeme notes is that Frederick, a curious man, "wanted to find out what kind of speech and what manner of speech children would have when they grew up, if they spoke to no one beforehand. He bade foster mothers and nurses to suckle the children, to bathe and wash them, but in no way to prattle with them or to speak to them, for he wanted to learn whether they would speak the Hebrew language, which was the oldest, or Greek, or Latin, or Arabic, or perhaps the language of their parents, of whom they had been born. But he laboured in vain, because the children all died. For they could not live without the petting and joyful faces and loving words of their foster mothers."[27] Curiosity in this curious story doesn't kill the cat; instead, it brings a group of infant victims to grief simply because they had the misfortune to be orphaned, put up for foster care, and then fell into the hands of a curious ruler.[28]

Readers are surely familiar with Shakespeare's "monarchy plays." These grow out of the mirror of princes genre. Shakespeare shows us nobility come to grief—*Hamlet*—and a king undone by an excess of pride and cruelty—*Macbeth*. We witness a king disintegrating when he showers favorites on one daughter and goes mad given her death and the tumult of the aftermath—*Lear*—and a ruler who is, from the first moment, a tyrant, not a real king, given the cruel and unnatural way in which he acquires power—*Richard II*.

Richard II also focuses on the monarch's "supposed divine right to unconditional obedience, irrespective of his actual fitness to rule. As a self-conscious theory, this seemingly ultratraditionalist doctrine was in fact fairly new [the writer means the divine right to unconditional obedience], and was far more vigorously promoted by the modernizing and centralizing Tudors and Stuarts than by their feudal predecessors. For traditionally, as Lord Chief Justice Coke pointed out to an amused James I, the king was subject not only to God, but also to the laws and customs of his people."[29] Shakespeare preferred the "old view" that the king was bound—we might call this the standard medieval view—and, ironically, this is a position that we tend to associate with "moderns" rather than "medievals" when it is really the other way around: Absolutism was a "modern," not medieval, theory of rule. What was modern in Shakespeare's day, therefore, was the claim to divine right and unconditional obedience—associated in England with the reign of King James I.[30] The famous Magna Carta, one signpost on the road to freedom in the standard story, was a restorationist act, seeking to bind the king in the standard medieval ways. In *Richard II,* Richard acknowledges "God omnipotent" as his master—a master allegedly on his side. We know that this is false and that the "treason" of Bolingbroke lies in his faithfulness to the medieval view of the distinction between tyranny and kingship.

In *Henry V*, Henry, referring to himself in the third person, articulates the distinction between king and emperor explicitly, telling the ambassador of France in act 1, scene 2, "We are no tyrant, but a Christian king / Unto whose grace our passion is as subject/As are our wretches fett'red in our prisons."[31] In the famous English camp scene on the eve of the Battle of Agincourt, Henry, disguised, speaks of the king's mortal nature: "I think the king is but a man as I am; the violet smells to him as it doth to me; the element shows to him as it doth to me; all his senses have but human conditions. His ceremonies laid by, in his nakedness he appears but a man; and though his affections are higher mounted than ours, yet, when they stoop, they stoop with the like wing."[32]

Macbeth, of course, is Shakespeare's *locus classicus* of tyranny, an object lesson in the mirror of princes tradition. Malcolm in act 4 scene 3 uses the *t* word explicitly: "When I shall tread upon the tyrant's head / Or wear it on my sword, yet my poor country / Shall have more vices than it had before; / More suffer, and more sundry ways than ever / By him that shall succeed." MacDuff follows suit: "Boundless intemperance / In nature is a tyranny."[33] The kingdom undergoes a moral meltdown if a king goes tyrannical.

The personalized nature of kingship is on display in this scenario, for MacBeth acquires his throne with blood—he is illicit from the first moment—and his tyrannical reign corrupts the kingdom as a whole even as the rule of a just one lifts up the kingdom morally. Laertes in act

1, scene 2 of *Hamlet* makes the point directly, for on the choice of a prince "depends / The sanity and health of this whole state."[34] And, presaging discourse on the sovereign self, Horatio tells Hamlet (act 1, scene 4) that following the beckoning ghost of his father is perilous, for the apparition, having got Hamlet in its clutches or under its spell, might "there assume some other horrible form, / Which might deprive your sovereignty of reason / And draw you into madness?"[35]

This Shakespearean digression helps us to appreciate that "political theory" in the late Middle Ages and early modern period was not the possession of a few articulate, self-possessed political theorists laboring away in their studies but, instead, was the making manifest of a whole climate of opinion that permeated the culture. Thus, the move to self-conscious "political theory" *does* mark a shift. One way or the other, sovereignty is a preeminent concern.

KINGS ON THE MARCH

The medieval view in which the king serves as mediator to the transcendent contends with the modernizing theory that the king is an absolute emperor within his own kingdom. Normal medieval thought "binds" the king. The new contender unleashes him in a quest for a more absolute form of political sovereignty. Those pushing against such claims advocate forms of "binding" that include covenants or "social contracts." One way in which monarchical absolutism takes hold is through the king's (alleged) embodiment of Christlikeness, for he is the earthly connection to the divine.[36] Roman law was embraced—or aspects of it—to consolidate the king's power as resting on force and not, as St. Thomas would have it, on justice. The king's word or command has the force of law. And, like the antique *patria potestas*, the king holds power over life and death. This voluntarist or command-obedience theory of law breaks, or mutes, the reciprocity characteristic of the old view; namely, that both king *and* subjects are equally subjected to the law: They are in the same boat. Not only are they moral equals but in some sense they are "political" equals.[37] Too, the medieval king is to govern according to law, law to which he is subordinate. He is an instrument of the law, not the other way around.[38]

The new view, by contrast, is that the king commands, we obey, and this has the force of law. Law is invented or fabricated—rather than being discerned and articulated.[39] The older view, remember, is that the basis for all forms of authority is justice. The new view is that the basis for authority is effective power which can be used well or badly. The old view is that unjust authority is in fact an oxymoron; if unjust, it is illegitimate and not authority at all—not authorized—but tyranny, illegitimate power. Law binds power. Note two great intellectual historians: "We have here arrived at the beginnings of the modern conception of sovereignty . . . the conception that there is in every independent society the power of making and unmaking laws, some final authority which knows no legal limits, and from which there is no legal appeal."[40]

The older view is that the will of the prince is in tune with *jus*.[41] The new view is that the prince wills as he wills and uses power in ways that the medievals would no doubt find "unjust." But excess—or the possibility of such—is held to be necessary to a king's continued hold on power (the position later articulated by Machiavelli). By contrast, the older view holds that the subjects of a king may find him iniquitous; the newer view, in its most intransigent form, holds that the position of the subjects matters not, for the king's power is absolute.[42]

The judgment of scholars is that forms of centralization and the shift to will take the later Middle Ages, in transitioning to the "early modern" period, away from the older view. At the same time the study of "politics" as an entirely autonomous activity, rather than assaying *regnum* or temporal rule within a single Christian commonwealth, grows more visible as we shall see in the writings of two quite different transitional figures (between the old and the new): Dante and Marsilius of Padua. Each considers competing notions of political rule, what it embodies, represents, and accomplishes.

Dante's Dream of the Unity of Christendom

Dante is a transitional figure with links to the medieval and postmedieval worlds. Known to us as the author of the sublime *Divine Comedy*, Dante also dabbled in political thought. *Dabbled* is perhaps too belittling a word for what he was up to—I simply mean that political thought wasn't his chief passion. No theory as sweeping as the papal doctrine of a plenitude of power could long go unchallenged. This doctrine emerged in the first instance from a determination on the part of the papacy not to cede any of its authority to emperors or kings. As I noted in the previous discussion of struggles over papal *plenitudo potestatis,* papal claims versus monarchical and imperial claims set off the theoretical equivalent of an arms race as each power spars with the other to determine dominance. A theory of the unity of power—a monistic by contrast to a dual or plural view—never squared with practice, of course, but it is the unity doctrine that subsequent thinkers and legists either took up to their own purposes or protested. Dante is one such[43]: a Florentine passionate about the prospects for an ordered and unified "Europe," but *not* under the aegis of the papacy. Dante could not abide the claim that the papacy enjoyed "direct monarchical authority over the whole of Christian society."[44] Experience told Dante that the papacy was, or could be, an instrument of division and conflict, for he had witnessed truculent popes and temporal rulers clashing over a multitude of issues.[45]

Prior to writing and publishing *De Monarchia,* Dante had seen a pope depose earthly rulers. During the extraordinary pontificate of Pope Boniface VIII, for example, Boniface took measures to innoculate ecclesiastics against the demands and prohibitions of secular power by bringing troops into Florence to pacify the locals.[46] Such bold gestures prompted Dante to write up a challenge to the Holy Roman Emperor to take charge of things in the interest of making possible unity, comity, and a general *humana civilitas,* a single human civilization under monarchical rule.[47]

Dante dreams a dream of unity. His project unfolds his respect for authority in the conviction that the telos, or purpose, of earthly rule is comity, peace. Even as there is a legal presupposition traceable from Justinian's Code of a law of the nations or peoples—the *jus gentium*—it follows as a matter of logic that all of humanity should be gathered together under a single capacious canopy of political authority to be lodged in an emperor. For empire is the only available locus of such authority in thirteenth-century Christendom.[48] Working with the *Politics* of Aristotle, Dante reverses Augustine's insistence that human beings do not require a political formation in order to perfect and complete their natures—indeed such perfection is impossible this side of the eschaton. For Aristotle, by contrast, human beings are born for and to the *polis*, enjoying—for the male, at least—a completion of their own inborn principle of teleological being only in political life. Augustine had insisted that our natures are fallen and are fulfilled, completed, and brought to perfection only at the end-time, not in earthly time. In the meantime, political governance has modest but nonetheless vital goals: to make life less brutal, more liveable; to punish the wicked and to lift up the good.

Dante's position follows the Aristotelian logic that the telos of political rule is grand. A unity of political rule makes possible an actualization of human potentialities with a world government directing the process.[49] Human beings require a forging of many into one, and discrete units of rule are a "many" that stand in the way of unity, at least as they are presently constituted with each kingdom proclaiming its own autonomy against some other. It is the task—the very telos of empire—to forge a one. This and this *alone* is a precondition for world peace. The body demands one head else the body cannot achieve its latent purpose. *Only* through the goodness of the total order can good pertain in the particulars.[50] Human beings are "twinned," both spiritual and temporal. Lest the self be hopelessly divided against itself, those two parts must be made singular. Too, only a single world empire can achieve unity. Absent this unity, we remain pinioned in endless contestations over rule. Dante does not so much innovate as invert: He turns upside down the papal doctrine of a plenitude of power, preserving some essential features. And these he assigns to a world monarch. The analogy—as God is to his creation, so the emperor is to his people—pertains.

The search for unity and harmony dies hard. Never dies at all, as a matter of fact. This may account for the tone of moral superiority assumed by contemporary advocates of universal order by contrast to defenses of "many" political orders. The unitarists insist that because politics involves moral-ethical goals, a "sovereign" advancing one overarching ethical doctrine is needed. International law often plays that role in such universalist proposals. In his time, Dante finds unity in what scholar Kantorowicz calls "the self-sufficiency and sovereignty of the *universitas generis humani.*"[51] For Dante, the monistic singularity of sovereign rule is not in the interest of power but, rather, serves a rationally driven quest for the peace that alone enables humankind to achieve justice. On the divinized monarch falls the burden of forging unity. The raw material on which he works is pliable, not recalcitrant, for Dante assumes that all persons without exception seek unity within themselves under the aegis of a rational intellect and, as well, that all seek a peace that endures with their fellows. This vision is rather pre-Fall, so to speak, stunningly optimistic that perpetual harmony is attainable if we just get the parameters right.

In answer to the question, how do we arrive at one sovereign ruler? Dante's answer is, through a world empire, for a unified monarchy comes closer than any other form of rule to emulating God's singularity. The ideal of unity is an ideal of absorption, of bringing all singularities, some of which might claim sovereignty for themselves, into an all-encompassing structure. Dante's empire is a "clean machine," to use a Beatles-ism. We learn nothing of the coercive force required to bring kings to heel; indeed, there is next to nothing on the punitive powers of earthly dominion. Instead, one reads paeons and panegyrics to unity, to wit: "The human race is at its best and most perfect when, so far as its capacity allows, it is most like to God. But mankind is most like to God when it enjoys the highest degree of unity"[52] Dante continues:

> All concord depends upon the unity of wills; mankind is at its best in a state of concord; for as man is at his best in body and soul when he is in a state of concord, the same is true of a house, a city and a kingdom, and of mankind as a whole. Therefore mankind at its best depends upon unity in the wills of its members. But this is impossible unless there is one will which dominates all others and holds them in unity, for the wills of mortals, influenced by their adolescent and seductive delights, are in need of a director.[53]

The intellect is the sovereign of the body. The prince, the apogee of intellection, is the sovereign of the whole, the many made one. Temporal rule stands alone: it is not beholden to *sacerdotium* for its power and legitimacy. An emperor of all would seem, by definition, to be a remote and inaccessible sovereign figure. Not so, insists Dante, for he mediates our relationship "to the prince of the world, who is God," thus taking up the task assigned to the second person of the Trinity in Christian theology.[54]

It is often the case historically that as things fall apart and the center does not hold, the most passionate articulations of visions of peace and perpetual unity are lodged: thus it is with Dante. The thirteenth and fourteenth centuries mark the period when it becomes clear that a world of many sovereignties absent a singular, overarching sovereign, is the shape of things to come.

MARSILIUS OF PADUA: PAPAL POWER TAKES A BLOW

Marsilius is sometimes called the first recognizably "modern" political theorist.[55] It isn't clear that this designation and others that label him "radical," "pivotal," and "revolutionary," the articulator of a "momentous" turn that fuels "secular political monism"—help us to appreciate his account of sovereign power.[56] His key text, *Defensor Pacis*, was published in 1324. Like Dante, Marsilius remains a Christian indebted to Scripture, but primarily to the Old Testament, not to the New. He shares with Dante an animus toward the papal "two swords" doctrine. Positing twin loci of authority and power troubles him far more than the papal unifying doctrine of a plenitude of power. The unity of a single Christendom with two distinctive authorities, meaning sovereignty is not monist but dual, strikes him as a "dangerous division" rather than a beneficial distinction.[57] Marsilius agrees that the "buck stops here" but the "here" is not Rome. Where, then, is sovereignty located, how is it authorized, and by whom?

Unlike Dante, Marsilius does not place his bets on one man—the perpetual emperor; rather, he emphasizes law. At first blush this would appear to square with the standard medieval view. But Marsilius means something quite different by law than did St. Thomas. Too, and controversially, Marsilius is associated with the view that the papacy should be barred altogether from any authority to meddle in *regnum*, even in matters of "sin"—the standard rationale for papal intervention.

By the beginning of the fourteenth century, the choices before Christendom were cast as some form of universal rule under papal power or imperial power, or "a collection of sovereign kingdoms" that "recognized no superior."[58] The canonists and legists had helped to pave the way for Marsilius and others who pushed the envelope in the direction of the triumph of temporal rule. In Marsilius's case, one finds the notion that there is a universal humanity. This being the case, authority must rest in the universal and encompass the members of a given unit of rule.[59] Manyness can be forged into oneness under a ruler, or what he calls the principal part of any community. Sometimes seen as the early articulation of the notion of "popular sovereignty," Marsilius's vision is far from our own. We see in Marsilius a tweaking of the ever-important *lex regia,* with the *populus Romanus* serving as the source of imperial authority. It is the will of the Roman people—the Romans having translated that will to contemporary life—that constitutes the perpetual source of law.[60] The people construed as a united "one" rather than "many" is sovereign. Law is the command of those assigned the task by the superior or "weightier part" of the people. Marsilius's voluntarism assumes the break-up of the Thomistic synthesis of reason and faith.[61] This fateful severing of reason and faith bears consequences we experience yet. *There must be one.* The beat goes on. In Marsilius's view, the overarching secular ruler possesses the authority to call church councils. The draining away of the temporal power of the church assumed by Marsilius does not mean that this flow of power seeps into the ground and disappears, so to speak; rather, it flows directly into the lake of secular rule and the water rises correlatively. The clergy are brought under the *direct* authority of the state: This at least becomes the goal.

Until recently, the received view held that Marsilius was a direct forerunner of the modern secular state, at least in "all advanced countries, and that the sovereignty of the people and the delegated power of the executive and legislative have likewise been accepted in *every civilized land*" [emphasis mine].[62] This equation of the stripping of all "earthly" power from the Church and siphoning it off to afford the state an unparalleled monopoly of coercive force is more difficult to articulate with such blithe assurance nowadays. Even as we joust over reason and faith, so we engage in intellectual combat—and political struggle, too—around the conviction, called Erastianism, that the primary "good" of religion is that it is something to be used and manipulated by statesmen who may not themselves be believers.[63]

Defensor Pacis is not a gripping work; indeed, it is dry as dust. But incendiary nonetheless in its insistence that the papacy is a menace and a danger. The Petrine doctrine cannot be used as the basis for declaring a "plenitude of power over the whole regime of men."[64] This willful doctrine does not pass muster, according to Marsilius. It strains and breaks the "limits of the church."[65] Too, by contrast to the classic Augustinian view, softened by Thomas given his absorption of Aristotle but present nonetheless, the state is natural: it is not reducible to a necessity given the Fall. Uplifting the status of temporal power in this way, Marsilius stresses that the authority to make laws belongs to the whole body of citizens. The state is a purposeful entity which helps men to realize their full possibilities. Within the state, it is the will of a ruling class (which Marisilius calls *pars principans*) on which sovereignty is based. This ruling class is derived in the first instance from popular sovereignty: "Having thus defined the citizen and the weightier part of the citizens, let us return to our proposed objective, namely, to demonstrate that the human authority to make laws belongs only to the whole body of the citizens or to the weightier part therof."[66]

To Marsilius, all of this can be "proved."[67] The structure of the entity he imagines is dependent on the will of a legislator expressed in singular ways. It is the essence of law to be an expression of that will, or the command of the "greater part" of the sovereign people. Marsilius writes: "In another way it may be considered according as with regard to its observance there is given a command coercive through punishment or reward to be distributed in the present world, or according as it is handed down by way of such a command; and considered in this way it most properly is called, and is, a law."[68] For Marsilius there can be no divided loyalties; no "twinning" of selves who may hold multiple loyalties without self-destructing; the state no longer is subject to external authority.

Unity "is the expressed object of sovereigns. Whatever their conception of the State and the sovereign power may have been, they have invoked the name of unity in attempts to absorb into their State . . . all separatist movements, all institutions, all powers which were too strong to be destroyed or which it would have been too costly to have rewarded or subjugated," writes James Marshall.[69] In this way, Marsilius anticipates later articulations of the "will" in politics and its eventual triumph, although the object of his political thought is not the modern notion of the state so much as the sovereign city or commune. His preoccupation is the preservation of the state itself—an imperative that grows ever more obsessive over time.

4
THE SOVEREIGN STATE UNCHAINED

THE PREVIOUS CHAPTER CONCLUDED BY NOTING THAT SOVEREIGN WILL CAVILS at internal opposition—by contrast to the view that there might be dual sites of authority and allegiance within a single polity. The upshot is that medieval *sacerdotium* is reduced to something more recognizably "the Church." She—the Church—may strive to maintain her independence from the state, but no longer can she impinge on the willful independence of a sovereign ruler.[1] God moves from suffusing the whole to taking up residence on the edge or margin of things, at least institutionally speaking. Of course, God continues to live in the hearts of the many, but the Church is defanged in its institutional incarnation in relation to public authority. As one arrives at the point that the Church must negotiate with temporal rulers concerning the place and position of the Church in particular polities, one finds about as dramatic a signal as possible that a unified Christendom is no more and exists only as an imagined dream of unity.[2] Two of the great, if unwitting, agents of the medieval crack-up are the titanic reformers Martin Luther and John Calvin. Luther, especially, is recognizably "medieval" in some respects even as his articulation of a political theology pushes in a direction no medieval pope could accept. Calvin relies heavily on law, as did St. Thomas, but in the interest of a particular body politic rather than a more general political project. Histories of the Protestant Reformation are thick on the ground. My concern here is to examine the reformers as transitional figures to the modern state and its sovereignty.

MARTIN LUTHER AND THE PROTESTANT NATION-STATE

One dilemma facing any interpreter of Martin Luther lies in the fact that he was larger than life in life and remains so in death, even at a remove of hundreds of years.[3] Concerning Luther, there is no uncontroversial interpretation. The assessments vary wildly. For some, it is a one-way street from Luther to Hitler: thus William Shirer in his 1960 best-seller, *The Rise and Fall of the Third Reich*.[4] The most popular story, however, holds that Luther makes one giant leap for humankind in the direction of freedom. There is the stirring view of Luther standing alone, facing the Diet of Worms (1521), and declaring forthrightly: "I am only a man not God. If I have spoken evil bear witness against me. Unless you can convince me by Scripture, I am bound by text. My conscience is captive to the Word of God. I cannot and will not recant. Here I stand. I can do no other. God help me. Amen."[5]

This is high drama, the stirring insistence of a man of conscience that he may compromise on many things but not on the truth. In historian Constantin Fasolt's words: "The promise of freedom and self-determination, that revelation of his self to the world, that ruthless honesty gave Luther credibility. Theology mattered to those who wanted reasons. Without theology, Luther himself could surely not have acted as he did. In that sense *theology is crucial to understanding the history of the Reformation*. . . . Henceforth conscience was never again to disappear from the stage of politics. Conscience was there for good" [emphasis mine].[6] We here see the pulling together of what modern political theory prises apart.

My undergraduate students in the 1970s and 1980s brought with them the conviction that Luther was a reformer who fought against an oppressive Church, venal Churchmen, ignorant superstition, and for "freedom."[7] Although linking Luther to one meaning of freedom is not wrong, it can be misleading. For it is also the case that Luther prepares the way for the political theology that underlies the emergence of the "Protestant" nation-state.[8] For our purposes, the guiding question is, what does Luther contribute to debates concerning sovereign God and sovereign state—perhaps even sovereign selves? Is his reasoning monistic, pluralistic, or open to the latter even if this isn't articulated explicitly? In the standard view the answer to this latter question is yes, but, again, it isn't so simple.[9]

If Luther can be said to have written "political treatises," two would most certainly count: "Temporal Authority: To What Extent It Should Be Obeyed" (1523) and "An Open Letter to the Christian Nobility of the German Nation Concerning the Reform of the Christian Estate" (1520).[10] One might also include the unfortunate "Against the Robbing and Murdering Hordes of Peasants" (1525).[11] Luther's theological treatises are pregnant with political implications even though the subject matter is not per se politics. With Luther one does not confront a strict divide between theological and "political" thought. He was a theologian who let the political chips fall where they may. Historian Fasolt declares: "Modern politics is unimaginable without the redefinition of the relation between politics and religion that Martin Luther . . . demanded and obtained. It was the Reformation that made the separation of religion, law, and history from politics inevitable."[12] Is there a warrant for this, and what sort of state would follow?

In earlier works, I credited (or blamed) Luther for a great deal: for sealing a public/private division; for uplifting the vocation of parenting and the goodness of family; for attacking narrow, moralistic construals of sexual morality; for unleashing the prince in ways that bore dire implications; for diminishing the authority of any entity that can be called "Church" in relation to state; concluding that "when politics is given over to the Devil, as Luther gave it, one ought not be surprised that the Devil takes over politics."[13] The reader may recall the earlier discussions of God's nature, bound or unbound. Having studied in the nominalist tradition and positioned himself ferociously against

Scholasticism, with special venom saved up for Aristotle, Luther was deeply immersed in this debate.

For Luther, there is nothing human beings can do to "bind" God: God is either bound or unbound in his very being. In "The Bondage of the Will," with reference to God, bound or unbound, Luther writes: "What God wills is not therefore right because he ought or ever was bound so to will; but on the contrary, what takes place is therefore right because he so wills."[14] Luther takes some of the sting out of this severe view by insisting that God remains trustworthy, even though he is a God of will. For God is righteous and in this sense, notes Luther scholar John Dillenberger, "Luther is not a nominalist."[15] Human beings may create institutions that are voluntaristic and potentially arbitrary or, by contrast, orderly and hemmed in by a dense thicket of law. The latter is the medieval view, as we have seen. Luther *tends* towards the former view, though it would be unfair to locate him in voluntarism unproblematically. He is a figure with feet in medieval and early modern notions, and that is why he seems "modern" and "medieval" at one and the same time, depending on the issue at hand.

Let's begin with the self—although the sovereign self isn't our specific topic just yet. It is impossible to separate the freedom of the Christian from Luther's views on temporal power. The human person is a twinned being but no longer in the received medieval sense. Rather than being twinned insofar as he and she is located in two different and distinctive spheres within a unified Christian society—the spiritual and the temporal—Luther interiorizes twinning, emphasizing not external forms of membership but interior distinctions, a twofold nature of the human being.[16] The outer person must submit to secular authority, save in rare and extreme circumstances. Luther's critics argue that this leads to a sovereign individual confronting a sovereign state. That is too strong a reading; rather, a (partially) sovereign self confronts a sovereign state that is limited by its place in God's orders of creation, although it is no longer hemmed in institutionally, the medieval Church having been stripped of its institutional authority. The paradox here is nigh overwhelming. In depoliticizing the Church, Luther does not so much break the bonds of authority as draw these tighter by providing for the flow of all political authority over to secular rule.

Let's take this dialectic step by step. We begin with Luther's famous propositions: (1) A Christian is a perfectly free lord of all, subject to none. (2) A Christian is a perfectly dutiful servant of all, subject to all. These are not, Luther insists, contradictory theses, for they reference man's twofold nature: spiritual and bodily. The inner man is righteous and free (ideally), and no "external" thing can touch this righteousness and freedom. The external, bodily man is subject to laws and powers: One can readily see Immanuel Kant emerging out of this Lutherian chrysalis—and even some of the more extreme aspects of twentieth-century existentialism.[17] Concerning the inner self: The Christian is justified by faith alone. We are utterly dependent on God's grace. Obedience to the "externals," the commandments themselves, does not justify. Luther's low anthropology (his bleak view of human nature), most strikingly articulated in his colloquy with Erasmus on the "Bondage of the Will," requires that the sinner throw himself on the cross and rely entirely on God's mercy. No act of the sinner makes any difference to justification. Christians are, of course, subject to laws, but they should never be lulled into the view that they are justified by them.[18]

The outer or external man shouldn't be idle, even if works do not justify. A person must be good before any of his or her works can be said to be "good." The "bad" person who does a good act, doesn't do good at all because his inner disposition is turned toward evil, not goodness. "A good tree cannot bring forth evil fruit, neither can a corrupt tree bring forth good fruit," Luther here deploying Matthew 7:18 to his purposes. The tree comes first. If one genuinely wants to do good works, one begins by believing. Then and only then can one engage in the repeated acts of *caritas*, neighbor love and affection.

We do not live for ourselves: a view that separates Luther from contemporary articulators of self-sovereignty. Luther's self is "unbound" in the sense that he or she is free from the *requirement* of works and from the rituals and ceremonies characteristic of medieval Catholicism. But the believer is "bound" by faith, through grace, and works for the welfare of others unceasingly, given this binding. We are left to worry about those persons of evil disposition who are not bound, as Luther has removed many of the externals that might once have stayed their hand, although he would argue that the dense intermingling of the temporal and spiritual powers in the late Middle Ages did not curb them either.

Is external authority, secular or temporal, bound or unbound? For Luther, secular authority is freed from chastening and deposing by a powerful institutional church, although earthly princes remain answerable to God. There is no spiritual estate above, or poised equally to, the temporal power, argues Luther: This is a pure invention, he thunders, and the German nobility should set itself against Rome by creating a *cordon sanitaire* that the papacy and the "spiritual estate" cannot penetrate. All Christians belong to the same estate through baptism. Here we enter the territory known as Luther's *die zwei Reiche* or "the two kingdoms" doctrine. It is this "two kingdoms" preaching that prompts some, unfairly, to put Luther on a straight-line continuum to absolutism in its more grotesque outcroppings.

Why do we require temporal authority in the first instance? It is pretty simple. Human beings are sinners and tempted to do evil. Temporal authority erects barriers to the evil that they might do. Temporal authority must be obeyed; Luther strips away (for the most part) the medieval "right of resistance." He fears anarchy more than he fears a tightly knit order. Resistance is limited to an individual commanded by God in a matter that touches faith and that the king or prince would undo or command against. Then and only then can the Christian resist. This resistance takes the form of passive, not active revolt. After all, such matters as earthly rule touch externals and do not penetrate to the inner self. The inner self is "utterly free in conscience, in [his or her] innermost being."[19] For the most part, the temporal ruler should be obstructed in his often grim work neither by the pope "above" nor the people "below."

Given Luther's bias against institutions and his greatest fear—disorder and chaos—he is compelled to rely on secular authority. Alas, the prince's conscience is the weak reed that checks his exercise of power. This is problematic because by no stretch of the imagination does Luther believe most temporal authorities will be authentic Christians and therefore self-binding, servants to all as well as lords of all. Luther's is *not* a theory of the divine right of kings; rather, it is a doctrine that temporal authority is divinely instituted. The state's tasks are both punitive and positive in that the prince must protect freedom to worship. Luther articulates his thesis concerning temporal authority in one of his seminal essays. Typically, he throws down the gauntlet and states forthrightly that rulers cannot command in matters of conscience. They have not the competence—they are not authorized—to do so.[20] Unfortunately, temporal rulers are usually a bunch of fools or knaves, so one must expect the worst and hope for a bit better until that rare bird, the Christian prince, comes along. Don't hold your breath, Luther advises.

For guidance on the law of the temporal swords, Luther turns to the story of the Israelites and their kingdom, including the scriptural warrant for the temporal sword and the law.[21] The sword must not be shy. The prince should exercise his authority boldly, lest chaos and criminality thrive. The world cannot be ruled without blood. It follows that the temporal ruler's sword is often bloody. He is God's rod and vengeance. There are some—likely the vast majority—who need this coercive and punitive sword more than do true Christians. Even as human beings are twinned, are two, so classes of human beings are divided into those who belong to the Kingdom of God and those who belong to the Kingdom of the world. The former are true believers. They do not require the law and the sword: "To live outside the law you must be honest," sings Bob Dylan, and Luther's citizens of the Kingdom of God are honest.

Alas, it will never be the case in this vale of tears that all the world is truly faithful; thus, the sword is required in perpetuity. Some—citizens of God's kingdom—go much beyond what the law requires to help their neighbors and give of themselves. But they cannot do this work of *caritas* if disorder is threatening and chaos pertains. Given Luther's assumptions, it is more rather than less likely that force is needed to bind human beings to one another and to the law. Were we "naturally" more good, less wicked, the hand of temporal authority could rest lighter on our heads. But we are not. So worldly authority has the power to punish and punish severely: not only power but authority. This is its legitimate task.

There are both mild and strong interpretations of Luther on the will and the state. The strong interpretations hold that, for Luther, human reason is the devil's plaything. It follows that our self-willing is invariably inflicted by the sin of pride: Adam's ur-sin of disobedience. Weaker interpretations hold that Luther hopes to tame strong notions of the efficacy of the will in order to keep believers both humble and prayerfully aware that their salvation lies not in self-worth and deeds but in grace, prayer, and God's forgiveness. Luther's self cannot be said to be sovereign, even in its innermost part. It may be free but this is not the same thing as being sovereign. The weakness of the human will is such that to pretend we can consistently will "the good" is folly. We are ongoingly reminded of our creaturely status by Luther: Believers are under God, not coequal to him.

But what about temporal authority? Human beings—all human beings—are subjected to a form of temporal authority. That this is so is not so much from interest in a common good as the hope that the least harm might be done. Only if all persons belonged to the Kingdom of God would the need for temporal law vanish. Temporal rule restrains the unchristian and the wicked. Those believers who, naively, hold that one can rule by the gospel alone would, were they in ascendance, unleash the beasts on the world to devour, slash, and slay as they might.[22] On this earth, if the lion lies down with the lamb, the lamb must be replaced frequently.

Although they are under temporal authority, Christians are not of it totally; however, they should, if called upon, fulfill temporal offices, including that of hangman. Government, ordained of God, is not to be despised. One should act in such wise as the inner and outer are both served. This means animation by *caritas*. Soldiers, too, can be Christians for they serve others even unto sacrifice of self. Christ did not bear the sword, true, but neither did he abolish it. As to the individual Christian's own orientation: If a matter touches himself or herself alone, better to suffer evil; however, if the matter touches others, the Christian may need to act in behalf of others even unto bearing the sword.

In a kind of Machiavellian move, Luther urges temporal authority not to punish too much or too little; not to command the soul, as it exerts no authority over souls. The prince acts under a norm of ordinary requirements *and* under the claim of *necessity*. Necessity may call for the temporary use of unusual authority by the sword to deal with a particular problem at a particular moment—a formulation that carries through to the present moment in, for example, arguments about the president of the United States and latent presidential authority under the War Powers Act. Luther concludes his essay on "temporal authority" in a typical way—by sliding into a "mirror of princes" mode, setting forth rules for the prince: He must give consideration to his subjects; beware of flatterers; not trust any man; deal justly with evildoers; be prudent; stay calm; refuse to go to war against an overlord, a liege lord—a very medieval formulation of temporal authority. If, however, what is going on is really a war of survival, all bets are off.

For example, Luther believed that the so-called Peasant Revolt, for which he was an inadvertent catalyst with his "priesthood of all believers"—a leveling argument designed to undercut traditional spiritual offices and vocations and any claim they might have to higher dignity—should be put down bloodily as it threatened temporal peace. Luther's reaction to the revolting peasants is a rather ugly one but intelligible given Luther's fear of anarchy and chaos and his insistence that one should not "literalize" Scripture politically speaking; theology isn't a one-way ticket to public policy, as we might put it nowadays. Luther finds the peasants—and by extension any person or group—identifying their cause with Jesus Christ an "outrageous folly and perversion of the gospel."[23] Those who do should be smitten, slain, and stabbed. Finally, and most fatefully, the tumult Luther reflected and contributed to stirred things up so much that "Europe" was soon riven by upheavals, wars, and confessional controversies, even unto use of the sword. There was no higher unity—no higher sovereign (save God) —to appeal to any longer, the papacy and empire having been denuded of much of their previous authority, in theory and in practice.

The upshot is the creation of the *Volkskirche* or *Landeskirche*, the Churches of a particular people, tied to a particular territory. Denying any form of sovereignty to either papacy or empire, sovereign powers flowed into the reservoirs of particular sovereignties and these became what we call "the state." This state was adumbrated in a variety of ways and through a variety of texts and arguments pre-Luther; Luther helped to seal the deal on the theological or, as we would now put it, "religious" side. In order to bring civic peace, a great council was called; the warring factions and princes turned up; the result was the so-called Peace of Augsburg, 1555. This council concerned the German princes but, as we have seen, the French monarchy was well on its way to centralized monarchical sovereignty before the sixteenth century; Italy was, for the time being, hopelessly split into contesting city-states; and England was going its own particular way having split from Rome and constituted a state Church of its own. (The severance from Rome was completed by Henry VIII in 1534.)

I will have more to say about an absolutist strain in English sovereignty in later chapters. For now, observe the unstable solidification of the principle *cuius regio, eius religio*, roughly that the faith of the prince is the faith of the principality. Princes are authorized to enforce their faith within a particular territory. Wars still followed—including the bloodletting of the Thirty Years War, culminating in the famous Peace of Westphalia, 1648, from which the classic system of sovereign states is dated.

A number of quite concrete things preceded Westphalia, though, including diminution of the authority of power of emperors and popes, with the temporal powers of the papacy gutted. Sovereign God–sovereign state are securely in place and religion—the Church—is tucked under the all-embracing arm of the state, a fact with far-reaching, sometimes pernicious, consequences over the span of the next four centuries. If modern politics comes into being with the presupposition of sovereignty, God's sovereignty over all recedes, Christendom cracks up, medieval universalism fades—and the "state" or particularistic sovereignty—triumphs and trumps. Luther and Lutheranism strengthened the territorial state, albeit retaining a role for the state as an ethical entity.[24]

The consolidation of the forces unleashed by the German reformation, bound and channeled, offered a strong autonomy for politics but fed into the oft-repeated insistence that God is on "our side," that is, the *Landeskirche* meant God, faith, was now a part of the state rather than apart from it. This puts the matter oversimply, to be sure, as one sign of a good state is that it guaranteed some form of toleration to a confession different from the official one. What about the freedom for protest and disobedience, including resisting the state? In Germany any such notion was radically diminished.[25]

CALVIN: A RETURN TO THE THICKNESS OF LAW

John Calvin, the second of the two great Reformers, followed upon the heels of Luther but took his reform in a different direction.[26] Calvin's background was law, not theology, and it is the mind of a lawyer, a jurist, that he brings to the question of how particular political bodies, independent of the universal Church or empire, are to be governed. His views are articulated quite straightforwardly in the admirably clear *Institutes of the Christian Religion* or, simply, *Institutes*, published when Calvin was all of twenty-seven years of age.

Calvin lifts up the dignity and purpose of the temporal authority by contrast to Luther. He seeks to reintegrate what had been ripped assunder. His state aims not just to repress evil-doing but to improve man via a religio-political order. In one sense this is a scaled down version of the *respublica Christiana*. According to Calvin, human beings are under both spiritual and civil governments. Civil government should support the worship of God in the interest of civic peace. Rulers are ministers of God in an important sense as a duty of office. The faithful should endure a wicked ruler with patience as his sovereign authority derives from God. It follows that no private person may resort to tyrannicide. God may, however, raise up someone to deal with the tyrant—this "someone" cannot be a private person. So Calvin, in this way, affirmed God's sovereignty and man's responsibility.[27]

The sovereignty of God is the pivot of Calvin's theology and ethics. One detects a similarity between Calvin's notion of God as *legibus solutus* and the modern, legalistic construal of state sovereignty. One also detects the voluntarist bent of Protestant ethics as natural law gives way to divine law or command, even as positive law under the state is routed through God's will.[28] It is a fairly smooth transmission belt from will to ethics and from thence to law and jurisprudence, with sovereignty as the "sacred dogma of positive jurisprudence, because it was the condition of the positiveness of law . . . the restriction of all law to positive law and the quest for a systematic construction of the legal order went hand in hand."[29] The form natural law takes with the coming into view of the modern sovereign state—to which Calvin made such a signal contribution—is that the sovereign commands and the subjects obey save in the most grave and unusual circumstances.

Although Calvin at points restates Aquinas on the law and affirms the need for a visible, manifest church, he nonetheless distinguishes sharply the two spheres of church and government, fighting for the independence of the "church" in relation to the "state." We note that by Calvin's era it is reasonable to speak of "church" and "state," for any notion of a united Christian society is well and truly dead. As students of Reformation history know, Calvin instituted a churched state in Geneva, with himself as master: this in 1555. According to Calvin, this was no theocracy, as it is often labeled. A full-blown theocracy existed in ancient Israel alone. Scholars of the history of religion argue frequently that the notion of the state as an "autonomous entity" is entirely "foreign to the Genevan reformer. . . . The Church and the state are both subject to the sovereign rule of God, the *regnum Dei et Christi*."[30] The fact that Calvin speaks of spiritual and civil government and their "completely different natures" would seem to buttress the first interpretation, namely, that Calvin sees two distinct modalities of government that are by no means antithetical but work together within a wider, if divided, Christian society—although greater unity may pertain in a particular entity like Geneva.[31]

Calvin enjoins obedience even as he abhors tyranny. God's sovereignty acts as a brake against any proclamation of the "self-sufficient absolutisms of rulers."[32] God is the only true sovereign, the only true monarch. God alone possesses sovereignty outright. Calvin has a low opinion of humanity—so low that he sees human beings as innately depraved. This depravity would overwhelm humanity save for the chastening hand of God and his grants of authority to both Church and state. The state has certain prerogatives. The subject obeys and is obliged to do so given the mutual obligation that pertains between rulers and citizens: This can be seen as a gesture in the direction of the medieval notion of government as a kind of proto-contract, between the self and externally imposed binding of kingly power. Also essential is curbing those enthusiasts who seek to bring heaven to earth—an enterprise that dangerously disregards our corrupted natures after the Fall.

Those who dissent from the requirements of a lawful, God-ordained magistracy would bring chaos upon an unsuspecting world by unleashing the depraved beasts within; indeed, all who rail against the magistracy, with its substantial but bound power and authority, rail against God himself.[33] God gives the magistrate the sword directly—it is not handed to him via spiritual authority. This sword punishes wrong-doers and wages wars, if just—executing public vengeance in a lawful way so as to preserve the tranquility of the domain. The law of God is a natural law. As to how we are to behave in general: We are to turn the other cheek, for the most part, in our dealings with others, never giving way to anger and wrath, even in war. Obedience is due even the unjust magistrate. To be sure, rulers have responsibilities to subjects. But one cannot conclude from this that subjects should obey only the just ruler. God—the sovereign God—must be praised in all things.

Now: it is worth noting here that Calvin's "political" references from Scripture are almost exclusively drawn from the Old Testament. It is the God of majesty and power of the Old Testament that proved to be such a nettle for the medieval thinkers—how to bridle such a God? Can he be bridled by any save himself?[34] These questions bring us back to the classical distinction—and dialectic—between God's ordained and absolute powers, distinctions that carry over into modernity and form the unacknowledged backdrop to the modern sovereign state.

Historian Peter Brown, the great biographer of Augustine, describes what he calls "The Rational Myth of the State":

> the seventeenth century onwards, was based upon a Rational Myth of the State. By myth I mean the habit of extrapolating certain features of experience, isolating them, in abstraction or by imagining an original state in which only those elements were operative, and using the pellucid myth thus created as a means of explaining what should happen today. The tendency, therefore, was to extrapolate a rational man; to

imagine how reason, and a necessity assessed by reason, would lead him to found a state; and to derive from this "mythical" rational act of choice a valid, rational reason for obeying, or reforming, the state as it now is.[35]

It is to this myth of the rational sovereign state or the rational myth of the sovereign state that we next turn.

5

THE BINDING AND LOOSING
OF SOVEREIGN STATES

SOVEREIGNTY IS ONE OF THE MOST FAMILIAR TERMS IN THE POLITICAL LEXICON. When we think of states we think of sovereignty. The locution—the sovereign state—springs readily to our lips. Instituted and historically reproduced, sovereignty came to seem something of an inevitability if a people is to attain its full stature and recognition in a world of states. As I have already observed, sovereignty remains "the essential qualification for full membership in international society, or, to express the point more comprehensively, the qualification which makes a state eligible for full membership. "[1]

The saga of sovereignty is usually presented as a heroic narrative: the bringing of order and civic peace and unity, on the one hand, and the inevitability of war and state violence, on the other. In this chapter we will trace further sovereign discourses and the dynamic of binding and loosing sovereign power: Domesticating the sovereign, one might call it. To that end, it is necessary to possess a working knowledge of the connection between theological, legal, and political disputes. Many of the thinkers I take up in this and subsequent chapters are familiar to us—too familiar, perhaps. As a result, we fail to notice just how extraordinary are many sovereigntist formulations and how deeply indebted to theology are legal and political disputants.

As we have already seen, there is no single *imago Dei* that dominates Western Christian theology. It follows that any theological template on which versions of political sovereignty emerged is going to be in tension with other versions. Painting in broad strokes one might say that, as taken up by early modern sovereigntists, God's volitionality trumps other features of God's being, like those articulated by St. Augustine or St. Thomas Aquinas. A voluntarist conception squeezes out relational and reasoned understandings and, as well, bids to place God beyond the pale of reason altogether. A monistic sovereignty exists in a cocoon—a kind of echo chamber—rather than in a space in which other interlocutors must be engaged. Monistic sovereignty is anti-dialogical. To be sure, as Kantorowicz notes, the "medieval patterns and concepts of kingship were not simply wiped out . . . [his reference is the move into early modernity] but they were translated into new secular and chiefly juristic modes of thinking and thus survived by transference in a secular setting."[2] And part of the divinity that "doth hedge a king" passes over to the secular state: An aura of sanctity surrounds it, else why would anyone die *pro patria mori?* Taken too far—as we shall see—this aura of sanctity invites "modern deification and idolization of state mechanisms," and what emerges is a triumphalist state with all its quasi-sacral trappings.[3] At its best, sovereignty has taken the form of the constitutional, limited state that affords its citizens both security and liberty.

ON THE TRAIL OF SOVEREIGNTY: HOOKER LOOKS BACK

We have followed the trail of sovereignty up to the point of its early modern emergence. But, as political historian Hendrik Spruyt insists, "History has covered its tracks well. We often take the present system of sovereign states for granted and believe that its development was inevitable. But it was not." The "new element" added that sealed the implosion of the feudal order was, he avers, "sovereignty" tied to a notion of "territorial exclusivity."[4] The trail of sovereignty is by no means straight

and smooth, as the examples of three famous articulators of themes en-
capsulated in modern sovereigntist ideology demonstrate, beginning
with Richard Hooker, author of the *Laws of Ecclesiastical Polity*.
Hooker is most often construed as a "backward looking" figure mounting a defense of the Church of England by recalling the normative and
regulative power of law as a medieval concept. This is only partly true,
however. Unlike the majority of his medieval predecessors, Hooker
moves back and forth between seeing the king as essentially the servant
of the law to construing him as a master to certain ends and purposes.
Defending the Church of England against the Puritans, Hooker begins
and ends with law.

Hooker is important because he illustrates one of the possibilities
among many possible configurations relating *regnum* and *sacerdotium*,
or church and state as they came to be called. Hooker helps us to appreciate the extreme nature of absolutism and the ways it was challenged by other alternatives. Hooker's definition of natural law follows
that of Aquinas in nearly every detail, connecting law to reason. The essential dignity and status of secular authority derives from a grant by
God—a God of power *and* reason. [5] The king is bound to and by the
law. This seems straightforward but it gets rather tricky. The king becomes king under the law; he reigns as king through the law. But his
identification with the law takes on a kind of quasi-voluntaristic cast
given that there are some situations and moments that require that he
go beyond or above the law in order to the preserve the law over the
long run.[6] Hooker doesn't stress the king's extraordinary powers, however, but his ordinary ones. These are considerable but not unbound.
The seeds of a limited constitutional government and a representative
system are on display in Hooker's writings.

Picking up on the ancient notion of *populus Romanus*, a form of tacit
consent rises to the fore insisting that, in accepting membership in a
society, you have given your assent to its constitution. The lawmaking
right, the definition par excellence of the monarch, is limited by the laws
of God and reason—a reason that the Puritans, antagonists of Hooker's,
denied with their scriptural "originology" and stress on God's obscure
(to humans) absolute will. The only justifiable reason to defy a command

is to demonstrate that the act of the sovereign runs in direct contradiction to the laws of God and reason. Hooker insisted that the Puritans had no such justification for their defense; moreover, they urged as an alternative an essentially theocratic, monistic order—an interesting criticism coming from a defender of the Church of England. But Hooker's Anglicanism differed from the ideal of a church controlling the actions of the civil government.

The Puritan ideal, Hooker fears, runs counter to the received status of *jus*, a system of laws that cannot, as Aquinas had earlier insisted, extend to the interior of the human heart. But the Puritans wanted to legislate nearly every aspect of human existence. Hooker's anti-Puritan stance illustrates what some have called Hooker's "restraint"; that is, Hooker is a thinker of the sort who gathers together and orders intelligibly principles and implications from the past, "one who thought out again for himself the great principles and traditions of medieval society," and that society, be it remembered, denied absolute sovereignty to any save God.[7]

Finally, for Hooker, the fact of human beings living together flows from our innate sociality and tends toward justice. The right to create orders of justice derives from "the people," another medievalism that Hooker embeds in his masterwork. In sum, law is supreme and there is at least the "implicit, and sometimes expressed . . . principle that the 'best form of government' was that in which all members of the political community had their share."[8] This best form of government is built on a foundation of a human prepolitical order. For human beings are not solitary isolates; rather, they naturally seek fellowship and communion with others. It is our sociality that spurs a drive to political society—for the common good. For Hooker, the world is not chaos, as Hobbes was later to characterize it, but an ordered structure, a cosmos. It follows that the tasks assigned to politics are neither overbearing nor heroic.

THE "NEWNESS" OF DIVINE RIGHT

Hooker's work and influence faded, rather like an aging photograph, precisely *because* of his moderation and restraint. It is extraordinarily difficult for any thinker, no matter how deft his or her pen, to dramatize restraint and to animate moderation.[9] It is unsurprising, therefore, that certain extreme formulations—like absolute divine right kingship—and certain figures—like Machiavelli and Hobbes—get the lion's share of attention and even a kind of adulation.

The articulation and enactment of divine right monarchy, mistakenly associated in the popular mind with medieval authoritarianism is, in fact, an early modern invention. It was the "progressive" view at the time of its emergence, something new and bold by contrast to the constraints embedded in the "prince is under the law" dictum of classical and standard medieval political thought. Divine right publicists took a leaf from the notebook of legists who paved the way for centralizing monarchism. In absolute and divine right monarchy, the king's body is itself sacralized. This divinization of the royal person means the king is at one with the collective identity of the state, an idea which is by no means gone with the wind in late modernity.[10] "Royal Christology," this is called. Kantorowicz stresses the liturgical nature of kingship—and this makes sense if the monarch can make stick the view that he receives his power directly from God, ergo he is himself an ecclesiastical figure. He mediates the heavenly and the earthly, the timeless and the time-bound. Promonarchical legists insisted that the transfer of sovereignty in the original *lex regia* was perpetual. Those who opposed the notion of royal power and authority in perpetuity and subject only to the "binding" the king imposes on himself claimed, by contrast, that there remains a residual or latent power in the people that comes into focus should the king transmogrify into a tyrant. Even those who called for the beheading of the English king, Charles I (1649), proclaimed that they killed the king in order to save the kingship.

Undoubtedly there had long been kings, both French and English, that believed they were the state—the famous *l'état c'est moi*. Interesting also in any consideration of royal absolutism in England is the fact that Frenchman Jean Bodin's tome on sovereignty received its "warmest foreign reception in England. . . . A translation of the *Six Books of the Commonwealth* was published in 1606 and the work won admirers at the English court."[11] Undivided sovereignty was worrisome in part because it tempted kings to believe that they were almost divine. A version of this claim was made by followers of King James I and such claims lie in the background of the political writing of the seventeenth century.[12] An "Epistle Dedicatory" to King James, on the publication of the glorious King James version of the Bible, that unparalleled monument, together with Shakespeare, to the richness and canniness of the English language, reads: "TO THE MOST HIGH AND MIGHTIE [*sic*] Prince, James, by the grace of God, King of Great Britaine, France and Ireland, Defender of the Faith, &." Continuing: "Great and manifold were the blessings (most dread Soueraigne) which Almighty God, the Father of all Mercies, bestowed vpon[*sic*] vs[*sic*] when he sent your Maiesties Royall person to rule and raigne ouer us." The Dedicatory goes on to call James the Sun that shines over all; says that his presence "disperses all murk and mistiness." England is "our Sion," James and God are virtually indistinguishable and "the translation itself holds a divinely sanctioned place."[13]

KING JAMES I AND ROYAL PREROGATIVE

We are dealing with bold analogies between sovereign God and the sovereign king, analogies that bode to become identities. The king in absolutist construals is "closer" to God than any other person in the kingdom and thus he legitimately plays the mediatory role to the divine. This confluence of sacral and sovereign offices and functions leads historian Francis Oakley to describe the pronouncements of King James I as a "political theology" in and through which he attempted to vindicate the absolute prerogatives of the "Crowne," while at the same time affirming his own robust commitment, as James put it, "to rule my actions according to my Lawes." James drew an intriguing series of direct parallelisms between kings and God. In so doing, he conflated "the *potentia Dei absoluta/ordinata* distinction . . . with the scholastic distinction . . . (in the terminology of the Protestant Reformers) between God's secret or hidden will and his will revealed in Scriptures."[14]

The king can do what God can do: "exalt low things and abase high things." This absolute prerogative, the king's will, is revealed in law and, as well, in those moments when the king goes above or outside the law.

The king possesses an absolute power in theory that renders him neither dangerous nor unreliable for defenders of divine right; rather, his will "revealed in his Law," is an expression of his "ordinary prerogative." That God performed miracles that unsettled the natural order doesn't make God willful and unpredictable in the main.[15] This is cold comfort to a committed Thomist, of course, because the presupposition of the king's absolute prerogative squeezes out the space for other "powers." Further, is it not possible that the king who freely chooses to bind himself can choose to do precisely the opposite? Particularly if he is not bound from necessity but binds himself "out of benevolence . . . while retaining . . . his absolute power, the prerogative of being able to act above or aside from the law—just as God does in the case of miracles."[16]

In this double use of the traditional distinctions, James touches on the two poles: first, the Thomistic insistence on rule by reason in the interest of justice and, second, that nominalistic strain that emphasized power, contingency, and the ruler's will. This is an inherently risky and fragile combination that could not be held together indefinitely. The strong prior tendency in English thought to keep the king under the natural law—to bind him objectively, not subjectively—weakens. As the power of the spiritual sword is challenged and then wrenched from the hands of Rome, the established Church of England comes more directly into partnership with the kingship, with each party vying for an edge over the other: the Becket–Henry II fracas comes to mind. This, too, is a configuration made possible by the spider's web of interconnections between what we now call "church and state."[17]

Given the possibility of multiple configurations, it is unsurprising that British monarchs in the "absolutizing" mode, like James I and Charles I, fought battles on many fronts against those who plucked a different strand of this spider's web of possibilities. James, as we have seen, contended with the Puritans, but the Jesuits were also a pain in the derrière of royal prerogative. Jesuit writers attacked the monarchy for its "sacral pretension," deriding the notion that there was no important difference between a king and a priest. "As though there were no distinction between Christ's Body Mystical and a body politic or human commonwealth. As though Christ had given His said Body, Spouse and spiritual Commonwealth to be governed either unto kings or emperors," noted one anti-royalist priest.[18]

James I advances the cause of the royal prerogative in breathtakingly expansive terms as his speech in Parliament on March 21, 1609,[19] in which he draws the God-king parallel explicitly:

> For if you wil [sic] consider the Attributes to God, you shall see how they agree in the person of a King. God hath power to create, or destroy, make, or unmake at his pleasure, to give life, to send death, to judge all, and to be judged nor accomptable [sic] to none. To raise low things, and to make high things low at his pleasure, and to God are both soule [sic] and body due. And the like power have Kings: they make and unmake their subjects: they have power of raising, and casting downe: of life, and of death: Judges over all their subjects, and in all causes, and yet accomptable to none but God onely. They have power to exalt low things, and abase high things, and make of their subjects like men at the Chesse.

If you are a subject destined to be moved about like "men at the Chesse" this doctrine is more than a little unsettling. James acknowledges that the just King observes the "paction" or covenant that the laws of the kingdom involve, at least tacitly, so that a king in a settled kingdom will not "degenerate into a Tyrant." But what forestalls such a dire possibility? That is the question. James has no satisfactory answer as he waxes lyrical about the "mystical reverence" attached to the person of the king, to anyone who sits on the "throne of God."[20] One fascinating feature of subsequent turmoil around the question of sovereignty lies in the fact that it isn't primarily the rights and powers of sovereignty that are contested, breathtaking as these may be, but, rather, who is to wield that power and assume those rights, and whether the person or entity that does wields it in a monistic manner: Is there one? Or, alternatively, is power divided and shared? If sovereignty is divided and shared within the boundaries of a given political regime, that still doesn't rise to the level of the medieval doctrine of two quite distinct offices and "sovereignties."[21] A pluralism of powers within a single government is a far more familiar and reassuring notion to us. We like the sound of the locution: "the sovereignty of the people." In England, and later in the French Revolution, however, the absolute sovereignty of the people, as an expression of the people's will, leads not to liberation but, if anything, to a deepening and strengthening of power over more aspects of human life. The sovereign "will" of the people is a monistic, not a plural idea. Historically, it moved in this direction and became illiberal, as we shall see.

In Cromwell's England, following the beheading of King Charles I, who had taken things one prerogative too far, the upshot was parliamentary absolutism controlled by Cromwell himself. Cromwell, unfortunately, added a Holy War ideology to the already volatile mix in the belief that he had a divine right to "execute judgement upon the Heathen . . . upon the King and his wicked Adherents."[22] The beheading of the king did not eliminate the sovereign and sovereign excess, as the sacral "people" now become the secular mimesis of God, penultimate in relation to the ultimate lawgiver whose commandments must be obeyed and whose power to judge is absolute.

With the Augsburg-Westphalian settlements, churches were disarmed in their relation to the state, hedged in by a *cordon sanitaire* that muted their civic presence and their potential political force and dissent. Churches were constituted as integral to the state.

The primary accent is on "armed civic virtue," the notion that the state decocts to a primal will with force at its disposal. The nation at arms is the highest expression of civic virtue. Concerns with a commonweal and justice—save justice as a command-obedience doctrine—fade correlatively. In the period under examination, a monistic site of sovereign power, whether it be the "many" (Parliament) or the "one" (the king) holds. In the words of one distinguished scholar: "The fatal identification of sovereignty with might is the *damnosa hereditas* of the English civil wars, but the beginnings of the departure from medieval thought which led to it go back much further." He, Charles McIlwain, then goes on to rehearse the way the two sides—parliament and king—argued for an exclusive supremacy, before continuing: "Under the stress of war, these opposing and one-sided but not yet wholly immoderate claims gave way to extremer views; on the one side, to a radical republicanism which had no precedent whatever in medieval England, and on the other, to the advocacy of a 'despotic' monarchy . . . which the political thought of the middle ages had recognized only to repudiate."[23]

MACHIAVELLI MAKES HIS MOVE

I leapt ahead of the story in the previous section by unpacking the theory of divine right monarchy using the example of the English monarchy. Let's return, for a moment, to the fifteenth century and to the most famous of all the political thinkers I have thus far considered, the Florentine Niccolo Machiavelli.[24] It isn't the case that Machiavelli is a bolt from the blue, a thunder clap shocking a somnolent postmedieval world into sudden awareness of truths about politics of which it had previously been unaware. Machiavelli may hammer the last nail into the coffin of the idea of a Christian commonwealth but he didn't build the coffin in the first place: that had already been done for him by the time he came on the scene.

Machiavelli is frequently read apart from the tumultuous currents of postmedieval upheavals, this despite the fact that he overlapped with so many significant thinkers, rulers, and events. Plucked out of nowhere, save the seemingly endless contestations between city-states on the Italian peninsula, Machiavelli is enshrined as one who cast off the shackles of medievalism and, by returning to pre-Christian antiquity, deeded to us the first "scientific" treatise on political life and governance. What is it about Machiavelli that continues to excite? It is surely because he is extreme, not typical. As I suggested above, extremism is more fetching by far than the ordinary, the everyday, the humanly decent and moderate. Why this is so would probably require a deep exploration into theological anthropology and psychoanalysis—some serious encounter with human nature. This is one reason Luther towers over Calvin in our imaginations. It helps to account for why Hobbes attracts more attention, positive and negative, than Locke: Exciting and extreme trumps sensible and moderate every time.[25] The danger comes into view when the extreme is *taken for the norm*. Not to find something uncanny and extraordinary in Machiavelli's cruelty and hyperbole suggests an inclination to see in the darkest arguments the hard and bitter "truth" of humanity. There is a tinge of this dark extremism in the early modern theory of sovereignty.

In some respects, Machiavelli is medieval. *The Prince* is a handbook in the "mirror of princes" tradition with this innovation: Machiavelli delights in lifting up as virtuous what the medievals condemned as unjust folly. At the same time, he carries about his own dream of, and nostalgia for, unity under the aegis of a Holy Roman Emperor. He pines for a political savior. Machiavelli's famous exhortation for a political savior evokes Moses, antique pagan exemplars together with the Biblical theme of deliverance from earthly tyranny: this in chapter XXVI of *The Prince*. "Italy has been waiting too long for a glimpse of her redeemer," he sighs.[26] For all his vaunted links to antiquity, Machiavelli's work bears the earmarks of the medieval struggle between bound and unbound powers. These are lurking in the backdrop with the prince as a figure who is all prerogative all of the time. He is unbound by definition and must be if he is to be successful, to rule with that quality Machiavelli identifies as *virtù*, meaning, variously, "craft, strength, astuteness, courage, effort, shrewdness, talent, vigor, energy, prowess, valor."

Machiavelli's prince is a highly personalistic vision of rule. He reaches back into the pagan past and resurrects the goddess Fortuna, a "bitch goddess" that controls about half of human affairs. This throws a wrinkle into strong notions of sovereignty as a mechanism to control and to manage as much of human life organized into a political body as possible. For Machiavelli, sovereignty is limited simply because ill fortune will strike sooner or later. He also abandons any notion of historic progress, reverting to a cyclical theory of time in which nothing new ever really happens: "Same as it ever was, same as it ever was," in the words of the famous song "Burning Down the House" by the Talking Heads.

Most important for our purposes is Machiavelli's argument for raison d'état or *ragione di stato* that lays down the claims of necessity in a grandiose way; that sidelines any normative structure or stricture of moral restraint in the Christian understanding; and that, in important respects, abandons reason—this despite the appellation of "scientific" to his work—in favor of luck. For example, another of his pagan mythical references is the goddess Occasion, who is bald in the back. Once she passes by, there is nothing to grasp onto, you cannot drag her back. So you must have the wit (*virtù*) to seize the main chance and snatch her before she passes by. This downgrading of law in favor of prowess derails the institutionalization of the imperatives lodged in the medieval notion of office.[27] If medieval theory was about binding, Machiavelli's is about loosing. Still . . . it must be said that raison d'état had medieval antecedents in the idea that the king can sometimes act outside the law and take extraordinary measures. But the inescapable difference lies in the fact that what, for the medievals, is the exception becomes, for Machiavelli, the norm.

The notion of the prince as a *legibus solutus* or *lex animata* has medieval derivations as filtered through Roman law. Given Machiavelli's obsessions with seizing and holding power, rather than acting through and in behalf of law, a version of this notion comes through in his insistence that the male is a form-giving entity that brings the whole to life: it is his virtuosity that gives form to the material deeded by fortune, "on which they [princes] could impose whatever form they chose."[28] Interestingly, *materia*, the material on which the prince works, derives from the same Latin root as *mater*, or mother, represented as an inchoate mass. It is the masculine *forma* that animates and shapes this material.[29] The Machiavellian system is wholeheartedly masculine. His *virtù* is the wiliness of the "public" player in things political even as the woman, privatized, keeps the traditional virtues alive outside the ken of rulership or, alternatively, plays Machiavellian sexual intrigue in the boudoir and in the mold of the intriguing prince. To that we must add the advancing "privatization" of "church." Once spiritual authority (*sacerdotium*) is no longer mappable onto a Christian society without distinction, and that spiritual governance is reduced to "church," it is easier to shove it off to the side of temporal affairs. So "normalized" is Machiavelli's sidelining of Christian ethics, so accepted is the notion that faith is an ethics of private life, that this point goes unargued more often than not.[30]

Some versions of the drive to prise church out of politics created a sphere of freedom for the church and for "spiritual life": here John Locke and, of course, the great reformers. Others, however, sought to expunge church as a significant institutional presence altogether: here Rousseau, as we shall see below. Machiavelli is insouciant on such matters save for the explicit ire he directs at the papal states.[31] There is no need to go over yet again all the many injunctions to treachery and cruelty one finds in Machiavelli, often accompanied by a wicked wit. He overturns the "golden rule" and pronounces instead a distinctly ungolden rule. He trashes the good Samaritan, for the man "who tries to be good all the time is bound to come to ruin among the great number who are not good."[32] It is better to be feared than hated, to be sure, but far better to be feared than loved. He fuses domestic and foreign affairs, averring that domestic affairs will be secure so long as foreign policy is successful. This no doubt helps to account for Machiavelli's continuing popularity: He takes the gloves off in dealing with "externalities," insisting that Christian restraint, so the argument goes, likely leads to more, not less, destruction and cruelty over the long run.[33]

Machiavelli revels in public nastiness—and all this to a singular public good as he identifies it, the independence, self-determination, and liberty of a bounded political unit. He fits the bill for all subsequent thinkers who see in raison d'état either a necessary evil or a perduring good. Machiavelli freed sovereignty of the need to justify itself according to received norms.[34] Evaluating everything from the standpoint of statecraft means evaluating internal to the very thing being held up for scrutiny. Statecraft per se provides no standard absent a normative account of this practice. We see the Machiavelli standards in his lifting up of Cesare Borgia, who seduced his opponents with promises and then stabbed them in the back. Machiavelli's preference, to be sure, is not for tyrants but for armed and virtuous republics of the ancient world. But, in a passage from the *Discourses*, Machiavelli offers up a recipe for sovereign excess: "For where the very safety of the country depends upon the resolution to be taken, no considerations of justice or injustice, humanity or cruelty, nor of glory or of shame, should be allowed to prevail. But putting all other considerations aside, the only question should be, What course will save the life and liberty of the country."[35] Small wonder that some contemporary analysts of international anarchy call for a revival of a "pagan ethos" that extols—no surprise—"public" virtue by contrast to "private" morality, thereby repeating as a given what in fact should be open to critical challenge.[36]

Machiavelli's ideal republic is entangled with and dependent on no one. The polity is akin to a singular armed body. The model par excellence of the citizen is an armed warrior; it is an armed militia that marks civil virtue and that ancient *virtù* is, in turn, equivalent to the *libertas* of the republic.[37] I don't mean to argue here that the full-blown version of a political body as an abstract, secular entity organized for self-sufficiency is here on display—by no means—for Machiavelli's account is too personalistic, relies too much on the prince as an artist who paints on what had been the blank canvas of the republic, to be that.[38]

The only way to tame Machiavelli's prince, the calming influence of intricate structures of law having been foresworn or ignored by Machiavelli, is for Fortuna, the bitch goddess, to bring him down a notch or two, or for another force to pose itself against the machinations of the prince, power to check power. In Machiavelli there is little of the "ancient constitution" of the sort repaired to so frequently by those contesting sovereignty and rule in the High Middle Ages. Instead, he highlights stories of defense of the liberty of the city by any means necessary. As we shift from the Italian peninsula to England, the thinker acknowledged universally as the great father of early modern sovereignty, Thomas Hobbes, appears on the stage in even stranger and more dramatic hues than Machiavelli's sly prince.

HOBBES, THE GREAT UNDOER[39]

Although Machiavelli is most often located as the first truly "scientific" student of politics, with Thucydides' *Peloponnesian Wars* as a precursor, Hobbes is placed in a line presaging the sovereigntist settlement of Westphalia in 1648.[40] He joins Machiavelli as an allegedly "scientific" student of politics, this despite his extreme views on human nature and his relentless focus on worst-case scenarios as if these were the norm.[41]

Cataloging sovereign discourses, Hobbes's vision is one of *strong sovereignty*, a maximalist account of what is required if society is to achieve the order required in order to forestall what would predictably happen otherwise, namely, a world of endless brutal violence and premature death. Here the famous Book XIII of Hobbes's masterwork, *The Leviathan*, comes into play:

> Whatsoever therefore is consequent to a time of Warre, where every man is Enemy to every man; the same is consequent to the time, wherein men live without other security, than what their own strength, and their own invention shall furnish them withal. In such condition, there is no place for Industry; because the fruit thereof is uncertain; and consequently no Culture of the Earth; no Navigation, nor use of the commodities that may be imported by Sea; no commodious Building; no Instruments of moving, and removing such things as require much force; no Knowledge of the face of the Earth; no account of time; no Arts; no Letters; no Society; and which is worst of all, continuall feare, and danger of violent death; And the life of man, solitary, poore, nasty, brutish, and short.[42]

One finds in Hobbes, as in Machiavelli, a world of extremes represented as normal, a world of exceptions represented as the rule. This invites ruthless behavior on the part of Machiavelli's prince and a coercive contract entered into out of primal, overwhelming fear in Hobbes's contractarian world. Hobbes lies in a tradition of covenantal or contract thinking but, like Machiavelli's upending of the "mirror of princes" literature, Hobbes evokes contracts in a way that makes mincemeat of notions of contract that involve promising, keeping trust entered into out of free will. Hobbes's *Leviathan* is a fearful *dominus*, the earthly version of an extreme nominalist God.

Hobbes inherited the tumult of the English Civil War, claiming that he and fear were "born twins." He knew, and despised, the Scholastic tradition and he cannot help but refer to the "Schoolmen" with a wink and a sneer. Let's briefly take the measure of Hobbes's claims concerning the necessity for sovereignty and the nature of the sovereign required, given this necessity. We have already taken note of his state of nature, a place none of us would want to inhabit. Get out of it we must, we plead. His Leviathan is brought into being given our collective predicament. Here is how the case is built—and I suspect that I am not so much offering anything new as lifting out well-known features in the interest of accenting a particular argument. Contrary to once-standard political theory accounts of Hobbes, accounts that brought in only occasionally Parts III and IV, "Of a Christian Commonwealth" and "Of the Kingdome of Darknesse"—sometimes *The Leviathan* was published in editions that excluded this second half of his masterwork altogether—these sections are noteworthy given our preoccupations with politics and religion viewed through the prism of sovereignty.

Hobbes tells us at the outset that the Commonwealth or *civitas* is a kind of "artificial Man," having sovereignty as its soul. Analogizing to medieval bodies politic, he locates magistrates as artificial joints; reward and punishment as nerves, and so on. The famous frontispiece to the first edition of *Leviathan* features a crown-bedecked king, sword and scepter in his hands, facing forward. A land is spread out before and below him as his body. It is composed of thousands of tiny homunculi, all of them facing toward him and gazing upward in a pose of worshipful awe and absolute dependence. It is the sovereign that makes the whole thing work, gives it motion. How, then, does Hobbes build his case for strong sovereignty, an argument that many embrace as the bitter, rock-bottom truth of politics and sovereignty itself?

Weak Words, Strong Commands

Hobbes is a masterful reductionist. His "man" is an atom flung about by appetite and aversion. Speech is a rule-governed business of applying the right order to names so, for example, one can say "the dog is free from fleas" but any substantive claim based on the use of the words *free* or *freedom* is an absurd and "inconstant signification." Nor is there a "free will," despite the fact that this is a *locus classicus* of Christian understanding.[43] Such usage leads to disputes, and disputes lead to bloody contestations, so words must be reduced to a strict denotative function. But how do human beings bridle themselves? Words are far too weak to do the job, so we enter into a contract out of fear, else we will use our own power in ways that bring every man into dispute with every other. And justice—*jus*—the noble concept central to medieval understanding of the *telos* or purpose of political life, this is reduced to obeying the rules and abiding by the contract, including the coercive contract that brings the Leviathan into being in the first place.

Law Is the Command of the Sovereign

Justice consists in following sovereign commands. The very notions of "just" and "unjust" do not exist until there is coercive power to compel men to the performance of the covenants by terror of punishment. Nothing like "natural law" offers a vision of justice to which human society might aspire, in Hobbes's world.[44] It follows that there is no such thing as an "unjust law": If it is a law (command), it is by definition "just," and with this argument Hobbes forecloses the space within which his Scholastic predecessors and contemporaries had evaluated law normatively and assessed whether *particular* laws met the standard of *jus* or not. What drives human beings, Hobbes tells us, is a desire for safety and whatever is good to ourselves. Whatever we give we do in anticipation of a reward. As to our vaunted reasoning capacity in which the classic theologians—Augustine and Aquinas—put considerable stock (though in quite different ways), reason is reduced by Hobbes to the reckoning of consequences.[45]

The Leviathan himself is presented in the language of grandeur and awe. He is a "mortal god" who uses the strength of all others—all those who have given over the right to use their own powers that brought him into being in the first place—and that transforms into his irresistible strength. Human beings do not require human society to fulfill their natures, *pace* Aristotle and Thomas (though not Augustine) but, rather, to protect them from their natures, to tie them by fear of punishment to a system of rules. There can be no commonwealth *unless* it is directed by one judgment—otherwise particular appetites triumph and lead inevitably to breakdown and a return of the "natural" state of a war of all against all. Men are continually in competition—unlike bees and ants (Hobbes's improbable contrast models!)—and they do not work together for a common good but, instead, for the immediate gratification of private benefits. The artificial man, the Leviathan, comes into being through the coercive covenant. United in one person, he is the mortal God. "Behold Leviathan!" This is a real unity, and no part of the sovereign power can be alienated or forfeited if it is to remain sovereign.[46] Behold Leviathan!—as if one is beholding the ark of the covenant or seeing before one's eyes the risen Lord. One stands in awe and wonder.

Forget About It: The Many Things You Cannot Do

The "rights" of this sovereign are not conditional, as in versions of the *potentia ordinata*, but unchained. The sovereign alone judges "all doctrines and opinions," has the right to make rules, judge, go to war, and reward whom he will. Subjects submit—that is their job description—for in the act of submission lies one's liberty. Once brought into being, the sovereign is *above the law*. Laws take the form of his untrammeled will.[47] He cannot break the covenant as he does not receive his power by the covenant. Law as command flows from the uniting of wills, *one having come out of many*, a melee of contending wills is pressed into one will that negates the authority of the old moral philosophy. For without sovereign power, law has no force.

Law can have no meaning contrary to the sovereign.[48] For the sovereign is not himself a party to the contract: He is unbound, a version of *potentia absoluta*.[49] One reason Hobbes frets explicitly about the so-called medieval right of resistance is that it may go so far as tyrannicide. This, in turn, would throw us back into a condition of multiple contending wills rather than keeping us under a single overriding will. One reason commonwealths dissolve is that the sovereign power "may be divided"—there can be neither dual nor plural sites of sovereignty—and because dangerous books are openly read, like John of Salisbury's *Policraticus*. Hobbes writes:

> From the reading, I say, of such books, men have undertaken to kill their Kings, because the Greek and Latine writ-

ers, in their books, and discourses of Policy, make it lawfull, and laudable, for any man so to do; provided before he do it, he call him Tyrant. For they say not *Regicide*, that is the killing of a King, but *Tyrannicide*, that is, killing of a Tyrant is lawfull. From the same books, they that live under a Monarch conceive an opinion, that the Subjects in a Popular common-wealth enjoy Liberty; but that in a Monarchy they are all Slaves. I say, they that live under a Monarchy conceive such an opinion; not they that live under a Popular Government: for they find no such matter. I summe, I cannot imagine, how anything can be more prejudiciall to a Monarchy, than the allowing of such books to be publikely read.[50]

For, as Hobbes claims in the little-known Part IV of *Leviathan*, "The Kingdom of Darknesse," a toleration of a "professed hatred of Tyranny, is a Toleration of hatred to Common-wealth [*sic*] in general and another evill [*sic*] seed, not differing much from the former."[51]

It is this version and vision of extreme sovereign power that enters the lists as a genuinely "scientific" approach to politics, because Hobbes's methodology breaks everything down into particulars. The problem is that that is all there is: No possibility of true commonalities and solidarities exists. Hobbes analogizes that, as precontract individuals are in relation to one another, so states are in their relation to other states, the difference being that the individual war of all against all can be concluded by the pact out of which emerges Leviathan. But the war of all states against all other states has no terminus, for there is no overarching Leviathan to which all states must submit and which they all must obey. This recognition forms the basis of a dominant strand in international relations called *realpolitik* or realism. What cuts across all spheres is a *lex naturalis*, not to be confused with medieval natural law. In Hobbes's world, the law of nature forbids "one thing only," namely, that a man destroy his own life.

Given the nexus between sovereign God and sovereign state that I am unpacking, it can be said that Hobbes's is a hyperbolic version of an arbitrary, capricious, absolute ruler—the sort of God featured in the most extreme post-Ockhamist accounts—and not one I wish to attribute to Ockham in a singular manner. For strong nominalists, like Hobbes, neither reason nor nature gives any guidance about what is good and evil—unsurprising, therefore, that Hobbes reduces evil—and good—to the more or less arbitrary names we attach to things: "*Good* and *Evil,* are names that signifie [*sic*] our Appetites, and Aversions; which in different tempers, customes, and doctrines of men, are different."[52]

Given the triumph or at least the pervasiveness of contemporary multiculturalist ideology (this by contrast to the fact of pluralism), such formulations seem to have a strong appeal, so we say: "Different strokes for different folks." This is an overhasty move. We know that there are enduring restraints and restrictions characteristic of every society—no society is indifferent to the taking of human life, sexuality, the treatment of the dead, and so on. There is considerable warrant for a transcultural or universal account of a basic morality; indeed, without some such, "universal human rights" is a mishmash, just an arbitrary imposition of one group of folks on other folks. To give up any notion of a substantive, objective—rather than arbitrary and subjectivist—construal of "good and evil," "right and wrong," is to give up altogether too much. One winds up in the garbage heap of bad ideologies. Hobbes's vision is voluntarism all the way down: an arbitrary and voluntarist sovereign god; a voluntarist and absolute state; and a self that can only be itself via one major voluntarist act (although even the language "be itself" is perhaps too teleological to pass muster in a Hobbesian linguistic universe). The state comes into being, given overwhelming fear, via an act of the will.

There Cannot Be Two

Because Hobbes believes we cannot live in two orders simultaneously—whether a state of nature or a state of commonwealth—so we cannot be faithful servants of a God external to and more powerful than his Leviathan, as well as faithful subjects of that Leviathan. A brief aside: Hobbes argues that the family constitutes a structure homologous to the state: He cannot permit the family to have its own being, its own raison d'être. In a strained construction—unusual for the deft Mr. Hobbes—he argues that the family, too, arises from a coercive contract, with both parents as masters over the children who "sign on," so to speak, because they know that, being weak, they could be starved to death or otherwise eliminated by the more powerful parents.[53] How does he sort out "religion"—the great and animating question that has driven sovereign discourse from its inception? (Please keep in mind here that an all-suffusive Christian faith has given way by Hobbes's time to "religion" and we are moving into a recognizably "modern" way of dealing with these issues—or at least the categories are somewhat familiar.)

Hobbes begins his treatment of "religion" in chapter XII of his masterwork, by telling us that fear of God has useful social purposes: His is a functionalist account. Like Machiavelli, he favors a civic religion. His God is a first mover, a cause, the one who sets things in motion. Religion he defines as fear of unseen things, driven by ignorance. Hobbes has no use for those he calls the Gentiles. He proffers a witty attack against the pagans with their multitude of mini-divinities, their portents, and their omens ("Men, Women, a Bird, a Crocodile, a Calf, a Dogge, a Snake, An Onion, a Leeke, Deified").[54] But he cannot endorse classical Christianity either, not without proliferating a massive number of caveats.[55] His attacks on Aristotle and the Schoolmen and his fear and animus toward the Church of Rome come through clearly. Classical "two swords" doctrine is a recipe for division and even civil war—incoherent and dubious at best. Hobbes's God is an irresistible power best displayed in Old Testament accounts of kingdom and rule. Toward the conclusion of Part II on commonwealth, he writes: "But seeing a Common-wealth is but one Person, it ought also to exhibite to God but one Worship; which then it doth, when it commandeth it to be exhibited by Private men, Publiquely. And this is Publique Worship. . . . where many sorts of Worship be allowed, proceeding from the different Religions of Private men, it cannot be said there is any Public Worship, nor that the Commonwealth is of any Religion at all."[56]

As he moves into the little-read (by contemporary political theorists) Parts III and IV, Hobbes steals the thunder from ecclesiastics by redefining religion, domesticating it, and putting it under the sovereignty of the civil authority. In the end-time God will reign as sovereign over a Kingdom of God and inflict punishment and eternal torment. Then

Christ will come to reign.[57] Hobbes's articulation of a "political theology" shows just how well versed he is in the theological and "church"/"state" disputes of his time.[58] His knowledge of Scripture, with especial stress on the Old Testament, is impressive. He deploys this knowledge to his purposes through sleight of hand as he redescribes basic scriptural norms and injunctions. For example, the positively cast "Do unto others as you would have them do unto you," Hobbes recasts negatively: "*Do not that to another, which thou wouldest not have done to thy selfe*" as if this is no major alteration at all in the verse.[59] There is, of course, a difference. Hobbes references passive inaction—do not do—rather than positive action—do.

Returning to his central points on "church," these are, first, that the church *cannot* be extraterritorial; there is no universal Christian *oikumene,* for to acknowledge such would be to sneak in Rome and the pope as universal pastor. The sovereign, instead, can command obedience to scripture and order the religion of his own people. Second, given Hobbes's obsession with "where is sovereignty?" ecclesiastical power is strictly limited to teaching. The sovereign, however, judges what doctrines are fit to teach insofar as they are conducive to civic peace and order. The sovereign, whether he be Christian or an infidel, is head of the Church.

Hobbes's voluntarist monism extends throughout the whole. He aims to eliminate any pretext for "Sedition and Civil Warre" as these derived in the past from attempts to obey both God and man when the commandments ran contrary to one another. Hobbes reduces the possibility of such conflict by confining faith to a command-obedience structure, so much so that he redefines Christian *caritas*, or neighbor-love, as a "will to obey." We are obliged not to disobey our faith. That is why we must obey our civil sovereign. He and he alone is the "Supreme Pastor." *Voilà!* Obedience to God and obedience to the sovereign are not in conflict. No longer need anyone struggle to reconcile the two.[60] To further this end, he strips sacramental power from the Church, for example, marriage as a sacrament. A civil contract alone should define marriage, not a church ritual, for there can be no power distinct from that of the civil state. In current debates in America about whether all faiths must conform to certain public laws or whether there are inviolable "private rights"—for we have, following Hobbes (and others) privatized religion in our own way and through our own terms—that are constitutive to a faith and should not be commandeered and trumped by sovereign civil authority, we find echoes of earlier battles. As I noted earlier, Hobbes's arguments represent an almost complete overturning of the classical medieval view of law, order, and so much else, but it is the medieval view that is ongoingly taxed as strange and foreign to us.[61] With Hobbes, finally, an absolutist strain in English political thought is made most boldly manifest.

It was Hobbes, and Bodin before him, that helped to give centralizing regimes, whether monarchical or parliamentary, a basis in legal and political theory. As we have seen, they were working from, and appropriating to their own purposes, a body of prestatist sovereign theory penned by defenders of the papacy as the site of a *plenitudo potestatis*, a plenitude, an untrammeled amplitude, of power. Roman imperial doctrine was plundered by kings and princes and deployed to many purposes—including the centralization I have noted plus a rationale for overriding positive law. Bodin's sovereignty as absolute and perpetual power vested in a commonwealth; Hobbes as a "reall Unitie," a reduction of all wills "unto one Will," the "Generation of that Great Leviathan, or rather (to speak more reverently) of that Mortall God, to which wee owe under the Immortall God, our peace and defense. . . . And he that carryeth this Person, is called Soveraigne, and said to have Soveraigne Power; and every one besides, his Subject."[62] The sovereign God–sovereign state nexus has rarely been referenced so clearly—and with an injunction to speak "reverently," as if in a hushed church, when one speaks of the "Mortal God," the sovereign.

The standard explanation for the emergence of sovereign absolutism, remember, falls into a number of categories, including the rediscovery of Roman law on which we have already spent considerable time. Primarily, however, one is treated to the heroic tale I noted previously: Facing situations of sometimes terrible disorder, with chaos threatening, guaranteed order and civic peace, at whatever price, takes on the force of an *imprimatur*. The fragmentation and chaos (in a typically negative characterization) of medieval Europe—divided as it was into many kingdoms under an overarching Holy Roman Emperor, with the Pope meddling, too—is most often cited as the explanation of the need, having nigh-teleological historic force, for sovereign states. The medieval system, as noted, was a "patchwork of overlapping and incomplete rights of government . . . inextricably superimposed and tangled" with "different juridical allegiances, asymmetrical suzerainties and anomalous enclaves" abounding.[63] Is this any way to run a continent? Thus the defenders of the move toward state sovereignty can be said to have reasoned. The Thomistic denial of absolute sovereign power to any of the component communities of Christendom, including papacy and empire, gives way to the construction of a perpetual, supreme power, first in incarnated form as the king's body which could not be dismembered and, second, in its recognizably modern form as an institutionalized, juristic entity that defines, both legally and normatively, the modern state.

Carl Schmitt and "Prerogative": Hobbes Redux

Hobbes's influence is great and continuing, in part because some who claim him as a "father" of the scientific study of politics choose to leave out the stuff about speech and human nature (appetite, aversion, and all the rest), as if this is dross or icing on the cake and you can hive off the piece of Hobbes that you want. But this doesn't work: Either Hobbes fits the bill as someone proffering "causal" explanations of the sort dear to the hearts of political scientists in the positivist tradition or he does not. He wasn't two people when he wrote *Leviathan*—God forfend, given his stress on oneness and unity! Rather than debating that point further, let me just note here the way in which Hobbes insinuates himself even with thinkers who are by no means Hobbesians. I think of Hannah Arendt who, in a decidedly non-Hobbesian discussion of power, force, and violence, finally throws up her hands and says, in effect, at the water's edge we are in Hobbes world. Here is the exact quote: "The chief reason warfare is still with us is neither a secret death wish of the human species, or an irrepressible instinct of aggression, nor, finally and more plausibly, the serious economic and social dangers inherent in disarmament,[64] but the simple fact that no substitute for this final arbiter in international affairs has yet appeared on the political scene. Was not Hobbes right when he said, 'Covenants, without the sword, are but words?'"[65] Arendt doesn't argue this point—she asserts it without challenge—although the argument runs counter to much of her discussion about "power" in "domestic" contexts.[66] Arendt endorses the classical theory in its general contours: (a) internally, sovereignty is the power to order a domestic arena—"domestic" implying that such order has already been achieved, the territory is "domesticated" (although, of course, Arendt rejects the absolutist version of sovereignty and raises critical questions about domestic sovereignty more generally), and (b) externally, sovereign powers function in a system of at least theoretical independence and equality of states whose relations are controlled by principles which are the reverse of those that comprise the internal structure of states, at least on the strong construction of sovereignty. Justice within; force without.[67]

The twentieth-century thinker who revived Hobbes in full-blown unapologetic form is the controversial Carl Schmitt, whose reputation has suffered—rightly—from his association as one of the "professors for Nazism." Schmitt sees his work as an explicit political theology.[68] "Sovereign is he who decides on the exception," writes Schmitt, for "only this definition can do justice to a borderline concept. . . . It must needs be borderline and not routine."[69] It is the sovereign who decides "whether there is an extreme emergency as well as what must be done to eliminate it." And he does so standing "outside the normally valid legal system" to which he "nevertheless belongs, for it is he who must decide whether the constitution needs to be suspended in its entirety. All tendencies of modern constitutional development point toward eliminating the sovereign in this sense."[70] The authority to suspend valid law means that those general principles embodied in natural law are, too, temporarily overridden. Reducing law to situationism, Schmitt places in the sovereign's hands the "guarantee(s) [of] the situation in its totality. . . . Therein resides the essence of state sovereignty."[71] Schmitt located support for his thesis of the exception among some Protestant theologians. Catholic support was and is much harder to come by, given the normative Thomistic structure of Catholic understandings of sovereignty under law. For Schmitt, any attempt to eliminate the possibility of the exception bodes to undermine the body politic itself in a case of emergency.

The problem, of course, is that a sovereign/Leviathan who stands outside the law (for Hobbes this is certainly the case; Schmitt is more ambiguous), *everything* is, in a sense, the exception as he—the sovereign—lies beyond normative restraint. There is a kernel of truth here; namely, that, in the words of Justice Robert Jackson, the "Constitution is not a suicide pact." There are dire situations—like Lincoln's suspension of *habeas corpus* during one period of the U.S. Civil War—that constitute an exception. But, because the American president is under the law, not above it, he can be called to account for such "exceptions" and, once the emergency is past, the measures taken to meet the emergency are in abeyance.

Anti-totalitarians, like the German Lutheran theologian, Dietrich Bonhoeffer, who died at the end of a Gestapo hanging noose, recognized moments that constitute what Bonhoeffer, following Machiavelli, calls *necessità*. But those moments must be rare. They call upon the leader or the citizen to perform a solemn duty. Writes Bonhoeffer, who was certainly neither a Hobbesian nor a Schmittian:

> In the course of historical life there comes a point where the exact observance of the formal law of a state, of a commercial undertaking, of a family, or for that matter of a scientific discovery, suddenly finds itself in violent conflict with the ineluctable necessities of the lives of men; at this point responsible and pertinent action leaves behind it the domain of principles and convention, the domain of the normal and regular, and is confronted by the extraordinary situation of ultimate necessities, a situation which no law can control. It was for this situation that Machiavelli in his political theory coined the term *necessita.* . . . There can be no doubt that such necessities exist; to deny their existence is to abandon the attempt to act in accordance with reality. But it is equally certain that these necessities . . . cannot be governed by any law or themselves constitute a law. They appeal directly to

the free responsibility of the agent, a responsibility which is bounded by no law.[72]

Bonhoeffer's account of "the exception" leads him to the conclusion that, as an act of free responsibility, he must participate in an effort to eliminate Hitler, hoping, thereby, that the Nazi regime will unravel. He cannot and will not make such an act normative, no more than did medieval theorists of tyrannicide. But he wants the option to lie within the realm of the free responsibility of citizens . . . without being "legalized." Imagine a world in which the law spelled out in excruciating detail the conditions under which it is licit to assassinate the sovereign! So, with Bonhoeffer, we get an ethical account of "the exception." With Hobbes, we find a permanent state of exception for the extralegal Leviathan. With Schmitt, we find a justification for exception that makes recourse to it too tempting—both in the first instance and as a perduring condition.

The thinker most clearly associated with a moment of unusual "exception," a "right of revolution," is John Locke,[73] although he neither writes nor thinks in precisely this way, as we shall now learn, for Locke's sovereign is as hemmed in by law as Hobbes's Leviathan is cut off from it.

6

BINDING, LOOSING, AND REVOLUTION

IF THOMAS HOBBES PICKS UP ON THE NOMINALIST-VOLUNTARIST STRANDS OF LATE medieval theological contestation and turns these to political purposes, John Locke,[1] or so it might seem at first blush, locates himself in the *potentia ordinata*–natural law tradition, though not without ongoing controversy over whether he is in fact thus indebted and if so how much. As we have already seen, there is no single "knock-down" account of natural law. Those whose work over time eroded Thomistic "realism" and reason, often clung to their own version of natural law (or law of nature) teaching. Indeed, it—this notion of law—had to be particularly forceful if one went the voluntarist route. For if the sovereign God is omnipotent and if his will prevails, it follows that God's sovereignty would be a terrible tyranny were God not bound. No humans can bind God; perforce, he binds himself. A number of scholars see the beginnings of constitutionalism in the claim that even as God binds himself freely, so the king or ruler must be freely bound. It follows that there are specific measures that must be taken to make manifest the earthly analogue of the binding that God enacts freely through an act of will.[2]

This will become clearer, first, as we take the measure of what this tradition yielded in Locke's hands. Second, I turn to the very different political thought of Jean-Jacques Rousseau, the French Revolution, and Georg Wilhelm Friedrich Hegel in order to illustrate radical alternatives that bend toward monistic absolutism—an unleashing of power. Finally, the Lockean strain is picked up a final time in a discussion of law and restraint in time of war.[3] What unites the different "takes" of Hobbes, Locke, and Rousseau is some notion of a social contract or covenant. The older notion of the unity of a Christian society (*respublica Christiana*), glued together by shared belief and culture and presided over universally by the papacy and a Holy Roman Emperor, as well as governed locally by kings, feudal lords, the eclectic panoply of the various partial "sovereignties" of medieval Europe, gives way to territorial, sovereign exclusivities. This "unity" that once characterized Christendom is transferred to the "interior" of competing territorial entities and cemented by a social contract of some sort. There are several contrasting models of this unity: Is it monistic or is it plural, a looser idea like the *respublica Christiana* which, whatever the monistic temptations and proclamations of Popes or Emperors, was always plural de facto? With sovereign political control over the interior emerges a vexing set of questions: How does one achieve and enforce unity within the sovereign state? Of what does this sovereignty consist? Must internal unity extend to confessional unity? If so, does this not require either expulsion of a confessional minority or, contrastingly, the institutionalization of some form of "toleration" such that unity need not extend all the way down?

All one need do is to look at current debates in Europe over immigration and what is to be done with a minority of an immigrant population that refuses to integrate into the society in which they are living and, indeed, openly aim to replace that society of toleration with a monistic Islamic state to catch a glimpse of the dilemmas. This radicalized minority uses toleration strategically and for the interim.[4] How does a sovereign state react to such realities and threats without undermining the principles that constitute Western democracy in the first place? But we jump ahead of ourselves. Let's go back and take the measure of how Locke and other early modern thinkers dealt with these and other problems.

LOCKE IN A NEW LIGHT

As is the case with Hobbes, so much has been written—and so wisely
and well—about John Locke, it may seem supererogatory to add more
words to the vast mountain.[5] Unfortunately, Locke's religious convic-
tions and foundations have often been downplayed in standard
accounts.[6] I recall no specific attention to this dimension of Locke's
thought in any course I took, save for noting in passing his formulation
of the "appeal to Heaven." This was construed as a gesture on Locke's
part to the religious demands of the day, to the extent it was discussed at
all. Despite such neglect, an understanding of the force of religious
conviction helps to position Locke with reference to the repertoire of
possibilities cast before him in his own epoch.[7]

Locke is a Whig defender of the "Glorious Revolution" of 1688. His
work is distinguished in part by the fact that he doesn't speak of sovereignty overmuch in his classic work, *Two Treatises of Government*[8]
Moreover, he did not, in the final analysis, equate parliamentary rule—a
parliament being the body that emerges most "naturally" from the
social contract—with sovereignty, certainly not strong sovereignty. If
sovereignty is located anywhere for Locke, it is with "the people." This
sovereign authority—for he stresses authority, a notion necessarily
bound, by contrast to unchained power—lies in the people. Locke's is
not a monistic conception but a modestly plural one as he tries to make
room for religious difference without courting the peril of religious difference turned into dangerous division. It is on this basis that he denies
the extension of toleration to atheists and Catholics alike—although
atheists are the bigger problem.[9] Atheists are untrustworthy because
they do not take an oath on the Bible, not believing in divine action;
and they deny the divine origin of fundamental truths necessary to underwrite decent government. Catholics are (or may be) civically unreliable because of their allegiance to an external power.[10] (There are
ongoing disputes about just how exclusionary were Locke's views on
Catholicism.)

The landscape Locke observed looked something like this: The
model for the territorial state that emerged out of the chrysalis of
medieval Europe was secular yet infused with Christian assumptions,

laws, and purposes. Indebtedness to Christian and Roman ideas and images is palpable. If a single prince is no longer the font of law, the *lex animata*, that notion passes over to a collective body—the representatives of the people—although it is lodged in the first instance in the people themselves.[11] The question then becomes how and in what ways this sovereignty is enacted legitimately.

To assay this matter, let's turn to Locke's best known and most frequently cited and used texts in political thought, the *Two Treatises of Government* and *The Letter Concerning Toleration*.[12] Lurking behind these and other of Locke's works—some of which treat theological questions explicitly—is the by now familiar debate concerning Thomistic "realism" and nominalist "voluntarism." Although traces of the Thomistic view pop up in Locke's arguments, he is primarily indebted to "theological voluntarism" of the Ockhamist variety. This voluntarist strain, the reader will recall, emphasizes God's will over God's reason and speaks (variously) of the ways in which that will is bound.[13] Fortunately for all his subjects, God wills through his "wisdom and goodness": God does not, indeed, *cannot* choose what is not good. God's acts are free and in the direction of the good.

Because God is by definition omnipotent, his will is without limit: This invited some of Locke's critics to score his thinking as marred by an image of an arbitrary and uncontrollably divine will—despite his invocations of the "Schoolmen."[14] However one finally sorts out Locke's indebtedness to late medieval strands of voluntarist theology, the upshot is that no one should underestimate the vitality and importance of religious issues and questions to Locke. His theism is central to his political theorizing. No thinker who pens a work on *The Reasonableness of Christianity* could be thought to be uninterested in what we call "religious" questions.[15] Locke's version of natural law, like Aquinas's is good for all times and in all places, although the basis for this universality differs—an issue that need not deter us here. The most important point is that the belief that God is bound by his will helps to spur contractarian theories of ethics and natural law and this, in turn, inspired constitutionalism, theological debates having migrated into political argumentation.

It follows that any treatment of Locke must keep in mind distinctions in place in his era that would have made little sense but a few centuries earlier; namely, those between "church" and "state" and between "politics" and other arenas of human life. Before the late medieval–early modern epoch, there was no separate sphere of politics, as we have already seen; rather, there was *regnum*, temporal rule over human life between the fall and the end-time, and there was *sacerdotium,* or governance of spiritual life that framed and infused the whole, being proleptic to the life post-regnum to which Christians looked forward with hope.

The separation of official political rule from religion, or the assumption of such, was required to attain political sovereignty under a social contract model. But what made such rule legitimate? What were the limits to sovereign power brought into being by a social contract? And so on. None of these questions could be settled, even provisionally, unless one possessed some notion of the raw material one was working with, including anthropological presuppositions: What is human nature? If Hobbes begins with a state of war and a view of human nature that is reduced in every sense of the word, Locke uplifts human beings by contrast. Our natural state is a social one, he insists, and politics is an outgrowth of this sociality. But politics does not create us in the first instance.

Although Locke, in common with modern political thought, makes provision for "prerogative," those occasions when rulers take leave of their ordinary powers and exercise discretionary powers, the power to act according to discretion and for the public good must not be abused. The norm must be restored once the "moment" of prerogative ("emergency powers") passes. In chapter 14 of *Two Treatises*, Locke insists that before civil society, government was pretty much all prerogative as there was no system of established law. All was arbitrary. The raison d'être of entering civil society is to get out of a world that is all prerogative and into a world that is regular, orderly, law-governed. Why would human creatures opt for a world riddled with the arbitrariness that characterizes the state of nature as a permanent condition of civil society? Prerogative is justified on one ground only: the right (power) to do public good in the absence of a governing rule or law to cover a particular exigency.

It is out of his discussion of prerogative that Locke repairs to the old tradition—the medieval right of resistance—to insist that the "people," who never give up their natural rights/powers, or their sovereignty, as Hobbes insisted they do, can make an "appeal to Heaven" if no other remedy is open to them. They can make this ultimate determination for they retain a natural law "antecedent and paramount to all positive Laws of men, reserv'd that ultimate Determination to themselves, which belongs to all Mankind, where there lies no Appeal on Earth, viz., to judge whether they have just Cause to Make their Appeal to Heaven."[16]

This is the sort of thing that drove absolutists around the bend, of course. For Hobbes, it constitutes an egregious violation of the minimal requirements of civic order. For patriarchalist Robert Filmer, it violates the natural order of things that derives from a direct grant of political power by God to Adam from which dominion then descends, logically and inexorably.[17] For Locke, political magistracy is of a different order than the authority of a father over a child, a husband over a wife, or a lord over a slave. Political power is a distinct sort of power dedicated, whether in war or peace, to one purpose only: the "Publick Good." We are not naturally in subjection nor in a solitary and brutish state à la Hobbes, but we do have freedom to order our actions "within the bounds of the Law of Nature," a law that obliges each and every one and is self-limiting. The social compact puts an end to the state of nature given mutual promising to enter into a "Body Politick." One does this noncoercively for we are "induced to seek Communion and Fellow-ship" with others, words that mark unmistakably Locke's indebtedness to Christian belief and worship.[18]

To be under the *arbitrary* rule of another is a condition of slavery. God did not create the human person in his image as a slave, for God himself is no slave but an omnipotent power who binds himself of his own free will.[19] It follows that any defensible account of sovereignty must needs be bound. Too, God gave the world to all in common. All of us have property in our own person. We mix our labor with that which is given. For Americans this is a very familiar argument. In the debate over slavery at the time of the Kansas-Missouri acts, the Illinois legislator, Abraham Lincoln, made the "free labor" argument against slavery, namely, that a man has the right to what he has earned through the sweat of his own brow and "as I would not be a slave, so I would not be a master."[20] This provides a capacious groundwork for political liberty based on mutual promising as well as erecting limits to the ways in which the representatives of the sovereign power (the people themselves) govern *over* the people. But there is a downside to Locke's argument that resonates today in our highly charged debates over religion, politics, and other controversial matters.

I will turn to one of those—religious privatization—in a moment. It would be remiss, however, were I not to note here in passing Locke's insistence, first, that one isn't permitted to waste the fruits of the earth and, further, that any place one happens on that lacks established rules and regulations for dealing with property, including the property interest we have in our own labor, is a "vacant place," a *terra nullius*.[21] Unless one takes pains to alter the spontaneous "Products of Nature" by mingling one's labor with them, the land remains vacant so long as it is uncultivated. For it is "this Labour indeed that puts the difference of value on everything." Land untilled is a wasteland. Without improvement on what nature has deeded, life will be tenuous and likely wretched as much more "vacant" space will be required to supply needs that a smaller space of tilled and cultivated land would afford.

This is not by definition a pernicious argument. It could be used to nasty purposes, but the argument fits within Locke's notion of the responsibility of human beings to provide for all by enhancing the available fruits of the earth. He further insists that this cultivation should leave none to arbitrariness. In all forms of cultivation there must remain a "common" for all to use: an insistence that helps to account for all the commons one finds today in New England villages. Unfortunately, Locke's *terra nullius* also provides the intellectual and theoretical backdrop to the removal of various Indian tribes in America from their ancestral land. One needn't fall into a *Dances with Wolves* romanticization of America's various Indian tribes to see that Locke's argument, intended to act as a brake on arbitrary power over others, could, in particular instances, be used to such purposes given the assumption that without being marked and "named" by sovereignty, a real land and a real people could scarcely be said to exist. It is important to be clear here: Locke doesn't "name" a land without cultivation as being in a state of anarchy or war but, rather, in a form of nonage until people get their acts together, forging the laws, rules, regulations, and limits to power that mark the good commonwealth.

Given the thicket of laws that distinguishes the sovereign people and political rule, it comes as no surprise that Locke despises "despotism," what the medievals called "tyranny," a deformation and violation of the people's sovereignty. In chapter 18 of *Two Treatises* Locke cites two speeches by King James I to Parliament, in which James lays out the distinction between his absolute and his ordained power. The tyrant makes the mistake of thinking that his absolute power does not bind him to the laws and customs guaranteeing the welfare of the people, while the (good) king is happy to bind himself within the limits of the law.[22] The king has a "paction" with his people and with God to govern the people "according to that Paction which God made with Noah after the Deluge."[23]

According to a number of important commentators, a workable consensus on the authority and limits of kings and parliaments pertained until the reign of Charles I. That balancing act had located sovereignty in no single place but, instead, in the enactments of limited divine right under law, the workings of Parliament, and so on. Matters of war and "foreign policy" were largely within the king's purview. Much of "domestic" politics belonged to and operated under the ancient common law and Parliament. Charles I, however, trenched on the "domestic" territory in which Parliament had previously exercised dominance. He reverted to a mysterious argument of royal prerogative, evoking the Trinity to these purposes and in other ways abusing the consensus that had emerged. Because judges were obliged to concede to claims of royal prerogative, Parliament eventually rebuked the king by impeaching these judges. We know the upshot of the failure to hold intact, if in tension, divine right monarchy and a Parliamentary commonwealth: Charles lost his head and the English people were subjected to the not-so-tender mercies of Oliver Cromwell.[24] In other words, Parliament's victory over the Royalists did not lead to a more "free," less "sovereign" commonwealth: quite the opposite.[25] All of this serves as backdrop to Locke's great work. Locke saw his task, in part, as cobbling together a workable notion of sovereignty following the upheavals I have noted.

PRIVATE RELIGION: CREATING SEPARATE SPHERES

Politics is now its own sphere. But does politics cover capaciously the human social world, including the world of governance in a number of forms, or is politics subjected to further divisions? Locke promoted the "further dimensions" side of the argument by insisting on a separate sphere for "religion." With the glaring exception of his withholding of toleration from atheists and Catholics (although the matter of Catholics is disputed by some), Locke is as widely known and beloved for his arguments in behalf of religious toleration as for his arguments justifying revolution in extremis.

To applaud without restraint is a mistake, however, at least if one believes in a strong version of religious free exercise and civic pluralism. For Locke's version of toleration pushes implicitly in a monistic, not a plural direction. On the level of whether there should or should not be an established Church, Locke is an anti-monist. My claim that Locke's argument is not, however, unambiguously pluralist derives from his famous *Letter Concerning Toleration*. A quick summation of his argument helps to highlight the question and the problem. Over religious activity, the individual retains sovereignty. The sovereign individual is one who possesses subjective rights under the law. In other words, the individual does not relinquish all her sovereign rights (powers) to form a "Leviathan" form of rule but, instead, deeds only so much. One might think of this sovereignty as a finite amount of a substance. To the extent that it is drained away from one site, like the monarchy, the level rises in another, the people collectively and individually.

Most of us find this unexceptional because we are all heirs of a world in which the sovereign state is a given and, as well, because the pre-sovereign world is invariably presented in the worst possible light.[26] Indeed, historian Constantin Fasolt argues that so long as politics defines itself by sovereignty, it requires "the medieval" out of which it "progresses," the upshot being that much of the time modern political theory presupposes what it should be trying to explain.[27] How did Locke treat the medieval heritage? St. Thomas would have found much of his response perplexing. For example, for Locke, religion is the realm of conscience and conscience is *private*. In this way Locke pushes a strong version of a public/private split. He courts the contemporary mistake of mapping the juridical concepts of separation of church and state—there must be no established church—onto the far more dynamic and nuanced world of religion and politics in civil society, a world the great French observer of America, Alexis de Tocqueville, described as a remarkable feature of the fledgling American republic. Although Locke put back into the picture some of the complexity Hobbes had shoved out given Hobbes' relentless reductionism, Locke nonetheless finds in the logic of sovereignty the requirement to privatize that which one holds most dear.[28]

The first strong claim in Locke's argument is that "the Care of Souls is not committed to the Civil Magistrate, any more than to other Men."[29] God did not do it thus, so man should not embrace the pretense that God did and that one is doing God's will. Here we see his argument against a state church in a nutshell. No man can dictate to another in a matter of faith—and this means no state—for faith has to do with an "inward" disposition: one reason Locke found Catholicism troubling. The faith of Catholics is far too "outward," a matter of a strong *ecclesia* and of communally endorsed habits. When Locke turns to the question of what a "Church" is, his prejudices are clear. A Church is a "voluntaristic" society, a kind of religious caucus: Nobody is born into the faith—a stance to which Jews of his time would surely have objected given their profound belief in the passing on of the faith of their people. A church is the voluntary defining of a set of "mutual rules." One needs no complex mediations, no authoritative interpreters, for the salvation of our individual soul is key and that is entirely a private affair. Although the public *worship* of God may be the end of this voluntary body, this same body has available to it none of the authoritative rights and powers available to sovereign power. Ecclesiastical laws and rule-governed church institutions are inessential to salvation. To be sure, the Lockean Church can expel those who violate the terms of the voluntaristic contract on which Church is based, but this form of expulsion carries no civic weight of any kind.

Church is "absolutely" separate from the commonwealth—"absolutely" distinct.[30] The magistrate has nothing to do with souls; the keepers of soul-craft nothing to do with magistracy. Free will according to the dictates of a private subjective conscience is the soul route to salvation, and that alone is the purpose and function of faith. The magistrate has no authority in rites of worship and the doctrines and articles of faith. He cannot forbid religious rites and ceremonies—unless they in some egregious way violate the civic law. For example: A church would never be permitted to sacrifice an infant, but it "may lawfully kill [his] Calf at home and burn any part of it that he thinks fit. For no Injury is thereby done to any one, no prejudice to another mans Goods. And for the same reason, he may kill his Calf also in a religious Meeting. . . . Whatsoever is lawful in the Commonwealth, cannot be prohibited by the Magistrate in the Church."[31]

In sum, the commonwealth with a Christian majority is "two" not "one." In the Old Testament, the commonwealth of the Israelites was "an absolute Theocracy. . . . But there is absolutely no such thing, under the Gospel, as a Christian Commonwealth."[32] Interestingly, and in light of our current preoccupations and concerns, Locke argues that "Mahumetans" [*sic*] cannot profess themselves such only in religion even as they claim they are faithful subjects to a Christian magistrate, because the "Mahumetan" is bound to yield "blind obedience to the Mufti of Constantinople; who himself is entirely obedient to the Ottoman Empire."[33]

What is the problem with Locke's argument? How can his case, one to which so many of us nod agreement, be objectionable? Let's try out the following considerations. Locke is not blatantly monistic. But his argument pushes that direction given his strong civic map, with religion privatized and magistracy in a separate airtight compartment. A person can be a citizen of each so long as the citizen does not merge or blend the two. In the religious domain, one answers God's call. But step out of that domain and take one step into the civic realm, and God doesn't figure directly any more. Religion is irrelevant in a strong public sense. This invites constitutional law scholar, Michael McConnell, to summarize: "Locke's exclusion of atheists and Catholics from toleration cannot be dismissed as a quaint exception to his beneficent liberalism; it follows logically from the ground on which his argument for toleration rested. If religious freedom meant nothing more than religion should be free so long as it is irrelevant to the state, it does not mean very much."[34] Why? Because religion has been privatized and its meaning reduced to the subjective spiritual well-being of the faithful.

This Lockean formula finesses as many problems as it tries to solve, for it assumes that human beings can seal themselves off into compartments and be believers one moment; subjects of the magistracy the next; and never the twain shall meet. Instead and necessarily, the categories bleed into one another. Modern strict separationism, going beyond Locke, would strip all of public life of religious symbols, signs, markers, and speech, for strict separationists are those who seek a thoroughly secularized society in which religion is invisible to public life, religion having long ago been relegated to the subjectivities of multiple individual consciences—a view Locke paved the way for although it is stronger than his explicit argument. Locke is the unwitting prophet of what can be called liberal monism, not because he fuses statecraft and soul-craft but, rather, given the terms under which he tolerates, or claims the commonwealth can tolerate, religious belief. Over time this has invited strict separationists to put religion in the closet: Only your best friends know! Lest someone draw the overhasty conclusion that I oppose a regime of religious toleration, let me hasten to add that Locke's is not the only possible version of toleration. There are alternatives to both Lockean privatization and the post–French Revolutionary radical laicism whose origins we will now consider.[35] To take up these matters, we must evaluate how religion's exclusion from a visible public role is required under the terms of strong sovereignty.

ROUSSEAU AND THE SACRALIZATION OF POLITICAL LIFE

Locke represents the "binding" wing of early modern political thought, with "prerogative" a temporary exception in times of emergency. (Times when the sovereign is unbound for emergency purposes.) Jean-Jacques Rousseau, by contrast, in and through the vehicle of a "general will" that in his view is one and indivisible and cannot err, illustrates a yearning to restore via politics a unity now lost. Rousseau's conclusions are troubling if one favors a pluralistic version of political sovereignty, religious free exercise, and deep toleration for religious difference. I will pare the discussion down to two main points: First, the Rousseauian sacralization of political life and, second, Rousseau's strong monism in his treatment of "religion" and "politics." Because these points of emphasis blend in his arguments, I will follow suit by entangling the two.

Rousseau pays considerable attention to bodies, human and collective. He fuses the many into the one: The body's many members must be as one and become such via the general will.[36] This accounts for why I read *The Social Contract* as a "religious" quest. Rousseau infuses transcendence into politics rather than reserving it for the sacred. He "naturalizes" the body politic and melds the self with a highly romanticized view of nature.[37] With this infusion of transcendence, Rousseau winds up with a unitary, monistic version of sovereignty that levels everything that stands in its way—particular wills, particular faiths, anything that might prove an irritant in the image of the indissolubility and indivisibility of sovereignty. Taken in the round, Rousseau's work adds up to an entire creedal system. For example: His famous second discourse contains his own account of the Fall, in Rousseau's case a fall from nature into culture.[38] In his *Confessions*, Rousseau undertakes a self-accusation before going on to absolve himself! He spends a good bit of time chiding his contemporaries for their lack of virtue, inviting philosopher Jacques Maritain to speak roughly of Rousseau's moralizing pomposity.[39]

But sovereignty is our concern, and Rousseau's is closed, indivisible, monolithic. It is also mysterious, one reason, I suspect, why my students over the years have spent so many hours trying to force Rousseau's general will into recognizable categories of contemporary politics in pluralistic societies, largely to little avail. One reason Rousseau's general will is so perplexing to modern eyes is that it is essentially a religious concept immanentized and made an object of sacred devotion.[40] The citizen goes through a sacred rite—enters as a sinner ruled by a bad form of instinct—and emerges as an avatar of justice, having been cleansed of the old and having put on the new. In this

way, Rousseau ties together self *and* civic monism, whereas Locke had
preserved the possibility of more complex identities—public citizen,
private believer. Rousseau makes no such provision. There is one [col-
lective] man, a singular, even as there is one sovereign collective will.[41]
No longer are heaven and earth, the spiritual and the governmental,
mediated. Instead, each collapses into the other in a manner that
gestures toward the French Revolution and the philosophy of Hegel, as
we shall see.

THE SOCIAL CONTRACT: THE BODY IS ONE, PERIOD

A succinct parsing of Rousseau's most famous work will make his
strong sovereigntism clear. In Book I he explores the social compact.
The ritualistic dimension of his political theorizing is visible from the
outset, to wit: "Each of us puts his person and all his power in common
under the supreme direction of the general will; and in a body we
receive each member as an indivisible part of the whole."[42] He continues in this vein: The passage from nature to the civil state "produces a
remarkable change in man, by substituting justice for instinct in his
behavior and giving his actions the morality they previously lacked.[43]

In Book II of *The Social Contract*, we encounter Rousseau's story of
sovereignty: It is inalienable; indivisible, permanent, and cannot err—
the characteristics of a vision of God's will for other thinkers. Sovereignty is lodged in the "general will"—the will of the entire body rather
than any of its parts. The sum of the parts, as all students of political
thought know, is "the will of all." The "general will" is something else: It
transcends and obliterates any partial societies in the state. This general
will gives "the body politic absolute power over all its members, and it is
this same power, directed by the general will, which as I have said bears
the name sovereignty."[44]

Perhaps because Rousseau couches all of this in the language of civic
equality, it has been "cleansed" of its totalistic elements in the writings
of many political theorists historically, for all citizens are equally under,
or at one with, the general will. An act of sovereignty takes place
between and among these equals. Rousseau goes on to claim that "the

sovereign power, albeit entirely absolute, entirely sacred, and entirely inviolable, does not and cannot exceed the limits of the general conventions, and that every man can fully dispose of the part of his goods and freedom that has been left to him by these conventions."[45] Given that the "general will" animates and gives life to the "one," to the collective body, it is unsurprising that Rousseau establishes a low threshold for treason—used to good effect, at least from their point of view, by the French Revolutionaries in their trial and beheading of King Louis XVI. Treason is now thought of in *internal* rather than *external* terms. Or, better said, one "externalizes" the internal by turning the king and other doomed persons into exterior enemies of the interior: as if they had become foreign combatants or spies. For Rousseau, the traitor is one who attacks the "social right," thus making the state's preservation "incompatible with his own, so one of the two must perish: and when the guilty man is put to death, it is less as a citizen than as an enemy."[46]

The traitor is an "alien" within, and the body must cast him off. The social compact gives the body movement, and anything that blocks that movement must be eliminated. For "the general will is always right."[47] The corporeal metaphor is important here. Even as one removes a diseased part of the body, a gangrenous limb, say, so one must remove the diseased part of the sovereign people lest the malady spread. The body politic can die and carries about the seeds of its own destruction if its "heart"—the legislative power—ceases to function properly.[48] If ever sovereign authority is divided, the body dies.

This leads directly to one of our central concerns, namely, how do *regnum* and *sacerdotium*, now reduced to "church" and "state" or "religion" and "politics," fare in the Rousseuian system? In one sense, Rousseau reminds us that Locke offers a pretty good deal by comparison. For in Rousseau's world there can be no independent religious body. Everything must conform to, and be of use to, the state. This is how he builds his argument "On Civil Religion" in Book IV of *The Social Contract*. He begins by reminding us of the singularity of the sovereign will and the fact that this will cannot permit independent authority nor what he calls "secret motives"—a usage that later fueled the horrific bloodletting of the French Revolution.

Rousseau continues that the spirit of Christianity is incompatible with the political system. Of the types of possible Christianities now spread before Europe, there is one that is worst of all, Rousseau insists: Roman Catholicism, a "bizarre type of religion" because it gives men "two leaders and two homelands, subjects them to contradictory duties, and prevents them from being simultaneously men and citizens." This faith is so "manifestly bad" one hardly wants to spend time attacking it, for everything that destroys social unity is perforce worthless.[49] Christianity he defines as a "totally spiritual religion," as the homeland of the Christian is "not of this world." One reason Christianity is so lousy as a possible civic religion lies in the fact that its spirituality cannot rise to the occasion to defend the body politic. Here Rousseau offers a vivid worst-case scenario: Imagine a "proud, impetuous, passionate enemy" taking advantage of the little Christian lambs: "Confront them with those generous and proud peoples consumed by a burning love of glory and homeland; suppose that your Christian republic is face to face with Sparta or Rome. The pious Christians will be beaten, crushed, destroyed before they have had time to look around."[50] So much is this the case, and so thoroughly, that the phrase "Christian republic" is oxymoronic: One should not utter these two in the same breath, they are incompatible with one another. There is an interesting wrinkle given our current preoccupations—one that I confess I passed over with scarcely an acknowledgement for years, not until September 11, 2001—and that is Rousseau's encomiums in behalf of the "wise system of Mohammed" whose "very sound views" tied together religion and the political system, "completely uniting" it. So what Christianity weakens, Islam strengthens,[51] and Rousseau supports this "wise system" by contrast to Christian division.

One readily sees that Rousseau's strong sovereignty must be unitary, monolithic, and cannot tolerate confessional pluralism. Because Christianity inevitably and invariably sows the seeds of anti-sovereign partiality within the body of the collective, an alternative civic religion is needed. In Rousseau's favor, but it is a rather backhanded compliment, he understands that the Lockean formulation of separate spheres doesn't work as tidily as Locke seems to think it does. But Rousseau's "solution" is not robust toleration; rather, he purges any religion from public life save one that buttresses sovereignty. Only a civil religion welds together different parts of the polity and the singular, not partial or divided, devotion the sovereign will requires. One might say that even as God sees into the human heart and understands if the believer is wavering or partial in his or her beliefs, so does Rousseau's godlike sovereign see even unto the innermost parts of selves and ferrets out partialities and covert withholdings that, even though they have not spurred action *yet*, nevertheless work to undermine the sovereign body.

Without this unity, the human being is schizophrenic: We must worship the *patria*, gaze upon it lovingly from the moment we first draw breath. It must be ever in our hearts, ever in our thoughts. If temporal and spiritual government are separated, men "see double"—a phrase from Hobbes, who fretted about the same thing and, as I noted, draws praise from Rousseau for having done so. In our obedience lies our freedom. In fact we consent to our own deaths, if need be—thus eliminating the teeny space Hobbes had allowed for an individual to try to escape being put to death by the sovereign. We cannot stand in opposition to what the general will has undertaken, for, as part of that general will, we have ourselves consented. A civil religion is one that causes man to "love his duties"—a locution that makes one squirm as it calls to mind George Orwell's *1984* and the requirement that one must not only *obey* but *love* Big Brother, something Winston Smith finally "learns" to do under torture.[52]

7
UNBINDING REVOLUTION, BINDING CONSTITUTION

POST-ROUSSEAUIAN POLITICS IS DOMINATED BY THE UPHEAVALS OF THE FRENCH
Revolution, the continuing evolution of British political thought culminating in John Stuart Mill (if one follows the standard canon), and
German idealism—Hegel, Kant, even Marx upending Hegel in favor of
a materialistic determinism. On the other side of the Atlantic, Americans made a revolution that was moderate by contrast to the French
version, and went on to explore political thought and to experiment
with the limits and extent of sovereignty primarily through constitutional law rather than abstract political theorizing. I will concentrate
on the high points—which are sometimes also low points from the
point of view of ethics and politics—beginning with the French Revolution. The catastrophe attendant upon the French Revolution
demonstrates what a monistic version of sovereignty that exempts
nothing, including the secrets of the human heart, looks like in practice. One might say that the sovereigntism of Rousseau, with its
sacralization of politics, demands human sacrifice. If ancient peoples
sacrificed goats, the French Revolution sacrificed humans to propiti-
ate the revolutionary gods.

OFF WITH THEIR HEADS!

I recall vividly an occasion when, in a discussion with a fellow political theorist, I was taken to task because I had assigned Edmund Burke's classic rejoinder to the French Revolution for my class in modern political philosophy.[1] In a very gentle way—for this was not a hostile encounter—he chided me: "How could you? Burke opposed the Revolution." I observed that Burke favored the American Revolution. But, at least thirty years ago, it sufficed to say, "Burke opposed the French Revolution" to damn him. As one of my heroes, Albert Camus, also criticized the French Revolution, I was not moved by this exchange. Nor has time altered my view about the destructive nature of the French Revolution in the main: Certainly it was nothing to celebrate given all the woes it deeded to humankind as a model for revolutions, a point Hannah Arendt makes tellingly in her book, *On Revolution*.[2]

Arendt's argument is that the emphasis on revolutionary "will" is the culprit, for this word "essentially excludes all processes of exchange of opinion and an eventual agreement between them. The will, if it is to function at all, must indeed be one and indivisible; there is no possible mediation between wills as there is between opinions."[3] The will must be capable of radical unbinding and even rebinding in a more strenuous, unitary way if it is to triumph. *"La nation une et indivisible"* is the byword. Unity is purchased on the backs of enemies, either internal or external. Arendt doesn't mince words: "The theory of terror from Robespierre to Lenin and Stalin presupposes that the interest of the whole must automatically and indeed permanently, be hostile to the particular interest of the citizen," and Robespierre "preached a virtue that was borrowed from Rousseau."[4] The words *terror* and *virtue* are linked—one doesn't require some foreign export to implant such an idea. The West has its own homegrown version. *Le people* must move as a single body and act "as though possessed by one will."[5]

Part of what is involved in this indivisibility is the "boundless" hunt for hypocrites, for if, as Robespierre, following his hero, Rousseau, declared sovereignty is at base a matter of the heart, then the "reign of virtue" must weed out, purify, and cleanse the body politic, removing thereby all pollutants. The belief is that there is some "uncorrupted and incorruptible inner core" that will pop through an "outward shell of decay and odorous decrepitude." For this purity to be made manifest, the ceaseless search for internal enemies, those who are opposed to the revolution in their hearts even if they have done nothing, must go forward.[6] Unsurprisingly, if the British version of sovereignty wound up with limited monarchy, and the American version with a separation of powers and a representative republic, the French version inspired absolutism: The nation must be a single person.

This triumph of the sovereign will in politics is necessarily militant: It is a ceaseless engine that does not rest, for at-oneness is always an uphill battle, a major challenge to architects and enforcers.[7] Voltaire's adolescent outburst that the general will requires that the last king should be hanged with the entrails of the last priest—or words to that effect—gives one a flavor of this delicacy. A brilliant exploration of the search for internal enemies and hypocrites, all those withholding full assent in their "hearts," is the 1983 film by the great Polish director, Andrzej Wajda, *Danton*. Wajda was a major support of Poland's Solidarność against the monism of the communist state apparatus. His sympathies lie with the victims of the terror, not its architects and enforcers. The film pits Danton, an architect of the Revolution, against Robespierre. As the film makes clear, Danton himself had a hand in the terror before it claimed him, too, as a victim. For Wajda this is the direction all ideological revolutions tend when they are driven by a compulsion—in this case the absolute sovereignty and purity of "the people"—that brooks no opposition. As a result, some of the stirring words of "The Declaration of the Rights of Man" are pale and ironic by contrast to the vividness of the hunt for hypocrites, their mock trials, and their beheadings.[8] The aura of dread, menace, the steady destruction of freedom, including freedom of the press, the proclamation of innocence as the prime virtue—all lead to the inexorable conclusion that disagreement, or imputed disagreement, makes you guilty as charged. As Robespierre insists, "Those who, in any manner and no matter with what mask they have concealed themselves, have sought to thwart the progress of the Revolution are guilty."[9] The Danton figure still trusts "the people"—the sovereign will of the people—and believes that Robespierre, St. Just, and the Committee on Public Safety have perverted that will by detecting plots everywhere; hence, the purging process never ends. There is one solution: *décapiter*.

In a previous work, I call this revolutionary version of virtue a form of "armed civic virtue," an absolutizing of the body militant. Celebrating martial virtue, reappropriating Machiavelli's discourse, Rousseau rails against softness and decadence. Effeminization and womanish mawkishness result when the tough go soft, allegedly one major effect of Christianity. A civic religion must turn boys into men; the soft into the tough. To this end, Rousseau's favored ancient polity was not Athens but Sparta. Sparta as refracted through Plutarch is proffered as exemplary because Sparta sets forth the disciplinary techniques necessary to create armed civic virtue. Rousseau also honors Spartan mothers whose "sayings" Plutarch detailed in Volume III of his *Moralia*, reproducing tales, anecdotes, and epigrams that constructed the Spartan woman as a mother who reared her sons to be sacrificed on the altar of civic need. Such a martial mother was pleased to hear that her son died "in a manner worthy of herself." Sons who failed to measure up were reviled. One woman, whose son was the sole survivor of a disastrous battle, killed him with a tile, the appropriate punishment for his obvious cowardice. Spartan women shook off expressions of sympathy in words that bespeak a martial civic identity.

Plutarch recounts how a woman, as she buried her son, told a would-be sympathizer that she had had "good luck," not bad: "I bore him that he might die for Sparta, and this is the very thing that has come to pass for me." Small wonder, therefore, that the demanding vision of total civic virtue preached by Robespierre required enemies and a version of the body politic that is vigorous. In his brief speech during the trial of Louis XVI, Robespierre appeals to "vigor" no less than six times and to "zeal" nearly as often. "The republican virtues," he feared, would be weakened by clemency, by natural feelings and sensibilities that must be suppressed if justice is to be done. As to King Louis himself, well, he is—bottom line—a hypocrite and must go. Reinforcing all of this is a new religion of the Republic, with its holy days, its exemplars, its new calendar—all the rest—a religion suited to a wholly monistic order that cannot abide alternative ways of construing self and world.

Wajda's film reminds us that purging and bloodletting does not lead to greater liberty or justice but to forms of cruel repression and absolutism.[10] In France, the upshot was Napoleon; then a version of radical laicism that became a model for those pushing monolithic absolutism and intolerant secularism.[11] Thinking along the lines of a body politic, one might say that a beheading—removing the part of the body that had long been believed to be its source of animation—cast a pall over the body politic. In France, this was mitigated by the fact that Rousseau's corporeal image had relocated the most essential organ in the heart: So the head can go.[12]

REGICIDES AND THE REPUBLIC OF VIRTUE

The course of the French Revolution was both swift and brutal. The period between the storming of the Bastille, in which a few prisoners were still being held, the execution of Robespierre, and end of the Reign of Terror covers but five years—from 1789 to 1794. The estimates are that Robespierre, tagged as the "Incorruptible," who headed up the Committee of Public Safety that terrorized France, had presided over some 40,000 deaths—of whom 70 percent were workers and peasants. Seventeen thousand were tried and executed; twelve thousand were executed without trial; others died in massacres as the Revolution sought to expunge all enemies, including children. By the conclusion of 1793, the Commune of Paris closed all the churches in the city and sponsored its new revolutionary religion, a "Cult of Reason." The monistic state required its own religion to buttress internal unity.

If as Pope Benedict XVI has argued, Jesus withholds automatic "Amens" to political rule by shattering "the political principle's claim to totality," having "put down the mighty from their thrones," French Revolutionaries saw their task as dethroning the semisacred body of the one—the king—the living mediator between heaven and earth, the transcendent and the immanent—and rethroning, via a "religion of reason" a collective sacral body, *le people*, the people, the general will to which all must pledge "Amen" without reservation. This is the crux of Albert Camus' critical argument.[13] In snapping the connection between the transcendent and the earthly, two things were accomplished. First, the transcendent becomes remote, gauzy, dematerialized, a vague gnosticism, a hotch-potch of meanderings, many of them gesturing "beyond" but, in reality, presentist and based on a particular manifestation of the self. Second, the immanentist strand, rather than emerging chastened from the experience of "revolutionary virtue" and less tempted toward sovereign excess and grandiosity, goes in the other direction and sacralizes a finite set of temporal arrangements.

This Camus clearly understood. The messy cobbling together that was European culture at her best, Jerusalem and Athens, cannot be sustained if Jerusalem is abandoned. Denial of the transcendent and a correlative divinizing of the experiences of "self" or the state, fuels a self driven to certain sorts of extreme "on the edge" experiences as a way to feel wonder and awe, and a state driven to a form of "overcoming" or transcendence that courts triumphalism: there are markers of monism, even nihilism. Camus himself favored what he called a "Mediterranean sensibility" to which Catholicism was more closely linked than its northern counterparts—Konigsberg and Jena—where the air is pretty thin and, Camus might suggest, where it's a bit gloomy much of the year and people spend too much time indoors living in the cabinets of their minds.[14]

Not himself a believer, Camus recognized the dilemma into which excarnation—destroying the embodied link to the deity—and loss of the Jerusalem wing of Europe, would tend. It would not lead to greater liberation but, arguably, to more control over the self and more power in the hands of the state.[15] Revolution, by contrast to rebellion which builds in limits, is a logical consequence of metaphysical rebellion translated into the earthly realm.[16] There is an inexorability to the French Revolution and to all revolutions that model themselves on it. A "logical delirium" takes over men's hearts and minds as they seek to make the world conform to a theory.[17] Such revolutions traffic in absolutes—absolute affirmation or absolute negation—and mistake totality for unity, coercion for commonality. Camus recognized that Rousseau's *Social Contract* had created a new gospel—unsurprisingly, given that the revolutionaries set about creating their own religion and even fancied that they were rebeginning the world.

In *The Social Contract*, Camus contends, "We are assisting at the birth of a new *mystique*—the will of the people being substituted for God himself. . . . The 'political entity,' proclaimed sovereign, is also defined as a divine entity. . . . It has all the attributes of a divine entity."[18] *Absolute, sacred, inviolable*: These are the words in which the Revolutionaries traffic. The scaffold is the altar of the new faith.[19] It offers transcendence through the vehicle of the general will. It identifies blasphemers who must be removed in order to cleanse the body politic. History is "disincarnated"—Camus' word—and, because man is a part of the general will, he, too, is divinized, infallible. His dignity is not affirmed, but his divinization as part of the collective is embraced. But to "ensure the adoration of a theorem for any length of time, faith is not enough; a police force is needed as well."[20] The king/god is dead; long live the sovereign God (*le people*). Enforcement requires terror, and terror is the measure of revolutionary virtue.

HEGEL'S SACRAL HISTORY[21]

Let's put the dangers inherent in Rousseau, the French Revolutionary project, and Hegel in another way. Transcendence is cut off. But humans long for it, so it is relocated in earthly matters. In the words of the anti-Nazi German theologian, Dietrich Bonhoeffer, one makes the penultimate, the world of here and now, into the ultimate. This ultimacy now drives history. We wind up with the phenomenon Camus explored and more, for one is tempted to see in the sovereignty of the state an infusion of the divine will or spirit in history. Camus taxes Hegel with a loss of limits, with totalism and absolutism. This helps us to make sense of Hegel's enthusiasm for Napoleon. Value is located at the end of history, in the yet-to-come, the direction toward which sovereignty tends and history moves. It makes a good bit of sense that "Hegelianism" destroys any received notions of transcendence (derived from Jerusalem, one might say) in favor of a dismantling of that transcendence as its remainders are then folded into the logic of history's dialectic. Camus is right:

Hegel's originality lies "in his definitive destruction of all vertical transcendence—particularly the transcendence of principles."[22] This is rather obscure—but, then, so is Hegel. Perhaps one can put it this way: Nothing is valued in and for itself but only to the extent that it gains external recognition. This holds for individuals and states alike. The nostalgia for unity, the yearning for transcendence, cannot be abolished, however, and it is Hegel's sacral state that is plugged into that gap in his theory.

Although absolute virtue leads to absolute terror, Hegel's notion of Geist or spirit and the full "transcendentalizing" of history, requires the *Kriegsstaat*, or war state. Those defending Hegel will say, yes, but his is also a law-state, a *Rechtsstaat*. His version of state sovereignty requires it. Here's the problem: Unless that sovereignty is recognized *externally,* the state does not really exist, Hegel insists. The manifestation of its sovereignty, its coming into being, requires acknowledgement. Here Hegel's monistic metaphysics comes into play as we find him offering a sacralized unfolding of the Prussian state as the full flowering of Geist or spirit in history. "Becoming" for Hegel is absolute negativity; an abyss, for "God is dead."[23] Hegel associates God with a kind of arbitrariness and even wrath—the cruel God of Israel, in Hegel's view. So he sees himself as rejecting this omnipotence in favor of an authentic "omnipotence," an absolute spirit unfolding in history, with all standards of good and evil cast as relative to the "particular task of spirit in any given historical epoch."[24]

How does Hegel treat received divisions—between family and state, "religion" and "politics," and so on? It would seem that he cannot permit authentic autonomy for "subsovereign" entities, at least not in modern pluralistic understanding. His account of sovereignty does not allow it. Although Hegel's account of reason and the mind constitutes a powerful and compelling alternative to the mind as *tabula rasa,* there are problems. Hegel leaves room for critical reflection in the fissure between social being and social consciousness. But his strong ontology, coterminous with the unfolding of the spirit in history, must "take up" and make its own, everything that comes across its path. We see this at work, for example, in his embrace of the world of freedom by contrast to the world of necessity: the household or family, as the *polis* or polity, constituting the realm of freedom. The family forms what Hegel calls a *natural* Ethical community: "as the inner indwelling principle of sociality operating in an unconscious way, stands opposed to its own actuality when explicitly conscious; as the basis of the actuality of a nation, it stands in contrast to the nation itself; as the immediate ethical existence, it stands over against the ethical order which shapes and preserves itself by work for univeresal ends; the Penates of the family stand in contrast to the universal spirit."[25]

The meaning of this passage is not obvious, to put it mildly. If one parses it, however, it comes down to the fact that the only reason the family—intimate and fecund relationships—have any importance derives from the relationship of the family to the universality embodied within the state. In other words, value is not only placed at "the end of history" but in an abstract universal collective. Because women are defined by the family, it follows that the male alone becomes a "real and substantial citizen." Should he abrogate citizenship and sink back into the family, he is "merely unreal insubstantial shadow."[26] The real, the actualized, is the most abstract. Particularities like the family, not mapped onto the sacralized sovereignty, must needs fall short. To be sure, there is a type of self-knowledge available in the family but it fails to rise to the level of full self-consciousness, something Hegel reserves to that universal being, the male citizen. The women cannot by definition achieve a full ethical life: "The law of the family is her inherent *implicit inward nature*, which does not lie open to the daylight of consciousness but remains inner feeling."[27] The woman realizes her ethical significance as wife and mother but not, Hegel insists, in her particular relation to her own husband and children. Instead, she must be tied to what Hegel terms a husband and children "*in general*," not to feeling but to the universal. One must abstract from these concrete relationships into the realm of abstract ethical life for the particular relationships to have any meaning whatsoever.

The male transcends the family, resists its tug, becomes individuated and separated from it, negates it, in order to be a citizen: He is a sovereign self, of sorts, identified as he is with the most sovereign of all political moments for Hegel, war and the state. "Everything that man is he owes to the state; only in it can he find his essence. All value that a man has, all spiritual reality, he has only through the state."[28] And because a state is recognized as sovereign only when it is internally "divinized" and externally recognized, war is the highest achievement of ethics and the culmination of a dialectic of negation. Sovereignty is manifest in and through a mobilized state, a triumphant *Kriegsstaat*. Hegel creates create a "we" in and through the holding bin of the state. All divisions—all pluralisms—are a threat: This is monism all the way down.

I think one can make good on the claim all of monism because of the way Hegel negates all other institutions and relationships in order that the truly universal can come into being. Hegel's is a grand vision of the sovereign state—the "actuality of an ethical idea" in his characteristic language. The state is the arena that calls upon and sustains the citizen's commitment to universal ethical life, satisfying expansive yearnings through the opportunity to sacrifice "in behalf of the individuality of the state."[29] How does Hegel locate value in war? The argument proceeds as follows: War transcends material value. War-constituted unity is immanent within the state form. The state, hence the nation, comes fully to life only with war, for Hegel, a moment of "overcoming" rather than a response to harsh necessity and threat. In war the state as a sovereign collective being is tested, and the citizen comes to recognize the state as the source of all rights. The state's proclamation of its sovereignty is insufficient: That sovereignty must be recognized. War is the means to that recognition. Hegel does not so much glorify war as sacralize history. He is the theorist of the sovereign state triumphant.[30] Man becomes what he is meant to be by being absorbed within the larger stream of this state. The state's "reserve power"—like God's plenitude of power—lies in abeyance much of the time. So the question is, is it capable of being activated?[31]

Hegel's divinization of history is the crux of his "political theology." He wrote on theology explicitly. Divinity is no longer out of time but subjected to it, historicized.[32] Hegel commits a very common mistake, namely, seeing "the universal," after one has climbed the ladder of particularisms and kicked off the lower rungs, as more "godlike." This godlikeness is not the Triune God of Christianity, however, but the principle of a monistic metaphysics. One need not belabor this point to see in

Hegel's divinization of history troubling implications. Hegel helps to fashion a climate of opinion that extends and deepens, through the abstract language of the dialectic, a quest for totality already noted in the discussion of Spartan women. Like the Spartan mother who "bore him so that he might die for Sparta," so Hegel's mother bears sons for the same reason—so that they might live and die for the divinized sovereign state.

BONHOEFFER AGAINST THE "DEMONIC" STATE

Can the genie of sovereign absolutism be put back into the bottle once it has escaped? Yes, but with great difficulty, sometimes attendant upon catastrophe. Some are familiar with the stirring story of Dietrich Bonhoeffer, the brilliant son of a distinguished German family, who studied theology, wrote complex works, joined in a conspiracy to assassinate Hitler, and paid with his life. He was only thirty-nine when he was hanged. In his unfinished *Ethics*, Bonhoeffer takes up the matter of the divinized Hegelian state—roundly condemned by Catholic scholars indebted to Thomism and, in Bonhoeffer's hands, condemned by a German Lutheran who does *not* see a direct connection: Luther to Hegel. Instead, he brings Luther to bear against state idolatry.

Bonhoeffer begins by offering a biting critique of the French Revolution. He is prescient in this regard. His analysis presages the critical rethinking of the legacy of the French Revolution in the important historic scholarship of recent years. This new scholarship reminds us that it was the French Revolution that deeded a new and terrible term to the Western political vocabulary—terror—together with the insistence that it is only through "just terror" that authentic societal transformation can be achieved. If the French Revolution is the inauguration of modernity politically speaking, and thus it has been enshrined, that aspect of modernity must be challenged. Much of the horror unleashed derives from the idea that a decisive, wholesale break with the past can and should be made. To the extent that this is a modernist prejudice, it traces in part from the architects of the terror who believed that one must eviscerate rather than reform extant institutions, excise words and invent new vocabularies wholesale, throw out old calendars and old holidays and invent new ones that celebrate the apotheosis of the revolutionary state.

What's the point, for Bonhoeffer, of bringing this up theologically? His critique is unsparing even as he acknowledges that many prejudices, "social conceits, hollow forms and insensitive sentimentality were swept clean by the fresh wind of intellectual clarity. Intellectual honesty in all things, including questions of belief, was the great achievement of emancipated reason and it has ever since been one of the indispensable moral requirements of western man."[33] Unfortunately, the French Revolution is based on a principle of the absolute sovereignty of the people and the consequent unleashing of *ressentiment* that erupted into the reign of terror. The enshrined version of "the liberation of man as an absolute ideal leads only to man's self destruction. At the end of the path which was first trodden in the French Revolution there is nihilism."[34] In other words, Bonhoeffer sees in the sacralization of sovereignty a terrible form of state idolatry, bringing into relief "western godlessness . . . itself a religion, a religion of hostility to God. It is in just this that it is western . . . the deification of man is the proclamation of nihilism."[35]

By embracing a radical view of human self-sovereignty and self-creation and disdaining the God of creation who reminds human beings of their dependence and creatureliness; by embarking on a course of destruction as a perverse mimesis of God's generativity under the presumption that the categories—good and evil—did not apply, the revolutionaries deeded to the world a dynamic we are contending with yet. Rousseau is central to this dynamic—as is Hegel. The basis of Bonhoeffer's revolt against Nazism lay in his repudiation of Hegel's proclamation that the state is a "real god." This divinized state exceeds its legitimate mandate, which is a limited one, Bonhoeffer insists, as is the mandate of any earthly, or penultimate, institution. Bonhoeffer sees in a Hegelianized history a principle that makes of history—the penultimate—something ultimate. Locating ultimacy in history invites only destruction and despair.

UNBINDING REVOLUTION, BINDING CONSTITUTIONS

We return, with something of a sigh of relief, to the natural law tradition, or that version of it which is one of "binding" political power and authority. Let's begin by taking the measure, briefly, of one of the central activities of political life: war. Contemporary Christian thinkers are loathe to think about war save (overwhelmingly) in tones of condemnation. This flies in the face of the dominant Christian tradition concerning the use of force by political bodies, namely, the just or justified war tradition.[36] I bring this into our discussion here not only because war has been a central feature of political sovereignty but, as well, because in the challenge of thinking about war and its unleashing there are competing understandings. One approach unleashes war, as if in wartime all rules collapse, "all's fair," and war is, one might say, all prerogative. In another approach, the just war tradition, the aim is to bind war ethically, in order to forestall war's worst manifestations. War, too, should function within bounded limits.

The just war tradition predates Hugo Grotius, a Dutch theologian and philosopher, being traced most often from St. Augustine and the famous Book XIX of his masterpiece, *The City of God*. Indeed, Grotius is not usually considered a just war thinker, perhaps because he concentrated less on the duties and ethical responsibilities of statecraft than on the natural laws that should guide the judgment of statesmen whether they are Christian or not.[37] But Grotius, often called the father of international law, illustrates an early modern attempt to grapple with that act of political sovereignty that most often relies on prerogative, namely, war. There is, for Grotius, autonomy for human action that is not entirely managed by the will of God; indeed, not even God can change the binding nature of natural law. In his *Rights of War and Peace*, Grotius stipulated that states have a right to defend themselves. A society of human beings may punish a member who has committed a crime against another internally. In the same way, a nation or group of nations has the right to punish a state or ruler that has injured it, or them, unjustly. Not well known to scholars today, is the fact that Grotius authored major works in theology, the most important being *Defensio fidei catholicae de satisfactione Christi adversus Faustum Socinum Senensem*.[38] Grotius helped to define the categories of what is now called, loosely, international law, but this tells us precious little in and of itself, and it omits the basic theme that, for Grotius, natural law is accessible to human reason, not exclusively to the reason of those who are Christian believers. Natural law is not reducible to God's will but may exist independent of God—thus locating Grotius both in, and in tension with, classic Thomistic theology.[39]

Suffice to say that in the Grotius argument, God is bound by the same ideas of lawfulness as any other ruler. Too, Grotius is a compact thinker who sees in the coming together of individuals who had previously lived isolated lives, the legitimate basis for civil society. By Grotius's era, as we have already seen, medieval universalism was no more, save as a dream of unity. So Grotius's arduous task is to think through how to bind those particulars known as sovereign states "who have no common superior and acknowledge no allegiance to any superior whatsoever."[40] For one thing, he insists, it is licit to base discussion of law concerning, say, law of the seas, on principles of human nature derived from classical humanistic sources. The judgment as between states in any controversy must turn on natural reason as the arbiter between good and evil. It is from this notion of a form of universal assent and thus of natural law that Grotius fashions his theory of international relations. Even as one can defend oneself against an attacker, so the nation can defend itself. On this earth, good should be rewarded and evil punished. Those outside organized states, a kind of single body with many parts, are in a lawless world, although their access to natural law predisposes them to forming bodies politic based on the principles of their own sociality.

As I already indicated, there are two possibilities in the matter of war. One is that war is a force all its own, not subjected to norms and rules, to binding: It is the exception, one might say, and the ordinary need not apply. The other possibility holds that war is indeed bound. It follows that states that violate the norms of wartime conduct are culpable for their actions. Grotius rejects the lessons drawn by contemporary so-called realists in international relations, beginning with the Melian dialogue from Thucydides' great work on the Peloponnesian War. For these "realists," the rule of force is "the strong do what they will and the weak suffer what they must." One of the reasons it is often frustrating to argue against this view lies in the fact that no matter what one's argument—or arguments made by statesmen and women as to why ethical norms must pertain in time of war—the hard-core "realist" can always claim, "Yes, of course, that's what people say to justify something. But deep down we know what is *really* going on." (This is a tactic similar to Marxian claims of "false consciousness.")

What is "really going on" for these contemporary "realists" is a human version of nature red in tooth and claw. War knows no law save that of force. The great theorist of this view is the Prussian general von Clausewitz. The sovereign is unbound in war, for war is an activity that knows no necessity save the rule of force. Karl von Clausewitz and Hegel died the same year, 1831. Both were caught up in the statist and nationalist enthusiasms unleashed in the postrevolutionary period. As heirs of a version of Enlightenment reason, each participated in the heady promise of reason triumphant, the human mind brought to bear on events freed from the burdens and bindings of older "superstitions." Clausewitz and Hegel are avatars of nation building, seeking national mobilization for reform and military purposes. Clausewitz, for example, supported both the abolition of serfdom and the mobilization of a large, national army as a task of the central state rather than a traditional duty of the Junkers, the Prussian landowning aristocracy. The result was a requirement that all male citizens (the clergy and educated middle-class men got exemptions) serve three years in the army and additional years in a reserve force. In the short run, Prussia and its allies defeated Napoleon in 1815 at the Battle of Waterloo. Over the long haul, what emerged was a powerful warfare-welfare state in the heart of Europe, Bismarckian Germany.

If Hegel is a theorist of the state triumphant, Clausewitz is the architectonic champion of, in his words, the theory of "war itself." War has an ideal form and to be understood properly must be grasped as a "pure concept"—unburdened, one might say, by caveats and modifications.[41] The just war tradition resists the notion that the "exception" of wartime effaces altogether the normal rule-governed, or bound, nature of political life. If the absolutism of the French Revolution leads to the *levée en masse* and war without limit, the same pertains to German absolutism and wars of devastation without intrinsic limits.[42] Clausewitz construes war not as an act of justice or in the behest of justice but, rather, as an act

of *will*—of forcing one's opponent to conform to one's will. It goes without saying, therefore, that one commits oneself to violence until the moment that that compliance is clear-cut.[43]

Grotius, coming out of the late medieval debates, binds sovereignty,
especially in time of war when the temptation to excess and overreach is
the greatest. If one follows Grotius in comparing the commonwealth to a
person with a will, how can that will not be bound, considering that God
himself is? One could go on from here to make a very reasonable case
for the view that the post–World War II blossoming of the notion of universal human rights is an outgrowth of the "binding" of international
norms, an attempt to bring limits to the activity of sovereign states.[44]
Where Grotius would find this entire enterprise wanting is in the area of
punishment. You cannot articulate a strong theory of international law
cast as human rights that are stipulated, neither arbitrary nor effaceable,
without an account of punishment for those who "unbind." It makes no
sense to announce boldly what people have a right to and what they are
protected from and then to shrink from the enforcement of these stipu-
lations where punitive justice is concerned. We routinely punish individuals who violate the law, and we insist that they need to be curbed by
legitimate force or compulson. How, therefore, can it not help but be the
case that groups or collectivities of human beings, too, need to be
bound, to be curbed, and their egregious violations punished? Perhaps
the American experience of binding is helpful in this regard.[45]

BINDING THE AMERICAN WAY

One could quite reasonably interpret the American experience from the
early Puritans to the present as a vast exercise in binding sovereign power
and determining whether or not there are moments when the sovereign,
as manifest in one aspects of its powers, can be partially unbound. We
call this latter the wartime power of the executive, and it revolves around
national security concerns as the first and foremost among all the duties
of the sovereign. Rather astonishingly, political theorist Hannah Arendt
had claimed in one of her essays that "sovereignty" was unknown to the
United States: the sovereignty she had in mind was linked in her mind to

sovereign exclusivities associated with the European nation-state system.[46] That sovereignty *tout court* is unknown to American law would be news to most American constitutional experts, although the notion that sovereignty is foreign to America was, in fact, articulated in the early decades of American constitutionalism.

From the beginning, Americans grappled with questions stemming from sovereignty. It could scarcely be otherwise, given the indebtedness of the American founders to John Locke and strains of European thinking and practice. Another source of colonial political thought, as political theorist Paul Sigmund points out, was Sir William Blackstone's *Commentaries on the Laws of England.* The first section of this work discusses natural law in detail.[47] The colonists were familiar—painfully so, one might say—with the powers and pretensions of sovereignty, both monarchical and parliamentary. It is unsurprising, therefore, that they aimed to bind—to set limits to—any single sovereign power within the American constitutional order. According to nearly all observers, the theories of bound power and authority together with natural law fueled the move to that vital American tradition—and a not altogether unproblematic one—of judicial review. Indeed, contemporary critics of the U.S. Supreme Court argue that it has usurped the rightful powers of the legislative branch by making rather than interpreting law, and this allegedly constitutes usurpation because the courts are not accountable as are elected representatives to those who elected them.

But that debate would take us too far afield. Staying with tracking the official fortunes of sovereignty, we learn that in *Chisholm v. Georgia* (1793), Supreme Court Justice Wilson uttered the famous words: "To the Constitution of the United States the term sovereign is totally unknown. There is but one place where it could have been used with propriety. But, even in that place, it would not, perhaps, have comported with the delicacy of those who ordained and established that constitution; they might have announced themselves "sovereign" people of the United States: But serenely conscious of the fact, they avoided the ostentatious declaration."[48] This "delicate" avoidance of ostentation didn't last very long— although the *sovereignty of the people* is not the way sovereignty has been articulated in American constitutional law, and constitutional law has been the primary vehicle in and through which Americans have done, and continue to do, political thought. For example, in an 1890 address commemorating the Centennial Celebration of the Federal Judiciary, one Edward John Phelps on "The United States Supreme Court and the Sovereignty of the People," goes to great lengths to unpack all the ways in which the judiciary is charged with limiting the "powers of political government" and ensuring that sovereignty remain "divided," for only then can the United States avoid the "conflict and disaster" endemic to imbalanced versions of sovereignty in "old Europe."[49]

With the thesis of "the sovereignty of God" steadily preached from the pulpit, the challenge was to ensure that the jurisdiction of the Court over the "great subject" of sovereignty remain sure-footed for, ironically, the best guarantee of the "rights of the people," with governance originating in the "sovereignty of the people," is not a popular assembly as a reflection of the people's own "uninstructed will," but in that institution "furthest of all beyond popular reach."[50] If, in the older logic, the king dies, Long live the King, in America the "Great Court" never dies—it is perpetually "in session," so to speak.[51] Sovereignty can never be above the law but, instead, must always be of the law. This notion of the sovereignty of the law relies heavily on a version of natural law derived from perduring truths deemed binding and not emerging via a monistic command theory of law.

But there are some bits and pieces here and there that exist in tension with this formulation, including Chief Justice John Marshall's declaration in 1821 that the people made the constitution and can unmake it because it is "the creature of their will and lives only by their will."[52] In an 1812 case, *The School Exchange v. M'Faddon*, Marshall embraces an ostentatious version of sovereignty as a territorial *imprimatur*: "The jurisdiction of the nation within its own territory is necessarily exclusive and absolute. It is susceptible of no limitation not imposed by itself. Any restriction upon it, deriving validity from an external source, would imply a diminution of its sovereignty to the extent of the restriction."[53] A court that offers formulations as breathtaking as this one must itself be bound, and that is done through the vehicle of *stare decisis*. Like God, the Court must bind itself—with a good bit of assistance from the executive and legislative branches of a divided sovereignty. (Divided also, in the United States, between the Federal and State levels—although it must be said that the sovereignty of states is largely conspicuous by its absence at present.) A 1936 decision, *United States v. Curtiss-Wright Export Corp*, reaffirms Marshall: "Rules come and go; governments end and forms of government change; but sovereignty survives. A political society cannot endure without a supreme will somewhere. Sovereignty is never held in suspense."[54]

Sovereignty takes on a metaphysical status here—"it" exists whether an actual political body does or does not. A government may go. But sovereignty endures. Here sovereignty as a metaphysical principle trumps arguments from political necessity or, perhaps better, the two are fused: Political society cannot be insured without a supreme will. The sovereign, in other words, is not brought into being by a social compact but exists above and outside that compact. It becomes "normalized" through the vehicle of a constitutional commonwealth based on compact: the implication of Marshall's remarks. The sovereign power cannot gesture to an "above" or "outside" itself as justification. "Perpetuity is implied, if not expressed in the fundamental law of all national governments," averred Abraham Lincoln in his First Inaugural Address:

> I hold that in contemplation of universal law and of the Constitution the Union of these States is perpetual. Perpetuity is implied, if not expressed, in the fundamental law of all national governments. It is safe to assert that no government proper ever had a provision in its organic law for its own termination. Continue to execute all the express provisions of our National Constitution, and the Union will endure forever, it being impossible to destroy it except by some action not provided for in the instrument itself. Again: If the United States be not a government proper, but an association of States in the nature of contract merely, can it, as a contract, be peaceably unmade by less than all the parties who made it? One party to a contract may violate it—break it, so to speak— but does it not require all to lawfully rescind it?[55]

This takes us to where the sovereign rubber really hits the road, the "exception," the president's powers in emergencies and given exigencies that can by no means be construed as part of the "normal" panoply of powers available to the executive. But this extraordinary power, this "exception," is largely held in abeyance. It is a reserve that may be called upon by the executive to act even though a public manifestation of that power may not have been seen previously. An emergency does not create the sovereign power—it has been there all along—but becomes, instead, an occasion for its use.[56] Going over the wartime powers of the U.S. presidency and the articulation, for purposes of emergency, of unusual and extraordinary powers in detail is beyond the scope of this work, but these highlights help to underscore the way in which one constitutional tradition—the American—made provision for strong binding and occasional unbinding of a sort that is temporary and rescindable.[57]

Binding the American way leads to a number of interesting tangles. There is no branch of government that is sovereign in all things and over all others. The rough-and-ready working out of sovereignty is primarily through constitutional law, although one detects traces down to the present of the insistence that sovereignty must be "as one." One area in which this is, or has been, the case is foreign policy, especially in wartime. The foreign becomes the domestic, however, insofar as war or the exigencies of the effective use of force demand violating explicitly, if temporarily, "peacetime" restrictions. The most dramatic example, of course, is Abraham Lincoln's suspension of habeas corpus during the American Civil War. Because at the water's edge sovereignty is one, whether one's internal arrangements are absolutist or, by contrast, the most meticulously calibrated constitutional separation of powers, one cannot have dozens of foreign policies declared, nor should presidential prerogative be challenged in a manner during a conflict that undermines significantly the executive's ability to deal effectively with that emergency. How this mandate is met generates bitter controversy and there are bound to be some judgements that are troubling or even later declared unconstitutional.

For example, Justice Felix Frankfurter in 1944 affirmed the constitutionality of the internment of the Nisei, American citizens of Japanese descent, during World War II as an act of executive emergency powers, writing that such action "is not to be stigmatized as lawless because like action in times of peace would be lawless."[58] So much is this the case that, in the United States, a general bipartisan consensus pertained in foreign policy until recently under the premise that "we are Americans" first. Critics of U.S. foreign policy, whether domestic or foreign, generally do not stake their claims on the elimination of sovereignty as such, but what sort of sovereignty might that be? Given that "peacetime" and "wartime" are not so easy to distinguish anymore, a national security apparatus having become permanent, especially so in post 9/11 America, the exception is operating, on some "normalized" level, pretty much all the time.

It follows that the form of strong sovereignty that has sneaked through in the American experience is, first, the assumption of presidential powers in wartime; second, the insistence that sovereignty is never held in suspense; and, finally, that the Supreme Court is the final arbiter of its application in action. That some find this too little and others altogether too much is no criticism of binding the American way but, rather, a recognition of the centuries-old nature of the political dilemmas of sovereignty.

CONCLUDING THOUGHTS ON SOVEREIGN STATES

A world of sovereign states presents a finite number of options, or proclaimed alternatives. Among these: First, the continuation of classical state sovereignty. Second, "world order" universalism, often represented as a generalized benevolence and human rights order of things, but absent an agreed-upon universal mechanism of enforcement. Third, a chastened version of sovereignty that questions from the actions of an individual sovereign state, from itself, indicting leaders of other states for doing politics in ways the indicting state finds unacceptable. This self-proclaimed authority lacks a generally recognized legitimacy. That said, it is most certainly the case that systematic, continuing, and egregious violations of the most fundamental of all rights—the right to life itself—demand concerted action in the form of interdiction and punishment. The most likely agents of such action at present are states who are constituted in and around a "binding" of sovereignty, including the articulation and enforcement of fundamental human rights. There is no foreseeable historic resolution to these dilemmas of political sovereignty.

Political sovereignty is a great historic achievement. It helped to bind millions of people to a particular "place," creating a civic home for which they had direct responsibility. In its constitutional form, it provided and provides for a type of civic identity not reducible to the terms of race, gender, ethnicity, or religion. Horrors committed in the name of sovereignty are well known and flung before us more or less incessantly. Less acknowledged is the political good accomplished when the dignity that comes from securing a civic place and status is honored. In its pluralist, constitutional forms of limited government and recognition that there are prepolitical dignities that belong to human beings as such and that the state can either honor or dishonor, sovereignty offers about as "good a deal" as human beings can reasonably expect in a world riven by conflict and confronted daily with the specter of wars of all sorts. This may be scant consolation, but it is far, far better than either statelessness or human-rights-abusing authoritarianism, whether in its theocratic or secular forms, in places where, in St. Augustine's words, people are daily "devoured like fishes."

If my hunch is correct, the aspiration to sovereignty, even unto god-likeness, did not limit itself to collectivities but migrated, got parceled out, as it were, into those microstates proclaimed as "sovereign selves." Can selves be sovereign in a manner analogous to states—or, as certain masters of "overcoming" have declaimed—God himself? It is time to take the measure of the sovereign self.

8

THE CREATION OF
THE SOVEREIGN SELF

A STREAMLINED VERSION OF MY THESIS WOULD GO LIKE THIS: AS SOVEREIGN state is to sovereign God, so sovereign selves are to sovereign states. Given that sovereignty in the political sense "named" self-determination for a territorial, collective entity, it is altogether unsurprising that this logic of sovereignty came unbound and migrated, becoming attached more and more to notions of the self.[1] As soon as one says this, of course, elaboration, caveats, emendations, and all sorts of explanations are required. For, as we have learned, there are multiple versions of sovereign states even as there are multiple versions of sovereign God. This complexity should come as no surprise. In this chapter we will trace the trajectory of emergent sovereign selves, recognizing, as we do, that the sovereign God as the fullness of reason and truth was contested and challenged in favor of God as irresistible will.

God as will is a monistic, singular God—the stress is One, not Three. God as reason and love is plural, dialogic, relational by contrast. Anti-Nazi theologian Dietrich Bonhoeffer delighted to speak of God's triune polyphony, drawing upon the music beloved by him and his family for his template. Again, by contrast, once you unleash wills, each construed as a mini-sovereign state, clashes are inevitable. Too, with the emergence of sovereign selves, the sovereign God stands as a provocation: man must himself become a God against the Creator God in order to strip himself of any indebtedness, whether to Creator or other persons. So, despite the fact that, theologically, a voluntarist will-centered God was ongoingly challenged by an emphasis on a triune God of reason and love, the voluntarist strand triumphed in strong state sovereigntist projects, and, as we shall see, in the emergence and solidification of sovereign selves.

We will begin with St. Augustine and his strong brief against any assumption of self-sovereignty or triumphant self-pride. That the self should rise in importance in relation to God or, even more dramatically, in an environment absent a transcendent horizon, would strike Augustine as pride triumphant. For what Augustine construed as a prideful self now proclaims its own self-fashioning. Various moments in the emergence of the self will be traced as questions are put concerning the self in relation to God's sovereignty; state sovereignty; and the moral or natural law.

Current demands that the state do the bidding of the sovereign self or the autonomous will(s) of citizens are made intelligible by considering the relationship over time of sovereign God, sovereign state, sovereign self. I detect at present, certainly in the mature Western democracies, something of this sort fashioned along the lines of a corruption of the social contract idea. In the classical idea from which the American founders took their cues, "I" becomes part of a "we"—we the people of the United States in order to form a more perfect union, establish justice, ensure domestic tranquility . . . etc. Nowadays, however, there is a contract between a multiplicity of sovereign selves and the state; indeed, this series of I's comprises or composes the state, for the state has been parceled out, so to speak, to help constitute these multiple selves in the first place. As God wills and the state wills, so selves will: we are willful; we make demands; we have wants. But the "we" is an aggregate of "I's." We have seen how the embodied metaphor for a state as a "we"—the body is one but has many members—was the stock in trade of theologians and political thinkers for centuries. These embodied metaphors have been abandoned in favor of multiple, individualized entities, each willing and each calling upon the state—a state defined as entirely self-determining under the classical definition of sovereignty—to satisfy that willing *and* to serve as a model of strong self-determination. How did this happen? What are the markers that point in this direction?

AUGUSTINE ON THE SIN OF SELF-PRIDE

In order to assess versions of self-sovereignty, one requires a contrast model, an alternative, to such understandings. The alternative must be one that is available to us now, not at some point in the past. There are those who would argue that the Augustinian self—my focus here—is not available because we are "practical atheists" in everyday life who think, act, and behave as though God does not exist. I want to acknowledge this concern but not argue against it directly. Unpacking Augustine on the self will either confirm the concerns of the anti- or non-Augustinians or bolster my view that we require some version of the self limned by Augustine if we are to avoid falling into the vortex of sovereign selves. What is wrong with sovereign selves? What would an alternative, one that preserves the importance of "the moral self" and individual responsibility, look like? Do we have any examples to look to currently?

You cannot discuss Augustine on the self without acknowledging the Fall. Let's assume the Fall for the moment. This means, among other things, that there is no such thing as absolute human freedom and that we no longer have available to us perfect versions of a fully transparent, fully cognizant, autonomously functioning self that is "at one" with his or her surroundings and with God. Even if one doesn't care about God, the Augustinian self offers a powerful corrective to any vision of self "at oneness." For Augustine there are intrinsic limits to our capacity to understand fully, and we cannot look to the self for a vision of wholeness. He also insisted, of course, that the trinitarian God tamed sovereign selves and helped to forestall an abstract, self-centered, monistic self and deity in so doing.

In his biography of Augustine, historian Peter Brown claims that Augustine "has come as near to us . . . as the vast gulf that separates a modern man from the culture and religion of the late empire can allow."[2] How so? One reason, surely, lies in Augustine's ruminations on the nature of selfhood. This is a theme close to our own preoccupations. Augustine anticipates current strategies in dethroning the "Cartesian" subject even before that subject was erected. For Augustine, the mind can never be transparent to itself; we are never wholly in control of our thoughts; our bodies are essential, not contingent, to who we are and how we think; and we know that we exist not because "I think therefore I am," but, rather, "I doubt, therefore I know I exist."

Only a subject who is a self that can reflect on that self can doubt. Augustine's *Confessions* is a story of a human being who has become a question to himself.[3] The *Confessions* is also an account of the claims others have on the self—among the many things that it is—the claims of friendship and *pietas* toward elders and respect for the *auctoritas* of great mentors. It is the story of a man struggling with the immediacy of desire, leading to a discernment that if the self lives only in the immediacy of desire, others became grist for one's mill. It follows that the claims of others have no authentic space within which to emerge. His account begins with an infant. Unlike so many political theorists past and present who assume adult subjects as their beginning point, Augustine starts with observations about infancy and the reality of birth itself. He intimates a developmental account of a fragile and dependent creature who is by no means a *tabula rasa* but a being that is at one and the same time social and quarrelsome.

INFANTS AND HUMAN FRAGILITY

If you watch infants and their rages and temper tantrums and all the rest, then you know that quarrelsomeness is part of our heritage. All human beings are driven by hunger and desire, and all experience frustration at their inability to express themselves fully and decisively. In the pre-linguistic infant this is certainly the case, but even when we become language users we find that we are not fully and completely understood or in control. We cannot simply have others at our beck and call. Augustine's dynamic trinitarianism helps him to account for our complex, interdependent selves.

How so? Let's take this one step at a time. Being an adult does not mean jettisoning childish emotions, for they are key ingredients of our nature; rather, being an adult means forming and shaping our passions in light of certain understandings about human beings, about human willing, and about our faltering steps to act rightly. Augustine presents a version of what it is to act and to desire rightly that many of our contemporaries do not share. But the point for now is that we can all make contact with his reminders of our dependencies, our fragilities, and the incompleteness of our ratiocinations. Unless we are in thrall to a hard version of modern voluntarism within which the self is in control, the individual will is absolute, we can choose willy-nilly, and it is nobody else's business. For Augustine, this version of freedom—power arbitrarily to choose—is a sure sign of the sin of pride, *superbia*, for the self, instead, must be pulled by love if it is to be oriented to what is genuinely good: Here the famous tug of war between *cupiditas*, which enshrines a form of self-love, and *caritas*, orientation to the good and love of the neighbor, including a recognition of one's own interdependencies.

Augustine's awareness of the sheer messiness of human life means that we cannot extract ourselves from this messiness, including grief, by rising above or holding apart from it all. This insistence lies at the heart of his withering attack on the Stoic theory of *apatheia*. This is what he says: "For the self to be in a state in which the mind cannot be touched by any emotion whatsoever, who would not judge this insensitivity to be the worst of all moral defects?"[4] Our thoughts can never be wholly purged of the emotions, and emotions remind us that we are embodied: We feel fear and anxiety in the pit of the stomach, we experience elation as a kind of tingling of the whole, anxiety "ties us in knots," and so on.

If one is going for the excarnated self, this just won't do, of course. The thinking self, for Augustine, expresses powerful emotions—emotions are thought, not just felt, and our language is never quite adequate to the occasion. Think of the moments when you have been at a "loss for words," and you will see what I mean. The upshot is that Augustine insists that philosophies that abstract from or offer wholly unreal assessments of our human condition by taking insufficient account of our vulnerability, our embodiment, and the centrality of our emotions should be rejected for these very reasons. He emphasizes over and over again that the body is epistemologically significant.

We must take account of what the body is telling us. The body is the mode in and through which we connect to the world and through which the world discloses itself to us. Mind is embodied; body is "thought."[5] All in all, we have available to us what Augustine calls "creature's knowledge." Full knowledge, complete transparency, is not available to human knowers no matter how brilliant and knowledgeable they may be. We are both limited and enabled by the conventions of language. None of us can leap out of our linguistic skin.

THE GOOD OF RECIPROCITY

We also learn about human reciprocity from the beginning, for this is how we all began. God did not intend for human beings to be alone but, rather, to "combine many relationships in his one self, [so] that those connections should be separated and spread among individuals and that in this way they should help to bind social life more effectively by involving in their plurality a plurality of persons."[6] The social tie is "not confined to a small group" but extends more widely. With this extension in kinship comes prohibitions. Marriage between cousins is one Augustine cites, and he explains:

> Yet no one doubts that the modern prohibition of marriage between cousins is an advance in civilized standards. And this not only because of the point I have already made, namely, that the ties of kinship are thereby multiplied, in that one person cannot stand in a double relationship, when this can be divided between two persons, and so the scope of kinship may be enlarged. There is another reason. There is in human conscience a certain mysterious and inherent sense of decency, this is natural and also admirable, which ensures that if kinship gives a woman a claim to honour and respect, she is shielded from the lust (and lust it is, although it results in procreation) which, as we know, brings blushes even to the chastity of marriage.[7]

Any society that loses a sense of decency, with its concomitant sense of shame, is a society in very big trouble. The importance of plurality, of the many emerging from a unique one, cannot be underestimated here. Bonds of affection tie human beings from the start. Bonds of kinship bind them further. (Still and all, given our quarrelsomeness and our frustration at noncomprehension, it is easier for a person to have a relationship with his or her dog than with someone speaking a foreign tongue.[8])

Now Augustine quite explicitly links his theological understanding of God to his account of human mind and human self. In his brilliant work *On the Trinity*, Augustine draws parallels between the persons of the trinity and the complexities of the human mind and its various capabilities and faculties. He calls the Trinity a form-giving category, "a principle capable of saving the reason as well as the will, and thus redeeming human personality as a whole."[9] In this work, Augustine is arguing, in part, against those who would absolutize the human will, *voluntas*. In this process they assume a direct path between willing, choosing, and action when, in fact, things are more complex by far. Augustine himself is credited with "naming" the faculty of the will, so these arguments are especially important. For Augustine, when we will, we simultaneously nill. Augustine insists that we cannot sustain a sinless condition; we cannot, pace Pelagius, who advanced this position, by our own unaided efforts, even with the grace of God, live without sin. The sinless life is a chimera and a dangerous one at that—it leads to self-pride and self-exaltation, a view that we are most ourselves when we are in command over others.[10] Augustine's massive four-volume *Answer to the Pelagians* gives his response to this absolutizing of the will, not in a nutshell, one might say, but in a torrent that pretty much obliterates the Pelagian position.[11]

AGAINST PELAGIAN MONISM

According to Augustine, the Pelagians argued in much the way that twentieth-century existentialists did. They posited a choosing self who, at any given moment, makes a definitive judgment as between alternatives but does not, in this process, create a kind of "heaviness," a history that bears down on us as we move through life. We can arbitrarily choose as we see fit, insisted the Pelagians; no, Augustine countered. It doesn't work like that; we are more complex; we are weighed down with history; and the will is no faculty of absolute and untrammeled "free" choice. For one of the many mistakes the Pelagians make is to assume a *monistic* self, moving zephyrlike through life and never encountering a bridge down or a cow on the tracks or a rail displaced. I suspect that the roots of modern voluntarism lie here: certainly one can go back and track the Pelagian insistence on the will as an entity of sorts that is itself constitutive of "freedom."

Augustine, of course, believes in a freedom of and for the will and in the ability—indeed unavoidability—of making decisions along life's pathway. But don't assume a straight line, he tells us. If life is plural, so are we: we are many parts and the mind is often divided against itself. As well, we are dependent in ways the Pelagians refused to acknowledge on God's grace, a grace "which does not destroy the human will, but changes it from an evil will to a good will."[12] And we are dependent as well on others—family, friends, and, yes, strangers, recalling Blanche Dubois's plaintive declaration, in Tennessee Williams's *A Streetcar Named Desire,* that "I rely on the kindness of strangers."

Human willing doesn't take place in a vacuum but in a context with which the self is oriented in some direction or another. Augustine walks a fine line between "all grace" and "all good works," "all voluntarism," or "all determinism," refusing to topple in one direction or another. This delicate balancing act is a burden. It isn't surprising that human beings, in one way or another, having found it so, have attempted to slough it off. I will say more on this theme in the discussion of "the Fall." Let it suffice for now to note philosopher James Wetzel's assessment: "I submit that the Pelagian will is a fiction. There is no faculty of will, distinct from desire, which we use to determine our actions. . . . Pelagius seemed . . . to deny that there were ever significant obstacles to living the good life, once reason illuminated its nature, [thus] he stood in more obvious continuity with the philosophical tradition than Augustine, who came to disparage the worldly wisdom of pagan philosophers for its overconfidence."[13]

LOVE IS WHAT YOU NEED

In his work on Trinity, Augustine stresses our capacity to love, and he dethrones, not reason, but too narrow an understanding of rationalism.

Belief is not unreasonable; it is not blind, nor does it idolize cognition. Thought, caught in splendid isolation, me-thinking, circling around oneself, is not the apogee of our humanity; rather, it is love, our capacity to give and to receive love. There are those who overestimate the intellect and its capacities. This, in turn, spurs abstracting from, or offering, unreal assessments of, our human condition by taking insufficient account of embodiment, despite the fact that the body is the mode through which we connect to the world and through which the world discloses itself. We, too, are creatures, known to ourselves in part through our relation to other creatures. Creatures cannot aspire to omniscience. "For in this world fear, grief, toil and peril, are unavoidable, but it is of the utmost importance for what cause, with what hope, and to what end a man endures those things."[14] Perhaps one can summarize Augustine here by noting that he wars against the pridefulness of philosophy. We must get over that pride if we would love *and* understand. God became incarnate to save all—not only the proud but the humble, not only the strong but the "weakest" of these. There is no huge gulf separating the learned from the untutored—much as those of us who are tutored would like to claim.[15] The ability to love, rather than to engage in certain highly abstract mental operations, is the heart of the human person as Augustine understands us. This by no means amputates reason, but it is a chastened, non-monistic reason that recognizes its own limits. Augustine calls a certain kind of pridefulness a conceit of the "Selfsame." There is no strong self-sovereignty, according to Augustine, for no "one starts off in an unimpaired condition in which he would only need to develop himself freely and make plans for his own happiness: everyone lives in a web that is part of his very existence."[16]

REMEMBERING AND FORGETTING THE FALL

Before moving on to philosophers of strong self-sovereignty or autonomy, one should take the measure of the classical Christian teaching on the Fall. The Fall is often wildly misunderstood, perhaps because we are allergic to the idea of original sin. Simply, "original sin" refers to the accumulated indebtedness we enter into when we are born. We "stand on the shoulders" of giants in a good way—they raise us up. But, unfortunately, we also sink into the Slough of Despond, like Christian in Bunyan's classic *Pilgrim's Progress*, dragged down by the weight of human sinfulness. In other words, we do not pop up into a sin-free context. One might think of it this way: No contemporary German can pretend Nazism and the Holocaust never happened, and no American can pretend that chattel slavery and segregation by race in part of her country never happened. We creatures are both "free" and "bound" in Luther's formulation—although not necessarily in precisely Luther's way. As bound selves we can never control everything. But nor are we entirely contingent selves. It is a complex *via media* again.

To implicate human beings in the Fall doesn't tell us much at the outset. And things rapidly grow more complex as we realize that the Catholic and Protestant traditions, respectively, present different "takes" on the Fall. But there is no time for a return to the Garden of Eden. Suffice to say that as the Fall has faded in Christian theology, so has sin and sinfulness. Alistair McFadyen, a contemporary theologian who has written on the legacy of original sin and the tendency to "forget" that we have fallen, reminds us of the ongoing forcefulness and explanatory power of the thesis of original sin to our understanding of modern selfhood.[17] Mc-Fayden argues that the claim that we can absorb sin into nontheological categories as we relegate "sin talk" to a private sphere, impoverishes thereby our ability to understand what is going on with ourselves and in our world.[18] Sin talk helps us to understand certain pathologies of self and culture that would otherwise elude us. Losing sin talk makes it easier to eliminate the relational and dialogic dimensions of selfhood as sin *always* evokes a self in relationship. The relegation of sin to the private world—at best—is part of the more general privatization of "religion" I discussed earlier. God takes up residence at the margin, not in the center, as we speak in psychological or moral categories freed from the legacy—so we claim—of the Fall and sin. Sin gets relocated in structures and detheologized. The upshot is that we are all "guilty as charged" if, for example, we "participate in structures of racism"—but one example. You may have "inner values" that push another direction but you are caught in the coils of the machine. The burden is removed from the self and displaced onto a conglomerate abstraction.

As well, modern treatments of the self of moral philosophers tend to begin with a sense of liberation from sin, as we do not want to believe that we are bound or weighed down in any way. We further claim that each and every act is the free act of a free agent—as if there is no historical record. Our voluntarism goes all the way down as we reject shortcomings, finitude, and the fact that much is determined by others, not ourselves.[19] If we accept that there is anything like a human nature or a human condition, we certainly do not want that condition to be itself conditioned by the legacy of sin as a statement about human beings as such. A theory of the voluntaristic, free self fuels dreams of perfection and these, in turn, lead to ruination for selves and for entire societies if they are not chastened in any way.

What remains alive and well in the Augustinian legacy—or one dimension of it that does—is Augustine's argument against the dangers of the Pelagian position. Augustine's doctrine of original sin counters the position articulated so many centuries later about the sin-free and free modern self. What was dangerous about the Pelagian notion, he continues, is that it identified some pure "essence" of the self that is untainted and permits us to choose, in an untrammeled way, between competing possibilities. This freedom is a kind of "neutral suspension" between different possibilities. The will possesses an "inalienable freedom" that converts potential into kinetic energy."[20] For Pelagius we can resist sinning—this is always possible—and we are inherently capable of willing and doing the good once we have identified it, for the "will is coextensive" with the capacity to make choices free from any compulsion whatsoever.[21]

By contrast, for Augustine, sin runs all the way down and is bound to distort our understanding at various points. That is why we all need to forgive and to be forgiven, why we need to confess, and why we can identify with the weak, for we ourselves have had the experience of a weak and divided will.[22] There is simply no such thing as absolute free will or absolute freedom to act. As well, because we assume (if we go the

Pelagian route) that everything can be controlled, managed, and even perfected we rush to blame in a moralistic way more readily. Somebody somewhere must pay! We don't want to accept the fact that sometimes things just happen and could not have been prevented. Unsurprisingly, if we embrace this view of a voluntaristically free self, we automatically place ourselves in competition with all other human beings, and this at every moment: "Hell is other people," in Jean-Paul Sartre's notorious words.

One might add that God is a problem, too, for any notion of God's sovereignty clashes with our presuppositions of self-sovereignty. For Augustine, it is love that helps to soften our tendency to fall into pride. We are, as well, less likely to get on a moralistic high-horse about people's weakness, refusing to acknowledge the ways in which sin "distorts" our "capacities for discerning and judging the good."[23] Augustine, in a manner we have by now come to expect, walks the line between freedom and necessity, between the determined and the open. One is accountable for one's deeds, yes, but grace and forgiveness are available so that we need not become hysterically self-blaming. Nor do we turn into "other-blaming" for we recognize that others, too, are limited in the ways that we are. One can find evidence of condemnatory Pelagian moralism all over the place in contemporary discourse. I will begin to take the measure of this by exploring the ideas of major articulators of self-sovereignty, with the self either wholly unbound or unbound in quite particular ways.

Here a closing observation on selves and the irreducibility of sin-talk drawn from the great film, *To Kill a Mockingbird*. Based on Harper Lee's famous novel, when matters build to a climax, the sheriff of Maycomb County—having identified the odd and reclusive Boo Radley as the person who killed the drunk, wicked man who had attempted to murder lawyer Atticus Finch's two children—engages in a colloquy with Atticus. The drunk, one Bob Ewell, had beaten his daughter after he caught her trying to kiss a black man, Tom Robinson. Subsequently, Ewell accuses Tom Robinson of raping his daughter—to explain away injuries she had sustained at his hand. Atticus defends Tom, who, after being found guilty by a bigoted jury, flees as he is being taken to prison and is shot dead. Ewell seeks vengence against Atticus for his defense of Tom Robinson; hence his attack on the children. Atticus, sizing up the situation, his son, Jem, with a broken arm and bruises; his daughter, Scout, unhurt, having been carried home by the rarely glimpsed recluse "Boo," assumes it is Jem who grabbed a knife wielded by Bob Ewell, the drunk villain, and stuck the knife into him, killing Ewell during the wrestling to try to protect himself and his sister. As Atticus, always a lawyer and staying within the language of a moral view of the law and responsibility, goes on in this vein, Sheriff Tate, running out of patience, says, "Your boy didn't kill Bob Ewell." He names the shy, wounded Boo, at that point sitting on the porch swing with Scout, as the defender of Atticus's children and the person who dispatched Ewell. The sheriff continues, drawing upon a wellspring of theologically graced language, speaking directly to Atticus:

> I never heard tell that it's against the law for a citizen to do his utmost to prevent a crime from being committed, which is exactly what he did, but maybe you'll say it's my duty to tell the town about it and not hush it up. Know what'd happen then? All the ladies in Maycomb, includin' my wife'd be knocking on his door bringing angel food cakes. [This, presumably, would take place in prison as Boo awaited some sort of hearing and determination as to whether he would be charged with anything.] To my way of thinkin', Mr. Finch, taking the one man who's done you and this town a great service an' draggin' him with his shy ways into the limelight—to me, that's a sin. It's a sin and I'm not about to have it on my head. . . . I may not be much, Mr. Finch, but I'm still sheriff of Maycomb County and Bob Ewell fell on his knife. Good night, sir.[24]

We can imagine recasting this as "It's a mistake, Mr. Finch," or "I don't think it's a good idea, Mr. Finch," or "It's an example of social determination, Mr. Finch," and it gets laughable after a bit. *Sin* is the only word with sufficient power to do the job.

On the Trail of the Sovereign Self

As we shall see, proclamations of the sovereign self, whether in "hard" or "soft" varieties—to be explained below—trace their genealogy at least all the way back to Augustine's debates with the Pelagians. Leading Christian theologians could never accept a doctrine of self-sovereignty, at least not until modernity, when some determined they could shoehorn the self into the box of sovereignty. By "hard" self-sovereignty, I refer to a maximalist version of such sovereignty. The "hard" or "maximal" version tends to be about power, self-encoded, enacted whenever the self sees fit. The self is both legislator and enforcer. The self is a kind of law unto itself, taking the form of a faux categorical imperative, faux in the sense that one could not coherently will that there be no daylight between one's own will and universal willing.

Some versions of the hard sovereign self are driven by *ressentiment,* and the lives of such selves are devoted to turning the tables on those they see as dominant. Sovereign selves, interestingly, often call for tougher laws and embrace a kind of legalistic moralism. Why? Because they hold to such a strong view of the ability of selves to control them-selves that they want to erect standards that guarantee such. From the standpoint of the sovereign selves, nonsovereign selves are living lives that are probably not worth living: the severely mentally disabled, the feeble elderly, a fetus, a comatose person, an Alzheimer's patient. Chil-dren are exempt, unless they fit into the handicapped category, because they will become sovereign selves at one point. None of these is a full-fledged individual, in their view, so all the full-fledged individuals might get together and make a legal determination that nonsovereign selves can either be done away with or "bred out" (here various eugen-ics projects), or in other ways positioned so they do not "drag" the sov-ereign self down. There are also implications here for how we think of, and treat, the dead, who, needless to say, cannot exercise self-sover-eignty. Sovereign selves are not linked to others, by contrast to the al-ternative view that as we are, in some sense, brothers and sisters, all of us are equally children of God whatever our mental capacities.[25]

Soft sovereign selves seems to be an oxymoron. How can there be a "soft" self that is nonetheless sovereign? It works like this: If the hard sovereign self is all about power and moralistic arguments, the soft sovereign self wants to relax or repudiate any standards on, or for, the self. One should "let it all hang out" and repudiate anyone who "wants to bring me down" and the like. This invites the soft sovereign self to find in any criticism or advice an assault on his or her being, for he or she is unable to distinguish between an assault and a critique. The soft, expressivist sovereign self ongoingly affirms itself, validates itself. Feeling is everything. One might call this, then, a therapeutic self that aims to get rid of the old—of relationships that are often called toxic—usually with one's own parents—and become a new self, like a butterfly emerging from a chrysalis. The only valid rules are those I make for myself. The hard sovereign self is the enraged, nonstop activist, for example; the soft sovereign self is the "flower child," the Woodstock self, although this self, too, can get very moralistic when it comes to anyone who doesn't share his or her project.

THEORISTS OF SOVEREIGN SELVES: DESCARTES AND EXCARNATION

René Descartes, Immanuel Kant, Ralph Waldo Emerson, and Friedrich Nietzsche, as well as the nineteenth-century American suffragist, Elizabeth Cady Stanton, and the twentieth-century existentialist, Simone de Beauvoir, are all associated with some version of a sovereign or autonomous self, a highly moralistic self in some versions at that. I will fold them into a general discussion that will help to prepare us for an explicit unpacking of contrasting versions of hard and soft sovereign selves, respectively.[26] There is a moment in Albert Camus' brilliant novel, *The Fall*, when his cynical world-weary protagonist, Jean-Baptiste Clemence, now resident in a foggy depressive Amsterdam, where he spends most of his time drinking gin in the seedy bar Mexico City and conducting monologues for the benefit of any willing listener,[27] remarks to one such companion: "Do you know what became of one of the houses in this city that sheltered Descartes? A lunatic asylum. Yes, general delirium and persecution."[28] Clearly the two are related in his mind: a strong view of rationalism, of the *cogito* in charge of itself, the flip side of which is a kind of lunacy.[29] For

Descartes, the "sovereign self . . . becomes . . . central to modernity" and is "derived from the nominalist notion of an omnipotent and sovereign God."[30] There is a self-controlling project of mastery in Descartes' position, as well as a focus on will—no surprise there. Important for our purposes is the fact that Descartes makes the astonishing claim that the "extended" parts of the self—the limbs, the body more generally—are inessential to who the self really is.[31] The heart of the self is an autonomous, rational cogito. Within this Cartesian rationalism, we live in our own heads—what philosopher Charles Taylor calls *excarnation*. And this is tethered to an exaggerated notion of what can be achieved through philosophy.

Living in our heads in this way denies relationality. We come to assume that "pure thought is greater than love. . . . [For] the philosophical God is essentially self-centered, though simply contemplating itself."[32] The anticorporeality of the Cartesian cogito, the stress on a certain sort of cerebral capacity, works to the detriment of persons with mental disabilities of course but, more generally, to anyone who cannot easily "disembody" herself. The positing of a self apart from and free from relationship means, in practice, a denial of the self, for we are who we are, we become who we become, in and through relationship and as participants in a particular linguistic community. Descartes jousts with those he calls "the Schoolmen," the Thomistic-Aristotelians. He claims we can indeed achieve mastery over ourselves even as he acknowledges that we cannot master all there is to know.[33] A theorist of the will, he links thoughts to volitions in his *Philosophical Writings*.[34] The body is a source of error and confusion—it can never illumine or enlighten. It follows that our volitionality makes us most like God, who is, after all, incorporeal. It is the task of human beings to keep the will on track—and this without specifically arguing against Augustine's insistence that the will is very rarely "as one" and is more likely to be divided and conflicted than anything else. For Descartes, by contrast, freedom lies in the monistic will and our ability to control it, for we, too, possess "infinite will."

Descartes' account of ratiocination continues to enjoy wide currency among some rationalistic philosophers, but it isn't credible to those who study emotion, reason, and the human brain: They have known for a long time that the mind functions as a dynamic system open to and responding to all sorts of currents and stimuli, internal and external.[35] One of Descartes' fundamental errors, then, was to "split the mind from brain and body."[36] Rather than a dynamic system, Descartes uses a mechanical model: clockwork mechanics. Thinking, as I already noted, because it is separated from the "unknowing" body in Descartes' view, it is allegedly "freer"—more sovereign, one might say—than some alternative account that, by acknowledging human finitude and weaknesses, recognizes that we are never fully masters, even in our own houses. If you follow Descartes in seeing the "soul" entirely separated from the body, the sovereign cogito can take flight as the finite body, with its various necessities, bumbles and fumbles along.

A curious spin-off of this Cartesian imperative was the most peculiar Society of Mutual Autopsy, formed in France in the latter decades of the nineteenth century. This outfit consisted of evangelizing atheists, dead set against the Catholic Church or anything at all that smacked of "traditional" religion. They claimed that autopsies of the brain "without question" were "the soundest way of increasing knowledge about the function of the brain," and this to defeat, empirically, any notion of the soul![37] Setting up their own cultish rites, members willed their bodies—"rotting garbage"—to be autopsied by fellow members of the society upon their deaths. The notion that you could conclusively demonstrate that there is no soul strikes us as naïve—even risible—but they made a rather major splash at the time as an example of extreme dualism within a Cartesian frame.[38]

KANT AND THE AUTONOMOUS MORALIST

Immanuel Kant contributed another layer to a stress on human willing, a "will conceived in abstraction from any foundation in other aspects of the person or in its broader environment."[39] It is said of Immanuel Kant that the good people of Konigsberg could set their watches by his daily peregrinations, so clocklike and precise was his schedule. This sort of regularity makes a good bit of sense to any reader of Kant.[40] His deontological system presupposes that we are law-naming autonomous beings and, in order to make this argument, he, too, has to subdue the body, the realm of necessity, the world of what he calls the determined or "phenomenal" and this by contrast to the realm of freedom, the world of the "noumenal." It is all very tidy, and that alone should make us suspicious, for living a life is, we know, not a walk in a park denuded of all weeds, bramble bushes, and unexpected bumps in the pathway. In a way, the Kantian self moves in circles, its moral point of reference being its own "good will." Kant helps to shift the locus from an appropriately chastened notion of fragile and partial moral autonomy to a strong account of self-sovereignty. For in our rational capacity, human beings become godlike and a particular class of human beings—intellectuals or, specifically, philosophers—form a separate objective class that, by its nature, is incapable of forming cliques or political intrigue. Evidently original sin is suspended for philosophers.[41] The idea that the philosopher could be entirely disinterested—wedded to the "moral law" and nothing else, neither family, nor faith, nor nation—is entirely unreal and somewhat reminiscent of the fond hope on the part of international communism before World War I that workers (the proletariat) in each and every country would identify only with the "universal" working class and would, therefore, not go to war on behalf of their countries. For some odd reason, such delusions must be defeated again and again as they pop up repeatedly.

In any case, Kant's understanding of human nature is explicit and helps to explain why he belongs in the ranks of self-sovereigntists. Involved is, as I already noted, his division between the phenomenal and the noumenal realms, with the latter being the realm of freedom and the former the realm of nature, the determined, necessity. The self is in part a being-in-itself, a "real, atemporal, noumenal self ": outside the causal order of nature, and thereby free and autonomous by definition. The thinking substance is presented entirely in noncorporeal terms.[42] Other human beings we construe as phenomenal objects—they are "mere appearances." Our appearance, phenomenally, in the empirical world in no way defines us. His philosophy requires that human claims be sundered from bodies with a history and within history. Kant's is a radically antidialogic account of human reasoning as he denies or negates human sociality and insists that the self form concepts independent of experience.

KANTIAN MORAL SELF-SOVEREIGNTY

The phenomenal is "independent of, and free from all . . . necessity" and "from all influence of sensibility"; the latter is bound up with nature.[43] Reasoning is severed from experience, and Kant's self is asocial; indeed, one might say that Kantian reason is "inflated and divinized"—godlike.[44] Give his view of the emotions and sensibility—and of embodiment—it should come as no surprise that women cannot be "universal" in the way men can. So fully sovereign selves, it seems clear, will be male. His a prioris are taken as "necessary conditions" for all moral judgments.[45] Indeed, freedom itself is an abstract apriorism in his system. Freedom's noumenal nature is such that one need not consult history or experience in order to assess contrasting ways of life as more or less free or conducive to freedom. Indeed, one can never establish the criteria for such an assessment at all. Kant rules out moral conflict, resting his morality on an Archimedean standpoint he presumes is independent of any social order and history itself. The categorical imperatives rest "on the sharpest possible separation between action and intention."[46]

Noumenal, autonomous will puts us as close to God as we are going to get, for God created morality in the first instance as an act of will.[47] The Augustinian emphasis on love disappears as the rational moral law is followed by autonomous sovereign selves who work like clockwork: There are no caveats, exceptions, no allowances to be made for human weakness. The moral law takes the form of "categorical imperatives" that one is required to follow. No legitimate categorical imperative can conflict with another, thereby eliminating by fiat serious moral conflict. The moral law steers us in the direction of moral perfection of an egotistical sort. Of course, stated this bluntly, my criticisms are open to murmurs of disapproval, but, in the main, this seems to me essentially correct—placing Kant in the company of one version or strain of self-sovereignty.

Critiques of Kant are plentiful. I will simply note Hannah Arendt's essay, "What Is Freedom?" in which she laments the fact that Kant wrenched freedom as a concept from any application in the phenomenal realm, thus distorting "the very idea of freedom . . . by transposing it from its original field, the realm of politics and human affairs in general, to be an inward domain, the will."[48] Having departed the field of action, the freely willing self need encounter no obstacles, making of this freedom something that is debilitating—no surprise if the free (noumenal) self is disembodied, dehistoricized, denuded of contingencies and particularities.[49]

One of my claims is that self-sovereignty of a strong sort invites moralism, including moralism of the legalistic sort. We cannot trust all these autonomous selves to be entirely self-governing in entirely the "right" way, to maintain themselves only from themselves, evidently. So the law, especially its punitive arm, plays a major role in Kant's argument. A kind of purism lies at the heart of his project. One example should suffice to make this clear as it illustrates the way in which the autonomous sovereign self, operating on a priori grounds, can make a moral dilemma disappear and engage in an act of cruelty that is celebrated as truth telling.

Although one can discern religious derivations for "providential deism" in Kantian philosophy, let's take a look at a critique of precisely that development that undermines any such claim as total self-sovereignty. Anti-Nazi theologian Dietrich Bonhoeffer argues that, within Kantian deontology, a sovereign self is the moral center. For Bonhoeffer, the moral center is a God who relinquished his power to go to death on a cross in order that cycles of vengeance might be lifted from humanity. The believer must act on the basis of brotherhood and sisterhood, of concrete responsibility, and not retreat into an inner purity of an insular self.

In his essay, "What Is Meant by 'Telling the Truth,'" Bonhoeffer reminds us that ferreting out the truth and nothing but the truth lies at the heart of all moralisms.[50] In order to appreciate Bonhoeffer in this matter, one must understand his severe words for Kantian ethics. He scores the moralist as a sadistic clown, a tormenter of humanity, when he issues dicta that strain friendship and rip apart our humanity; thus: "Kant, of course, declared that he was too proud ever to utter a falsehood; indeed he unintentionally carried this principle ad absurdum by saying that he would feel himself obliged to give truthful information even to a criminal looking for a friend of his who had concealed himself in the house."[51] He thereby gives his friend over to be murdered but his "private virtuousness"—he has not lied—is maintained all the while. We all have encountered nasty people who must tell the truth at every moment in order to give an unsuspecting spouse the full story of undetected infidelities, for example. "Only at the cost of self-deception," writes Bonhoeffer, can he, the man of private virtuousness, "keep himself pure from the contamination arising from responsible action."[52] The word *contamination* is important here, given the purist drive in all moralistic codes for sovereign selves.[53]

Alexander McCall Smith, in his delightful novel, *The Sunday Philosophy Club*, pictures his heroine, Isabel Dalhousie, who edits a journal of ethics, ruminating on lying. Clearly, Dalhousie believes there are lies . . . and then there are lies. Many lies are malicious, distorting, instruments of deceit and cruelty. But some "white lies" help to preserve sociality, make human relationships possible, stem cruelty. At least this is a proposition worth entertaining, she believes.

Reading a paper submitted to the journal on this theme, she imagines that one day she should write a paper "In Praise of Hypocrisy." Here's why:

> Of course, not all lies were wrong, which was another respect, Isabel thought, in which Kant was mistaken. One of the most ridiculous things that he had ever said was that there was a duty to tell the truth to a murderer looking for his victim. If the murderer came to one's door and asked, *Is he in?* one would be obliged to answer truthfully, even if this would lead to the death of an innocent person. Such nonsense; and she could remember the precise offending passage: *Truthfulness in statements which cannot be avoided is the formal duty of an individual to everyone, however great may be the disadvantage accruing to himself or another.* It was not surprising that Benjamin Constant should have been offended by this, although Kant responded—unconvincingly—and tried to point out that the murderer might be apprehended before he acted on the knowledge which he had gained from a truthful answer.
>
> The answer, surely, is that lying *in general* is wrong, but that some lies, carefully identified as the exception, will be permissible. There were, therefore, good lies and bad lies, with

good lies being uttered for a benevolent reason (to protect the feeling of another, for example).[54]

Without endorsing the views espoused by the wonderfully imagined Isabel Dalhousie, I remind us that the air was—rather rarified—in Kant's Konigsberg. Kant, a punctual man, alone, imagines monism on the level of the self in the interest of strong sovereign selves. This is just not a credible position and it easily becomes rigorist and even cruel, insufficiently aware of human foibles, shortcomings, and the unpredictabilities of the world. It is harsh and unforgiving to push the self into a godlikeness that is never warranted for limited beings like ourselves. So, once again, monism and disembodiment are characteristics of the Kantian sovereign self. As we move to the next chapter, we will take the measure of representative nineteenth- and twentieth-century sovereign selves and the implications of these understandings, particularly for those human beings who can never be sovereign in the way imagined or demanded.

9
SELF-SOVEREIGNTY: MORALISM, NIHILISM, AND EXISTENTIAL ISOLATION

A FRUITFUL POINT OF ENTRY INTO JOHN STUART MILL'S SOVEREIGNTIST arguments emerges as one rereads his classic essays.[1] Take, for example, his indictment of authority in *On Liberty*, enshrined as one of the lodestones of contemporary liberalism.[2] If anything approaches a sacred principle for Mill it is that the individual is entirely *sovereign* over himself: "Over himself, over his own body and mind, the individual is sovereign." This does not apply to children, nor to backward societies where the "race itself" may be said to be akin to a child, in its nonage. Then despotism is a legitimate mode of government, Mills insists, insofar as it is directed to the improvement of such peoples—here a justification for British imperialism. Human beings are poised in a world of stark antinomies, the most important being the "struggle between liberty and authority."[3] Mill's lack of subtlety in this matter, including his assault against religious authority, as if authority is equivalent to despotism rather than to responsibility given the office one holds legitimately, is on full display.

The logical extension of Mill's position is a version of liberal monism. His fusion of authority and tyranny is instructive in this regard. He associates tradition with a lack of enlightened reason as well as a tendency to seek power rather than liberty. Authority, however, as every political theorist understands, is not collapsible into power, for authority means that power is exercised legitimately, and this is central to well-functioning constitutional societies in modernity. But legitimate authority always pertains to a whole range of institutions. You cannot sustain certain relationships, including parent-child or teacher-student, without a complex authority relationship. Despite this, authority, for Mill, signals that someone else is encroaching on my self-sovereignty.

The sovereign self is the sole judge of his or her own good. Although Mill imposes severe restrictions on pubs (public drinking houses) and forbids marriage licenses to those who cannot demonstrate that they have the means of supporting a family, a rule that, in practice, would prohibit marriage to persons falling below a certain socioeconomic level, he sees no assault on self-sovereignty in such measures. As well, Mill stoutly denies that there is anything like human nature. Nature, in fact, is a problem for—another dichotomy—nature lies in opposition to reason. Nature Mill downgrades to instinct, the most "degrading" and "pernicious" of human possibilities. A split between reason and desire undergirds his argument. Herein lies the rub: Mill repudiates human desire as enslavement to the body, to the passions, rather than the mind.[4] Passion and emotion—things of the body—threaten to reduce us to the level of animals. His approach to all this is dualism of a particular kind. Its origins seem to me to be Manichean. The Manichees, with whom Augustine conducted one of his titanic arguments, held that the human body is polluted by definition. Only the spirit is pure. It follows that only one who distances himself or herself from the pollution of the body is uplifted to a higher realm. Mill's picture of our degraded condition is understandable given that he believes impure male desire holds sway. As the result of certain reforms all of this will be purified and make way for a future condition in which a small elite has battled the brutality of natural forces and emerged victorious.[5]

The Sovereign Woman as Robinson Crusoe

Given Mill's commitment to women's suffrage, it is unsurprising that his essays *On Liberty* and *The Subjection of Women* made a huge splash on both sides of the Atlantic. One American feminist who picked up on a Millian view was Elizabeth Cady Stanton, the most important theorist of the women's suffrage movement of the nineteenth century. The Seneca Falls Convention, from which the American Woman Suffrage movement is usually dated, was held in 1848. Stanton lived to a ripe old age and argued all the while, making many pronouncements—in the interest of self-sovereignty. It is easy enough to see why some version of self-sovereignty would be attractive to women who were for so long identified solely with their immersion within families and the domestic realm. But one can overdo it, and that is indeed what happened. Paradoxically, although suffragists like Stanton repudiated the view that women should be the domestic ones, they accepted the evaluation of women that flowed from that immersion, namely, that women were somehow morally purer beings, uncontaminated by the tainted male-dominant public sphere.

Stanton extolled "the domestic altar" as a "sacred flame where woman is the high and officiating priestess."[6] If the male element is ambitious and cruel, the female element will bring out "the diviner qualities in human nature." But not all natures have diviner qualities, it seems. Those human beings most associated with the body—including harsh manual labor—should be disenfranchised. The overbreeding of the more animalistic immigrants, she feared, might one day swamp the "better sort." It behooved political society to enfranchise the female part of that better sort in order to stave off the threat. Stanton was not beyond openly racialist arguments—perhaps *nativist* would be the better term—attacking "unlettered and unwashed ditch-diggers, boot-blacks, butchers, and barbers" who got the vote when women (of the better

sort) did.[7] "Sambo, Patrick, Hans and Yung Fung" were not of the better sort. Illiteracy, too, constituted a sufficient criterion for denial of the
franchise. She had doubts about whether Catholics, among others, could
fit the strenuous bill of her version of strong (Protestant) selfhood.

Her most famous essay, a paean to self-sovereignty, "The Solitude of
Self," was delivered as a lecture in 1892. This essay is at one and the same
time exhilarating and chilling. Stanton traces her notion that we are all
Robinson Crusoes on our own little islands (this from a woman who bore
six children); we enter the world alone and we go out alone, an aloneness
she traces to the Protestant, Christian ideal. It is the self that comes first,
followed by citizenship, and only then by "incidental relations of life, such
as mother, wife, sister, daughter."[8] These incidental relations do not in
any way fundamentally define the self. "Self-sovereignty" for Stanton
means we are solitary voyagers. We "walk alone." We realize our "awful
solitude." When things go well, others cluster around; when they go
badly, there is "not one to share her misery," again a rather astonishing
claim for someone who seems always to have been in human company.
Life is a "march" and a "battle" and we are all soldiers who must be
"equipped" for this battle. In "the tragedies and triumphs of human experience, each mortal stands alone."

Her words are chilling because they conjure up a universe that is
either hostile or benignly indifferent—depopulated save for the self. The
universe has been stripped of objects of meaning save what the individual
chooses to apply to it. She aims to disenthrall the self, to disencumber it
in the sure and certain hope that a lofty and invigorating ideal of individual sovereign freedom will be the end result. Somehow all of this will redound to a general good. At least she genuflects in the direction of a
general good. The essential solitude and aloneness of the self is one version of a liberal view of the self. It isn't nearly so virulent—indeed it isn't
virulently self-sovereign at all—in the ways later radical feminism discourse became. I refer to that strain of feminism that requires excising the
body—nature—altogether, or eliminating male bodies specifically, or destroying all institutions that mark our embodiment, like the family. One
thinker may be worth taking up here as a vision of self-sovereignty that
triumphs over everything in its pathway, including the body.

AN EXISTENTIAL DIGRESSION: SIMONE DE BEAUVOIR AND RADICAL VOLUNTARISM

If Cady Stanton seems indifferent to the body and its claims on the self, Simone de Beauvoir, following Sartre in all things, finds the body odious. One might suppose that theorists who claim to have rejected liberalism would incorporate within their thought those features of human life that liberal monism strips away. But matters are often neither simple nor reasonable. The philosophy of Jean-Paul Sartre is a case in point.[9] In many ways, Sartre's existentialism goes beyond the liberal accounts of self-sovereignty represented by John Stuart Mill. Sartre's categories, in turn, were taken up by his disciple, Simone de Beauvoir, to form the basis of her classic feminist text, *The Second Sex*. Sartre's profusion of obtuse terms, his labyrinthian twists and turns, his capitulation to moral nihilism as he sanctions the shedding of innocent blood in terroristic attacks against "colonialists"—for those being killed are not innocent even if they have done nothing in particular— together with his celebration of the nobility of violent force, compel one to ask what sort of self is here triumphing. Sartre's theory declares that human beings are set apart from all else—from any embeddedness in the "muck" of nature. He refuses to consider seriously whether there are any limits to, or on, the self. The icing on this existentialist cake is his excoriation of those who refuse to seize their absolute freedom as living in "bad faith." Sartre's atomistic sovereign self could not be clearer: we are isolated monads confronting an external social and natural world set off against and in opposition to our free projects. The natural state of human beings, à la Hobbes, is of a war of all against all— a bleak reiteration of an a priori and fundamental human asociality. There are no ties binding the individual to the past or holding him in the present.

"The Hell of Other People"

For Sartre, relations between persons are instrumental and calculated, although they may be "masked" with such notions as brotherhood. Beneath the "false unity" of such mystifications lurks a constantly recreated world of violence and terror. Because the unity of the group comes to it from the outside, Sartre denies any internal or intrinsic links between persons. He denies human sociality absolutely. Sociality is reduced by Sartre to oppression. Sartre is forced to live in a world "haunted" by others—hell being other people. To live in such a world "is not only to be able to encounter the Other at every turn of the road; it is also to find myself engaged in a world in which instrumental-complexes can have a meaning which my free project has not first given to them."[10] Others are what stand in his way. Fear of violence and death drives individuals to form groups. This same terror prevents groups from dissolving. All ways of life, for Sartre, represent an "endangering morass into which men sink who refuse to assume their full human stature."[11] One assumes one's full stature when the past and other persons, in the most fundamental sense, no longer exist for oneself. Possession for Sartre is a form of being. A person possesses unceasingly. All activities are modes of appropriation, even play. Thus Sartre describes skiing as the possession of a visual field and the conquest of space. The Cartesian distinction between consciousness and matter figures centrally in Sartre's thought. Sartre grounds individual choice in freedom. But that freedom is nothingness. Although Sartre asserts that men must be totally responsible, he gives no grounds for preferring one course of action as against another. His assertion of total responsibility—that one is responsible for every act of humiliation, torture, degradation, destruction in the world—denies any reasonable moral stance: "If I am responsible for everything, I am responsible for nothing in particular." Morality, at base, is a match which can be won or lost.[12]

The Feminist Sartrian: Radical Self-Sovereignty

Simone de Beauvoir, following in Sartre's footsteps, deploys his categories of the Being-in-itself and the Being-for itself, identifying women, as does Sartre, with nature. This transmogrifies into a feminist project, astonishingly enough, given the censorious repudiation of female bodies it advances. Civilization begins where nature ends—which would seem to leave women stuck outside civilization. Although Sartre urged that woman's nature was fixed by her "unfortunate sexual anatomy," Beauvoir dissents from that view. She has to make women Sartrian subjects. The only way to do that is to spring them from nature in order that they, too, can be fully sovereign, can be aggressive, appropriating selves.

For Beauvoir, the "body of man" has its own integrity whereas the female body "seems wanting in significance by itself."[13] Human civilization is male; woman is "the incidental, the inessential as opposed to the essential. He is the Subject, he is the Absolute—she is the Other." Woman is now trapped in Immanence, that nature-bog. Beauvoir would spring woman from this world of the given in order that she, too, might enter Transcendence. She associates all the loftiest human attitudes—heroism, revolt, disinterestedness, creativity—with the male world of Transcendence. She would have women become great like those men who have taken the weight of the world on their shoulders. Everyday life has no dignity and is, therefore, neither to be redeemed nor affirmed.

Women's lives have heretofore been almost embarrassingly paltry and pallid. Mind you, Beauvoir offers no criteria for assessing greatness. Instead, she applies it willy-nilly, whether to a Hitler, presumably, or a Goethe, for both no doubt fit within the category of having taken the world on their shoulders. Eschewing moral categories of evaluation, she can only make one abstract leap after another. It is unsurprising, therefore, that in her repugnance of Immanence one finds contempt for the lives of ordinary human beings, male and female. She accords to women no sense of integrity, joining the chorus of repugnance at the female body.

Her discussion of "The Data of Biology," which opens *The Second Sex*, shows how Beauvoir must hold her material at arm's length as she views women as the "victim of the species" and males as somehow "transcended" in their sperm. Women are biologically alienated. Pregnancy is described in entirely negative terms, with the unborn child characterized as a "tenant" who feeds parasitically upon his mother's existence. One particular statement concerning female biology is especially stunning: A woman's "mammary glands," her breasts, may be "excised at any time of life" for they play "no role in women's individual economy." The upshot is a version of repressive feminism: The body must be repressed for it invites scorn, despair, inhibitions, and all the rest. As well, if oppression is located in nature itself, the only way to transform societies is to radically alter nature. Women must be freed from biological "tyranny."[14] We've come a long way, baby, one might say—or a long way against babies begotten the old-fashioned way as one feature of the modern conquest and transcendence of nature, part and parcel of strong self-sovereignty, as we shall see below.

For the moment, however, we must get back on the (historic) track by taking up a thinker sometimes called the American Nietzsche—although that designation doesn't make much sense to me—Ralph Waldo Emerson. Where Emerson is upbeat, Nietzsche is gloomy. Nietzsche unpacks nihilism, and Emerson extols a new world that will overtake the limited old one.

EMERSON AND AMERICAN "IDEALISM": UNQUENCHABLE SPIRIT

Jane Addams, founder of the U.S. settlement home movement and the first American woman to be awarded the Nobel Peace Prize, so idealized Emerson that when Bronson Alcott visited her college, Rockford Seminary in Illinois, she was content to shine his boots (Alcott was a friend of Emerson's); for Addams, contact with Alcott's boots somehow brought her into connection with Emerson himself: Such was Emerson's reputation.[15] I will touch briefly on Emerson's version of the sovereignty of selves, in part because this feeds into Jane Addams's eventual disillusionment with notions of self-sovereignty.[16] For when Addams, as a young adult, went through a period of debilitating soul-searching called neurasthenia in those days, although today we would likely diagnose depression, she found Emerson's stirring account of the "self alone" cold comfort indeed. How can one be a sovereign self if one is bedridden, grieving, despairing?[17] Two of Emerson's essays are particularly important, his Divinity School address of 1838 and his American Scholar oration delivered before the Phi Beta Kappa Society at Cambridge, August 31, 1837. Let's begin with American Scholar to determine whether Emerson warrants inclusion in the company of sovereign selves. As a preliminary comment, it should be noted that when Emerson broke away from his traditional faith to become a Unitarian, he declared that he would not find the Eucharist objectionable if one got rid of the bread and the wine and all that body and blood stuff—which is, of course, the entire point and an ongoing reminder of how powerful is embodiment and a reminder of our bodies in Christian theology and practice. Emerson is ambivalent about the "tug" of bodies.

Emerson declares that "Man Thinking" must appropriate rather than repudiate the best from the past—all to the end of instructing and heightening the "one thing in the world, of value, . . . the active soul."[18] The Man Thinking finds "consolation in exercising the highest functions of human nature." He resists the vulgarity of the common—vulgar prosperity that "retrogrades ever to barbarism." He is enlightened by genius and lives and breathes the melodious, the best. He stands alone, never deferring to "the popular cry." In plumbing the secret of his own mind, "he has descended into the secrets of all minds," for we share a nature although what we make of it varies from person to person. Along the way, man has wronged himself. He has lost "the light." Emerson endorses the eccentric system of Emanuel Swedenborg, a "purely philosophical Ethics" that departs from alleged theological obscurantism with its sin talk and gloominess about human prospects. Nowadays each man "shall feel the world is his, and man shall treat with man *as a sovereign state within a sovereign state* [emphasis mine]," thereby articulating explicitly the connection between states and selves. We are all part of one Divine Soul—but this is no barrier to our self-sovereignty.

In his Divinity School address, Emerson waxes lyrical from the first moment: "The grass grows, the buds burst, the meadow is spotted with fire and gold in the tint of flowers."[19] The mysteries of the world are available to us if we realize that the "world is the product of . . . one will, of one mind; and that one mind is everywhere active . . . . And whatever opposes that will is everywhere balked and baffled." This takes us to the heart of the matter and to his view of Man Thinking. Emerson preaches a version of immanence within which that which is transcendent—nature—infuses itself into the immanent and creates an at-oneness.

In this world there is no sin—that is the "injustice of the vulgar tone of preaching"—that violates the lofty philosophy of Jesus. Old understandings are "for slaves." He admonishes his listeners to "go alone" and "to love God without mediator or veil." One can do this in part because God is within—not without. It is unsurprising that Emerson does not discuss Incarnation, Crucifixion, Resurrection, the heart of Christian theology. His flowery language presses to the conclusion that we can clean up "religion" if we rid it of the old, all the traditional understandings that yet cling to it.[20]

Compared to Sartre and Beauvoir's extreme formulations, Emerson's version of self-sovereignty is much easier to take—one feels considerably less battered after reading him. But there are consequences—always—and among these in liberal Protestantism, people who essentially agree with much of what Emerson had to say but did not decamp to Unitarianism, one consequence was a buoyant belief that one could in a benign way remake human nature in order that it better comport with the uplifting image of the "Self Alone."

Despite Emerson's paeans to the multifariousness of nature, he saw the world as the product of a single will and mind. But this mind is not Logos, not the God of classical trinitarian reason; rather, this mind is all sentiment, for that is what religion comes down to as the "majesty" of God enters into and divinizes man. Here modern excarnation is on full display: no birth, no crucifixion, no resurrection—on the theological front—and, on the political and personal, man owns the world. Man's soul is without limit. Emerson's American gnosticism disembodies faith and divinizes the self, laying down another few bricks thereby to the primrose path culminating in contemporary self-absorption.

COUNTERPOINT: LIMITS, IMPERFECTIONS, AND THE UNPARDONABLE SIN

There were among Emerson's contemporaries those who took exception to the transcendent "at-oneness" of his project and his determination to leap over traditional Christianity with its original sin and the like. The greatest of these was the writer, Nathaniel Hawthorne, best known to us as the author of the classic novel *The Scarlet Letter*.[21] Those who know only *The Scarlet Letter* and who see it, wrongly, as a tale of Puritan repression and the burden and cruelties of shame, might think Hawthorne saw himself as one who would liberate humanity from the shackles and snarls of tradition. Not so. Hawthorne had a great nose for humbug, however fancy the suit in which it clad itself. His brilliant short stories are warnings about overreach, about thinking one can abandon the difficult for the easy and enjoy the same outcome, about the endless morass of human folly, much of which is the enlightened opinion of any given age.

A favorite of Jane Addams's, Hawthorne's story "Ethan Brand" tells the tale of a lime burner who has returned to the little village from which he departed many years earlier to go on a quest to find the "unpardonable sin." As the story begins, Bartram, a "rough, heavy-looking man, begrimed with charcoal," and his son watch over and stoke a lime kiln that sits about a village. The jet smoke and flame issuing from it "resembled nothing so much as the private entrance to the infernal regions, which the shepherds of the Delectable Mountains were accustomed to show to pilgrims"—a gesture, clearly, to Bunyan's classic *Pilgrim's Progress*, known to all Americans of that day. There had been an earlier lime-burner, one Ethan Brand, who had led a solitary and meditative life, "before he began his search for the Unpardonable Sin," an "IDEA [*sic*]" that overtook him and drove him out of the village, into the night, and down an ever-darkening road. Brand had been the butt of ridicule to the villagers. But on this particular night the phantom, Ethan Brand himself, reappears. He has discovered the unpardonable sin. It is one that "grew within my own breast. . . . A sin that grew nowhere else! The sin of an intellect that triumphed over the sense of brotherhood with man and reverence for God, and sacrificed everything to its own mighty claims! The only sin that deserves a recompense of immortal agony!"[22]

The triumph of intellect, of a system, an overarching philosophy—that was the unpardonable sin. Ethan Brand had cultivated an IDEA but lost his heart and soul. He had cherished his own powers exclusively. He would rise to the level of "star-lit eminence, whither the philosophers of the earth, laden with the lore of universities, might vainly strive to clamber after him. That, indeed, had withered,—had contracted,—had hardened,—had perished! It had ceased to partake of the universal throb. He had lost his hold of the magnetic chain of humanity." Thus he "became a fiend" as he cast off all others in search of his own obsessive idea. That night, as Bartram and his little son sleep, Ethan Brand commits himself to the flames of the furnace: "Come, deadly element of Fire, henceforth my familiar friend! Embrace me, as I do thee!" All that is left in the morning are ashes that have taken the shape of a human heart.

Although Hawthorne speaks of a "magnetic throb" and the like, his primary insistence is that one cannot absent oneself in search of the wholly abstract and thereby rank a certain kind of philosophical ratiocination above all other human activities and virtues. In a second story, "The Celestial Railroad," a vivid 1843 tale, Hawthorne writes wittily of a gleaming new railroad that will take pilgrims to the Celestial City without all the arduous dangers that Christian in John Bunyan's *Pilgrim's Progress* encountered on his pilgrimage.[23] Hop aboard: Mr. Smooth-it-away will get you to the promised place as you avoid the Slough of Despond, the battle with Apollyon, and every other obstacle. One "great convenience" of the new rapid transit way to get to the Celestial City was that you didn't have to make your way with all your burdens upon your back—no, you could just check the luggage and be done with it. As for Apollyon, well, he is now tamed as the "chief engineer" on the train. All of this shows "the liberality of the age; this proves, if anything can, that all musty prejudices are in a fair way to be obliterated." As they streak through the countryside, the modern pilgrim notices some old-fashioned pilgrims making their labored way—these are called preposterous and obstinate. Mr. Smooth-it-away, Mr. Live-for-the-world, Mr. Hide-sin-in-the-heart, Mr. Scaly Conscience, and some gentlemen from the town of Shun Repentance were all reassuring on this score.

Now a tunnel, quickly, through the Hill of Difficulty—no arduous ascents or descents. The old terrible giants were "Pope" and "Pagan" for Bunyan. Here, they are gone. But there is a new terrible giant who tries to seize travelers. He is called Giant Transcendentalist, German by birth, and his world is a "heap of fog and duskiness," so it is very difficult to know what he is talking about. More characters pop up, all designed by Hawthorne to spoof the liberal theology of his day for believing there were shortcuts for the modern pilgrim. Alas, it turns out that the Lord of the Celestial City will not take in the passengers from the train—for, indeed, there really are no shortcuts. Even worse, some of those assisting on the voyage turn out to be cohorts of Satan himself, including Mr. Smooth-it-away, for the train leads straight to hell. Hawthorne's narrator presents this as "Thank Heaven" a "Dream," but the satire is keen and penetrating.

"The Hall of Fantasy" (1843) and "Earth's Holocaust" (1844) are parables of warning, telling a tale of those who want to cast off everything from the past and burn it and those who wish to create a machine to make sunshine "out of a lady's smile" and "to irradiate the earth, by means of this wonderful invention," this "Utopian invention." Alas, the Hall of Fantasy ushers in destruction as those who spend all their days there find they are no longer living in the world—it is as if the end of the world has already happened. More chilling is the tale of the great fire, the Holocaust. People seek to purge themselves entirely of the past. Reformers have been working overtime to get rid of all the debris of the old: Whether it is beautiful or not, it must go. The moralistic streak in such reform comes through as all tea and coffee are destroyed and tobacco is burnt up. This burning of everything includes the accumulated wisdom of the world found in great books and constitutions: Universal benevolence demands no less. The accoutrements of faith go last—garments, mitres, crosiers, finally the Bible itself. But one thing the "Wiseacres"—a term Hawthorne uses—haven't done and cannot do is to destroy the human heart. That persists, and it is in the very soul of humans that the endeavor for perfection can flip over and show the triumph of destruction, of evil, that begins with an unforgiving assault on all that has gone before.

Finally, "Birth-Mark," a story so prescient it seems as if Hawthorne imagined in advance tales of the sovereign self as a quest for human genetic perfectibility such as we confront today.[24] A beautiful young woman, perfect in every way save for a birthmark on one cheek that takes the shape of a tiny red hand, weds an ambitious scientist committed to man's control over nature. Her tiny birthmark looms larger and larger in his mind. He begins to loathe it, and his wife, Georgiana, picks up on this loathing, internalizes it, and would have the mark removed even if she dies in the effort. Get rid of this blemish, and all will be perfect! "Deep science" will do the job! Her husband, Aylmer, presents her with "Airy figures, absolutely bodiless ideas, and forms of unsubstantial beauty," and these "came and danced before her, imprinting their momentary footsteps on beams of light." Dazzled by this Gnostic display, his wife puts all her faith in Aylmer to remove the blemish that she would wrench out with her own hands if but she could. He tells her of the alchemists of old and his aspiration toward the infinite. Nothing less than perfection will do. Georgiana takes the potion. Slowly the little red hand fades from her face and, as it does so, her life drains from her. She is now perfect . . . and dead. The true blemish here on display, surely, is the sin of pride displayed by Aylmer in his quest for perfection.

Hawthorne—Melville would be another—represents a countertradition to dominant American boisterousness, boosterism, and optimism. It isn't that Hawthorne is gloomy—he does leave room for hope—but hope is not the same thing as optimism-without-limits. At the moment, we find the optimists busy as beavers extolling the as yet unproven wonders of stem cell research and positive genetic enhancement and controlling and shaping exactly the kind of progeny we want. Upward and onward! The quest for human cloning is another feature of a cluster of efforts, some relatively new, some in the works for decades, to achieve perfect control over nature, to get our bodies into shape so that we are no longer subject to their failures, frailties, and necessities. Whether eugenics in the early twentieth century—which acquired a bad name with Nazi biopolitics and the racialist cruelties with which it was larded from the beginning—or "positive genetic enhancement now," eugenics is part of the program. Euthanasia is yet another, as is the selective prevention of the births of less-than-perfect persons: Some 90 percent of all pregnancies in America today in which the woman is carrying a Down syndrome child, according to prenatal forecasting, end in abortion. Indeed, there is evidence that many medical providers push and urge women in that direction. The quest for perfection is alive and well and it is linked now, as it was in the past, with certain agendas for social change. The quest for self-sovereignty links together science, technology, and ideology even as the earlier phase, and craze, of state-engineered eugenics stitched these same elements together. In the most notorious case, that of National Socialist Germany, much of the ideology was provided by the use—some argue the grotesque misuse—of the philosopher whose name is inescapably linked to the "will to power," namely, Friedrich Nietzsche. Emerson's sunniness here gives way to overwrought gloom as Nietzsche peers over the edge of the abyss and takes the leap.

NIETZSCHE AND THE WILL TO POWER

It is impossible to settle definitively the question of whether the Nazis misused Nietzsche or whether Nietzsche gave them ample ammunition to deploy in their quest to set the strong against the weak, to goad the powerful to destroy the powerless. Surely both claims bear some truth, and I will leave it at that. Wherever one comes down in that dispute, no one cavils at placing Nietzsche in the company of the great philosophers of the will.[25] Indeed, Nietzsche construed philosophy as a heroic enterprise in which a philosopher makes the world his own through fundamental acts of the will. He "worked out" a rather malicious theodicy as a young man—and never grew out of it—in which he made God the father of all evil, a Manichean move of sorts save, so far as I understand it, he does not counterbalance this God who generates evil with a God of reason and good. On the "good" side of the ledger there is a rather ominous blank.

Having made God the author of evil, and wanting to get rid of both God and evil—or, more precisely, finding God "dead" in the hearts of his contemporaries, Nietzsche insists we speak of "good and bad" only, leaving evil out of it. Moral norms are, he insists, reducible to "value judgments" that are entirely perspectival—not open to truth warrants: These are all basic themes underscored in *On the Genealogy of Morals*.[26] There is, of course, more; namely, Nietzsche divides societies and groups of human beings into the *healthy* and the *unhealthy*. The healthy aristocratic values exhibit life abundantly through "war, adventure, hunting, dancing, war games." The sickly, impotent mode of existence—mastered by "the Jews, that priestly people"—seeks to undermine and destroy all that is vibrant and healthy, to bring it down.[27] It is the Jews that spurred a "slave revolt" in morality. Christianity embodies the triumph of a sickly slave morality as the weak dominate over the strong. Hatred disguised as a kind of sickly love Nietzsche detects at work.[28] (Interestingly, Nietzsche has some favorable words for Islam as a masculine religion for "real men," sounding a bit like an advertisement for the Marlboro Man at this point.)[29] Nietzsche's rantings about Jesus of Nazareth are often painful to read because the level of vitriol is so great: One wonders if Nietzsche himself isn't guilty of being charmed by that which he so vehemently rejects—an observation that is fair enough given that Nietzsche insists all philosophy is ad hominem.

The weak use strong words that Nietzsche abominates—*equality, justice, brotherhood*—words that he spits out with juicy bile mixed in. To this end, he loathes democracy and socialism—they are for the least and the stupid and the envious—and any mode of life Nietzsche associates with the abomination of the weak reigning over those to whom they should properly be subjected and whom they should hold in awe.

Those who cavil at my inclusion of Nietzsche in a discussion of strong self-sovereignty will likely say that he is not guilty as charged because he "decenters" the subject. Nietzsche is critical of Kant, and I have included Kant in the strong self-sovereignty camp: How, then, can both thinkers forge links to contemporary self sovereignty? That should become clearer as we continue.[30] In the passages in his writings that were cobbled together to become *The Will to Power*, Nietzsche leads us to the self he celebrates by, first, unpacking the architecture of nihilism. Much of this writing is elusive, cast in epigrams and misty notions that trail off, having arrived at no conclusion. We know that Nietzsche rejects human free will and credits morality as an antidote against practical nihilism. But this means turning one's back on the "will to existence" itself.[31] Further on he indicts faith in reason as the cause of nihilism. One way or another, human beings are never on sure and certain ground when they make truth claims or plumb reason. These are all perspectival and arbitrary claims made from our own particular points of self-interest and absorption. Some are better than others—those that celebrate human power and joy in that power. But none can be defended on the grounds of truth for which reasons may be proffered.

The upshot is this: For man to seize his will to power, he must be sovereign, radically self-fashioning. Anything else is bad faith. As far as society as a whole goes, every healthy society generates "[human] waste, decay, elimination" and this is not to "be condemned." All societies form "refuse and waste materials." There will be failures, and these are to be expected.[32] The worst possible response to this generation of misery and "waste" is to try to level things up, to preach equality and justice. "Those poor in life, the weak, impoverish life; those rich in life, the strong, enrich it. The first are the parasites of life; the second give presents to it.—How is it possible to confound these two?"[33] Reading these words, I contrasted them to those of Emma Lazarus, which appear on the base of the United States' Statue of Liberty: "Send me your tired, your poor / your huddled masses yearning to breathe free / the wretched refuse of your teaming shore / Send these, the homeless tempest tossed to me / I lift my lamp beside the golden shore." Not a sentiment Nietzsche could ever share. Who wants the refuse?

Contempt for the weak is laced throughout Nietzsche's writing—it would take mental gymnastics far beyond what my mind is capable of to claim this is not so or that, somehow, he didn't really mean it, or we shouldn't take it that he did. Herein lies the rub: We ask of thinkers, quite reasonably, whether they build in prophylaxes to their own most ungenerous and spiteful tendencies, and Nietzsche does not. This makes it easier for people to "take him wrong." When a thinker tells us that "there is nothing to life that has value, except the degree of power—assuming that life itself is the will to power," one had best take him at his word and figure out how, if the unscrupulous take him at his word, there are built-in barriers to the triumph of those whose will to power is most unbridled. Every human drive is a "lust to rule," and some are lustier than others.[34]

The genuine self-sovereign must be a destroyer, bold, even merciless. Any "degeneracy movement composed of reject and refuse elements" that represents "the decline of a race" is an abomination.[35] (Here Christianity again. Just as no serious student of Christianity accepts Nietzsche's hyperbolic excesses, so no serious student of classical paganism will recognize the paganism he presents as a contrast model, as he sees the classical and the noble played out.) Christianity appealed only to the "lowest class of Jewish society and intelligence"; it was base in origin.[36] This enchantment with origins, with what is weak and strong and base, was so characteristic of twentieth-century futurist and fascistic movements that it is impossible not to see links. Without saddling Nietzsche with any of the guilt rightly associated with such efforts, let's examine a few more of the passages and arguments that activists and propagandists seized upon in order to craft a vision of hyper-self-sovereignty that could usher in only a master-slave scenario, in which slaves exist to work for the master and those who are below slaves, the *Untermenschen*, live only to die: That is all that suits them.

Consider what Nietzsche despises: weakness, justice, equality, cowardice, notions of evil and forgiveness, any idea of guilt. ("We immoralists" reject this.) "All souls became equal before God, but this is precisely the most dangerous of all evaluations! If one regards individuals as equal, one calls the species into question, one encourages a way of life that leads to the ruin of the species."[37] This obsession with species life and the contempt for the notion of the unique particularity and dignity of each and every one, makes it much easier to think in terms of racially pure and impure elements—race here referring to genetic conglomerates (even of a specious kind, like "Aryan"). Any effort, like Christianity, that would break the strongest and noblest in favor of the weak and ground down must be opposed with every fiber of one's being. If, as Nietzsche argues, "Life is will to power," then any qualms one should have about morality are readily dissipated. In fact, there "are no moral phenomena, there is only a moral interpretation of these phenomena."[38] The "weakness of the inferior herd" threatens to swamp the strong. Every effort must be made to forestall this otherwise likely outcome.

Accepting, apparently, a version of Lamarckianism, Nietzsche held that every individual recapitulates the entirety of evolution in his person. Some represent "the ascending course of mankind," and their value is "extraordinary, and extreme care may be taken over the preservation and promotion of his development. . . . If he represents the descending course, decay, chronic sickening, then he has little value: and the first demand of fairness is for him to take as little space, force, and sunshine as possible away from the well-constituted."[39] The horror, of course, is that these sentiments, removed from the overheated pages of Nietzsche's polemics, became grist for the mill for Nazi biopolitics as its architects set about systematically to remove all "life unworthy of life," first with killing programs aimed at the developmentally disabled—even a harelip counted—and, then, at entire "races," the Slavs and the Jews. Is this an outcome Nietzsche would have endorsed? One must believe the answer is no. Is it an outcome against which he has a strong antidote? Sadly, the answer there, too, is no. Perhaps one further passage will suffice, as there is no need to belabor this sad story, a story of self-sovereignty cast as a will to power that trails, as it is literalized by the unscrupulous armed with a philosophy of the strong as against the weak, feeds into the hideous dénouement that is twentieth-century European totalitarianism. Bear in mind that Nietzsche is writing in 1888. It was but four decades later that medical doctrine began to preach the elimination of the weak, of "life unworthy of life," so all these ideas were part of a darkening and ominous zeitgeist spurred by the unspeakable horrors of World War I.

Scoring the commandment to love one another, Nietzsche writes:

> There are cases in which a child would be a crime: in the case of chronic invalids and neurasthenics of the third degree. [This would have eliminated Jane Addams as a biological mother for she, together with so many women of her era, were diagnosed with the catchall ailment "neurasthenia."] What should one do in such cases?—One might at least try encouraging them to chastity, perhaps with the aid of Parsifal music: Parsifal himself, this typical idiot, had only too

many reasons not to propagate himself. The trouble is that a certain inability to "control" oneself . . . is one of the most regular consequences of general exhaustion. . . . Society, as the great trustee of life, is responsible to life itself for every miscarried life—it also has to pay for such lives: consequently it ought to prevent them. In numerous cases, society ought to prevent procreation: to this end, it may hold in readiness, without regard to descent, rank, or spirit, the most rigorous means of constraint, deprivation of freedom, in certain circumstances castration. . . . The Biblical prohibition "thou shalt not kill!" is a piece of naïveté compared with the seriousness of the prohibition of life to decadents: "Thou shalt not procreate!"—Life itself recognizes no solidarity, no "equal rights," between the healthy and the degenerate parts of an organism: one must excise the latter—or the whole will perish.—Sympathy for decadents, equal rights for the ill-constituted—that would be the profoundest immorality, that would be antinature itself as morality![40]

Albert Camus, a sympathetic reader of Nietzsche, holds that Western society owes Nietzsche a profound apology for the misuse to which he has been put. Camus is correct that Nietzsche hated "mediocre cruelty," that cruelty that may come clothed in the high rhetoric of justice and equality. But Nietzsche's method of "methodical negation" and determined destruction, and his insistence that we must affirm all that is—bring it on!—means he has no ground on which to stand to oppose the murderer. The problem isn't so much either his atheism or his critique of the infirmity of a sickly moralism—"those calumniators of the world"—the punitive and condemnatory cast sometimes taken up by Christianity and morality in general. One can grant all of this, says Camus, but Nietzsche's "unreserved affirmation of human imperfection and suffering, of evil and murder," leads only to a celebration of the ruthless creators. "He dreamed of tyrants who were artists." The upshot is that, although Nietzsche would despise the Nazis with all his might, there is in his work much that can be—and was—used by those enamored of a philosophy of murder without restraint. "From the moment that assent was given to the totality of human experience ["we immoralists"], the way was open to others who, far from languishing, would gather strength from lies and murder." [41]

With Nietzschean self-sovereignty, we are once again on the turf of the "unbound" and reminded of the dangers of evocations of unconstrained sovereign selves. The implications and policies that flow from strong visions of self-sovereignty will be explored next.

10

THE SOVEREIGN SELF:
DREAMS OF RADICAL
TRANSCENDENCE

FOR THOSE ASPIRING TO SELF-SOVEREIGNTY, THE WORLD OFFERS UP A VAST arena within which many projects and forms of an absolute self, a law unto himself or herself, beckon. Self-sovereignty, in practice, is a protean thing. Consider a bit of recounting by Cormac McCarthy's protagonist in his novel, *No Country for Old Men*. Describing a moment recognizable to any of us on the conference circuit, no matter our line of work, he writes:

> Here a year or two back me and Loretta went to a conference in Corpus Christi and I got set next to this woman, she was the wife of somebody or other. And she kept talking about the right wing this and the right wing that. I aint even sure what she meant by it. The people I know are mostly just common people. Common as dirt, as the sayin goes. I told her that and she looked at me funny. She thought I was sayin something bad about em, but of course that's a high compliment in my part of the world. She kept on, kept on. Finally, she told me: I don't like the way this country is headed. I want my granddaughter to be able to have an abortion. And

I said well mam I don't think you got any worries about the way the country is headed. The way I see it going I don't have much doubt what she'll be able to have an abortion. I'm goin to say not only will she be able to have an abortion, she'll be able to have you put to sleep. Which pretty much ended the conversation.[1]

In this dry, colloquial, down-home speech, we catch a glimpse of where one version of self-sovereignty heads—with utter control over the bodies of not only ourselves but others who are not yet, or have ceased to become, self-sovereign in ways that we increasingly equate to "human." The language of conquest, control over, complete self-ownership—tests of self-sovereignty—prevails.

Characteristic of all projects of self-sovereignty is a "triumph over" something, nature being one of the chosen antagonists. This triumph takes several forms that I identify as "hard" or "soft" self-sovereignty, respectively. Each features a monistic, voluntaristic notion of the self, the self "as one" with its projects. Even as we have observed that the monistic, voluntaristic understanding of God as will, and the monistic version of state-sovereignty that trumps all other loyalties and identities, are characteristic of strong forms of theological and political sovereignty, so the monistic self appears in dreams of radical self-sovereignty.

In the world of hard self-sovereignty, the self stands alone, sans any mutually constitutive relationship to the world. This does not mean that hard sovereign selves refuse to marry or shun friends. No; rather, the point is that such relationships are seen as incidental to the self, not essentially definitive of one's identity. The messiness, incompleteness, paradox, and shortcomings of the world are treated with a kind of scorn. The self is proud, characterized by *superbia*. The self lives in a world shorn of transcendence. There is only an empty sky. What occupies the vertical site of transcendence? The self, outside, above the world, a place where one rises above the "herd" and seizes one's projects with nary a backward glance.

But there is another version of self-sovereignty that seems, at first blush, to be anything *but* the self as radically in control. Soft sovereign selves are absorbed in a collective or group project. One finds the full triumph of the self and the will-to-power and self-transcendence in and through a group project. Here one sees a monism of the collective within which the self is absorbed, reminiscent of Milan Kundera's chilling description of the dance of the angels in the "magical circle" in *The Book of Laughter and Forgetting*. One is inside the magic circle. We have already noted some of these sorts of efforts and their consequences in analyzing the sovereign state. In the twentieth century, transcendence was promised by fascist, communist, and other "totalizing" projects. In this world the sky is emptied of any transcendent "moment" or truths. Trancendence is infused into immanence, experienced on the horizontal level as we become godlike through our identification with the surround, the magical circle. God is somehow "in everything," as we become little godlike particles, so to speak, "at one" with other such entities.

We are reminded constantly about how "special" we are insofar as we identify ourselves with the movement or party or ideology or zeitgeist. A recent example of this latter phenomenon is *Time* magazine's love letter to "You: Yes, you. You control the Information Age. Welcome to your world." *Time* made each and every one of us, insofar as we are absorbed within the dominant cultural project as they construe it, their "Person of the Year" for 2007. Just in case anyone was so dense as to miss the point, *Time*'s cover featured a reflective sheet of shiny foil-like paper that reflected the self-absorbed gaze of each person who picked up the magazine in order to learn something about—yes—your*self*.[2]

SOVEREIGN SELVES AGAINST NATURE

One area that has long inspired dreams of radical self-transcendence is humanity's engagement with nature, an engagement that is spoken of frequently in the language of mastery, control, domination, triumph over. Nature, including our own natures, has long frustrated an aspiring humanity: We haven't brought it under our sovereign domain. One area in which this drama has played itself out, and is playing itself out currently, is eugenics—the attempt to control nature by controlling the sorts of people who are permitted to become part of our world. These attempts would seem, at first blush, in direct contradistinction to the traditional Christian view of the human person. Jesus, after all, came to save all—including the weak, the broken, the blind, the ill, the lame. But this did not stay the hand of American Christians in the early decades of the twentieth century, many of whom embraced the promise of genetics with alacrity and attempted to square it with Christian theology. This attempt came from the side of liberal theology. A significant swath of those occupying the pulpit managed to convince themselves that Jesus presaged the eugenics message. After all, didn't He heal those afflicted? How much better to heal in advance by preventing certain conditions and the birth of certain types of human specimens who are more likely to drag the human race down.

Pridefulness on the individual level squeezes out space for others, hence, for an appropriate self-regard consistent with our recognition of others and loving attention paid to them. Selves trapped by pride refuse to pay proper attention to the other. Pride can take a number of forms. There is the boastful, power-mad sort, as one recklessly knocks over barriers to self-promotion. There is another way to refuse to pay proper attention, a type of sloth or acquiescence when, instead, one should perk up and raise questions. Sloth clings to us, Martin Luther opined, for we are born to it. It is one of the fruits of original sin. In the endorsement of a eugenics project by Protestant clergy I detect slothfulness more than anything else, but a healthy dose of self-pride is involved as well. Those preaching eugenics are never from one of the categories of persons slated for eventual "eugenics cleansing," of course!

TAKING A STAND AGAINST THE HELPLESS

If human freedom consists in part in refusing overidentification with the sea in which we swim, then slothfulness is a refusal of freedom.[3] So—to stay with the metaphor of the sea—the slothful never come up for air. We see this absorption in the zeitgeist of the eugenics movement. Eugenics was also part and parcel of the American birth control movement spearheaded by Margaret Sanger. In the 1920s at least twenty-three of the clergymen, scientists, and physicians listed on the national council of

Sanger's American Birth Control League were involved prominently in eugenics.[4] On the public policy level, this group agitated "for compulsory sterilization and immigration restriction"—successfully, one might add.[5] The United States adopted immigration quotas that restricted the movement of Slavs and southern Europeans to our shores even as a number of states embraced compulsory sterilization laws. The compulsory sterilization statutes came to a head in the now-notorious case of *Buck v. Bell* decided by the U.S. Supreme Court in 1927. The Court, by an 8 to 1 vote, allowed that the state of Virginia was within its constitutional rights to sterilize a single mother found "feeble-minded." The opinion was written by the lauded Oliver Wendell Holmes and included these words: "It's better for the world if, instead of waiting to execute degenerate offspring for crime or to let them starve for their imbecility, society can prevent those who are manifestly unfit from continuing their kind. . . . Three generations of imbeciles is enough."[6] Sanger was also on record as favoring the birth of at-one-point-to-be-sovereign selves, but those without the wherewithal to be "sovereign" were to be eliminated or restrained. She advocated sterilization of "defectives."[7] This was part of the overall package that included immigration restriction. Sanger shared a generalized fear that the lower classes and races were outbreeding the Anglo-Saxons and healthy stock more generally.[8] Another feature of the argument was that "defectives" drained resources away from the fit, resources that could more usefully be deployed by sovereign selves to their own chosen projects.[9]

Eugenics, then, was one feature of a cluster of attitudes that linked together euthanasia societies, the birth control movement, evolutionists who had turned Darwinian theory into a radical ideology for social engineering, and strands of the women's movement. A question ongoingly put by such groups was, How do we save civilization? One answer that emerged, as Ian Dowbiggin notes in his definitive work on euthanasia, was killing the undesirable as part of the eugenics project, a "gentle painless death" for America's drunkards, criminals, and those with disabilities. The *only* thing that stood in the way of this effort was the "unreasonable dogma that *all* human life is intrinsically sacred"; thus, the "march of science . . . dictated that Americans give up long-standing religious belief."[10]

One might assume that a defense against such measures would have been mounted by the Christian clergy, Protestant and Catholic. The Catholics, for the most part, fought the eugenics craze. The record with Protestants is, as I have already pointed out, less good. One definitive history of this phenomenon points out that it was when "liberal and modernist religious men abandoned bedrock principles to seek relevance in modern debates that they were most likely to find themselves endorsing eugenics. Those who clung stubbornly to tradition, to doctrine, and to biblical infallibility opposed eugenics and became, for a time, the objects of derision for their rejection of this most modern science."[11] We now know that early twentieth-century eugenics wasn't good science at all. This should be a shot across the bow warning against acquiescing to the latest science in any era, including our own.[12] For example, a geneticist pronounced in 1986 that the Human Genome Project is "the grail of human genetics . . . the ultimate answer to the commandment, 'Know thyself.'"[13] Any claim to "ultimacy" based on a project of human mastery smacks of the pride that "goeth before a fall." In the early 1920s, there was a "eugenics sermon contest" sponsored by the American Eugenics Society that was awarded to the pastor who preached the most compelling eugenics message from the pulpit.[14] Although the roots of the eugenics movement are traceable from the nineteenth century, eugenics enthusiasm really burgeoned during the Progressive Era in America and became a staple of American progressivism. One of the most important members of the liberal clerical establishment to extol eugenics was Harry Emerson Fosdick, a Baptist. Another was Bishop William Lawrence, an Episcopal priest.[15] Scripture was turned into knots to support eugenics, even the Sermon on the Mount. Here is one example, rather unintentionally hilarious but frightening in its implications: "Eugenics compelled the biblical Good Samaritan" (who stopped to aid the victim of a theft) to "assume new functions." Once, the Samaritan simply "befriended the victim on the road to Jericho"; in the early part of the twentieth century, he would have provided "better policing and lighting of the road" to discourage the thieves who preyed on travelers; now, with eugenics, the Good Samaritan knew that his duty was "to prevent those thieves from ever being born in the first place."[16] Among the many things that this passage does—in addition to suggesting that those who violate the law are failures in the race to the status of sovereign self—is to remove the obligation of *caritas* from the shoulders of individual believers. Now compassion can be sublimated into state policy. This is extolled as more efficient. Besides, one needn't be bothered with the entanglement of a personal relationship. The Ten Commandments, too, became a duty of eugenics, "the final program for the completed Christianizing of mankind."[17] Liberals and modernists within their faiths "became the eugenics movement's most enthusiastic supporters."[18]

Nowadays the preferred language is *positive genetic enhancement*— the old word *eugenics* does not appear. Efforts to eliminate the unfit also take the form of aggressive prenatal testing and promoting abortion for all flaws, defects, and "abnormalities." I have already noted that 90 percent of Down syndrome pregnancies in the United States are aborted, but this extends to a vast array of other disabilities as well.[19] One mother of a Down syndrome child wrote to me, after having read one of my essays against genetic control, "The function of prenatal tests, despite protestations to the contrary, is to provide parents the information necessary to assure that all pregnancies brought to term are 'normal.' I worry not only about the encouragement given to eliminating a 'whole category of persons' (the point you make), but also about the prospects for respect and treatment of children who come to be brain damaged whether through unexpected birth traumas or later accidents. And what about the pressures to which parents like myself will be subject? How could you 'choose' to burden society in this way?"[20] All of this makes sense if you presuppose self-sovereignty with an enhancement of that sovereignty at its terminus. Abortion, then, is no longer a tragedy or a dire circumstance but a positive good, a way to close the "control deficit" against flawed nature. Overall, it becomes a story of "us," the forces of control and perfection, against "them," the forces of randomness and imperfection. Once you put wills in motion, as I argued earlier, you are headed for a clash, a fight even unto death. Someone *must* triumph. This scenario works best if one's "opponent" can be dehumanized or demeaned, as those who push eugenics and euthanasia have done historically and presently, characterizing their opponents negatively and with considerable success. The upshot historically was that in the name of choice and a vision of the good society in which "defectives" and the less worthy have been weeded out, too many within the clergy acquiesced in, and became triumphant advocates of, eugenics in the early decades of the twentieth century.

"HARD" SELF-SOVEREIGNTY AND ITS VARIETIES

The sovereign self isn't one but many. One version is pushed by today's genetics turned into a popular crusade—and not favored by all scientists by any means. Let's trace the broad contours of the argument here under the rubric of sovereign selves.[21] Genetic fundamentalism as a feature of today's sovereign self presents a mixed picture to the world, for it is an odd combination of excarnation—the bodies we are now in are demeaned—with a type of biological or, better, genetic obsession. Most of these discussions take place in a zone sanitized of any normative accounts of human nature or the human condition more generally. A quest for control has always been a feature of the quest for the sovereign self. The technocratic view of our ability to manipulate and get the outcomes we desire is widespread. In a review in the *Times Literary Supplement* a few years back, the reviewer opined matter-of-factly that "we must inevitably start to choose our own descendants." He added that we do this now in "permitting or preventing the birth of our own children according to their medical prognosis, thus selecting the lives to come," and that so long as society doesn't cramp our freedom of action, we will stay on the road of progress and exercise sovereign choice over birth by consigning to death those with a less than stellar potential for a life not "marred by an excess of pain or disability."[22] The eugenics thrust is clearly at work in talk about Designer Genes. Note, in this regard, the following advertisement that appeared in college newspapers all over the United States, as reported by the *New York Times:* EGG DONOR NEEDED / LARGE FINANCIAL INCENTIVE / INTELLIGENT ATHLETIC EGG DONOR NEEDED / FOR LOVING FAMILY / YOU MUST BE AT LEAST 5 FEET 10 INCHES / HAVE A 1400+ SAT SCORE / POSSESS NO MAJOR FAMILY MEDICAL ISSUES / $50,000 / FREE MEDICAL SCREENING / ALL EXPENSES PAID.[23] This is one avenue favored currently for genetic "enhancement," namely, selective breeding.

These methods contrast to such crude measures as a bill proposed in the Minnesota state legislature in the Progressive era that handicapped newborns be "electrocuted." This was regarded as a painless way— genetics not having been perfected—to rid society of excess unsovereign selves. But who determines an "excess"? Isn't it likely to be the case that as we eliminate what no doubt nearly all of us would regard as serious disabilities, we will chip away at others that currently don't seem that bad but surely will once their contrast models have been removed? Opposition to nearly all once-startling developments—including the prospect of human cloning—has dissipated like the early morning dew in today's climate. Ardent advocates of embryonic stem cell research have finessed moral questions by suggesting that there are two different ways to clone—to clone for "research" and to clone for "reproduction." This is sleight of hand, for there is only one way to clone. And it is easy enough to imagine that at one point those who wish to clone for reproduction will say, "Hey, what's the big deal? We've been cloning for years, after all!"

Bring on the Clones!

One even gets preemptive strikes in favor of the rights of clones! A distinguished Harvard Law professor opines that if we ban cloning, we diminish choice, and we do so illegitimately by appealing to divine commandment or inspiration. This means we will automatically "criminalize" a method for "creating human babies." It follows that we diminish human freedom and generate a "grave" evil—that of creating a "caste system" of the cloned. If we ban cloning, we will make clones a "marginalized caste." So the "social costs of prohibition" are too high. It is hard to imagine a stranger argument. All the heavy artillery—choice, freedom, marginalization, criminalization—comes into play. Decent, caring people who want to prevent suffering favor this new freedom. By contrast, those who consider themselves under an "irrational" divine sanction promote the "evil" of diminished choice and marginalize clones, beings of our own creation. They, therefore, are cruel and disturbed, and they must be stopped before they negate a freedom we have yet to exercise! In this way we acquiesce, in the name of untrammeled self-sovereignty, to a new and entirely abstract "freedom" and take several huge strides in the direction of undermining even the merest intimation of our never-perfect embodiment and its integrity.[24]

For self-sovereigntists seeking perfection, the body we currently inhabit is the imperfect body subject to chance and the vagaries of life, including illness and aging. This body is our foe. The *future perfect body* extolled in manifestoes, promised by enthusiasts, embraced by many ordinary citizens, is a gleaming fabrication. For, so the story goes, we will have found a way around the fact that what our foremothers and forefathers took for granted—that the body must weaken and falter and one day pass from life to death, will soon be a relic of a bygone era. The future perfect body will not be permitted to falter. The new reproductive technologies bespeak a yearning for a world of guaranteed self-replication, at times fueled by fantasies of sameness: All will be perfect and pretty much alike, given the shared cultural norms to which positive genetic enhancement will aspire. One wonders what ever happened to the insistence that we learn to love one another, a matter I take up below.

Technology, Abortion, and Radical Feminism

As one takes the measure of one form of feminism and its radical search for complete transcendence over the body and nature or, alternatively, achieving transcendence through complete immersion in a specifically *female* nature to counter the "toxic" male body and genes, it is important to note that a form of triumphalism surfaced early on in radical feminist argumentation, fed by technology. Here, for example, is a celebration of a dream of radical self-transcendence envisaged by a feminist theorist who finds hope in pervasive intervention into biological life, creating such possibilities as the following:

> For instance, one woman could inseminate another, so that men and non-parturitive women could lactate and so that fertilized ova could be transplanted into women's or even into men's bodies. These developments may seem far-fetched,

but in fact, they are already on the technological horizon; however, what is needed much more immediately than technological development is a substantial reduction in the social domination of women by men. Only such a reduction could insure that these or alternative technological possibilities are used to increase women's control over their bodies, and thus over their lives.[25]

The reader will have noticed the articulation of the language of control in the citation. It is unsurprising, therefore, that the language of control and what one wills or wants made its way into the abortion debate.

The Unwanted

Nowadays in our continuing travail over abortion, the term *unintended* has been substituted for the once-pervasive *unwanted* because it is a gentler way to cast matters. *Unwanted,* however, is the word that lingers in the mind as it dominated debates and conferences on abortion for decades. One of the first moves made in arguments of the sort that aim to enhance self-sovereignty in a conflict of wills is to dehumanize the "opponent"; thus, the fetus was characterized variously as a "parasite," a "tenant," an airborne "spore," or "property." The biologically human status of the fetus was covered up. Reviewing the arguments of an array of extreme pro-choice philosophers, political theorist Philip Abbott recalled the examples that these philosophers deployed to make their case. Not one example is drawn from everyday social existence; not one makes contact with ordinary life, language, and ethical conflict. It is all smooth sailing for the sovereign self in these cases:

> Sixteen examples (and there are variations) are used to analyze the morality of abortion. But what examples! The world of the philosophers is filled with people seeds, child missile launchers, Martians, talking robots, dogs, kittens, chimps, jigsaw cells that form human beings, transparent wombs—everything in fact but fetuses growing in wombs and infants cradled in their parents' arms.[26]

The argument in behalf of such moral distancing holds that our minds are too muddled by emotional debris (all that "sanctity of life" stuff) and that is why we must mount "science fiction" examples so that we can clean away the dross of complexity and moral conflict in the interests of self-sovereignty. As proof of our collective emotional debility, one philosopher cited our revulsion to infanticide, seeing this as an irrational taboo "like the reaction of previous generations to masturbation or oral sex."[27] Thus, the so-called abortion philosophers had no problem extending the abortion right to cover the newborn child, who is, by definition, no sovereign self, by giving adult sovereign selves the final say about the child's life or death.

Closing the Control Gap

In the United States, the articulation and solidification of a constitutionally protected abortion right and radical feminism emerged in tandem—in the early 1970s.[28] No doubt nearly everyone is familiar with the arguments by this time. What is fascinating is the fact that radical pro-choice rhetoric proceeds on the assumption that women are born into the world with a "control deficit"; hence, it is more difficult for women to become fully sovereign.[29] Birth control helped to achieve that end. Abortion is the icing on the cake, so to speak, for without the abortion right women are doomed to second-class status, or so the argument goes. Women are to join ranks with the males as sovereign, free, choosing agents. In more complex evocations, the case gets made that women have yet to enjoy the full status of classical personhood. But an extreme liberal position also sees in women's links to biology, birth, and nurturing only the vestiges of "animal origins," the residue of preenlightened history. Women as embodied beings can become first-class citizens only if they, too, embrace and act on sovereign choice and sever their links with nature . . . nature always being a drag on self-sovereignty.

Within this framework, abortion becomes a resolution to the control deficit: No wonder it was called by some of its advocates, "the final freedom." Absolute freedom to abort presumes a female subject for whom "dependency entails absolute control. If something is within our power, i.e., the fetus, we have the right to control, even destroy it.

Humanity gets defined by self-sufficiency. This is a very different sensibility from one that links dependency with responsibility, with care not control."[30] Many abortion arguments, including the feminist variety, pit the woman, alone, against the world. Remember that one way human beings have all along made it easier to rid themselves of that which is "unwanted" is by denying its humanity. It follows that advocates refuse to acknowledge that what is going on involves the life of a to-be-full human person, so as to throw up a linguistic barrier between us and the realities and conflicts of abortion, for only in this way is it possible to shore up the sovereign self against conflict and critique. Indeed, when challenged, those folks who argue along these lines are likely to come back with a riposte that bespeaks an indebtedness to a kind of Cartesian, or some other, anthropology that disembodies us; it then becomes far less of a problem to distance oneself from the reality of the fetus and even of wombs, for that matter.

One even gets dire warnings that pregnant women with "unwanted children" threaten society for unwanted children might overrun society if you add them all up. "Above all," writes one such observer, "society must grasp the grim relationship between unwanted children and the violent rebellion of minority groups."[31] Those who insist on giving birth to unwanted children are stigmatized as creatures stuck "at the level of brood animals," for human birth, unfortunately, is often "the result of blind impulse and passion . . . little more than the automatic reflex of a biological system."[32] Unsurprisingly, some of the "abortion philosophers" also countenance infanticide or acknowledge that their arguments justify it. Princeton ethicist Peter Singer is undoubtedly the most famous—and he is prepared to euthanize persons with disabilities, too—but there are others.[33] There are also implications in such arguments concerning the ill and the infirm—anyone too weak to stand on his or her own, to be "productive," to be of social use. All arguments from so-called value theory tend to proceed in this way. Using language drawn from neoclassical market economics, its proponents treat children as objects that may or may not have value imputed to them, as if one were speaking of automobiles. A cost-benefit calculus is offered, and those who refuse to take account of the costs, or for whom the costs are too

high, are said to be behaving irrationally. The price of self-sovereignty is
high—but someone else, the most defenseless among us, pays it. Were
this all not so serious one would think it a spoof—rather along the lines
of Jonathan Swift's famous solution to the Irish problem.[34] There is a
kind of latter-day Malthusianism running through much of this argumentation—no surprise, then, that some of its advocates find nothing
particularly troubling in infanticide for no serious moral values are
involved, they claim, especially in a situation of scarcity.[35] (Remember, in
neoclassical economics, one begins with the presupposition of scarcity.)

Radical Feminism and Strong Self-Sovereignty

Feminist analysts and advocates who preach self-sovereignty come in a
number of varieties, both liberal and illiberal. I have analyzed radical
feminist texts and arguments under the rubric of "Sex Polarity:
Manichean Moments," because of the harsh dualism necessary to the
creation of the monistic sovereign self advocated. As most readers know,
the original Manichees severed the world in dualistic fashion between a
Kingdom of Light and a Kingdom of Darkness. The soul sprang from
the one; the body from the other. This doesn't map precisely onto radical feminism, but the dualism may help us to understand what is going
on. Instead of body-matter, the divide is male-female.

This distinction is hardened to the status of ontology. One advocate
defends her move to these categories by insisting that maleness and
femaleness ineluctably lead to certain outcomes. Men are tainted by an
inherent lust for power; women, in their inner core, are unsullied.[36] We
are offered the cyberneticist as the modern savior, for this would lead
sooner rather than later to human birth without pregnancy: Women
must be freed from "biological tyranny." This freeing will, in turn,
undermine all of society and culture that is erected upon biological
tyranny and the family; finally, all systems of oppression, including the
economy, state, religion, and the law, will erode and collapse, but only if
women seize control of reproduction and come to own their own bodies.
Once test-tube babies replace biological reproduction, we will have
moved out of barbarism into a brave new world indeed.[37] It follows that
no reciprocity between men and women is ever possible. Somebody is

going to dominate over somebody else. Someone must be a strong self-sovereign. Up to now, the men have held full sway. It is the women's turn. The solutions run to the ridiculous—like reducing the number of males in the population to 10 percent—for only then can women take charge. Men are the "enemy" and called the "enemy." In my book *Women and War*, I present this story in and through the categories of "the Beautiful Soul"—the woman who embodies all that is good and spiritual—versus the male body run amok. Metaphors of war and battle are common in these arguments.[38] Patriarchy—and every society known to humanity heretofore has been a patriarchy, we are told—is by definition a state of war.

Another variation on self-sovereignty emerges in visions of a female-dominant society. Matriarchal society is one in which "all relationships are modeled on the nurturant relationships between a mother and her child," and only when all societies are matriarchal will estrangements cease and all be healed. You must get under the tent thus afforded or spend your life groveling in the wilderness made untenable by the machinations of patriarchy.[39] Such advocates of sex unity, by contrast to sex polarity, see the solution in men becoming "women," assuming men are capable of being healed. Self-sovereignty takes the form of a maternal "caregiver" who will stop men being men: We will be one feminized entity. Sex and violence figure centrally in the scenarios of radical sex polarists. Oddly enough, for a discourse pushing for the creation of female self-sovereignty, women are often represented in the language of victimhood. The remorselessness of male victimization of the female—her enthrallment to his will and design—is a kind of bondage situation, tapping deeply rooted narratives of goodness enchained. An unmediated conduit is presupposed between the "normal" violence of the heterosexual male, the repressive family, up to and including militarism, wars, nuclear technology, despoliation of nature, advertising, and pornography—all outgrowths of unchained masculinism.[40] Original sin is much magnified in males; women are somehow exempted. In a sense, the pure woman victim—for the victim is somehow untainted—is the flip side of the male sovereign self. Few questions are put regarding what happens when women take over the reins of power, save that somehow women will cleanse and purify all that they touch. One can see the dynamic of what Nietzsche called *ressentiment* at work here, no doubt one reason that this version in its harshest form didn't penetrate very far into the female population as a whole but became almost exclusively a discourse of elites within universities. Who can live consistently within a vortex of resentment and rage? This is the direction the language of control and strong self-sovereignty tend, for the dominant require others to dominate over.

Strong self-sovereignty denies reciprocity and intrinsic sociality and aims for control—goes on a quest for such. One must "kill the king," so to speak, on the assumption that somehow freedom or liberation will result for all human beings or at least for women in the feminist scenarios.

SOFT SELF-SOVEREIGNTY AND ITS VARIETIES

If sex polarists are about hard and unforgiving divisions, sex unitarists blend everything into an indistinguishable stew. Within soft self-sovereignty all is connectedness. One is absorbed within and "at one" with a cocoon of relationships. Nature is sometimes also divinized as that which one must be "at one" with—one sees this strand in feminist theology as well as feminist political rhetoric. Having literalized the notion of God as male, a reductionism abandoned by serious theologians a long time ago, including Augustine, the thinkers I refer to seek to divinize a specifically female nature, a goddess not a god, perhaps, certainly a "she" and not a "he." If one version of radical feminism denies nature any efficacy and a second hardens the category into an ontological one between male and female, so in soft self-sovereignty, women are presented as a different sort of "giving self" but—at least in some versions—males can become this way, too. One doesn't aim for self-sovereignty as autonomy—for that is the male way to do it—but for love and an immanentized deity, with or without a specific evocation of a goddess, instead. Divine transcendence is abandoned in favor of a divinized immanence.

Some might wonder why this is self-sovereignty at all. My answer is that, one way or the other, one winds up worshipping at the altar of the self. God as "she" is a direct mapping of the self onto God and loses, thereby, the concreteness of traditional Christian story that starts with a baby, a male baby, born in a manger. Any notion of *askesis* or emptying oneself of power is seen as wholesale relinquishment of the self followed by the insistence that this is what women historically have all been about—forced to self-relinquishment. There is some truth to these claims or they would lack any evocative power whatsoever. The problem appears when this view is magnified and absolutized out of proportion.

Attunement or at-oneness—not differences—are emphasized, save the basic difference that must be effaced between males and females. There are two versions of this argument. One sees the female as eventually triumphing, as in the strong self-sovereignty discourse. A second calls for resocializing away from gendered categories, erasing "men" and "women" and eliminating any biological need for sex to be associated with procreation—either that or map the female part of procreation wholly onto the species, an ur-mother vision. Despite a nigh-deterministic model of the sex/gender system, these narratives push some version of transformed self-sovereignty as a utopian possibility. There will no longer be a need for anyone to oppress anyone else.[41] Given the animus against distinctions, it should come as no surprise that many self-sovereigntists embrace a vision of androgyny and an androgynous future in which difference has been obliterated. There is a rich storehouse of feminist literature that does not tend in such absolutist directions, offering modest or modified versions and variations on self-sovereignty, some seeking a responsible self that is not sovereign in the ways here examined. But the temptations of self-sovereignty cannot and must not be understated and that is why they take center stage here.

A BRIEF HISTORICAL DIGRESSION: SOVEREIGN SELVES IN NATIONAL SOCIALIST GERMANY

One of the ongoing puzzlements—what happened in Germany?—comes closer to intelligibility if we recognize the trappings of radical self-sovereignty of both varieties—hard and soft—in the National Socialist project. The self is an Übermensch, above the "herd," all *Untermenschen*. The self is a hardened will. As British author and historian Michael Burleigh notes, the project that held "every individual has sovereign powers to dispose of his or her life as he or she sees fit," included as a corollary that those who cannot act as sovereign selves require sovereign selves to act for them under the premise that they know how *Untermenschen* would act if they could, for the less than sovereign life is not worth living.[42]

The Nazi project was a dream of perfection, a systematic rational project, not a descent into barbarism as is often alleged. One finds a biotechnological project of planning and action. You have a problem—the presence of "lives unworthy of life"—and you figure out how to solve it. The solution did not turn on bloodlust—quite the contrary. Highly emotional, rabid anti-Semites were not regarded as sufficiently in control of their emotions to be reliable as people to whom to entrust carrying out the Final Solution, a society purged of bodily imperfections. To this end, the National Socialists implemented the *best* public health programs in Europe in cancer prevention, diet, the banning of smoking in all public places, for German doctors had discovered that smoking was carcinogenic in the 1920s.[43]

Nazi politics towards Jews, Gypsies, and the mentally handicapped were designed to methodically eliminate pathogens that threatened the realization of a perfect bio-order.

WHERE WERE THE CRITICAL VOICES?

Those who spoke out against Nazi bio-politics challenged it at its heart—its view of the human person. Take, for example, the arguments of anti-Nazi theologian, Dietrich Bonhoeffer, in his unfinished *Ethics*. Bonhoeffer discusses that which is "natural," insisting that the concept of the natural tells us we enjoy only a "relative freedom," not an absolute freedom, in natural life. There are "true and mistaken" uses of this freedom and "these mark the difference between the "natural and the unnatural." He throws down the gauntlet: "Destruction of the natural means destruction of life."[44] It is wrong to approach life either from a false "vitalism"—the will to absolute power—or an equally false "mechanization" and lassitude that shows "despair towards natural life" and expresses "a certain hostility to life, tiredness of life." This he links to the sin of sloth. Our right to bodily life is a natural right and the foundation of all other rights: It is not a right revocable by the "sovereign *Volk*." Our bodies are good but we can use them for well or ill.

The most striking and radical excision of the integrity and right of natural life is "arbitrary killings," the deliberate destruction of "innocent life." Bonhoeffer here notes abortion, killing defenseless wounded or prisoners, destroying lives we do not find worth living—a clear reference to Nazi euthanasia and genocidal policies toward the ill and the infirm. "The right to live is a matter of the essence" and not of any socially imposed values. "Even the most wretched life" is "worth living before God." Other violations of the liberty of the body include physical torture, arbitrary seizure and enslavement, separation of persons from home and family—the full panoply of the horrors the twentieth century has dished up in superabundance. Notice that Bonhoeffer steers a course between radical transcendence over the "natural" and complete submission within a collective view of nature—the two routes traveled by sovereign selves.

But the views of the Bonhoeffers did not prevail. I noted above the melting away of mainline opposition within Protestant Christianity when confronted with the ecstatic possibilities of eugenics in the late nineteenth to early twentieth century in the United States. Where were the voices in Germany? Historians and cultural critics note that the "sovereignty of the *Volk*" argument that gripped German elites and trickled down into the general population held that law was no longer bound to norms; rather, all values came from a totalized *Volk*. Only the *Volk*—the radical sovereignty of the particular—could lay down norms for the *Volk*, as no universal truths or ethics existed.

These developments were aided and abetted by the so-called "new religionists" who pushed for an anti- or post-Christian German faith. Nineteenth-century liberal theology, in their view, had helped to pave the way by divesting Christianity of some of its "Jewish elements."[45] They embraced Nietzsche as a god-father because he attacked Christianity and justified eugenics, as I noted above. Christianity and Jewish-Christian morality were biologized as "diseased" entities, eating away at the vitality of the German *Volk* and blocking the triumph of a pure, primordial will. "We German Faithlers are of the opinion that the Christian sin, guilt, and repentance feelings are not the religious feelings of our German nature," for these fly in the face of a heroic ethics, not the mewling milk-sop of a womanish Christianity.[46]

Racial argument entered with the insistence that the idea of original sin was insulting to the German race, for it meant that "the newborn child of the most noble Germanic descent with the best racial qualities of intellect and racial qualities of intellect and body is as subject to eternal damnation as is the hereditarily handicapped half-breed of two degenerate races."[47] The eternal, sovereign, creative will of the *Volk*—and the German faith movement, as it was called—that harkened back to a primordial, authentic *Urwille*, or original Germanic will, must triumph over all confessional creeds. Only a race-related experience of God was authentic: one is either "Christian or German"; you could not authentically be both.[48] Once Jewish particularism and Christian confessionalism were bested, new, holistic, neopagan cultural revolution would triumph, in harmony with a nature "red in tooth and claw" in which the strong triumph over the weak. In this manner, by pushing a new religion, extirpating the "womanish" weakness and "Jewish taint" of Christianity and hence of any claim that there are universal moral norms, the sovereign self and collective triumphed in an orgy of destruction of the unfit, those who could not actualize a sovereign will to power. I am not, of course, equating contemporary developments in the West with these horrors—-that said, we should squirm at those moments when we see a "family resemblance" in our own choices of rhetoric and practice.

SOVEREIGN SELVES IN A CRITICAL LIGHT

As with sovereign selves themselves, criticisms of self-sovereignty come in a number of varieties—theological, political, literary. Although my alternative will figure in the next chapter, here is a preview, so to speak. For now, I will offer two final reflections, one on humanness and the treatment of the dead and a second from one of my favorite writers, P. D. James, best known for her Adam Dalgliesh mysteries. An animus against the dead is often one feature of sovereigntist discourse—of what use are those who by definition are no longer self-sovereign? It should not surprise us that, in our own day, one finds stories of people seeing their bodies as so much garbage to be tossed out, or perhaps ground up into fertilizer, or certainly not to be lovingly honored and remembered.[49] Some years ago, I asked readers of another text to picture a time long ago and far away, a scene described by Richard E. Leakey and Roger Lewin in *Origins: What New Discoveries Reveal About the Emergence of Our Species and Its Possible Future*. Perhaps this passage may serve as a guide through the theme of the relationship of the living to the dead. Leakey and Lewis write:

> From the Shanidar Cave in the Sagros Mountain highlands of Iraq, . . . on a June day some sixty thousand years ago a man was buried in unusual circumstances. The humidity of the cave was far from favorable for preserving the bones of a dead man; but pollen grains survive very well under these circumstances, and researchers at the Musée de l'Homme in Paris who examined the soil around the Shanidar Man discovered that buried along with him were several different species of flowers. From the orderly distribution of the grains around the fossil remains, there is no question that the flowers were arranged deliberately and did not simply topple into the grave as the body was being covered. It would appear that the man's family, friends, and perhaps members of his tribe had gone into the fields and brought back bunches of yarrow, cornflowers, St. Barnaby's thistle, groundsel, grape hyacinths, woods horsetail, and a kind of mallow.[50]

This deliberate burial, with its delicate specificity, is described by Leakey and Lewin as an act by survivors that "betrays a keen self-awareness and concern for the human spirit." Later, the authors remark that the sociality of human beings runs like a vital thread through our most distant origins. The human being, they declare, has unique reasons for living in communities. What all this means is not simply that we are social beings but that we are, profoundly, beings with needs and yearnings of spirit and body.

Honoring the dead, as did those ancient ancestors of ours, with their offerings of thistle and hyacinth, horsetail and groundsel, forms one dimension to a set of deeply felt imperatives that includes, as a prohibitive injunction, not harming the dead. How is it that we, all these millennia later, can recognize immediately actions whose inner rationale we ourselves deeply feel—but may be in danger of forgetting. In scattering flowers and grains as remembrances in an orderly fashion over the grave of a loved one, these "primitive" forebears of ours were acting within and upon presumptions that form the bedrock of any recognizably human existence. Stories of survivors of death camps and gulags reinforce this claim, noting the inhuman horror of leaving bodies in the open to rot, finally becoming indifferent to the corpse lying next to you. This is not a *human* way to live, as all our most basic instincts are diminished and thwarted by the horrors imposed on human beings in the terrible circumstances of twentieth-century totalitarianism. One takes up evidence from the past, like the burial at the Shanidar Cave, as a clue to a vast mystery that embodies basic human imperatives.

We know of no continuing way of life, past or present, in which the dead were casually tossed out, were defiled, degraded, and left unburied to rot, in which the dead were bartered, bargained after, or turned into dog food. The hideous counterexamples, like gulags or death camps or Thucydides' powerful description of the horror felt by the Athenians when they were forced to leave their own dead unburied—are exceptions that prove this general rule.[51]

Respecting the dead enlarges life and compels us to acknowledge our indebtedness—precisely what strong sovereign selves cannot bring themselves to do. The living, knowing that at their deaths they will be honored, too, gain an awareness of a life connected not only horizontally but vertically—to generations now gone and generations to come. Such recognitions are so fundamental, so basic, that they are constitutive of one's own self-identity. Within a framework that stresses our sociality and that couches an account of the human subject as a being who exists in a body in and through definite, specific relations, human beings can be understood not so much as self-interested bearers of rights, certainly not as sovereign selves, but as beings whose sufferings and joys, pains and pleasures, triumphs and tragedies, make them members of a human community, participants in a social compact. In not harming the dead, in respecting the dead, we do more, much more, than enact unthinkingly, tribal custom, or carry out, unfeelingly, abstract obligation. We link ourselves up with human meanings and imperatives that go back as far as recognizably human creatures go and will continue so long as human beings are born, live, and die. No wonder sovereign selves have such trouble with the dead. Unsurprising, then, that regimes in which totalistic self-sovereignty triumphed defiled the dead and broke the links between generations. It is often said that we can judge societies by how they treat their most vulnerable—and none is more vulnerable than the dead.

A World Without Children

If there is an animus against the dead in a world of self-sovereignty, the to-be-born don't fare too well either, as I have noted. So consider a world in which there are no more births, as does P. D. James in her novel *The Children of Men.*[52] James depicts a forlorn globe. The novel is set in Britain in the year 2021. No children have been born, none at all, on planet Earth since the year 1995. The reason for this is not the perfection of some draconian regime to prevent fertility but because in that year all males became infertile, for reasons no one understands. The human race is dying out. People are despondent, chagrined, violent. "Western science had been our god," writes the protagonist, one Theodore Faron, an Oxford historian and a cousin to the dictator of Great Britain. He "shares the disillusionment" of one whose god has died. Now, overtaken by a "universal negativism," the human race lurches toward its certain demise. Because there will be no future, "all pleasures of the mind and senses sometimes seem . . . no more than pathetic and crumbling defences shored up against our ruin."

Children's playgrounds are dismantled. People disown commitments and responsibilities to, and for, one another except for whatever serves some immediate purpose—what I want—by contrast to anything that is given. A cult of pseudobirths emerges as women take broken dolls and even baby kittens to be baptized in pseudoceremonies, surreptitiously, for religion, except for a cult of state worship, is forbidden. People thought they had eliminated evil, Faron notes, and all churches in the 1990s moved from a "theology of sin and redemption" to a "sentimental humanism." In the name of compassion, the elderly, no longer needed or wanted, are conducted to a state-sponsored ceremony of group suicide called the Quietus. Faron concludes that we are diminished, we humans, if we live without knowledge of the past and without hope for the future. The old prayer, that I may see my children's children and peace upon Israel, is no more, and without the possibility of that prayer and the delicate entanglement of all our lives with such fructifying possibilities, the world ceases to be. We are not there yet. Let's see what sorts of selves we need in order to forestall such a horrific outcome insofar as humans can shape their collective destiny.

11

THE LESS-THAN-SOVEREIGN
SELF AND THE HUMAN FUTURE

THIS BOOK HAS BEEN A SUSTAINED EXAMINATION, CRITIQUE, AND INTERPRETATION
of monistic understandings of the sovereignty of God, states, and selves.
But it does not suffice simply to deconstruct, to leave behind the rubble
of what has been discarded. One must fashion an alternative. Is it possible to tame the variants on self-sovereignty we have examined, those
deeded to us by our complex history of faith, philosophy, and politics?
If we would capitulate neither to pridefulness nor to inappropriate self-
loss, what are our alternatives?

One problem we face today is a certain postmodern attitude that sees
in the past only ruin, ignorance, and error. But if the past is jettisoned
entirely we can never rebuild—unless we fanatically and fantastically
claim that it is possible to create a new self de novo. Not only is such a
stance astonishingly arrogant, it is flat-out wrong, incoherent about
selves and societies. We are always indebted, for good or ill, to what has
gone before. In seeking a self that is neither triumphalist nor abject, we
rely on insights, moments, and accomplishments that went before. We
must acknowledge the undeniable accomplishments of sovereign bodies
politic, lordly kings, and strong selves historically—even as we spell out
the troubles lurking therein.

The terrible irony that prompts these concluding reflections is this:
the notion of the sovereign self leads to the destruction of the human

person, to a nadir, not an apogee. The paradox lies in the fact that in divinizing will and choice, we sometimes subtly and sometimes egregiously assault the delicate tendrils of relationship that, alone, lift up and display our humanity. If challenging the sovereign state leads to a chastened patriotism and a limited sovereignty, with sovereignty tied inextricably to the responsibility of states, so with selves one must ask: If we are not fully masters in our own house, what, then, are we? If we are not perfectly autonomous, are we autonomous in any way? What sort of achievement might chastened autonomy be? If we lose at-oneness with our selves, if we are estranged necessarily, how, then, do we fashion a self? If radical, limitless freedom, driven by will, is a destructive dead end, what does freedom with limits offer? And what limits might those be? Albert Camus is surely right: One who denies everything and assumes absolute authority lays "claim to nothing short of total freedom and the unlimited display of human pride. Nihilism confounds creator and created in the same blind fury. Suppressing every principle of hope, it rejects the idea of any limit, and in blind indignation, which no longer is even aware of its reasons, ends with the conclusion that it is a matter of indifference to kill when the victim is already condemned to death."[1] This nihilism is the nadir of which I spoke.

DEFINING SOVEREIGNTY WITH LIMITS

Let's restate this in order to underscore certain salient points: personal autonomy (rightly understood) and national sovereignty are achievements rather than presuppositions. We presuppose—we believe—that God is sovereign (and this for hundreds of reasons), but we cannot assume that a nation-state is sovereign until it demonstrates its ability to be independent from the protection of another state, to treat its citizens decently, and to foster a vibrant civil society: sovereignty as responsibility. This marks a state as a mature member of the international community. Something analogous is also true for the person—persons are not born as mature members of society, but they can grow to become such. Until they reach maturity there are defensible reasons for treating them as immature. As with the nation-state, so with the person. Being a mature member of society does not entail complete independence from everybody else but, instead, requires a willingness and ability to build and to sustain rich relationships with other people. It is thus possible to make an analogy between selves and sovereignty—up to a point. There is a less helpful analogy to be drawn between the sovereignty of God and the sovereignty of the state—depending upon the understanding of God's sovereignty one advances. The God who humbled himself, God as "the man-for-others"—in theologian Dietrich Bonhoeffer's locution, that analogy serves to highlight responsibility and limits and, therefore, is helpful.

Given the historic achievements of sovereignty and its dangerous excesses when man decides he is utterly autonomous, indeed, godlike, we need other sorts of selves to forestall the worst.[2] Contra Immanuel Kant, the subject is relational. Bonhoeffer's critique of Kant reminds us that the person before me sets a limit to my own projects. The responsible self acknowledges the one before her and lives in the dialogic space thus created. Albert Camus also reminded us that the will to dominate and the will to submit are part and parcel of the same triumph of the will and certainly not the stuff out of which grows the responsible life. The self cannot be what St. Augustine calls the proud "Selfsame," a point of reference unto itself. In strong versions of sovereignty, the self shoulders on alone as the self is entirely volitional and grounds all reality. In soft sovereign selves, it is the self as victim that, oddly, triumphs, controlling through weakness rather than strength—a dynamic discussed in the previous chapter. Neither the self-maximizer of *homo economicus*, nor the self as willful invention, nor the biologically reductionist self of genetic fantasies is a candidate or an alternative to sovereign selves; rather, each is an exemplar of the phenomenon I wish to undermine and to refashion.

The self I have in mind seeks meaning and dignity and finds a measure of both not in total liberation from nature, nor in some utopian attunement and at-oneness with nature but, rather, in growing to become a full person according to our human natures. Because that nature is intrinsically social; because we are persons, not individuals; we must refrain from doing everything of which we are capable. If we refuse to observe a limit, we are destroyers, we become death dealers. Camus describes this process of becoming a self as a much harder birth than one's first, "to be born as a man and then to be born in harder child-birth, which consists of being born in relation to others."[3] These are words St. Augustine would understand—as would he appreciate Camus' insistence that we are born to and for joy and gratitude: "The child felt tears coming to his eyes along with a great cry of joy and grati-tude for this wonderful life."[4]

Above all, we are created to love and to be loved. Think of the human beings whom we downgrade and whom National Socialism aimed to destroy: persons who cannot reason because of inborn mental incapac-ity ("idiots and imbeciles and morons," in the gentle language of his-tory). Think about abuse of obviously sentient and loving creatures, like dogs, because they cannot reason—the assumption being that they lack emotion and feeling. Think of our treatment of the dead, discussed in the previous chapter. What all these selves have in common is that they cannot be sovereign in the manner extolled by so many philosophers. They appear to lack sovereignty altogether. They become *a problem* to and for liberal societies that presuppose selves are sovereign and to and for illiberal societies that require militant selves to be prepared to sacri-fice others who cannot be "the new socialist man" or the ardent, willing Nazi.

In our own liberal society at the moment, and in most of the West-ern democracies in general, we are pursuing a paradoxical project: We are more aware of those with physical and mental disabilities; we want to provide them access. Yet at the same time, our most enthused-about and ideologically fraught projects aim at creating a world with no such persons in it. We will genetically engineer them away and, until that time, we can eliminate them through selective abortion. And all this with no apparent regard for how persons with disabilities might well come to the conclusion that the so-called right to die—another way to say "right to eliminate non-sovereign selves"—might just threaten them.

Moral Fables and Fighting Contemporary Excarnation

If we think of the famous moral fables that warn us of hubristic over-reach, we discern that they have much in common: an excess of *superbia*, human pride; a run-amok *curiositas*, a curiosity turned deadly as it recognizes no limit, no constraint. Writes literary critic Roger Shattuck, concerning Mary Shelley, the author of the famous story of Dr. Frankenstein, "Her [Shelley's] judgment of the presumptions and selfish actions of Frankenstein in creating and then abandoning a new form of life" is instructive. "Apparently, it required a woman to inventory the destruction caused by the quest for knowledge and glory carried to excess, and to invent the counterpower to Faust."[6] Well, it doesn't really require a woman, as we find a similar motif and warning in the moral fable of Jekyll and Hyde by Robert Louis Stevenson: We experiment with our natures at our peril. By experimenting with our natures, I do not mean "attempting to forestall terrible illness," say, or healing injury and so on. The reductionist argument often thrown in the face of one calling for limits is ridiculous stuff much of the time, to wit: "I see, well, because it means messing with our natures, I guess you would never have wanted pneumonia to be treated or a polio vaccine developed because that messes with nature." One sees how beside the point such a riposte is. By assisting us in being as whole in body and spirit as we can be, given what was given us at birth, we are helping to complete our nature, not to alter it radically. By contrast, Aldous Huxley's classic *Brave New World*, once considered a fantastic allegory, a moral fable with the stress on "fable," now bids to come uncomfortably close to the utopian dreams of some genetic fundamentalists. We return to these classics, these moral fables, or we should, to instruct us on the excesses of sovereign selves.

Pondering the phenomenon of modern excarnation, the image of the bereft ghost of Hamlet's father comes to mind—a poor spirit haunting the netherworld, the ghost cries out to his son to "Remember me . . . remember me"; and what father, what king, does Hamlet remember? The king enfleshed, embodied, standing before him in the earthy splendor that had been his. Hamlet loved, loves, *that* incarnate father, and when our loved ones leave us, that is how we remember them as well. The reader will recall that one feature of celebrations of and arguments for self-sovereignty is a strange abstractness, a refusal to keep one's feet on terra firma, perhaps because that reminds us ongoingly "from dust to dust," we are earthy and earthbound creatures. We can soar only if we are dis-embodied, the phenomenon philosopher Charles Taylor calls modern excarnation. This invites a hyperexaggerated notion of what can be achieved through various philosophical modalities, in Taylor's view, whether Kantianism or utilitarianism. We live in our own heads. We pro-mote disciplinary codes: just consider how excessively legalistic our own society has become. We are moralistic—consider the almost hysterical moralism involved in campaigns against trans fats or God knows what.

But if we lose authentic relationality, which should make us less all-knowing and harsh, we lose dialogue, we lose a sense of what is appro-priate to, and achievable by, creatures like ourselves. We also lose history—the living incarnational realities of human life in common. As Pope Benedict XVI argues, without embodied history, political theory becomes an entirely gnostic enterprise—all words, no flesh; all spirit, no-body. Then, disastrously, this disembodied enterprise invites abstract schemas imposed upon the living within history.[7]

To truly fight excarnation, to find some new direction, requires that certain possibilities have not been smashed altogether. Here there is rea-son to be hopeful—not optimistic, but hopeful. Consider the horrific world limned by Primo Levi in his classic, *Survival in Auschwitz*.[8] It is impossible to imagine a world more cruelly designed to defeat totally the human person than that demonic social experiment, the death camp. Levi alerts us, yet again, to the fact that the camps flowed directly from a process of reason, a terrible rationalism played out to the bitter end. There is a major premise; a syllogism; and the end of the line is the death camp. If indeed there are "lives unworthy of life" it follows inex-orably that those who are "worthy of life"—sovereign selves—must remove those "unworthy of life" who have already been defined out of the human universe in any case.

Levi characterizes life in the camp as a "journey toward nothingness." But then he says something remarkable: "Yet no world of perfect unhappiness can exist. Our human condition is opposed to everything infinite. There is a limit on every joy and on every grief."[9] In the camps, human beings were reduced to phantoms: the demolition of man, Levi calls this, although language doesn't seem quite up to the task of expressing "this offense." Your life was reduced to the "very lowest material level." You were a "man who is no longer a man."[10] First, Levi continues, they annihilate you as a man—a person—and then they kill you. It isn't enough just to kill you. They must kill the human spirit first and our spirits are fragile. And yet . . . and yet. . . . The conviction that "life has a purpose is rooted in every fiber of man," and for some inmates of the camps surviving the "insane dream of grandeur of their masters" somehow kept them going.[11] Levi keeps his own sense of purpose alive by desperately attempting to recall the "Canto of Ulysses" from Dante's *Divine Comedy:* there was beauty and form and sense in the world; there might be again. Levi concludes this haunting memoir, a moral fable of the twentieth century, the most horrible of all centuries, in this way: "No human experience," he reminds us, "is without meaning or unworthy of analysis." In the camps thousands of human beings, who differed in "just about every way people can differ," were "thrown into a vast social experiment." And out of this he learns that human beings are not "fundamentally brutal at base." It is "far more complicated," and many social habits can be "silenced, quashed." But they *cannot be destroyed utterly.*[12]

If Primo Levi can redeem this much from the demonic horrors of the death camps, surely we—all of us concerned about the human future—can find resources to draw upon as, hopefully, we look to common sense, decency, dignity, to our sense of shame, our capacity for joy, our ability to recognize when our dignity is affronted, our ability to love, not just to use, others. The nonsovereign self has readier access to all of this precisely became he or she finds intimations and realizations of such a self all around, sees beauty, sadness, hope, mystery, truths to be found and discerned—as part of the very fabric of the universe.

WHERE DO WE FIND MODERN INCARNATIONALITY?

Our incarnational writers—I have already noted Albert Camus' beautiful story of growing up desperately poor yet without resentment in Algeria—and there are others. Two come readily to mind: the poet Czeslaw Milosz and the novelist Marilynne Robinson. Each understands that persons—by contrast to isolated individuals—are unique and unrepeatable. They cannot simply be replaced by a new recruit. Each understands that pure thought is not greater than love.[13] The poet Czeslaw Milosz is also the author of one of the great books assaying the nature of totalitarianism, *The Captive Mind.*[14] It was derided when first published (the early 1950s) by those still enamored of the world-historical project of Marxism. It also got located and ground into pieces as but one of the many polemical entries in Cold War argumentation; indeed, Milosz told me over the course of a dinner conversation that he had been informed by a member of his tenure-review committee at the University of California, Berkeley, that he received tenure in spite of the fact he had written the politically incorrect *Captive Mind!* As the philosopher Ludwig Wittgenstein might note, Milosz's critics were prisoners of a picture, an abstract picture they could not get "out of their heads." If we take a look at *The Captive Mind,* we enter a world of incarnationality and leave behind a world of lifeless ratiocination. Here I have in mind Milosz's determination to be fleshly, concrete, and particular. An incarnational text is a world of concrete presences; it derives from an impulse to make "real" that which is symbolized or represented. A symbol, a metaphor, a figure does not stand apart from but participates in "the thing itself," so to speak. The writer aims neither for a pure realm nor an ideal form but for a way to express reverence for that which simply *is,* most importantly the flesh-and-blood human beings around us. I think, for example, of my favorite passage from *The Captive Mind,* in which Milosz describes walking through a train station in Ukraine in the desperately disordered time of the beginning of World War II. He is caught up short by the following scene:

> A peasant family—husband and wife and two children—had settled down by the wall. They were sitting on baskets and bundles. The wife was feeding the younger child; the husband who had a dark, wrinkled face and a black, drooping

mustache was pouring tea out of a kettle into a cup for the older boy. They were whispering to each other in Polish. I gazed at them until I felt moved to the point of tears. What had stopped my steps so suddenly and touched me so profoundly was their *difference.* This was a human group, an island in a crowd that lacked something proper to humble, ordinary human life. The gesture of a hand pouring tea, the careful, delicate handing of the cup to the child, the worried words I guessed from the movement of their lips, their isolation, the privacy in the midst of the crowd—that is what moved me. For a moment, then, I understood something that quickly slipped from my grasp.

Perhaps, one might suggest, something about the fragility and miracle of the quotidian. Milosz is rightly celebrated for capturing such moments in his poetry, moments that quickly slip or threaten to slip from our grasp. His poems, he tells us, are encounters with the often peculiar circumstances of time and space. This is true as well in *The Captive Mind.* The portrait of that forlorn bit of humanity, huddled together, uprooted, yet making and pouring tea—this, too, says something about the quotidian that can neither be added to nor abstracted from. For Milosz, the touchstone for twentieth-century politics was terror and the immediacy of stark, physical pain—a phenomenon that self-encloses us, cuts us off. And yet . . . those cries can still be heard if our thinking is not so disordered—so excarnated—that we cannot try to enter into the reality of that pain.

The twentieth-century mind was susceptible to seduction by sociopolitical doctrines that abstractly dealt out death. The twenty-first century has already treated us to examples of the same, a willingness to accept terror for the sake of a hypothetical future. Milosz puts on display the impoverished, one-dimensional, flattened-out view of human beings which a totalizing ideology of politics and self-sovereignty requires and feeds on. In *The Witness of Poetry,* Milosz indicts the "vulgarized" knowledge that gives birth to the feeling that everything is controllable, for example, "the young cannibals who, in the name of inflexible principles, butchered the population of Cambodia" and who "had graduated from the Sorbonne and were simply trying to implement the philosophic ideas they had learned."[15] They had been overtaken by excarnation.

In her award-winning novel *Gilead,* novelist Marilynne Robinson opens up a world of simple beauty and goodness that often goes unremarked. "Any human face is a claim on you," her protagonist, the dying pastor, John Ames, writes, "because you can't help but understand the singularity of it, the courage and loneliness of it."[16] Her incarnational writing highlights the body "blessed and broken"—in Christian theology and in everyday life. Pastor Ames talks about "the gift of physical particularity and how blessing and sacrament are mediated through it."[17] It follows that God's love and mortal love are not so separate. There is splendor revealed in a child's face, for God so loved the world. Robinson's protagonist also reminds us that the great Hebrew prophets of Scripture chastised and loved a concrete people, something too many moderns who don the mantle of prophecy seem to have abandoned as, all too often, they seem to despise those they criticize.

We also have theologians to turn to, those who insist on the concrete, living realities of real communities and the relational dimensions of all human propensities and projects. What theologian McFadyen in *Bound to Sin* alerts us to is the damage—the "deeply distorting, distorted and damaging relationship"—that results when some human beings are systematically harmed by others, calling this recognition a "relational ecology."[18] This reminds us every human being enters the world under a burden of history, and this history teaches us—or should—to beware "highly optimistic assessments of the possibilities of reason."[19] Even the architects of Nazi genocide found it difficult, if not impossible, to kill face-to-face, or to witness such killing, or to view the aftermath of it. In handing out their plans for mass murder, they required a far distance that eliminated the moral space of the "in between" myself and another. Narrow rationalism tethered to boundless will generated a tyrannical nightmare. The upshot for McFadyen? We must reject certain dichotomies: It is neither autonomy, nor abject surrender—as I have already argued. God is neither utterly transcendent—so removed God offers no coherent analogy to our selves—nor is God so entirely immanent that we are simply subsumed into this God-substance and become indistinguishable from it. This ecology of relationship doesn't deal with human agglomerates defined by race or sex or class or some other category made absolute; no, the dignity of the human person is irreducible and cannot be wholly subsumed into such abstract categories.

Anti-Nazi theologian Bonhoeffer reminds us throughout his work that "bodilyness and human life belong inseparably together" and this has "very far-reaching consequences" for our understanding of every aspect of human life, for we can use our bodies and the bodies of others well or ill.[20] The right to live is, for Bonhoeffer, of the "very essence"; indeed, even the most "wretched life" is "worth living before God."[21] What should continually amaze us is that many lives we imagine as wretched are, in fact, not: people find purpose and even joy in the midst of extraordinary difficulty and suffering. That is not all they find, of course, but we can see redemptive moments when we would least expect them. Bonhoeffer is also insistent that human beings are not free as such:

> Freedom is not a quality of man, nor is it an ability. . . . it is not a possession, a presence, an object, nor is it a form of existence—but a relationship and nothing else. In truth, freedom is a relationship between two persons. Being free means "being free for the other," because the other has bound me to him. In relationship with the other I am free. No substantial or individualistic concept of freedom can conceive of freedom.[22]

These are strong words, words that bespeak incarnational realities. Human life is always lived in concrete communities—not in nowhere. Even as God is dialogic and related and gives of himself, so are we called—in Christianity—to be likewise. In a society such as ours, with our history, these recognitions can be ongoingly kindled, and no doubt resources from other faiths offer similar possibilities of renewal. To oversimplify, we are never in a zero-sum game in this life of ours, never in a situation where the exact sum I "give" is something taken away from me absolutely and appropriated by someone else: that is Sartre's "hell is other people," a desolate, dead, and lonely world. "Zero

SOVEREIGNTY

sum" is not the world of people who embrace the quotidian rather than despise it; who find joy in simple things; who find dignity in a decent job well done. Our bodies define a limit, yes, but also a possibility as we enter into community, for we can only "be" by virtue of others. Writes Pope Benedict XVI, "In a world that in the last analysis is not mathematics but love, the minimum is a maximum; the smallest thing that can love is one of the biggest things; the particular is more than the universal; the person, the unique and unrepeatable, is at the same time the ultimate and highest thing."[23]

PLURALITY, NOT FRAGMENTATION; COMMONALITY, NOT TOTALITY

Even as selves are irreducible, so are cultures. A world of many nations, each with its own particular marks of self-identity, reminds us that we are not alone and that we cannot and ought not make the world one by cruelly obliterating diverse ways of life. One of the most insidious aspects of communist "universalism" was precisely its need to crush difference, to "make everything the same," in the words of Vaclav Havel. He continues:

> The greatest enemy of communism was always individuality, variety, difference—in a word, freedom. From Berlin to Vladivostok, the streets and buildings were decorated with the same red stars. Everywhere the same kind of celebratory parades were staged. Analogical state administrations were set up, along with the whole system of central direction for social and economic life. This vast shroud of uniformity, stifling all national, intellectual, spiritual, social, cultural, and religious variety, covered over any difference and created the monstrous illusion that we were all the same.[24]

No, we are not the same. But we do share a capacity for identification with the ideal of a plural political body; we all resist ill dignification; we all yearn for a decent life for our children. If we would resist agglomeration as replaceable units—individuals—within a whole, so we resist reduction to the universe of "one," the universe of he who rules over a desert depopulated of flesh-and-blood persons. In our relational ecologies, we search for commonalities—something quite different from being forced into a totality by external compulsion. We live our lives in and through concrete levels of being of which all have some experience and to which each can testify. Our experiences in and through these concrete relations, too, offer intimations of alternatives to the excarnationality of our time. Bear in mind: the displays of bodies writhing and contorting and self-mutilating are all around us in a manner that speaks to a loathing of that which is authentic embodiment: the *I* in relation to some other, a *we*. I respond to the fullness of this other. I resist the despair and loneliness that lies at the heart of the culture of "hooking-up" and the reason—surprise! surprise!—so many young people are left despairing given their sojourn in such a culture.

So, what do I mean by concrete levels of being? Here at the conclusion of our journey we return to one of the companions with whom we began, St. Augustine. St. Augustine criticizes the notion of gods who are territorially bounded and exclusive. God travels with the pilgrim. One doesn't adopt a new god each time one crosses a boundary. God is not thus limited and nor are we. The prototypical Christian identity is that of pilgrim; one wanders with the mind as well as the body in movements that defy certain limitations. But the concrete expression of one's identity is revealed in and through the body of various institutions. For the early Christians, the most important body was that of church, the *ecclesia*. But Augustine begins with families and the good of families and what they are charged with preserving and sustaining. Augustine's "universalism" is always realized in and through layering of institutions. Our work in small ways and about small things contributes to the completeness of the whole and to the overall harshness or decency of the social order.

What we find in Augustine is certain universal claims about human dignity and value—we are all God's children—but this recognition can only be specified and realized concretely, in and through speech and fellowship and loving and serving one another. Privileging territorial identity no longer pertains. We do love our homelands but we have more than one. With the triumph of a certain sort of rationalism, the number of people who were incorporated into the definition of what was fully human, per se, narrowed. That we are all children of God was replaced by *cogito ergo sum* or some similar formulation. We have already noted the way this downgraded nonsovereign selves in the overall scheme of things, including, it must be said, women, who, for Kant, among others, are beings who traffic in sentiment and emotion, and these have no cognitive value. By giving up the capacity to love and substituting the capacity to engage in ratiocinations, in a certain way, the capaciousness of Augustine's notion of "the human" narrowed. As well, nationalistic projects narrowed territorial identities in a manner that set up the suspicion that all who were foreign were enemies—precisely the equation Augustine criticized as part of the project of the Roman Empire: all that was "alien" was "enemy."

Suffice to say that in the Augustinian scheme of things, there is a flow between the concrete beginnings of the household and that more vast arena, the *mundus* or world. Each layer of relational identity contributes to the ordering or disordering of the whole. And *disordering* does not mean tension, conflict, alienation, unintelligibility: Augustine assumes these are constant features of the human condition; rather, *disordering* means the wrongful subordination of one institution or layer of identity to another that possesses more power in the sense of earthly rule. And let's be clear about what *concrete* means: This is more than a sentiment or an abstraction about something. *Concrete* means embodiment in some institutional or relational form that has some sturdiness and capacity for perdurance. There is a moral purpose in the concrete pilgrim self of Augustine's understanding. This realization of the self is very different from the fleeing of identity (or being forced to flee) of the refugee or the dilettante.

Augustine's fear would be that as we give up God's sovereignty, other forms of human sovereignty—not of the chastened or limited sort—drive to become superordinate and destructive in the ways assayed in this book. Augustine was keenly aware of the fact that any human institution can be turned into an idolatry—whether of family or of state or of anything else. The altar at which we worship daily is the sovereign self whose key terms are control, doing your own thing, and choice as a kind of willfulness rather than as the sometimes-tragic weighing of options where there is no knock-down good or bad on either side. The Augustinian pilgrim is one who can challenge the idolatries of his or her day without opting out (as if one could) or fleeing into a realm at least theoretically removed from the vortex of social and political life. The pilgrim of Augustinian Christianity offers up that possibility, as the late antique world makes startling contact with late modernity. The obstacles that stand in the way of realizing such a complex identity, forged on the anvil of concrete and particular commitments, are formidable. It is unsurprising that we flinch and heartening that so often human beings rise to the occasion as they answer generously and forthrightly not only the question, Who am I? but also, Who is my neighbor?

LESSONS LEARNED FROM CAMUS

Some may find it jarring as I move, in conclusion, from a great saint to a great twentieth-century writer associated with unbelief. But Albert Camus offers us an example of one who lived through and was defined by the culture of self-criticism so characteristic of the West. He understood his indebtedness to those who had gone before, who had created the possibilities for such a culture, for Europe at her best. Exploring a world of moral relativism and absolute nihilism, Camus indicts philosophies that are used as goads or alibis for murder, indicts those who take refuge in an ideology and erect slave moralities under the flag of freedom. In his great essay *The Rebel*, so unfairly trashed by Sartre's minions and other ideologues, Camus writes,

> If we believe in nothing, if nothing has any meaning and we can affirm no values whatsoever, then everything is possible and nothing has any importance. There is no pro or con: the murderer is neither right nor wrong. We are free to stoke the crematory fires or to devote ourselves to the care of lepers. . . . Since nothing is either true or false, good or bad, our guiding principle will be to demonstrate that we are the

most efficient, in other words, the strongest. That is the only
measure of success.[25]

Camus here sketches a world of the will-to-power triumphant, a
world of "executioners and victims," as he put it. And how does one tell
the story of this triumph? It is "the history of European pride."[26] In
rebelling against a world that is cruel or murderous or systematically unjust, the authentic rebel observes a limit. He affirms the "existence of a
borderline . . . that there are limits and also that he respects—and
wishes to preserve—the existence of certain things on this side of the
borderline."[27] When a person rebels, he identifies himself with others,
according to Camus, rather than repudiates others utterly. He eschews
resentment, a corrosive envy of what one does not have. No, the authentic rebel wishes to defend what he in fact is—a human being, a person.
And in rebellion he finds, not isolation, but solidarity. So strong is
Camus' claim in this regard that he declares that anyone who "claims
the right" to destroy this "solidarity loses [the] right to be called rebellion and becomes instead acquiescent in murder." For rebellion "must
respect the limit it discovers in itself—a limit where minds meet and, in
meeting, begin to exist. I rebel, therefore we exist."[28]

That Camus fell out of critical and political favor is an indictment of
those who ostracized him for his refusal to become complicit in murder
and terror; for his resistance to "metaphysical rebellion" that abjures
God and one's fellow man alike; that traffics in absolute negation, a
world of submission and domination, for "unlimited freedom of desire
implies the negation of others and the suppression of pity."[29] What is a
totalitarian society but a story of unbridled freedom to kill? The nihilist
would become godlike, a rival of the Creator, perpetually demanding
some sort of unity (of victim and victimizer); a hatred of the creator
transmogrifies into hatred of creation.

And what politics comes out of all this? We see it all too clearly in the
terror that accompanied the French Revolution, as I noted in an earlier
chapter, a period fueled by what Camus calls a "logical delirium." One
must kill and kill again in order to create revolutionary virtue and everywhere "the sovereignty of the state is substituted for the sovereign king

who has already substituted for the sovereign God, although a link still maintained."[30] We behead the king, break the link to transcendence, and make of the "here and now" an absolute, a new deity that requires human sacrifice. A political utopia replaces God by some sort of abstract future and the demand for justice ends in injustice. "Things are not good or evil but either premature or out of date."[31] For Camus, one had to learn how to live without grace and without justice—something, of course, Augustine would take exception to as grace was God's free gift to us. Be that as it may, the two—Augustine and Camus—would come together in an answer to what happens when people live without grace and without justice. Nihilism supplies the answer. A frenzied will to power triumphs. Finally, one must insist, Camus concludes, on the fact that there is a human nature and resist all attempts to turn it into the rubble of historic forces:

> Absolute revolution supposes the absolute malleability of human nature and its possible reduction to the condition of a historical force. But rebellion, in man, is the refusal to be treated as an object and to be reduced to simple historical terms. It is the affirmation of a nature common to all men, which eludes the world of power.[32]

These are words the totalitarian would scoff at and the radical post-modernist could never speak. But speak such words we must, and Camus reminds us that the fruit of Western culture requires that we remember both Jerusalem and Athens, belief and unbelief, skepticism and faith. And, for Camus, the beauty of this world and our ability to respond to it is one possible source for the regeneration of our culture which recalls the "common dignity of man and the world he lives in and which we must now define in the face of a world that insults it."[33] Those insults mount daily, as I have pointed out, perhaps in more detail than the reader desired. But we cannot and do not stop with these insults. We look for commonalities and for sources of renewal. I have noted but a few, emphasizing philosophy, theology, literature. But in the worlds of commerce (essential to which is trusting and promise keeping), in politics (at its best a world of commitment to a good we can know in common that we cannot know alone), and law (each and every one, no matter how lowly, stands as an equal before the law), we also find possibilities of renewal.

And lest we should ever get too prideful about our abilities to refashion and renew, so that we are tempted by the controlling, abstracted features of the very "sovereignties" we are challenging, Camus, in his novel *The Plague*, whose narrator, Dr. Rieux, "bears witness" to the sufferings of innocent people laid low by the terror of the plague, tells us that after the plague is gone and people greet one another in open plazas and laugh and drink and eat, we should never be complacent, never smug:

> Nonetheless, he [Rieux] knew that the tale he had to tell could not be one of final victory. It could be only the record of what had had to be done, and what assuredly would have to be done again in the never ending fight against terror and its relentless onslaughts, despite their personal afflictions, by all who, unable to be saints but refusing to bow down to pestilences, strive their utmost to be healers.
>
> And, indeed, as he listened to the cries of joy rising from the town, Rieux remembered that such joy is always imperiled. He knew what those jubilant crowds did not know but could have learned from books: that the plague bacillus never dies or disappears for good; that it can lie dormant for years and years in furniture and linen-chests; that it bides its time in bedrooms, cellars, trunks, and bookshelves; and that perhaps the day would come when, for the bane and the enlightening of men, it would rouse up its rats again and send them forth to die in a happy city.[34]

Selves that are less than sovereign understand this moral allegory and live with this mordant recognition. Far easier to be comfortably sovereign and "in control." But then one lives in a kind of dream world that will fade or crash to bits as all dreams of incandescent glory can and must. Selves immersed in a world with and among their fellow human beings, that relational ecology we have noted, affirm, respect, and find joy in life's everydayness and its simple pleasures, even as many aspire to enact their projects on a wide arena and before "larger audiences," so to speak. It is often difficult to keep one's feet on the ground as the stages grow loftier and words are taken up in the glare of publicity—perhaps one reason so many are so mistrustful of politicians and even celebrities we laud and loathe in equal measure. But, even in these sorts of circumstances, there are those who use their arenas and their platforms to remind us of the dignity of everyday life and to extol those forms of politics most mindful of that dignity.

Love may not be all we need, but without it we are naught but husks or willful "spirits" rushing onward into the abyss.

AN AFTERWORD (1992)

THIS IS A STORY OF EMPTY POCKETS. DURING A RECENT TRIP TO ROME, I enjoyed an evening in the company of a group that included a young Jesuit who had spent a year in El Salvador and was due to return there soon. At one point over the course of the evening's discussion, Father Michael described the time he had spent at one of the l'Arche communities founded by Jean Vanier. L'Arche began in 1964 when Vanier bought a home in rural France and invited two adults with mental retardation to live there with him. Some sixty l'Arche communities now exist worldwide. The guiding spirit behind l'Arche differs dramatically from the therapeutic paternalism that often structures relationships between the "normal" and the "mentally handicapped." L'Arche is a community dedicated to the unlikely proposition that the more able should not *do* things to or for the less able but should, instead, live with them in covenant. Writes Vanier, "Handicapped people are teachers of . . . the strong. With their tremendous qualities of heart and lives of faith and love, the handicapped give testimony to the truth that the privileged place for meeting with God is in our vulnerability and weakness."

I thought of Vanier's words as I listened to Father Michael tell a story of empty pockets. At l'Arche, Michael helped to dress and clean a profoundly handicapped young man. One day it struck him that this young man went out of his room and into his world and through his life, every single day, with "empty pockets."

Father Michael thought of how odd that was—no change, no wallet. "No keys," another dinner guest and I exclaimed simultaneously, showing, no doubt, both our automotive and professional preoccupations. In my own case domestic concerns also helped to account for my outburst concerning keys—keys to one's home being central to one's sense of self and place.

The real problem, Father Michael decided, was not with his handicapped brother, but, as he put it, "with me and my ideas of him and what he felt." As Father Michael said these words he put his hand over his heart, and I mused and remarked on how the heart's understanding of humanity is often much more generous and expansive than definitions that rely on measures of intelligence or productive capability. This led those at the table to turn to the growing eugenics enthusiasm, with its technocratization of birth and its tacit conviction that the world would be "better off" if "they"—the handicapped with their empty pockets—were no longer to be born, to appear among us. It is important to note that the urge to eliminate those handicapped biogenetically is a view often born of compassion. But this compassion quickly turns perverse because it is a free-floating, untethered sentimentalization, devoid of context and concrete experience or engagement with those with the empty pockets.

As I was driven back to my room near the Santa Maria Maggiore on that becalmed, warm Roman night, I felt a spreading sorrow, which has remained with me. For I am convinced that our reigning metaphors of success and productivity, of what "counts" as definitive of the human, will more and more leave our fellow human beings with their empty pockets in the shadows, eclipsed, outside the circle of concern. Here the unbearable lightness of a certain sort of triumphalist and narrow secularism—I know not what else to call it—can be seen as exacting a terrific toll in its heady great leaps always forward, always upward, pockets full of keys, inexorably extending and deepening, not our awe and humility, but our drive for sovereign control. And I remembered one of Vanier's warnings: "One of the dangers in our world is wanting to do big things, heroic things. We are called to do little things lovingly—to work to create community." You don't need full pockets to be a citizen of this polity.[1]

ACKNOWLEDGMENTS

With each book one writes, the indebtedness to others grows. I cannot possibly provide an exhaustive list. My colleagues at the University of Chicago, especially William Schweiker and Franklin Gamwell, are always supportive and helpful. David Tracy, Susan Schreiner, Clark Gilpin, Richard Rosengarten, Steve Meredith, and Constantin Fasolt must also be noted. Research assistance came from Dan Maloney, Ryan Anderson, and Jeff Langan. They, in turn, were supported by Luis Tellez and the Witherspoon Institute at Princeton. (Thanks, also, to Seamus Hassan for getting the ball rolling for support.) Randall Newman offered intelligent suggestions along the way. My graduate students are a source of energy and intelligence, particularly, for the purpose of this project, John Carlson, Erik Owens, Melanie O'Hara Barrett, and Matt Rose. Cardinal Francis George of Chicago is a cherished interlocutor on the issues taken up in this book and many others. My editors at Basic Books, Joann Miller and Laura Heimert, and my agent, Glen Hartley, are indispensable. And I must note, after all these years, two extraordinary undergraduate mentors—Dr. Harry Rosenberg and Dr. Leo J. Cefkin—for their tutelage and faith in me.

Other forms of indebtedness belong to Michael Gillespie, Francis Oakley, Derek Jeffreys, William Gordon, Michael Walzer, Charles Taylor, Daniel Philpott, Martin Palous, Peter Berkowitz, William

Galston, Paul de Hart, Carl Gershman, Mary Ann Glendon, Robert George, Thomas Levergood, Patrick Deenan, Joshua Mitchell, Robert A. Markus, and Gilbert Meilaender. Thanks also to Alan Johnson for his support and the great conversation in London. Many others have offered comments and nuggets of wisdom. Whenever one prepares such a list, it is with a sinking feeling that persons very important to the project and to one's intellectual formation have been omitted inadvertently. Memory does not improve with age!

Thanks also to the National Humanities Center, with special kudos to Bob Connor (then the head of the NHC) and Kent Mullikin. As a fellow at the Center, 2000–2001, I completed my intellectual biography of Jane Addams and began work on the sovereignty theme—before being notified of my Gifford selection—a helpful head start. My time at the Library of Congress as the Maguire Chair in Ethics, fall 2003, enabled me to crystallize my conceptual framework and to do bibliographic research. Thanks to the Librarian of Congress, James Billington, and to Prosser Gifford, then director of the Kluge Center at the Library of Congress.

I am grateful to the Gifford committee, Jay Brown, and Timothy O'Shea for the invitation to become a Gifford lecturer and, especially, Isabel Roberts, for her generosity and exquisite attention to detail. Too, I must acknowledge my gratefulness to my family of origin and my own family for keeping me tethered and earthy, and to my country of origin—the United States—for enabling young people from the "provinces" (Colorado), not born into privilege, to be educated and to use their educated powers to their fullest. Finally, I acknowledge formation as a child in a faith that lifts up human dignity and chastens human willfulness.

NOTES

Preface

1. Jean Bethke Elshtain, *Public Man, Private Woman: Women in Social and Political Thought* (Princeton: Princeton University Press, 1981).

2. Elshtain, *Democracy on Trial* (New York: Basic Books, 1995), see especially the discussion of "the politics of displacement."

3. I was quite fortunate during my graduate school years to find professors who had not succumbed to the behaviorist approach. Most importantly, I must single out my dissertation director, the late George Armstrong Kelly.

4. For a splendid discussion of all this see Jeremy Waldron, *God, Locke, and Equality: Christian Foundations in Locke's Political Thought* (Cambridge: Cambridge University Press, 2002). Waldron explores seriously the religious dimensions of Locke's work, acknowledging, as he does so, that this is rarely done.

5. See Elshtain, *Augustine and the Limits of Politics* (Notre Dame, Indiana: Notre Dame University Press, 1996).

6. Elshtain, *Women and War* (New York: Basic Books, 1987; 2nd edition, University of Chicago Press, 1995). See also my *New Wine and Old Bottles* (Notre Dame: Notre Dame University Press, 1996).

7. I have taken heart from recent publications, for example, Michael Burleigh's riveting *Sacred Causes: The Clash of Religion and Politics, from the Great War to the War on Terror* (New York: Harper Collins, 2007). Burleigh describes his book as operating in a space that has no satisfactory label, a space where "culture, ideas, politics, and religious faith" meet (p. xi). Burleigh also says he wants to avoid "crocodiles" like "the history of ideas." I hope my book demonstrates that an interpretive, historically attuned "history of ideas" can at least be mammalian rather than crocodilian.

CHAPTER 1

1. Hundreds of works elaborate the emergence of the doctrine of the Trinity and its definitive culminations with the Councils of Chalcedon and the Nicene Creed. Neil Ormerod, *The Trinity: Retrieving the Western Tradition* (Milwaukee: Marquette University Press, 2005); Roger E. Olson, *The Trinity* (Grand Rapids: Eerdmans, 2002); Bernd Oberdorfer, *Filioque: Geschichte und Theologie eines ökumenischen Problems* (Göttingen: Vandenhoeck & Ruprecht, 2001); Bertrand de Margerie, *The Christian Trinity in History* (Still River: St. Bede's Publications, 1982); Walter Bowie, *Jesus and the Trinity* (New York: Abingdon Press, 1960); Domenico Spada, *Le formule trinitarie: da Nicea a Constantinopoli* (Cittá del Vaticano: Urbaniana University Press, 2003); J. W. C. Wand, *The Four Councils* (London: Faith Press, 1951). Questions of God's sovereignty are linked to the theodicy conundrum that haunts Christian history and Western thought, even as it shadows this book; namely, if God is all-good and all-powerful, how did evil arise? Why does it appear to flourish and even to triumph? Although not my explicit concern, theodicy cannot help but show its face above the surface of things from time to time. As all students of history know, the early Christians emerged from the chrysalis of Judaism and went on to incorporate wide swaths of the philosophic thinking of the antique world. Christian apologists struggled to define the "good news" of their faith; namely, that the transcendent God had appeared immanently in the second person of the Trinity and, upon his return to the transcendent God, had sent the Holy Spirit (the third person of the triune God) to work its way on this earth. This is not such an easy thing to capture; indeed, so many found it so daunting and complicated that the early Church confronted an alphabet soup of schisms and heresies, some of which are known to us largely because that giant, St. Augustine, spent so many of his working hours dealing with the challenges each presented in turn. Augustine's arguments with the Pelagians and Manicheans provide interesting material for debates about sovereign selves—as well as the origin of evil and the extent of human freedom of action. Now, as I indicated, this may seem like dusting the cobwebs off old objects nobody cares about any more. Yet, despite proclamations that God is dead and theodicy abandoned, we remain haunted by these questions. Albert Camus takes them up brilliantly through the sermons of Fr. Paneloux, a learned man who is a student of St. Augustine, in his novel, *The Plague* (New York: Vintage Books, 1991). See also Robert A. Markus, *Christianity and the Secular* (Notre Dame: Notre Dame University Press, 2006).

2. On the specifics of Augustine against the Manichees there is no substitute for reading Augustine himself, although the secondary literature is vast. *The Works of Saint Augustine: A Translation for the 21st Century* (Brooklyn: New City Press, 1990). Augustine's anti-Manichean writings are also collected in

Vols. 4 and 5, *A Select Library of the Christian Church*, ed. Philip Schaff (Peabody, Mass.: Hendrickson Publishers, 1995).

3. One cannot "chunk off" one person of the Trinity and consider it in isolation, for each piece is distorted if separated from the whole. The Trinity is a non-monistic unity, a claim that will come into view as we go along. When Christians slide into monism, it is never reassuring, as a monism of the will then becomes an ever-present temptation.

4. Augustine's dates are 354–430. See also Pope Benedict XVI's discussion of the Trinity in *Introduction to Christianity* (San Francisco: Communio Books, Ignatius Press, 2004). The lengthy Augustine material that follows is warranted, given his extraordinary importance to all that follows.

5. Joseph Cardinal Ratzinger (Pope Benedict XVI), *Introduction to Christianity* (San Francisco: Communio Books, Ignatius Press, 2004), p. 26.

6. To these complexities should be appended a recognition that Christianity is not primarily a philosophical system but a relational, embodied community sustained by the practices of the faithful themselves. These matters resurface in my treatment of the sovereign self as I ponder whether the sovereign God any longer tames sovereign selves.

7. God's self-giving, even unto death, is called *askesis* in Christian theology and it is not so much a relinquishment as a withholding, refusing to bring all one's powers to bear.

8. St. Augustine, *De Trinitate, The Trinity,* trans. Stephen McKenna (Washington, D.C.: Catholic University of America Press), p. 20.

9. You can find the entire poem at http://www.bartleby.com/188/119.html.

10. To which, of course, one must add "the Holy Spirit."

11. This pride and folly enters into our discussion directly when we arrive at the "sovereign self" in chapters 8–10.

12. Augustine, *The City of God*, ed. David Knowles (Baltimore, Md.: Penguin Books, 1972), Book XIX, chapter 7, p. 861.

13. This has taken pop form in our own time with the silliness about men being from Mars and women from Venus.

14. For the "usage of our language has already decided" certain things, Augustine argues, including the Trinity. Thus, essence and substance confound us linguistically as we think of Trinity, finally deciding on one essence or substance and three persons. See Augustine, *The Trinity*, p.187. The footnote to this edition adds that it was after the Council of Chalcedon in 451, twenty-one years after Augustine's death, that the term *hypostasis*, designating the meaning of the persons of the Trinity, became doctrinally definitive.

15. On this see Augustine, *The City of God*, Book XI, chapter 8, p. 437.

16. Gordon Leff, *Medieval Thought: Augustine to Ockham* (Baltimore, Md.: Penguin Books, 1958), p. 19.

17. Material on this theme is scattered throughout Augustine's work. I think here of Book X of *The City of God* and Book XII of *The Trinity*.

18. This from Charles Norris Cochrane's oldie but goody, *Christianity and Classical Culture* (New York: Galaxy Books, 1959), p. 384, where Augustine writes that the Trinity is "a principle capable of saving reason as well as the will, and thus redeeming human personality as a whole." Given our epistemic limitations and the noetic consequences of sin, God teaches us through allegory, analogy, figurative language, and narrative. Trinity, Augustine proclaims, is a necessary category of thought—that without which we cannot do. His book moves back and forth from the mind's knowledge of itself, to self and mind, to self and others, to self and God, and so on. The back-and-forthing is vital to Augustine's understanding of the God that came to be called sovereign. As beings circumscribed by boundaries of time and space, we require certain fundamental categories in order to *see* the world at all. Form that circumscribes is also a presupposition of freedom, necessary to our ability to reason things through and to imagine.

19. Augustine, *The Trinity*, Book V, chapter 1, p. 176.

20. For an excellent discussion of this point see James Wetzel, *Augustine and the Limits of Virtue* (Cambridge: Cambridge University Press, 1992), especially p.15.

21. To this day philosophers imagine worlds behind veils of ignorance in which we are abstract entities with no knowledge of ourselves, our history, our time and place, etc. Or they make assumptions that one can come to know "the good" and that there is a clear conduit between this knowledge and human action. Or that truths that we come to know cannot, by definition, conflict with one another. Augustine would criticize all such assumptions or claims.

22. And, increasingly, or so I shall argue below, we see the self itself as sovereign, a territory unto itself with its own laws, its own perspective, etc., me, my, and mine.

23. The will becomes ever more important as we go along. Here it is important to note Hannah Arendt's discussion in *The Life of the Mind* (New York: Harvest Books, Harcourt, 1978). She tags Augustine the only real philosopher the Romans ever had and the first philosopher of the will, so much so that he "names" this faculty of mind.

24. This features in the long tale of sovereignty: Is there one? Are there two, three, or more? Such questions are refracted in debates about earthly rule and authority, as we shall learn.

25. For this discussion of Augustine I draw willy-nilly on passages from my book *Augustine and the Limits of Politics* (Notre Dame: Notre Dame University Press, 1996). Augustine directs some withering fire against the Stoics and their quest for a form of self-sufficiency and a condition of mind and being that en-

ables one to avoid injury and to make oneself radically independent of circumstances. Whether this is a fair or adequate characterization of Stoicism is one debate, and one that doesn't interest me for my purposes here; rather, I find intriguing the ways in which Augustine critiques *any* quest for self-sufficiency as a cruel illusion.

26. Ratzinger, *Introduction to Christianity*, p. 147.

27. John 3:16. Herein lies a central part of the tale. God limits himself through a gift without limit. God empties himself to give up the son.

28. Augustine, *The Letters of St. Augustine. Fathers of the Church Series,* 20 (Washington, D.C.: Catholic University of American Press, 1953), Letter no. 55, p. 475.

29. St. Thomas Aquinas, 1225–1274, known as "the Angelic doctor." Thomism was *the* doctrine and philosophy of the Catholic Church, then Roman Catholic, through its history subsequent to Aquinas and as manifest in the teachings of popes, philosophers, bishops, Church councils, and all the rest. Indeed, in many ways Thomism remains regnant, although John Paul II offered many interesting "additions"—more than direct challenges—through his incorporation of strands of twentieth-century philosophy, importantly personalism and phenomenology, with a touch of carefully vetted Marxism (labor's priority over capital) insinuated. Too, under his tutelage the commitment of the Church to human rights and democracy as a system, not an all-encompassing creed, is cemented.

30. Matthew 22:21.

31. Augustine, *City of God*, Book I, Preface, p. 5.

32. *Ibid.*, Book XIX, chapters 23 and 24, p. 890.

33. The words in quotes are from Augustine, *City of God*, Book XIX, chapter 6, p. 860. This paragraph and several that follow draw upon my book, *Augustine and the Limits of Politics.*

34. *Ibid.*, Book XIX, chapter V, p. 858. I have already drawn attention to Augustine's thoughts on the inescapability of and confusions wrought by language. These divisions manifest themselves in every earthly kingdom as well as *between* earthly units of rule. The tongue is an instrument of human coming together *and* a weapon of domination and breaking asunder.

35. See Markus, *Christianity and the Secular*, p. 39.

36. Augustine, *City of God*, Book XIX, chapter 16, p. 876. It should be noted that Aristotle's *Politics*—with its severing of the realm of necessity from the realm of freedom, the *oikos* (the world of women) from the *polis*, the most perfect association suited to male citizens—was unavailable as a text to Augustine; nevertheless, his arguments are a rebuke to such Aristotelian categories.

37. Relations between husbands and wives are a form of friendship. Augustine assumes the ontological moral equality of men and women but accepts that they occupy different offices or stations. The father in the household should injure

none and do good to all. Should a father violate his vocation, he is worse than an "infidel." The genuine father is concerned for the well-being of all in the household as well as the peace and decency of the household, and this contributes, in turn, to the concord and justice of the city. The authority of the husband must never be arbitrary nor absolute—it is not and cannot be sovereign in ways that form a too-easy trajectory for the triumph of the *libido dominandi*, or lust to dominate. Augustine "relativized . . . political institutions, social practices, customs," argues Markus, both "restricting their spheres and asserting their autonomy." See his *Christianity and the Secular*, p. 40.

38. Augustine's argument begins with God's first two people: Adam and Eve are equally culpable of the Fall, he argues. But sin does not lead to death everlasting, as would have been the case without the free gift of God's grace but, rather, to divisions within the self, between self and other, between entire nations and cultures.

39. *Ibid.*, Book XVI, chapter 14, p. 873.

40. There is a huge and continuing controversy over Augustine and coercion, especially coercion within the Church against schismatics and heretics. R. A. Markus, in his classic *Saeculum: History and Society in the Theology of St. Augustine* (Cambridge: Cambridge University Press, 1970), laments that Augustine didn't bite the bullet (poor metaphor, no doubt) and go on to embrace the "non-coercive exercise of office, pastoral and political." Other commentators lament Markus's lamentation, arguing that it is simply not possible to uphold earthly rule without the use of coercion, appropriately limited and chastened. See John R. Bowlin, "Augustine on Justifying Coercion," *Annual Society of Christian Ethics* 17 (1997), 49–70; *The Limits of Ancient Christianity: Essays on Late Antique Thought and Culture in Honor of R. A. Markus*, ed. William E. Klingshim and Mark Vessey (Ann Arbor: University of Michigan Press, 1999); Arthur P. Monahan, *Consent, Coercion and Limit: The Medieval Origins of Parliamentary Democracy* (Montreal: McGill-Queen's University Press, 1987), pp. 29–46.

41. *Ibid.*, Book XI, chapter 27, pp. 461–462. Well-ordered kingdoms may be even more vulnerable. Were one doing a book on Augustine, one would need to discuss war and peace in detail. Suffice to say that the worst kinds of wars are social and civic wars. Other wars may be just or justified, tragic necessities, and even then should occasion tears of regret (see Book XIX, chapter 7, pp. 861–862). Augustine also issues warnings about "peace." *Peace* is a word brandished as a talisman and repeated as a mantra. It has a soothing and cleansing effect as it is contrasted with war. What too often follows is that good and decent people are naturally for "peace." What, then, about confronting systematic, egregious abuses, massive injustices? As well, there can be a peace of imposition: One attains peace by dominating others with whom one might conflict. No decent person advocates this in its absolutist and cruel forms, but many fail to guard against it. If by "peace" one advocates a condition in which all conflicts are

adjudicable and all persons are open to reason, Augustine would argue one is chasing a chimera—and a dangerous one at that.

42. Although this was the way I was taught it, I should note that some scholars of Byzantium have challenged such terminology in recent years.

43. Pope Gelasius was Bishop of Rome for four short years, 492–496.

44. See the discussion by the O'Donovans, Joan and Oliver, in their reader, *From Irenaeus to Grotius: A Sourcebook in Christian Political Thought* (Grand Rapids, Mich.: Eerdmans, 1999), pp. 169–176.

45. Another key passage for early medieval thinkers determined to sort out the distinction between God and Caesar is Christ's insistence that his kingdom is not of this world: "Jesus answered, My kingdom is not of this world: if my kingdom were of this world, then would my servants fight, that I should not be delivered to the Jews: but now is my kingdom not from hence" (John 18:36). Hannah Arendt and Peter Brown, in their distinct and respective ways, note the importance of this Roman legacy to the Western Church, crediting it in major part with the culture-creating and law-producing capacity that stayed alive and then flourished in the West. See Arendt, "What Is Authority?" in *Between Past and Future* (New York: Penguin Books, 1977), pp. 91–142. She writes, "The Church became so 'Roman' and adapted itself so thoroughly to Roman thinking in matters of politics that it made the death and resurrection of Christ the cornerstone of a new foundation, erecting on it a new human institution of tremendous durability" (p.125). Brown surveys the emergence of powerful and authoritative bishops in his *Power and Persuasion in Late Antiquity* (Madison, Wis.: University of Wisconsin Press, 1992).

46. Such uninformed and mischievous characterizations are frequently used today to make exaggerated claims about the danger posed by "religion" to the American polity.

47. See the discussion in Volume 1 of the multivolume *History of Medieval Thought in the West, The Second Century to the Ninth* (Edinburgh and London: Wm. Blackwood and Sons, 1930), by R.W. and A. J. Carlyle. This series remains an achievement, although this form of intellectual history is said to be out of style and out of touch. The upshot, alas, has been that one gets all sorts of social histories absent serious in-depth consideration of traditions of thought and political life. What was once a corrective has become its own form of orthodoxy.

48. Excerpts are printed in the O'Donovans' reader, p.179.

49. *Ibid.*

50. The Code was first produced in 529, with revised editions in 534 and 533, according to the O'Donovans, for whom the corpus "shows us how an unusually clear-sighted, ambitious, and theologically self-conscious Christian emperor saw his task of government." *Ibid.*, p.189.

51. Galatians 3:28.

52. This whether human rights advocates acknowledge it or not, as the case may be. Whether universal human rights can remain robust over time without *some* such grounding remains to be seen: Is the residuum of theological proclamation sufficiently resonant in secular forms?

53. The words in quotes are drawn from A. P. D'Entreves' small classic, *Natural Law: An Historical Survey* (New York: Harper Torchbooks, 1965), p. 21.

54. On this see the discussion in the Carlyles' *History of Medieval Thought.*

55. *Ibid.*, p. 31.

56. St. Ambrose's dates are 340–397.

57. Quotes from the Carlyles, Vol. I, p. 183.

58. The literature on this goes beyond "vast." In my own reading and rereading I checked many books. In addition to the Carlyles' multivolume work, I consulted Gordon Leff, *Medieval Thought: St. Augustine to Ockham,* already cited; A. P. D'Entreves, *Natural Law,* already cited; Fritz Kern's classic, *Kingship and Law in the Middle Ages* (New York: Harper Torchbooks, 1970); Walter Ullmann, *A History of Political Thought in the Middle Ages* (Harmondsworth, Middlesex, England: Penguin Books, 1965); John B. Morrall, *Political Thought in Medieval Times* (New York: Harper Torchbooks, 1962) for this earlier period; *Sacred and Secular in Medieval and Early Modern Cultures,* ed. Lawrence Besserman (New York: Palgrave, 2006); Hendrik Spruyt, *The Sovereign State and Its Competitors: An Analysis of Systems Change* (Princeton: Princeton University Press, 1994).

59. Many have made this point, including John Morrall, *Political Thought in Medieval Times,* see pp. 76–77.

60. John of Salisbury's dates are 1115–1180. Excerpt from *Policraticus* cited in the O'Donovans' reader, p. 281. The section on John of Salisbury, including the O'Donovans' helpful introduction, covers pp. 277–296. John's view is cited frequently as central to an ecclesiastical right of resistance, underwritten, in part, by his conviction that the prince or monarch accepts his sword of rule from the hand of the Church. Although he is sanctioned in his rule, he rules on sufferance. See the discussion in Kern, *Kingship and Law,* p. 97ff. Salisbury follows a train of argumentation dating from the ninth century on that articulates procedures and their justification for dealing with recalcitrant and unjust rulers. For John of Salisbury, the prince is bound to serve divine justice. He is a "binding law unto himself" who must, in all matters, "prefer the advantage of others to his private will" (*Policraticus,* 4:2); *The Statesman's Book of John of Salisbury,* trans. John Dickinson (New York: Knopf, 1927), pp. 7–8. Although the medieval worldview is sometimes called "organic," this is not quite right. Following Augustine and absorbing Aristotle, as the Thomistic system does, means one calls order or unity that which is "in common," the coming together of overlapping and mutually constitutive parts within a single society. This is quite different from an organic view that assumes a "totality" and then differentiates features internal to it and dependent upon it. Nor is it a vol-

untaristic system, the flip side of organicism, in which "unities" consist exclusively of the multiple contracts of a series of individuals who are in no way transformed as members of a body politic.

61. See Kern, *Kingship and Law in the Middles Ages*, p. 108.

62. A furious epistemological debate flows from this claim—the insistence that descriptive terms exude normative consequences. See, for example, Elshtain, "Methodological Sophistication and Conceptual Confusion," in *Real Politics: At the Center of Everyday Life* (Baltimore, Md.: Johns Hopkins University Press, 1997), pp.12–35.

63. Chrimes is the translator of Fritz Kern's classic on *Kingship and Law in the Middle Ages,* and this quote is drawn from his introduction, p. xxii.

64. *Ibid.,* p. 69.

65. "There are truths about God that have been conclusively proved by philosophers making use of their natural reason." From *Summa Contra Gentiles,* trans. Anton C. Pegis, Book I, chapter 3 (Notre Dame: University of Notre Dame Press, 1975), p. 64.

66. *Summa Contra Gentiles,* trans. Charles O'Neil, Book IV, chapter 54 (Notre Dame: University of Notre Dame Press, 1975), pp. 228–233.

67. Or should I say "male" nature for, alas, Thomas incorporated Aristotle's flawed biology that held that women were somewhat wanting in the rational capacity that each locates as the apogee of humanness. Women are certainly human, but something is wanting in their makeup that ill suits them to the full unfolding of the telos associated with earthly dominion. The way in which Thomas twists himself into a pretzel in order to stay square with Aristotle and faithful to the Christian understanding of God's good creation is rather painful, but he winds up with the wholly unsatisfactory conclusion that in her human nature woman is equal to man but with "respect to her particular nature woman is somewhat deficient and is begotten." It is too bad that the power and emerging mystique of Aristotle stopped Thomas from just ignoring or arguing against Aristotle's flawed biology as it makes its way into his politics. See *Summa Theologia*, I.92, "The Creation of Woman" (Benzinger Brothers, 1947). See also my discussion of Thomas in *Public Man, Private Woman: Women in Social and Political Thought*, 2nd edition, pp. 74–80.

68. From "On Kingship or the Governance of Rulers: *De Regimine Principum,* chapter 1, p. 15, in Paul E. Sigmund, ed., *St. Thomas Aquinas on Politics and Ethics* (New York: W.W. Norton and Company, 1988).

69. *Ibid.,* p. 15.

70. *Ibid.,* p. 16. As early as the ninth century, arguments had been proffered on the need to check unjust and tyrannical abuse of authority—here Isidore of Seville (560–636) is a key figure. Marie Regina Madden, *Political Theory and Law in Medieval Spain* (New York: Fordham University Press, 1930). According

to the Carlyles, the "theory of the ninth century recognized . . . the necessity of checking the unjust and tyrannical use of authority." The King should be bound by positive law, itself in conformity with higher law. See the Carlyles' *History of Medieval Political Thought*, Vol. 1, p. 292.

71. *Ibid.*, p. 45. There is no need at this juncture to rehearse each aspect of the law within Thomas's system. There are four distinctive levels of law: eternal law which is not subject to the vagaries of time but refers to the rational ordering of everything by God; natural law, in which all sentient creatures participate; human law, or that particular articulation arrived at by reason; finally, divine law that orders us to eternal bliss. Importantly, God alone is the judge of human hearts.

72. *Ibid.*, p. 47

73. *Ibid.*, pp. 62–63.

74. Here I draw upon Oakley's analysis of St. Jerome's famous discussion of the "sad case of the fallen virgin," in "St. Jerome and the Sad Case of the Fallen Virgin," chapter 2 of *Omnipotence, Covenant, and Order: An Excursion in the History of Ideas from Abelard to Leibniz* (Ithaca, N.Y.: Cornell University Press, 1984), pp. 41–65.

75. The controversy surrounding Pope Benedict XVI's Regensburg Lecture calling for reasoned debate and religious freedom, delivered September 18, 2006, resurrects all these issues. Benedict ties God to Logos and to reason and scores a voluntarism, a radical monism, that winds up justifying violence in the name of God. We must rediscover reason, Logos, Benedict insists. This means there are, indeed, limits to God's freedom. God cannot contradict Himself; God is not arbitrary, univocal will. For God is bound by His own truths. Obedience to God flows from love and discernment, not abjection. See Pope Benedict XVI, "Faith, Reason, and the University," www.vatican.va/holy-father/benedict-XVI/speeches/2006/september/documents/hf-ben-xvi-spe–20060912-university-regensburg-an.html.

76. *Ibid.*, citing Jerome, p. 43.

77. Thomas had considered both of these dimensions of God's power without separating them. Given that God is the apogee of reason and truth, it follows that his power will not be put to unjust (irrational) ends. Increasingly, a wedge was driven between the understandings of God's power.

78. See Michael Gillespie, "Where have all the sins gone?" (typescript) and "Slouching Toward Bethlehem to Be Born: On the Nature and Meaning of Nietzsche's Superman," *Journal of Nietzsche Studies* (30: Autumn 2005), pp. 46–69.

79. Francis Oakley, *Politics and Eternity: Studies in the History of Medieval and Early-Modern Political Thought* (Leiden: Brill, 1999), pp. 43–44.

80. *Ibid.*, p. 44.

81. D'Entreves, *Medieval Contributions to Political Thought*, pp. 38–39.

82. The king's power and authority derive from two broad sources: from below, what Walter Ullmann calls the "ascending theory," with originary power located in the *populus Romanus*, then transferred to subjects of the medieval emperor. There was by contrast a "descending theory"; namely, the insistence that a king governed legitimately because originary power is located in a superior being, God himself, via delegation. If there is no power but of God, as St. Paul proclaimed, then one could speak only of delegated power. Ullmann's argument is that these contrasting theories were in conflict throughout the Middle Ages. If he is correct, the descending versus ascending theories of power and legitimacy form but one such clash as the battle over God's ordained and absolute power is another, distinct yet related. See Walter Ullmann, *A History of Political Thought in the Middle Ages* (Baltimore, Md.: Penguin Books, 1965).

83. See William J. Courtenay, *Capacity and Volition: A History of the Distinction of Absolute and Ordained Power* (Bergamo: Pierluigi Lubrina Editore, 1990), p. 11.

84. *Ibid.*, pp. 13–14, 88, 92. Thomas had to deal with the distinction between ordained and absolute power, although they did not fit neatly into his vision of a rational created order, including the close fit he discerned between the created order and divine nature.

85. Ewart Lewis, "King Above Law? 'Quad Principi Placuit' in Bracton," in *Speculum XXXVIII* (No. 2, 1963), pp. 240–269. God's representative, so to speak, can do nothing except in accordance with the law. He is not to act in an arbitrary manner. Interestingly, it is the king's relationship to God—the descending theory of power and authority—that securely "bridles" the king in this account.

86. *Ibid.*, p. 268. Lewis suggests that missing from Bracton's thought is recognition of "some degree of discretionary decision or choice, an act of *arbitrium* which is in fact an act of law-determining power."

87. Bracton's dates are 1199–1268.

88. Lewis, "King Above Law?" p. 241.

89. *Ibid.*, p. 242. Justinian had claimed that the *lex regia* gave the prince absolute freedom of legislation. Bracton sees a restriction by appeal to different texts in Roman law, according to Lewis.

90. Boniface VIII held the Petrine chair from 1293–1202.

91. Morrall, *Political Thought in Medieval Times*, p. 66.

92. His dates are 1242–1254.

93. Lewis, "King Above Law?" p. 240.

94. Others who have turned to the Roman law of primitive property as genealogical backdrop to concepts of state sovereignty include international relations scholars John Gerard Ruggie, *Constructing the World Polity* (London: Routledge,

1998); Friedrich Kratochwill, "Sovereignty as dominium: Is there a right to humanitarian intervention?" in Gene M. Lyons and Michael Mastenduno, eds., *Beyond Westphalia? State Sovereignty and International Intervention* (Baltimore, Md.: Johns Hopkins University Press, 1995). I first explored this theme some years ago—although neither of the authors cited seems aware of this fact—probably for the simple reason that international relations theorists and political theorists, of whom I am one, often do not "talk" to one another, so to speak. This book, indeed everything I write, attempts to bridge that distance.

95. Charles Howard McIlwain, *The Growth of Political Thought in the West* (New York: MacMillan, 1932), p. 98. McIlwain notes that there were strenuous dissenters to this view even as others strenuously put it forward. For our purposes the singularity is important. Implications of the notion of "supreme" pop out all over the place; indeed, the *OED* offers "a husband in relation to his wife" as one meaning of sovereignty, although they delicately declare this usage obsolete. This dimension will reappear below, but I want to plant the flag for future references.

96. D'Entreves, *Medieval Contributions to Political Thought*, p. 39.

97. Thus Figgis asserts that canonists meant by *plenitudo potestatis* everything that moderns mean by sovereignty. See John Figgis, *From Gerson to Grotius, 1414–1625* (New York: Harper, 1960, 1907), pp. 44–45. Figgis seems to me only partially correct for the proclamation requires a coercive and enforcement dimension that popes lacked, for the most part. For an alternative approach, see Francis Oakley, *Council over Pope: Towards a Provisional Ecclesiology* (New York: Herder and Herder, 1969).

98. Duns Scotus (1265–1308); William of Ockham (1285– or 1287–1349).

99. Morrall claims that the term *sovereignty* was coined by French legists in the thirteenth century. Many there were who talked about the "thing" before sovereignty cast as voluntaristic and supreme became the coin of the conceptual realm.

100. The rational theology of St. Thomas gives way to a stress on revelation, for only revelation tells us what we need to know. Revelation need not be definitive, because God could change his mind, although the odds are strong that he will not.

101. Political theorist Michael Gillespie offers the strong version of the thesis in his book *Nihilism before Nietzsche* (Chicago: University of Chicago Press, 1995), an expert unpacking of a nihilistic strain in Western thought that he traces from nominalism.

102. My argument is located in-between the strong and weak statements of the thesis.

103. Drawing upon Scotus *Ordinataio* 1, 44, Vol. VI, 363–369 and *Opera Omnia*, Vol. 17 (Vatican, 1966), pp. 535–536 and 254–256.

104. *Ibid.*, p. 118.

105. William of Ockham, *Quodlibeta Septem*, trans. Alfred J. Freddoso and Francis E. Kelly (New Haven: Yale University Press, 1991), 6:1, 4 and 4:25.

106. It should be noted that Marilyn Adams has labored to undermine strong conceptions of Ockham's voluntarism in her two-volume work on Ockham (*William Ockham,* Notre Dame: University of Notre Dame Press, 1987) and in a number of articles. She denies that he abolished natural law, was a moral skeptic, or was a moral subjectivist.

107. This is a point that Gillespie develops to good effect in his essay "Where have all the sins gone?" The human-divine gap was bridged continually through the intercession of the Mediator (the second person of the Trinity), and through grace.

108. Gilson more or less summarizes Ockham in this fashion. Whether it is precisely fair to Ockham seems to me less important, at this point, than what was subsequently made of Ockham and Ockhamism. See Etienne Gilson, T*he Unity of Philosophical Experience* (London: Sheed & Ward, 1938), Chapter III, "The Road to Skepticism."

109. Oakley, *Omnipotence, Covenant and Order*, p. 61.

110. *Ibid.,* p. 63.

CHAPTER 2

1. Another issue at stake here is the fact that those who prefer their philosophies neat, unsmudged by historic realities, shy away from the issues I take up here, as they are so intricate and complex that they *require* a historic dimension to the analysis.

2. Joseph Cardinal Ratzinger, *Introduction to Christianity* (San Francisco: Ignatius Books, 2004), pp. 92–93. See also Jaroslav Pelikan, *The Christian Tradition: A History of the Development of Doctrine* (Chicago: University of Chicago Press, 1971). Pope Benedict XVI points out that faith and "mere philosophy," philosophy construed as a "process of purely private search for the truth," hence essentially individualistic, the work of solitary individuals, are wide apart. Faith is "first of all a call to community . . . an essentially social one." The church is not so much a system of knowledge as "a way."

3. So much so that Brian Tierney entitles his collection of medieval documents on *regnum* and *sacerdotium, The Crisis of Church and State: 1050–1300* (Toronto: University of Toronto Press, 1988).

4. When Dan Maloney was doing research work for me, he helped to formulate these issues, and my dialogue with him was fruitful.

5. This in the words of a twentieth-century Calvinist, following closely a notion of God's absolutism. Reverend John Murray, "A Biblical Theological Study," in Jacob T. Hoogstra, ed. *The Sovereignty of God, or the Proceedings of the First American Calvinistic Conference* (Grand Rapids, Mich.: Zondervan, 1999), pp. 25–44.

6. Carl Schmitt, *Political Theology: Four Chapters on the Concept of Sovereignty*, trans. George Schwab (Cambridge, Mass.: MIT Press, 1985), p. 56. In my book, *Women and War* (New York: Basic Books, 1987), I note the "Protestant Nation State," for it is with the breakup of medieval Christendom and the reemergence and triumph of Roman private law of *patria potestas* as the tool of centralizing monarchies, that the architecture of the modern nation-state really solidifies. In this and succeeding chapters I make good on the claim I made in an underdeveloped way—for my focus was on something else—in this previous work.

7. It is these terms and notions that blossom fully with the creation of universities in Padua and Bologna, where law faculties labored overtime and not always in favor of a papal plenitude of power but, rather, on behalf of the autonomy of earthly power.

8. Leo's dates in the papacy are 440–461.

9. The papacy took a distinctively legal turn with the insistence that what issued from the papal office had the stamp of legitimacy and law. The pope, as the holder of the Petrine office, continued Leo, possesses a plenitude of power. That plenitude of power is concerned with government and government's law. The pope can neither be judged nor deposed by any earthly authority. In medieval papal usage, the concept of sovereign is not attached to a territory but to God and to an office—that of the papacy. (If one accepts that papal *plenitudo potestatis* constitutes de facto a vision of sovereign authority.)

10. We would now say "church and state" but this is misleading in the medieval context as the state in its modern form did not exist and "Church" was a far more comprehensive thing—in a sense coterminous with a way of life—in a way that is deeper and wider than anything we conjure with nowadays, faith having been shoved to the margins or edges of earthly existence for us moderns.

11. I owe this point to Dan Maloney who claims as support Aquinas, Duns Scotus, and Anselm on justice and God's will. See *The Mirror of Justice: A Plea for Mercy in Contemporary Liberal Theory*, Ph.D. thesis (University of Notre Dame, 2004), pp. 226–237. On the willing self, see the chapters on the sovereign self below. St. Anselm's dates are 1033–1109.

12. See excerpts in Tierney, *Church and State*, p.102.

13. The American constitution has its own version of "the exception"—not in the form that the executive is ever above the law but that, in certain emergency situations, he may temporarily suspend the law, a question taken up below. See the *U.S. Constitution*, Article II, Section 3; Abraham Lincoln, "Suspend Writ of Habeas Corpus" *Letter to General Winfield Scott*, April 27, 1861 in *Collected Works*, Vol. 4 (New Brunswick: Rutgers University Press, 1953), p. 55.

14. Tierney, *Church and State*, pp. 116–117.

15. *Ibid.*, p. 122, citing a Commentary on Gratian. The emperor may hold his power by election, but a pope could as a "last resort" depose the emperor by the will and consent of the princes.

16. *Ibid.*, p. 123.

17. For excerpts from Innocent documents see Tierney, *Church and State*, pp. 131–138.

18. Oakley, *Omnipotence, Covenant and Order* (Ithaca, N.Y.: Cornell University Press, 1984), p. 43.

19. J. K. Rowling, *Harry Potter and the Prisoner of Azkaban* (New York: Scholastic Press, 1999), p. 331. Footnote supplied by my grandson, Bobby Bethke. Thanks to Bobby for his assistance.

20. *Ibid.*, p. 44. The quotes within the quote are from Arthur O. Lovejoy's classic work, *The Great Chain of Being*.

21. This remains a controversial claim as a battle rages between, for example, those who credit or blame Ockham for stressing a voluntarist and arbitrary God and those who see him as very much in line with orthodox Christian doctrine, meaning Thomism. The full story of medieval nominalism is dauntingly complex. What had once been dominant Scholastic Aristotelianism—is condemned as having given too much weight to reason. Only revelation tells us about what God wills, but God might change his mind. A host of influences and thinkers are at work. If this book was about medieval nominalism versus medieval realism, one would have to take up Abelard, Duns Scotus, and Ockham in depth. This is much beyond the purpose and scope of the chapter.

22. Oakley, *Omnipotence, Covenant and Order*, p. 47.

23. Oakley has some typically rich things to say about this, e.g., *Ibid.*, p. 50.

24. Michael Allen Gillespie is a notable exception to the insouciance of academic political theorists to these concerns. I want to acknowledge here his generosity in sharing with me the preliminary fruits of his own labor in the vineyard I am trampling through. This work follows upon his brilliant treatment of Western nihilism, *Nihilism before Nietzsche* (Chicago: University of Chicago Press, 1995).

25. It isn't vital for my purposes to wade into the controversy between those like Marilyn Adams, arguably the leading interpreter of Ockham in current scholarship, who reject the notion that Ockham's view of divine sovereignty is significantly different from orthodox Thomism and those, by contrast, who maintain what had been a standard interpretation, that Ockham is indeed the originator of absolute sovereignty.

26. William of Ockham, *A Short Discourse on Tyrannical Government*, ed. Arthur Stephen McGrade (Cambridge: Cambridge University Press, 2001), p. xxix from the editor's Introduction. See also Ockham's "Eight Questions on the Powers of the Pope," in Arthur Stephen McGrade, ed.,

William of Ockham, *A Letter to the Friars Minor and Other Writings*
(Cambridge: Cambridge University Press, 1995); and the discussion by Joan
and Oliver O'Donovan in their reader, *From Irenaeus to Grotius: A Sourcebook
in Christian Political Thought* (Grand Rapids, Mich.: Eerdmans Publishing,
1999). The Ockham material is located on pp. 453–475. Also pertinent is the
inordinately dense and difficult Heiko Augustinus Oberman, *The Harvest of
Medieval Theology: Gabriel Biel and Late Medieval Nominalism* (Grand
Rapids, Mich.: Eerdmans Publishing Co., 1967). Additional items of import
include Alan Wolter, OFM, "Ockham and the Testbooks," *Inquiries into Medieval Philosophy: A Collection in Honor of Francis P. Clarke* (Westport,
Conn.: Greenwood Press, 1971); Marilyn McCord Adams, *William Ockham*,
Volume 2 (Notre Dame: University of Notre Dame Press, 1987). A top scholar
of medieval political thought, Gordon Leff, believed originally that Ockham
embodied the beginning of the end for the grand medieval synthesis; he then
changed his mind. Some supported this move; others lamented it. For example, Alister McGrath, "Forerunners of the Reformation?A Critical Examination of the Evidence for Precursors of the Reformation Doctrines of
Justification," *Harvard Theological Review* 75 (1982) pp. 219–242; "The
Righteousness of God" from Augustine to Luther, *Studia Theologica* 36
(1982), pp. 63–78; "Homo Assumptus?A Study in the Christology of the Via
Moderna, with Particular Reference to William of Ockham," *Ephemerides The-
ologicae Lovanienses* 60 (1984), pp. 283–297; and "The Transition to Modernity, 1400–1750," in J. L. Houlden and Peter Byrne, *Encyclopaedia of
Theology* (London: Routledge, 1995), sees the (so-called) *via moderna*, the
broad intellectual movement of which nominalism is a philosophic component, as playing a significant role in deconstructing the structure I describe
above. Finally, John Bossey, *Christianity in the West: 1400–1700* (Oxford:
Oxford University Press, 1985), insists that, yes, Ockham is in part responsible for a major shift as morality becomes the carrying-out of God's commands
rather than a fight against the seven deadly sins and for the virtues.

27. *Ibid.*, p.17. In an extended footnote the editor points out that thirteenth-
and fourteenth-century popes who proclaimed a "fullness of power" insisted
that the pope could intervene in secular matters ("regarding the work of secular
government as something done by the pope through secondary causes"), thus,
e.g., Innocent III. "On this view secular government is part of a single system of
which the pope is the head on earth" (p.18).

28. *Ibid.*, p. 21.

29. *Ibid.*, p. 23. "Not only does the gospel law not make Christians the pope's
slaves, but neither could the pope by fullness of power impose on any Christian,
against his will, without his fault and without reason, a burden of ceremonies as

great as that of the Old Law" (p. 25). Ockham worked with Marsilius of Padua in mounting arguments against papal supremacy.

30. *Ibid*, p. 29. Spouses do not enjoy any such fullness of power over one another either, including the husband in relation to the wife.

31. *Ibid.*, p. 56.

32. Gyula Klima's paper "Natural Necessity and Eucharistic Theology in the Late 13th Century" is instructive. It can be found ·at: http://www.fordham.edu/gsas/phil/klima/EUCHARIST.HTM. As a nominalist, Ockham broke things down where the medieval realists, like Thomas, found complex unities. A unity in medieval thought did not mean an organic, indistinguishable whole. Medieval notions of unity are quite different from organicism, for the common good—at which rule aimed—is comprised of overlapping and mutually constitutive parts.

33. See Oberman, *The Harvest of Medieval Theology: Gabriel Biel and Late Medieval Nominalism* (Grand Rapids, Mich.: Eerdmans Publishing Co., 1967), p. 46.

34. Etienne Gilson, *The Unity of Philosophical Experience* (London: Sheed and Ward, 1938), chapter II, pp. 84–87.

35. William Courtenay argues that by 1320 or thereabouts, theologians are maintaining that God the Father has a form of absolute sovereign power that is beyond the power of either Son or Holy Spirit. William J. Courtenay, *Capacity and Volition: A History of the Distinction of Absolute and Ordained Power* (Bergamo, Italy: Pierluigi Lubrina Editore, 1990), p. 118. Here it is important to remember that the distinction itself comes into routine use in the twelfth century and essentially means that God could have done things otherwise.

36. *Ibid.*, p. 94.

37. See *Ibid.*, p. 120.

38. Harry Klocker, S. J., *William of Ockham and the Divine Freedom* (Milwaukee: Marquette University Press, 1992), p. 9. Heiko Augustinus Oberman, *The Dawn of the Reformation: Essays in Late Medieval and Early Reformation Thought* (Edinburgh: T & T Clark Ltd., 1986), pp. 6–8. Marilyn McCord Adams, *William of Ockham* (Notre Dame: University of Notre Dame Press, 1987).

39. Here Ockham was a transitional figure insofar as he never freed himself "from the deeply ingrained medieval view that government was exercised for the people and not by the people." See Michael Wilks, *The Problem of Sovereignty in the Later Middles Ages: The Papal Monarchy with Augustinus Triumphus and the Publicists* (Cambridge: Cambridge University Press, 1964), p. 108.

40. Perhaps an experience I have had many times in graduate seminars will clarify. Students read Thomas Hobbes's great work, *Leviathan*. We discuss the theological backdrop. Inevitably, a student voices the view that Hobbes by no means abandons natural law; indeed, he references it repeatedly. Hobbes is an

unusually canny and, at times, deceptive writer. Even as he rather casually rearranges Scripture to suit his purposes, he also turns natural law into a *lex naturalis*, a law of nature, by no means the same thing as classical natural law. *Lex naturalis* signifies that which cannot be helped, a preemptory urgency—by no means identical to the natural law we reach through the light of reason.

41. Oakley, for example, makes this point repeatedly.

42. Paul E. Sigmund suggests something similar in his introduction to the comments of Ockham on "natural law" in *Natural Law in Political Thought* (Cambridge, Mass.: Winthrop Publishing, 1971), p. 57.

43. Oakley, *Omnipotence, Covenant and Order*, p. 81.

44. The thinker is one Ralph Cudworth, a Cambridge Platonist, as cited in Oakley, *Ibid.*, p. 86.

45. Perry Anderson, *Lineages of the Absolutist State* (London: NLB, 1974), pp. 20, 23, 26.

46. See John Gerard Ruggie, "Continuity and Transformation in the World Polity," in Robert Keohane, ed., *Neorealism and Its Critics* (New York: Columbia University Press, 1986), pp. 131–157, especially p. 144.

47. Cited in Antony Black, *Monarchy and Community: Political Ideas in the Later Conciliar Controversy, 1430–1450* (Cambridge: Cambridge University Press, 1970), p. 74. See also Walter Ullmann, "The Development of the Medieval Idea of Sovereignty," *English Historical Review*, No. 250 (1949), pp. 1–33.

48. Also, of course, rich with implications for relations between men and women insofar as these partake of notions of headship and a right to govern.

49. *Ibid.*, pp. 80–81.

50. Gregory's dates are 1073–1085.

51. Charles Howard McIlwain, *The Growth of Political Thought in the West* (New York: MacMillan, 1932), pp. 223–225.

52. Thanks to Dan Maloney for this pithy way of putting the struggle.

53. Historians of Western political thought trace the elements of "the modern legalistic conception of sovereignty" all the way back to Cicero, contending that the elements are present "in their entirety . . . and for the first time." See McIlwain, *Ibid.*, p. 135. Although McIlwain concedes that this might be correct in that no philosopher before him had exactly defined it as he did.

54. See Antony Black, *Monarchy and Community: Political Ideas in the Late Conciliar Controversy, 1430–1450*, p. 33.

55. Black, *Ibid.*, p. 68.

56. See William Galston, *Liberal Purposes* (Cambridge: Cambridge University Press, 1991), pp. 257–298.

57. Morrall, *Political Thought in Medieval Times*, p. 61.

58. The literature on this is so vast that it fairly boggles the mind. In addition to the multivolume Carlyles, Morrall, Ullman, Leff—the standards—Tierney,

Oakley, and D'Entreves proved helpful when I was a student of these developments and remain helpful to anyone doing something as "old-fashioned" as a kind of history of ideas. More recent works—to the extent these political and legal matters are central at all—can appear to be reinventing the wheel as so much of the heavy lifting done by earlier generations of medieval scholars is scanted or ignored.

59. Pope Boniface VIII, "The Superiority of the Spiritual Authority," 1302, *The Portable Medieval Reader*, pp. 233–236, p. 234. (DS 873). Also Heinrich Denzinger, *Enchiridion Symbolorum* (Freiburg, Germany: Herder, 1963).

60. Wilks, *The Problem of Sovereignty*, p. 286.

61. Walter Ullmann, *A History of Political Thought in the Middle Ages* (Baltimore: Penguin Books, 1965), is good on this theme, displaying the way that mature papal power "laid particular stress upon the law." The "cluster of ideas" construing the ruler as *lex animata*, or living law, relies on what Ullmann calls "the descending theory of government" within which the "will of the prince" is the material ingredient of the law. Machiavelli has his own version of this theme, as I will show in chapter 3.

62. Gregory, also known as Hildebrand, was born sometime between 1020 and 1025 and died in 1085. Henry was born in 1050 and died in 1108.

63. Document in Tierney, *Church and State*, letter of Henry to Gregory refusing to recognize him as pope (1076), trans. T. E. Mommsen and K. F. Morrison, *Imperial Lives and Letters of the Eleventh Century* (New York: Columbia University Press, 1962), pp. 150–151, in Tierney's reader, pp. 59–60.

64. *Ibid.*, trans. E. Emerton, *Correspondence* (February 1076), pp. 90–91; in Tierney, pp. 60–61.

65. Although this is *not* what later became an absolutist doctrine of divine right.

66. *Ibid.*, Letter of Henry to German Bishops, trans. Mommsen and Morrison, *op. cit.* pp. 152–154; in Tierney, pp. 61–62; trans. from p. 62.

67. Tierney offers a clear version of events.

68. His dates are 1155–1190.

69. Whether the people retained any residual power to revoke this grant to the ruler is the very point that bursts open into constitutional struggles. The *lex regia* held that the grant was good for all time. The alternative affords a framework for what became theories of representation.

70. This is the coronation oath required of English kings: "In the name of Christ I promise these three things to the Christian people subject to me. In the first place, I will devote my rule and power to all men in order that all Christian people and the Church of God may serve the true peace according to our common for all times;

again, I forbid all rapacity and injustice to all classes of men; thirdly, I command that there be mercy and fairness in all judgments, so that a compassionate and clement God may grant His mercy to me and to you." Coronation Oath of King Henry I, 1110, pp. 76–77.

71. John Gillingham, *The Middle Ages: A Royal History of England* (Berkeley: University of California Press, 2000), pp. 42–50. Michael Staunton, *The Lives of Thomas Becket* (Manchester: Manchester University Press, 2001). See also Jean Anouilh, *Becket: ou l'honneur de Dieu* (Paris: Table Ronde, 1959) and the movie based on the play, *Becket* (1964).

72. Innocent III's dates are 1198–1216.

73. See Ullmann, *History of Political Thought,* pp. 103–105, 114. Innocent IV's dates are 1245–1254.

74. On this theme the *locus classicus* is, of course, Ernst H. Kantorowicz's enduring text, *The King's Two Bodies: A Study in Medieval Political Theology* (Princeton, N.J.: Princeton University Press, 1957).

75. In *Women and War*, I track modern formulations of the will in politics from Machiavelli and the French Revolution and these considerations will be pursued in detail.

76. R. W. Carlyle and A. J. Carlyle, *A History of Medieval Political Theory in the West: Vol. IV, The Theories of the Relation of the Empire and the Papacy from the Tenth Century to the Twelfth* (Edinburgh and London: Wm. Blackwood and Sons, 1928), p. 389. R. W. Carlyle died before this volume was completed, and A. J. Carlyle dedicates it to his brother. As to the options noted above, Carlyle argues that the first was generally admitted; that is, the spiritual authority was presumed to possess a superior dignity; the second presents a much more difficult question. All authority was subject to the laws of God and natural law, ecclesiastical or secular, and if either ran contrary to such law, it was null and void. This position we find difficult to assess because our own conception of sovereignty is of a unity, a final world. As to the third option, it insists that spiritual authority is superior not only in spiritual but in temporal affairs (p. 390).

77. Making of Ockham a moderate "Ockhamist" or nominalist.

78. Carlyle and Carlyle, *A History of Medieval Political Theory in the West: Vol .VI, Political Theory from 1300–1600* (Edinburgh and London: Wm. Blackwell and Sons, 1936). This is a point made throughout by the Carlyles. The notion that power is at its heart arbitrary is a radical departure from the norm.

79. In a moment of political incorrectness that would set off howls nowadays, the Carlyles call this notion one "substantially alien to Western thought," some sort of "orientalism" to be carefully distinguished from the "conception of St. Paul, that political authority is derived from God, because it exists for the maintenance

of justice." Of course, this way of putting it is no longer "politically correct" but the point is well taken (p. 292).

80. Jean Bodin, *Six Books of the Commonwealth*, trans. M. A. Tooley (Oxford: Basic Blackwell, 1956), is the key text here. Bodin's dates are 1530–1596.

81. I do not mean to suggest that Bodin commits the heresy of equating the king to the incarnate savior but, rather, that the king is a direct emanation of God's design, if you will. There really *is*, for Bodin, that "divinity that doth hedge a king."

82. This is the standard reading of Bodin and hard, indeed, to miss. The Carlyles' *Vol. VI* covers Bodin. But they do not emphasize the points I take up above. The "triumph" of the will in politics is suffused with profound and troubling gender implications just as it is rife with troubling political and ethical implications.

83. Bodin's isn't a full-blown patriarchal theory as he backs off proclaiming that the family is in its essence a political as well as a natural entity. He does not equate the patriarchalism of the sovereign father-king with the "natural" patriarchy of the private lordly father. See Elshtain, *Public Man, Private Woman: Women in Social and Political Thought* (Princeton: Princeton University Press, 1981), pp. 101–102.

Chapter 3

1. Jean Bodin's dates are 1530–1596.

2. Although I cannot belabor this point without detracting from the main line of argument, it should be noted that Bodin was deeply involved in theological disputes. His most popular works were on witches and witchcraft (*On the Demon-Mania of Witches*). It is the prince who controls and punishes both traitors and witches and Bodin articulates a panoply of punishments at the sovereign's disposal. Too, Bodin turns to Old Testament accounts of rule to make the point that there is a kind of "positive" legitimacy for states not reducible to the Fall. Law as the command of the sovereign is the distinguishing mark of what we call sovereign.

3. And if you tell it differently, noting the good things that were lost to, or muted by, early modern political life, you are suspected of theocentric nostalgia, or some other dreadful malady—no doubt catching.

4. See my *Public Man, Private Woman: Women in Social and Political Thought* (Princeton, N.J.: Princeton University Press, 1981); *Women and War* (New York: Basic Books, 1987); and *Meditations on Modern Political Thought* (University Park, Penn.: Penn State University Press, 1986. Published originally by Praeger, 1982). In an interesting way, however, this latter story, in most feminist narratives, follows the familiar telos of progress—although there were some, myself among them, who argued that this could not account for the complexity of male-female relations, let alone states and politics and what remained of *sacerdotium*.

5. The questions that required answers included what could be shared with non-Christians by contrast to what was distinctively non-Christian. Robert Markus sketches a distinctively Augustinian approach: "From the beginning, Augustine's objective was to define a civil community in a way that would enable Christians to give full weight to its claims on them, no less than on pagan citizens and functionaries, while at the same time deflecting the more grandiose, quasi-divine claims made for it, either by pagans or Christians." See his *Christianity and the Secular,* p. 39.

6. On this see the discussion in Volume I of the Carlyles' multivolume *History of Medieval Political Thought in the West, passim.* There are too many other sources to list. Collections of papal documents are particularly helpful if one is eager to go through the original source material. Also see Walter Ullmann, *Jurisprudence in the Middle Ages* (London: Variorum Reprints, 1980); Lester L. Field, *Liberty, Dominion, and the Two Swords: on the Origins of Western Political Theology (180–398)* (Notre Dame: University of Notre Dame Press, 1998); Mathews Shailer, *Select Medieval Documents and Other Material Illustrating the History of the Church and Empire* (New York: Silver, Burdett, 1900); Matthew Innes, *State and Society in the Early Middle Ages* (Cambridge: Cambridge University Press, 2000). When I was a student of medieval history, the joke about the Holy Roman Empire was that it was neither holy, nor Roman, nor an empire.

7. Michael Wilks, *The Problem of Sovereignty in the Late Middle Ages* (Cambridge: Cambridge University Press, 1964), p. 169.

8. *Ibid.,* p. 219.

9. Sadly, the author of these stirring words, James Marshall, in his *Swords and Symbols: The Technique of Sovereignty* (New York: Funk and Wagnalls, 1969, rev. ed.), goes on to to insist that this view of unity is far superior to "Hitler's Corporative State," p. 144. Marshall asks the reader to compare Augustine's *City of God* to Hitler's *Mein Kampf,* the one noble and far more expansive than the other, which is puny by comparison. To be sure, the papal theory does possess a nobility Hitler lacks, to put it mildly, but it seems to me obscene to put these into any kind of series—there are differences of kind here, not merely, or only, degree.

10. *Ibid.,* p. 287.

11. Innocent III's dates are 1160–1216.

12. At the end of the thirteenth century, Pope Boniface VII in *Unam Sanctam* waxes eloquent on medieval power even as, de facto, it is on the wane. See Leff, *History of Political Thought in the Middle Ages,* pp. 106–113.

13. *Ibid.,* p .74.

14. Jeremy Bentham, *The Principles of Morals and Legislation* (New York: Hefner Publishing Co., 1965), p. 74.

15. Tierney, *Monarch and Community*, p. 84.

16. Wilks, p. 275.

17. If memory serves, this is a phrase from Abraham Lincoln.

18. Indeed, Ringo describes a young man on crutches, at the front of a Beatles concert, moving maniacally. Hampered by his crutches, he threw them off—only to fall flat on his face. See *Beatles Anthology*, Vol. 3, interview with Ringo Starr, a.k.a Richard Starkey.

19. A problem here is that it is but a short distance from the "prince" or mind as animating the whole to the prince as subjecting the whole to his sovereign will.

20. Kantorowicz, *The King's Two Bodies*, p. 48. It is this king who is both temporal, and "subjected, like any ordinary human being, to the effects of time. In other respects . . . he was unaffected by Time . . . he was beyond Time and therewith perpetual or sempiternal" (p. 171).

21. Roger D. Masters, *Machiavelli, Leonardo, and the Science of Power* (Notre Dame: University of Notre Dame Press, 1996), pp. 64–67. We will see the theme that the will of the ruler animates the body politic in Machiavelli, although this theme is ignored by political theorists who have tagged Machiavelli the father of "the scientific study of politics." The prince animating a "body" doesn't sound terribly "scientific" in our current lingo.

22. Black, *Monarch and Community* (Cambridge: Cambridge University Press, 1970), p. 4.

23. See Kantorowicz, *The King's Two Bodies* (Princeton: Princeton University Press, 1957), p. 311. Black, too, argues that the notion of an undying crown or office is the predecessor of the modern notions of the state (p. 134).

24. Jean de Joinville, "A Saintly King," in the *Portable Medieval Reader* (New York: Viking Press, 1960), pp. 367–378.

25. *Ibid.*, p. 372. Louis's dates are 1214–1270.

26. *Ibid.*, pp. 362–368. Frederick, who liked to call himself "Stupor Mundi," or "wonder of the world," lived in 1194–1250.

27. *Ibid.*, p. 368.

28. The "mirror of princes" genre persists so long as rule has an intensely personalistic quality. As we shall see, Niccolo Machiavelli, to whom the invention of the "scientific study of politics" is attributed routinely, contributes to "mirror of princes" literature—although he inverts the mirror and preaches concerning what the prince *should* do, what medieval writers insist the prince must eschew. In this way as in so many others, Machiavelli is not a radical innovator so much as one working in a tradition he upends yet contributes to.

29. Robert Grant, Introduction to Richard the Second, in *The Complete Works of William Shakespeare* (London: Collins, 1951), pp. 478–479.

30. His dates are 1566–1625.

31. *King Henry V* in *The Complete Works*, p. 594.

32. *Ibid.*, p. 611. Henry discourses on the King's burdens in act 4, scene 1, p. 613.

33. *Ibid.*

34. *Ibid.,* p. 1086.

35. *Ibid.,* p. 1089. The juicy film *The Madness of King George III* pursues the theme of kingly nuttiness in a cunning and sympathetic way.

36. Critics averred that monarchical divinization marked a foreign graft onto the sturdy stem of classical medieval thought. This view smacks of an innocent West corrupted by an alien set of notions and practices. See W. W. Tarn, *Alexander the Great,* Volume II (Cambridge: Cambridge University Press, 1948), pp. 360–370. If you wanted to, you could trace it back to Alexander the Great's campaign into the Persian empire as Alexander grows more "foreign" to his troops in his assumption of a divinized identity they associate with the Persian empire and find "un-Greek."

37. The way the scenario is played out represents order on one side and chaos on the other. To sustain order, one requires absolute rule. This sort of starkness isn't anything new. All one need do is to recall Plato's alternatives in *The Republic,* trans. Allan Bloom (New York: Basic Books, 1968). Mapping his quest for unity and singularity of truth onto political arrangements in his ideal city, Plato cries, "Have we any greater evil for a city than what splits it and makes it many instead of one? Or a greater good than what binds it together and makes it one?" (Book V, 461e–462d) Why this tendency to traffic in opposites I cannot say, but I suspect it has something to do with bringing order to what the first Gifford lecturer, William James, called the "bloomin' buzzin' confusion."

38. It should go without saying at this point that the king is under God, who is, after all, the divine lawgiver.

39. See, for example, the Carlyles' *History of Medieval Political Thought,* Volume III, p. 41.

40. *Ibid.,* p. 45. The Carlyles go so far as to say that the "new" theory would have been entirely unintelligible to medievals. In contemporary America, we have our own version of this formulation in sparring between the Congress and the Supreme Court over who has final say on a whole range of controversial issues. For the medievals law is not a command "imposed by a superior, but rather represents the adaptation of the permanent and immutable principles of 'nature' and justice to the needs of a communithy, under the terms of the circumstances and traditions of that community." See A. J. Carlyle, *The Political Theory of the Roman Lawyers and Canonists,* Vol. II (Edinburgh and London: Blackwood and Sons, 1950), p. 97. Certain moral precepts like "Thou shalt not kill"—a far better translation and one that would have done considerably less mischief is "Thou shalt not murder"—would be one example of a moral precept good for all time and all peoples. There are, of course, other positive laws that pertain to a particular time and a particular people, but none should stand contrary to the natural or divine law. There are laws of custom as well as nature.

41. John B. Morrall, *Political Thought in Medieval Times*, articulates this explicitly, p. 68.

42. Remember, the tyrant might even be slain in John of Salisbury's view. St. Thomas moderates this and argues that certain holders of subordinate offices may, as a group, challenge the tyrant . . . but this isn't the subjective, individual judgment that leads the lone assassin to kill.

43. His dates are 1265–1321.

44. Morrall, *Political Thought*, p. 81.

45. Dante also represents the vernacular—Italian—linked, often quite romantically, to an ideal of a particular political body, against the universalism of medieval Latin—but to take this up explicitly and in detail would be one theme too many.

46. Boniface's dates are 1294–1303. *Unam Sanctam* was issued in 1302.

47. Indeed, so adamant was Dante that he chided his fellow citizens who refused to subject themselves to Henry VII, elected Holy Roman Emperor in 1308. As payment for his contribution, Dante was banished from Florence!

48. Dante, *Monarchy and Three Political Letters* (New York: Noonday Press, 1954). Morrall characterizes Dante's respect for authority as "excessive" yet typical of "medieval thought in general." If it is typical, it is the norm, so one wonders how Dante's respect for authority can be "excessive," but this is a minor point.

49. Dante, *Monarchy*, p. 7.

50. *Ibid.*, p. 11.

51. Kantorowicz, *The King's Two Bodies*, p. 463.

52. Dante, *Monarchy*, p. 13. It might also be said that Dante anticipates sovereign selves as these begin to appear in "the Renaissance."

53. *Ibid.*, p. 25.

54. *Ibid.*, p. 91.

55. 1280–1343.

56. The quoted words are from Joan and Oliver O'Donovan in their *From Irenaeus to Grotius: A Sourcebook in Christian Political Thought* (Grand Rapids, Mich.: Eerdmans Publishing, 1999), p. 423.

57. Morrall, *Political Thought*, p. 106.

58. Wilks, *Problem of Sovereignty*, p. 433.

59. Marsilius of Padua, *The Defender of the Peace (Defensor Pacis)* (New York: Harper and Row, 1967). For his troubles, Marsilius was anathematized and his book put on the Index. He managed to elude efforts to capture and silence him, assuming these were afoot. Marsilius owed a great deal to the Conciliar movement within the medieval church—although it is anachronistic to speak of "church" as a separate entity in medieval Europe, as I have argued—for ideas about representation. Conciliarism and its importance came into its own several decades ago with the work of Francis Oakley and others. Francis Oakley,

*Natural Law, Conciliarism and Consent in the Late Middle Ages: Studies in Ec-
clesiastical and Intellectual History* (London: Variorum, 1984). See also An-
thony Black, *Council and Commune: The Conciliar Movement and the Fifteenth
Century Heritage* (London: Burns & Oates, 1979). For Nicholas of Cusa, see
Christopher M. Bellitto and Thomas M. Izbicki, eds., *Introducing Nicholas of
Cusa: A Guide to a Renaissance Man* (New York: Paulist Press, 2004); and
Nicholas of Cusa, *The Catholic Concordance*, edited and translated by Paul E.
Sigmund (Cambridge: Cambridge University Press, 1991). In 1443 the Council
of Basel insisted it had supremacy, both legislative and juridical, over the Pope.
The work of Nicholas of Cusa (1401–1464) is sometimes also seen as modern in
the sense that it involves an account of representation. Some observers go so far
as to claim that with Nicholas of Cusa one finds "an important and neglected relationship in the history of modern political thought: between democratic liberalism and Christian mysticism." See the O'Donovans, *Sourcebook,* p. 542.

60. *Ibid.,* p. 425.

61. See D'Entreves' discussion of Marsilius, in his *Medieval Contributions to
Political Thought*, p. 48.

62. Thus speaks George Clark Seller in his text, routinely assigned in courses
in early modern history, *The Renaissance: Its Nature and Origins* (Madison,
Wis.: University of Wisconsin Press, 1962), p. 41.

63. Loosely defined, *Erastianism* denotes an undue subservience of the
Church to the state. Its origins lie in the support that Erastus showed towards
Zwingli and his followers against the Lutherans. Erastus was primarily concerned with the question of whether known sinners could be excluded from
receiving the sacraments. His theory of Church and state was a corollary. He ad-
vocated that Christian kings possess the same power as Old Testament kings.
See Bernard Ward, "Erastus and Erastianism," *Catholic Encylcopedia* (New
York: The Encyclopedia Press, 1913); and J. N. Figgis, "Erastus and Erastianism," in *The Divine Right of Kings* (New York: Harper and Row, 1965). There is
a possibility that the doctrines of Erastus came to influence Hobbes. See Jeffrey
R. Collins, "Christian Ecclesiology and the Composition of the *Leviathan*: A
Newly Discovered Letter to Thomas Hobbes," *Historical Journal* 43 (2000):
217–231. William M. Lamont, *Godly Rule, Politics, and Religion: 1603–1660*
(New York: St. Martin's Press, 1969), pp. 113–115.

64. Marsilius, *Defensor Pacis*, p. 109. Discourse Two, chapter III, par. 2.

65. *Ibid.,* Discourse Two, chapter XXV, par. 1.

66. *Ibid.,* Discourse One, chapter XII, par. 5, p. 46.

67. On essentially contested concepts, see my essay, "Methodological
Sophistication and Conceptual Confusion," In *Power Trips and Other Journeys.*
See also, in *Public Man, Private Woman*, the discussion "On Thinking and
Nastiness."

68. Marsilius, *Defensor Pacis*, Discourse One, chapter X, par. 4, p. 36. See also D'Entreves' discussion in his *Medieval Contributions*, p. 61: "The essence of law appears to lie in its "imperative" and "coercive" character. . . . It might almost be Hobbes's or Austin's conception of law; it is certainly the exact reverse of the Thomist conception," emphasizing not reason but will. The absolute "will of the people" is a curious outcropping that appears from time to time even in contemporary constitutional systems, e.g., in the aftermath of the contested U.S. presidential election in 2000. At the time those supporting Sen. Al Gore and defending counting "hanging chads" and the rest of the nearly comic enterprise claimed that the "will of the people" must be discerned, even if large numbers of people hadn't voted correctly and wound up in ballot incoherence. The idea was that there is a latent will ready to be manifest and that the vote, even if improperly cast, is a way to do that insofar as others can "divine" the intent of the voter. This struck me as bizarre until I located it within the willful strand of Western political thought. For a classic constitutionalist, by contrast, whether of a liberal or conservative stripe, a vote is the articulation of a necessarily provisional judgment by citizens—a completed act, not an act in *potentia*—that can be objectively measured and on which outcomes turn. There is no view that the actually cast vote—the achieved objective count—is only icing on the cake, and perhaps sloppy icing at that, of a deeper and somewhat mysterious "will of the people," a view far more indebted to the French rather than the American Revolution. In noting all this, I am not taking a stand on the Supreme Court's final decision on the 2000 election but observing yet another manifestation of the will in politics.

69. James Marshall, *Swords and Symbols* (Oxford: Oxford University Press, 1939), p. 143. I am by no means suggesting that this position was knowingly articulated by sovereigntists, including Marsilius, but that it emerged as the outcropping, the fruits, of sovereign theorizing over time.

CHAPTER 4

1. Freedom for the Church segues in the twentieth century into a stress on freedom of individual consciences. As we go forward, we find that the Church felt compelled to negotiate a settlement, a concordat, with sovereign political bodies to try to prevent its full absorption within the aegis of the state: This was most exigent for the Catholic Church in Protestant "state church" regimes.

2. Looking ahead to modern Church-state controversies, I here note a debate with the Chief Justice of the Canadian Supreme Court, the Rt. Hon. Beverly McLachlin. I avowed that her insistence that disputes about "church" and "state" took their orienting point from just how much religion the state can "accommodate," was a position dependent on a view that both religion and politics are comprehensive and monistic views that make "total claims upon the self." It follows that something's "gotta give." But must one view things in a way that

almost inevitably ends up in the courts so that someone somewhere has final say? I argued that the "goods at stake are not best understood as totalistic religious goods versus totalistic legal and political goods but, rather, as competing understandings of a public good, variously derived." That we are now in a world of legalistic overreach is unsurprising given the long history of the playing out of this issue. See the Rt. Hon. Beverly McLachlin, "Freedom of Religion and the Rule of Law: A Canadian Perspective," pp. 12–34. With a response by Jean Bethke Elshtain, pp. 35–40, in Douglas Farrow, ed., *Recognizing Religion in a Secular Society* (Montreal and Kingston: McGill-Queens University Press, 2003).

3. Martin Luther's dates are1483–1546.

4. William Shirer, *The Rise and Fall of the Third Reich* (London: Secker and Warburg, 1960).

5. In standard treatments of the story, as I well recall as a young Lutheran, somehow this Lutherian stance fed into the cries for freedom of the American Revolution and the Bill of Rights. Luther made possible Thomas Jefferson and my right to say whatever I wanted to, etc.

6. Constantin Fasolt, *The Limits of History* (Chicago: University of Chicago Press, 2004), p. 137. Alas, absent a temporal institutional matrix through which to "voice" conscience, it is defanged with reference to temporal authority.

7. Luther's life spans a number of tumultuous decades, made more so by his activities. His contemporary, Machiavelli, sets the basis for subsequent theorizing about the morality or amorality of politics even as Luther irrevocably altered our thinking about the human subject, among other things. See my discussion in *Meditations on Modern Political Thought*, 2nd ed. (University Park, Penn.: Pennsylvania State University Press, 1992), pp. 5–19. I also treat Luther in *Public Man, Private Woman*, pp. 80–92 and, as well, in *Women and War*, pp. 135–138. I draw upon but do not replicate these discussions, in part because my thinking has changed somewhat.

8. Thus *Women and War*, p. 136.

9. There are several possible ways to approach Luther. One can go back to his original texts and interpret them. Or one can concentrate on implications drawn by interpreters, polemicists, activists, religious and political figures, and the like. One need not choose between these, but in any discussion of Luther as part of a much bigger project, one has to decide which emphasis to take. In the interest of concision, I will parse several key texts and then round up critical evaluations that touch explicitly on sovereignty, God's and the prince's.

10. *Martin Luther's Theological Writings*, ed. Timothy F. Lull (Minneapolis: Fortress Press, 1989). "Temporal Authority" appears on pp. 655–703, inclusively. "Letter to German Nobility" can be found in *Works of Martin Luther* with introduction and translation by C. M. Jacobs, Vol. II (Philadelphia: A. J. Holman Com-

pany, 1915). One ought not be surprised that the Devil takes over politics. See W. D.J. Cargill Thompson, *The Political Thought of Martin Luther*, ed. Phillip Broadhead with a preface by A. G. Dickens (Brighton: Harvester Press, 1984); Luther Hess Waring, *The Political Theories of Martin Luther* (Port Washington: Kennikat Press, 1968); Jacques Maritain, *Three Reformers: Luther, Descartes, and Rousseau* (New York: Charles Scribner's Sons, 1937). The secondary literature on Luther is a mountain—or an entire mountain chain—by now. No single person could possibly encompass it all, even a full-time Luther scholar. Like Augustine, Luther is a magnet drawing people to him. Some emerge emboldened, some repulsed, but nobody is indifferent.

11. Found in E. G. Rupp and Benjamin Drewery, eds., *Martin Luther* (London: Edward Arnold, 1976).

12. *The Limits of History*, p. 49.

13. As a summary judgment this is too harsh, of course—the quote is drawn from p. 91 of *Public Man, Private Woman*—but there is sufficient evidence behind it to unsettle ongoingly. See also Charles Taylor, *Sources of the Self* (Cambridge: Harvard University Press, 1989), pp. 216–218, for Luther's role in what Taylor calls "the affirmation of ordinary life." See also my essay on Taylor that strikes this theme in James Tully, ed., *Philosophy in an Age of Pluralism* (Cambridge: Cambridge University Press, 1994), pp. 67–82. In *Public Man, Private Woman*, from 1981, I speak of the "redemption of everyday life." Taylor and I are pretty much talking about the "same" thing.

14. "The Bondage of the Will" (1525), Lull, ed., *Martin Luther's Basic Theological Writings*, pp. 195–196. Also quoted in J. B. Schneewind, *The Invention of Autonomy* (Cambridge: Cambridge University Press, 1998), pp. 30–31; see pp. 21–31 for a wider discussion of Luther's theory and Martin Luther, *Commentary on Galatians 2:16*, in *Works* 26.128, where he comments on Duns Scotus's view. See also Heiko Augustinus Oberman, *The Harvest of Medieval Theology: Gabriel Biel and Late Medieval Nominalism* (Durham, N.C.: Labyrinth Press, 1983).

15. John Dillenberger, *God Hidden and Revealed* (Philadelphia: Muhlenberg Press, 1953), p. 19. If Ockham's formulation borders on arbitrariness in its severing of faith and reason—for Scriptural warrant and revealed truth trumps any authoritative claims of the pope, indebted to the Scholastic construction of reason, Luther is indebted simultaneously to nominalism and to scholasticism. Luther lifts up the "absolute will of God" but this does not mean that God is "capriciousness" par excellence. God wills necessarily though often in a hidden way, *potentia secreta*, Luther called it, and linked it to *potentia absoluta*: this according to Dillenberger's analysis of Seeberg's *Lehrbuch der Dogmengeschichte* (vierter Band, erste Abteilung), p. 156. God binds but is not himself bound—but we needn't fear this as God has revealed himself incarnationally through the second person of the Trinity;

this is the face of God, and that face is righteousness and mercy. For Luther, God is wholly and even terrifyingly "Other"—transcendent—and at the same time present, here, coming in the form of a baby. Luther wrote many letters to his children and other items for children on Jesus the baby. Too, God is community, Dillenberger argues; he "wills community for man, already has community because of his Trinitarian nature" (p. 134). God alone is sovereign in any full and complete sense. If the sovereignty of God is revealed in Jesus the Christ, what does this say about the nature of God's sovereignty? That God is love even unto death: God is with us.

16. What I will be doing here is parsing "The Freedom of the Christian"; my interpretations are drawn from a reading and rereading of this vital text. All other commentators will be noted explicitly.

17. I have in mind Jean-Paul Sartre and his argument that you can be as free in a prison cell as anywhere else. See *The Wall (Intimacy) and Other Stories*, translated by Lloyd Alexander (New York: New Directions, 1975).

18. "The Bondage of the Will" (1525), large chunks of which appear in Lull, ed., *Luther's Theological Writings*, pp. 173–226.

19. *Works of Martin Luther*, Vol. 36 (St. Louis: Concordia Publishing House, 1955), p. 70.

20. In *Public Man, Private Woman* and *Meditations*, I offer discussions of Luther's rich ruminations on *auctoritas*, or authority, including authorization of translations of the Bible. Readers may turn to those two texts if they wish to follow up these matters.

21. What follows is all drawn from Luther's "Temporal Authority: To What Extent It Should Be Obeyed," unless otherwise noted.

22. Lest anyone believe this matter is dormant, he or she should check out current "peace politics" by contrast to a more Lutherian view.

23. William A. Mueller, *Church and State in Luther and Calvin* (New York: Doubleday Anchor Books, 1965), p. 58.

24. Alas, this ethical mission of the state is to be overseen by clergy as well as magistrates (lower down the scale from the king). I say "alas" because, absorbed within the purview of the state apparatus, the independence of such "ethical watchdogs" was sorely compromised. See Steven Ozment, *A Mighty Fortress: A New History of the German People* (New York: Harper Collins, 2004).

25. This makes the twentieth-century conspiracy against Hitler by the Confessing Church that had broken with the Lutheran State Church all the more remarkable. The key figure here is, of course, Dietrich Bonhoeffer, a brilliant young Lutheran theologian who paid with his life for his part in the conspiracy—about which more in chapters 5 and 6.

26. Calvin's dates are 1509–1564. I am painfully aware of the shortcomings of so brief a discussion of Calvin. There are hundreds of available works of critique

and interpretation. My main concern is to be certain that the Reformers are acknowledged for their critical role in the emergence of sovereignty in the West.

27. See Mueller, *Church and State in Luther and Calvin*, p. 74.

28. The revival of natural law in the sixteenth and seventeenth centuries—in Hooker, Grotius, Suarez—departs from voluntarist theories of law and any notion of will as the expression of the unified will of the people or the will of an omnipotent God, as we shall learn.

29. D'Entreves, *Natural Law*, p. 103.

30. Mueller, *Church and State*, p. 127.

31. John Calvin, *Selections from His Writings* (Missoula, Mont.: Scholars Press, 1975), from Book IV, chapter XX, *Institutes*.

32. *Ibid.*, p. 140.

33. *Ibid.*, pp. 478–479).

34. The great American Calvinist—America's greatest and most original theologian—Jonathan Edwards, in eighteenth-century New England, commented frequently on God's sovereignty in the *Salvation of Man*. See *To All the Saints of God: Address to the Church by Jonathan Edwards, Pastor of the Church at Northampton* (Morgan, Penn.: Soli Deo Gloria Publications, 2003). Fascinatingly, all of his references are Old Testament—God to Moses. God is not the author of the hardening of any man's heart. God, for Edwards, is pretty much unbound and can do what he wills. "The sovereignty of God is His absolute, independent right of disposing of all creatures according to His own pleasure. . . . The will of God is called His mere pleasure, first, in opposition to any restraint. Men may do things voluntarily, and yet there may be a degree of constraint. . . . God may save any of the children of men without prejudice to the honor of His majesty. If men have affronted God, and that ever so much, if they have cast ever so much contempt on His authority, Yet God can save them, if He pleases, and the honor of His majesty suffers not in the least." Edwards goes on to document God's exercise of sovereignty in all things—including withholding salvation as he pleases. Here is the key comment— demonstrating that Edwards goes Calvin one step further in insisting, apropros of strong versions of God's *potentia absoluta:* "It is agreeable to God's design in the creation of the universe to exercise every attribute, and thus to manifest the glory of each of them." What his humble subjects are to do is to adore and to worship him, this awesome God who does what he pleases.

35. P. L. B. Brown, "Political Society," in Robert A. Markus, ed., *Augustine: A Collection of Critical Essays* (Garden City, N.Y.: Doubleday Anchor Books, 1972), pp. 311–335.

CHAPTER 5

1. Alan James, *Sovereign Statehood: The Basis of International Society* (London: Allen and Unwin, 1986), p. 7. I draw some paragraphs here and in the next few pages from my book *New Wine and Old Bottles* (Notre Dame: Notre Dame University Press, 1996).

2. Ernest H. Kantorowicz, *The King's Two Bodies* (Princeton: Princeton University Press, 1957), p. 115.

3. Kantorowicz, *The King's Two Bodies*, p. 189. Renaissance and early modern thinkers commonly evoked claims of *necessitas* to legitimate unusual princely power, up to and including taking away the private property of citizens (p. 260).

4. Indeed, it is difficult to imagine the project of political theory absent its object—the state. What would political theory have been about? See Hendrik Spruyt, *The Sovereign State and Its Competitors* (Princeton: Princeton University Press, 1994), p. 3; Charles Howard MacMillan, *The Growth of Political Thought in the West* (New York: MacMillan, 1932), p. 392. He notes that, although the constituent features of modern sovereignty are present in the late medieval period, sovereignty couldn't make itself fully manifest without the existence of a "nation" and thus awaited the emergence of what he calls "a sentiment of national unity." But this turns into a chicken and egg problem immediately, for that "sentiment" requires some prior welding of a "people" into something coherent, something that can be identified. It is no doubt fruitless to debate about which came first; clearly, the sentiment and the growth of the concept of sovereignty grew up hand in hand. See also Martin Thom, *Republics, Nations and Tribes* (London: Verso, 1995).

5. Hooker's dates are 1554–1600. He died the year the doomed Charles I was born.

6. As I write, there is an acrimonious debate going forward in the United States concerning presidential war powers. President George W. Bush, under presidential war powers, authorized the wiretapping of American citizens who were making telephone contact with al-Qaeda or other terrorist entities overseas. This is no different from what presidents have tended to do, and have done, in the past and rather milder than some past measures. My point is: The debate goes on. Presidential prerogative is a question that will never be settled once and for all—otherwise one thinks it would have been settled by now. And, sadly enough, much of the heated nature of our current debate turns, not on principle, but on whose partisan ox is being gored.

7. This sort of Hookerian restraint challenged absolutisms, past and present, but fell victim to the historic "forgetting" I have associated with the emergence of the standard canon in Western political thought: you will not find Hooker on the

syllabus in courses in the history of Western political thought, as a general rule. See R. W. Carlyle and A. J. Carlyle, *A History of Medieval Political Theory in the West,* Vol.VI (Edinburgh and London: Blackwood, 1932), p. 351.

8. Carlyles, *Medieval Political Thought,* Vol. VI, p. 523.

9. I speak at some length of this dilemma in *Jane Addams and the Dream of American Democracy* (New York: Basic Books, 2002). I note that one of the American reformer and democratic theorist Jane Addams's favorite words was *ameliorate.* Yet it is the person who wants to denounce, trash, overthrow who gets "the ink," so to speak—and why?—well, because it is "high drama" to our eyes and ears, ever more so, I believe, in light of the way the visual media emphasize extremes, whether of politics or human behavior more generally.

10. See Wilks, *Idea of Sovereignty,* p. 41. To be regretted is the manner in which Wilks plays rather fast and loose with the category "totalitarian"— depicting even the medieval Church as "totalitarian." This no doubt derives from a certain insouciance concerning the huge gap that separates medieval understandings of the rule of law and authority from twentieth-century deformations that deeded to us the horrors of totalitarianism. That an entity is concerned with the totality of a person doesn't mean that the political regime within the body politic within which this concern is manifest is necessarily "totalitarian." Real totalitarianism enters when the state attempts to control every aspect of life, exerts the most horrific forms of force to do so, and punishes all who depart even in the most minor ways from the "totality." The modern state may, as Wilks avers, be an outgrowth ("a direct inheritance") from medieval political thought, but the pretensions of modern state sovereignty are foreign to medieval understandings, which always function in and through structures of law and limitations imposed by God's sovereignty. To be sure, there were breathtaking evocations of a plenitude of power in the most expansive versions of papal power, but this power is quite different from our way of thinking about power. We associate power with force and compulsion, pretty much exclusively. But the medieval understanding, inseparable from legitimate authority, associated power with *jus*, with overall justice and a "right ordering" of things. Too, Jesus himself shattered claims to totality on behalf of political power and principle, as Pope Benedict XVI argues: Jesus says no to the absoluteness of political power; shatters claims to totality "once and for all." Thus all political communities are subject to "relativization by contrast to the unity of God" (*Introduction to Christianity*, p. 113).

11. King James I's reign began in 1603. Paul Kléber Monod, *The Power of Kings: Monarchy and Religion in Europe, 1589–1715* (New Haven: Yale University Press, 1999), p. 79. It is worth a reminder at this point that Bodin's sovereignty embedded a strong patriarchal element, being derived in important part from the Roman law of *patria potestas*, the sovereign power of the father

over all in the household. Fathers in patriarchal theory—its apogee is Robert Filmer's famous or infamous *Patriarcha*—go into ecstasies over the nature of this power, linking it directly to a kind of godlikeness. See Sir Robert Filmer, *Patriarcha and Other Political Works* (Oxford: Basic Blackwell, 1949). See also my discussion of Filmer in *Public Man, Private Woman*, pp. 102–108. This explicit link to patriarchal theory, dependent on Roman private law of the family, helps to account for the tendency of absolute rulers to view their subjects as "children" in a kind of familialized kingdom.

12. King James wrote rather prolifically, including "An Exhortation to Obedience" and a famous "Address to Parliament" in 1609. What is interesting about these outpourings is that they were required to be read word for word in Anglican Churches in a twelve-week cycle at the time. If one is absorbed in a world in which the king's power, authority, and strength come from God and taught that his laws reflect God's order, it follows that neither the pope nor anyone or anything else has any direct role in granting legitimacy. I owe this point to Dan Maloney, who adds that "if everyone in England heard these homilies four to five times a year every year of their life, you don't need to look very far to find all sorts of connections between God and the king." Unsurprising, then, when Sir Francis Bacon (1561–1626) begins his "Essay of a King" with the line, "A King is a Mortal God on earth, unto whom the living God hath lent His own name as a great honor."

13. See Adam Nicolson, *God's Secretaries: The Making of the King James Bible* (New York: Perennial, Harper Collins, 2003), p. 217. In this lively, entertaining work., Nicolson demonstrates that a foundation stone of the Bible's translation is the idea of majesty given its "consistent attention to a grand and heavily musical rhythm [which] are the vehicles by which that majesty is infused into the body of the text. . . . The Translators of the Bible clearly believed that and the majesty of their translation stems from its loyal belief in that divine-cum-regal authority" (p. 189). Nicolson doesn't stop there but goes on to discuss what we have lost with many subsequent flat-footed, dessicated English translations that veer toward a stifling "political correctness": "Again and again, the seventeenth-century phrases seem richer, deeper, truer, more alive, more capable of carrying complex and multiple meanings, than anything the twentieth century could manage. It happens in linguistic history that languages lose aspects of themselves, whole wings of their existence withering, falling off, disappearing into the past. Has it now happened to English? Does English no longer have a faculty of religious language?" (p. 236) And again: "It is impossible now to experience in an English church the enveloping amalgam of tradition, intelligence, beauty, clarity of purpose, intensity of conviction and plangent, heart-gripping godliness which is the experience of page after page of the King James Bible. Nothing in our cul-

ture can match its breadth, depth and universality, unless, curiously enough, it is something that was written at exactly the same time and in almost exactly the same place: the great tragedies of Shakespeare. That is no chance effect. Shakespeare's great tragedies and the King James Bible are each other's mirror-twin. Both emerge from the ambitions and terrors of the Jacobean world" (p. 239).

14. Francis Oakley, "Omnipotence and Promise: The Legacy of the Scholastic Distinction of Powers," PIMS Etienne Gilson Series 23 (1 March 2002, The Pontifical Institute of Medieval Studies), p. 16. Oakley cites various statements of James, including "A Speech to the Lords and Commons of the Parliament at White-Hall . . . Anno 1609," a very famous speech that unsettled the parliamentarians considerably. James's collected writings can be found in Charles Howard McIlwain ed., *The Political Works of James I* (Cambridge, Mass.: Harvard University Press, 1918).

15. *Ibid.*, p. 7.

16. *Ibid.*, pp. 7–8. Oakley argues that neither term of the *absoluta/ordinata* distinction was intended "to be understood in isolation from the other. . . . If the postulation of the absolute power erected a stout bulwark against any form of Greek necessitarianism, affirming the utter freedom of God and the concomitant contingency of the entire created order of nature, morality, and grace, the juxtaposition of the ordained power served at the same time to affirm the de facto stability and reliability of that contingent, will-based order. . . . The only force capable of binding omnipotence without denying it is, after all, the omnipotent will itself" (pp. 13–14).

17. Apropos of this interconnection, Kantorowicz, in *The King's Two Bodies*, writes that "Infinite cross-relations between Church and State, active in every century of the Middle Ages, produced hybrids in either camp. Mutual borrowings and exchanges of insignia, political symbols, prerogatives, and rites of honor had been carried on perpetually between the spiritual and secular leaders of Christian society" (p. 193).

18. Monod, *The Power of Kings*, pp. 52–53. Quoted material is from a pamphlet by a priest, William Allen, published in 1583. Contributors to the maintenance of classic Scholastic doctrine and the assault on royal absolutism included important Spanish Jesuits like Father Juan de Mariana and the great Father Francisco Suarez, who insisted that the power of political dominion was not granted directly by God to a given individual but to a body of people as a whole. The Jesuit drive to desacralize earthly dominion parallels a similar impetus in Reformers like Luther. Suarez, following the classic Thomistic doctrine, argues that it is through natural law that human beings participate in eternal order and find an objective standard of good and evil, although he adds that God could change the direction of his willing and thus alter natural law. But it is given that God cannot lie, and this

means the created order is regular, not irregular. See Bernice Hamilton, *Political Thought in Sixteenth-Century Spain; A Study of the Political Ideas of Vitoria, De Soto, Suarez, and Molina* (Oxford: Clarendon Press, 1963), pp. 25, 27.

19. Cited in Oakley, *Omnipotence, Covenant and Order*, p. 97.

20. *Ibid.*, pp. 104–105.

21. Although the word *sovereignty* connotes so much the monistic strain that one uses it at one's peril when the reference point is anything medieval.

22. Cited in my *Women and War*, p. 136. I have also drawn on a paragraph or two from that work. That the Church is a kind of strike force for the state is apparent in an exhortation by the Bishop of London to the faithful in 1914—he addresses youth in particular: "Kill Germans—to kill them, not for the sake of killing, but to save the world, to kill the good as well as the bad, to kill the young men as well as the old, to kill those who have shewn kindness to our wounded as well as those fiends who crucified the Canadian Sergeant [reference to a widely circulated propaganda myth]. . . . As I have said a thousand times, I look upon it as a war for purity, I look upon everyone who dies in it as a martyr." This is creepy stuff.

23. McIlwain, *Growth of Political Thought*, p. 387.

24. His dates are 1469–1527.

25. Fasolt, *The Limits of History*, writes: "Machiavelli, Luther, and Hobbes have withstood the test of time more successfully than their contemporaries. Their views remain more thoroughly alive. The business they started was never finished. The threat they posed in early modern times has never been defused. It lurks barely concealed beneath the surface of modern consciousness, from where it exercises an abiding fascination. They still provoke intense hostility. With friends like these, who needed enemies? But notwithstanding their intellectual longevity and their importance as both challengers and victims of the boundaries laid down in the historical revolt in the short term of early modern Europe and even modern history, all three must be considered failures. The most successful were saner and arguably more boring men like Calvin, Melancthon, Lipsius, and even John Locke, who followed the radicals up to a point but closed the door on their most daring experiments. They defused the explosives that Machiavelli, Luther, and Hobbes had placed under all principles of order, transformed them into classics, and made their teaching safe to study in public and in school" (p. 24).

26. Machiavelli, *The Prince* (New York: W.W. Norton, 1977), p. 75.

27. To be sure, Machiavelli's *Discourses* offer a more detailed and measured historical account but, once again, antiquity is lifted up as exemplary and one is struck by how much is remaindered to ill or good fortune. There is a kernel of wisdom here, to be sure, for we cannot control everything. The problem is that his version of sovereign control is of an arbitrary sort or potentially arbitrary sort.

28. Machiavelli, *The Prince*, p. 17.

29. *Ibid.*, note 7, p. 17. Curiously, the editor fails to note the role (bad) Aristotelian biology played in all this, given Aristotle's conviction that in the reproductive process all the female provides is a kind of incubus. The male deposits the fully formed homunculus that then matures into a baby.

30. For example, one scholar, J.W. Allen, in his classic work, *Political Thought in the Sixteenth Century* (London: Methuen and Co., 1928), simply notes that, contrary to what some have argued, Machiavelli didn't really separate ethics and politics; rather, he separated the "ethics of political life" from the "ethics of social and private life." Allen misses the fact that Machiavelli is one of the architects of this public/private split that relegates faith to an "ethics of social and private life" (pp. 471–473). In *Public Man, Private Woman*, I unpacked these matters through the prism of the gendered public-private distinction. In interesting ways, the religion-politics or church-state pairings not only confirm the heuristic usefulness of the public-private categories but strengthen them by adding another significant dimension designed to further the interest of monism.

31. At the same time there is much that is admirable in the Renaissance papacy, certainly from the perspective of patronage of the arts. But this seems at rather a distance from the primary mission, or commission, to the faithful. Another dispute for a different occasion.

32. Machiavelli, *The Prince*, chapter 15, p. 44.

33. A "Machiavellian" might, for example, argue quite persuasively that it would have been better by far to take Hitler out early on rather than to wait until he had destroyed so many lives. But this presumes that the necessary political will could be generated in the absence of an empirical record of cruelty and excess.

34. Some argue that this is far better than cranking up a Christian justification for sovereign power, an argument with considerable force. The problem is that if you strip away "morality" altogether, if your only progenitors are the multiple gods and goddesses of Athens and Rome and you abandon the traditions of Judaism and Christianity, you lose over time the ability to recognize an excess or to "name" an evil, for your thought is cast within an entirely immanent horizon.

35. Niccolo Machiavelli, *The Discourses*, taken from *The Historical, Political, and Diplomatic Writings of Niccolo Machiavelli*, Volume II, trans. Christian E. Detmold (Boston: James R. Osgood and Company, 1882), p. 421.

36. See, for example, Robert D. Kaplan, *Warrior Politics: Why Leadership Demands a Pagan Ethos* (New York: Random House, 2002).

37. See my discussion in *Women and War*, p. 57.

38. Thanks to Bill Gordon for this insight.

39. The secondary literature on Hobbes is vast and growing exponentially. Perhaps someone devoted full-time to Hobbes could keep up with it—I certainly cannot—but the reader might care to check out one or more of the following titles

drawn from the last fifteen years or so of Hobbes scholarship: Jeffrey R. Collins, *The Allegiance of Thomas Hobbes* (Oxford: Oxford Univerity Press, 2005); Aloysius Martinich, *Hobbes* (New York: Routledge, 2005); Vickie Sullivan, *Machiavelli, Hobbes, and the Formation of Liberal Republicanism* (Cambridge: Cambridge University Press, 2004); Noel Malcolm, *Aspects of Hobbes* (Oxford: Oxford University Press, 2002); Quentin Skinner, *Visions of Politics* (Cambridge: Cambridge University Press, 2002); Adela Claramunt, *Interés Privadoy Bien Común: Algunas Líneas de Comparación de los Argumentos Desarrollados por Aristóteles, Hobbes, Locke y Rousseau* (Montevideo, Uruguay, 2000); Deborah Baumgold, *Hobbes's Political Thought* (Cambridge: Cambridge University Press, 1988); David Boonin-Vail, *Thomas Hobbes and the Science of Moral Virtue* (Cambridge: Cambridge University Press, 1994); Stuart Sim, *The Discourse of Sovereignty: Hobbes to Fielding* (Burlington, Vt.: Ashgate, 2003); George Shelton, *Morality and Sovereignty in the Philosophy of Hobbes* (New York: St. Martin's Press, 1992); Franck Lessay, *Souveraineté et legitimité chez Hobbes* (Paris: Presses Universitaires de France, 1988); Ian M. Wilson, *The Influence of Hobbes and Locke in the Shaping of the Concept of Soveriegnty in Eighteenth Century France* (Banbury, Oxfordshire: Voltaire Foundation, Thorpe Mandeville House, 1973); "Introduction to Hobbes's *Leviathan*," in *Leviathan*, ed. Edwin Curley (Indianapolis: Hackett, 1994); M.M. Goldsmith, *Hobbes's Science of Politics* (New York: Columbia University Press, 1966); Jean Hampton, *Hobbes and the Social Contract Tradition* (Cambridge: Cambridge University Press, 1986); E.C. Hood, *The Divine Politics of Thomas Hobbes* (Oxford: Oxford University Press, 1964); Gregory S. Kavka, *Hobbesian Moral and Political Theory* (Princeton: Princeton University Press, 1986); C.B. Macpherson, introduction, *Leviathan*, ed. C.B. Macpherson (London: J. M. Dent & Sons, 1968); Michael Oakeshott, *Hobbes on Civil Association* (Oxford: Oxford University Press, 1975); Leo Strauss, *The Political Philosophy of Hobbes: Its Basis and Genesis* (Oxford: Oxford University Press, 1936); Richard Tuck, *Hobbes* (Oxford: Oxford University Press, 1989); Howard Warrender, *The Political Philosophy of Hobbes: His Theory of Obligation* (Oxford: Oxford University Press, 1957); J.W.N. Watkins, *Hobbes's Theory of Ideas* (Brookfield, Vt.: Gower, 1989).

40. I have challenged the "scientific" claims argument but located Machiavelli instead in the long train of sovereign discourses, with this caveat: Machiavelli's drama of the prince, befitting Jacob Burkhardt's famous "state as a work of art," may lie so far outside the frame of the standard arguments as to warrant exclusion from a continuum. This is not a central issue but it should be noted at least.

41. Hobbes's dates are 1588-1699. I am not debating political science per se, but it is worth noting that early modern sovereigntists, like Hobbes, gained great and enduring recognition from political scientists whereas the meticulous articulators of a law-governed and ordered social life, like St. Thomas Aquinas,

were often ruled out because they were "religious" thinkers who appealed to transcendent norms. This made or makes them "premodern." Hobbes, however, is modern and shows us the way in which politics "really" works, deep down, despite sunny illusions to the contrary, so the story runs.

42. These are among the most famous words in the English language, no doubt, and can be found in Hobbes, *Leviathan* (New York: Penguin Books, 1983), chapter XIII, p. 186. When I teach Hobbes I use the film *Road Warrior,* the 1962 cult classic starring Mel Gibson, to illustrate Hobbes's war of all against all. But it is interesting that, in order to find a world at all resembling the claims Hobbes insists exist by nature, one has to go to a world reduced to horrific "fundamentals"—cruel scarcity—by a nuclear holocaust. But even in this world the hard-bitten Max (Gibson) cannot bring himself to behave in purely Hobbesian, self-interested ways. His is definitely a world of violent self-help but he shares limited food with his dog and, at the end, he makes a deal, a contract, with others that suggests he isn't "just here for the gasoline" but has developed fondness for at least the feral child of a group in control of a limited petrol supply. Although *Leviathan* is Hobbes's most famous work, he wrote a great deal. Apropos of our topic are two other titles: *The Elements of Law* (Cambridge: Cambridge University Press, 1928) and *De Cive: On the Citizen* (Cambridge: Cambridge University Press, 1998).

43. Hobbes, *Leviathan,* chapter X, p. 113. Hobbes argues that such notions as freedom as aspiration or a free will are not only senseless and inconstant but dangerous. Free will invites discussions of Christian freedom and then freedom more generally.

44. At this point in the discussion we recognize what Hobbes is throwing out: divine law, higher law, natural law as usually understood and, with it, the right to resist, what we call "civil disobedience," etc. Hobbes preserves the tiniest possibility of "disobedience," though it can scarcely be called that, a teeny window for refusal to obey, namely, that if the Sovereign orders me not to defend myself, this is "voyd," for no man "can transferre, or lay down his Right to save himselfe from Death." He continues, "For though a man may Covenant thus, Unlesse I do so, or so, kill me; he cannot Covenant thus, Unlesse I do so, or so, I will not resist you when you come to kill me" (chapter XIV, p. 199). In other words, the sovereign has every right to come after me to kill me, but I can try to escape. This isn't principled open defiance of "unjust law," for that is an oxymoron for Hobbes, but trying to escape by the skin of one's teeth, a self-preservative act undertaken in stealth.

45. The contemporary "rational choice" theory, dominant in so much contemporary social science, holds pretty much the Hobbesian view: what human beings are all about in all things is making calculations of marginal utilities based on self-interest. I'll not belabor the point here, save to say that rational

choice theory invites a particular version of "the sovereign self" as a chooser modeled on self-sufficient calculations of utility.

46. All of these characterizations are drawn from chapter CVII of Hobbes' *Leviathan*, pp. 223–228.

47. Or largely untrammeled—the one thing he isn't supposed to do is to permit himself to weaken so that he is no longer capable at every moment of keeping men within those strict boundaries necessary to prevent violent death. In chapter XXIX, pp. 363–376, Hobbes goes over why commonwealths dissolve, and the first reason is "want of absolute power."

48. On this see especially chapter XXVI, "Of Civil Laws."

49. See the discussion in chapter XVIII, "Rights of Sovereign," pp. 228–239.

50. Hobbes, chapter XXIX, p. 369.

51. Hobbes, Conclusion, p. 722.

52. Hobbes, chapter XV, p. 216.

53. See my *Public Man, Private Woman*, p. 108–116. See also my discussion in *Women and War*.

54. Hobbes, chapter XII, p. 173.

55. On Hobbes and religion see Oliver O'Donovan's brilliant, and difficult, *The Desire of the Nations: Rediscovering the Roots of Political Theology* (Cambridge: Cambridge University Press, 1996).

56. Clearly an endorsement of the Augsburgian *cuius regio, eius religio*.

57. See Hobbes, chapter XXXVIII, p. 384.

58. Interestingly, this discussion traffics in the sorts of metaphors Hobbes warns us against in part I, although he acknowledges as much and goes on to claim, daringly, that hell fire is a metaphorical expression.

59. See chapter XV, p. 214. To the best of my knowledge, very few pick up on Hobbes's playing fast and loose in this way.

60. This from part II, chapter XLIII, p. 612. It is easy enough to see that Hobbes would, if he could, eliminate any "private" realm of religious belief that runs counter to "public religion." But this cannot be controlled entirely so long as people are secretive and do not engage in public worship.

61. All one need do is to consider the way the medieval Church is almost invariably represented in movies: corrupt popes, venal churchmen, zealous inquisitors. Even in a movie friendly to the claims of "religion," like "Becket," the scene when Becket excommunicates one of King Henry II's retainers shows monks in full costume, their faces hidden, looking like brown Ku Klux Klansmen—save they have hoods not cones on their heads, as they trail after Becket and smash out their candles when Becket (Richard Burton) orders it. It is a chilling scene but hyperbolic in its representation of ordinary monks.

62. Hobbes, *Leviathan*, chapters 17 and 18, especially pp. 236, 227.

63. Perry Anderson, *Lineage of the Absolute State* (London: NLB, 1974), pp. 20, 23, 26. See also John Gerard Ruggie, "Continuity and Transformation in the World Polity," in *Neorealism and Its Critics*, ed. Robert Keohane (New York: Columbia University Press, 1986), pp. 131–157, for the Roman law influence. F. H. Hinsley, *Sovereignty*, 2nd edition (Cambridge: Cambridge University Press, 1986) is a standard reference point. On the rejection of any telos leading to 1648, indeed a deconstruction of the whole "idea" of 1648 and the Westphalian solidification of the sovereign state, see Benno Teschke, *The Myth of 1648* (London: Verso, 2003). The work of Daniel Philpott is essential in studying sovereignty and international relations, and he has developed subtle arguments in both articles and books, including his groundbreaking book *Revolutions in Sovereignty* (Princeton: Princeton University Press, 2001). See also "Sovereignty: An Introduction and Brief History," *Journal of International Affairs* (Winter 1995), pp. 355–368 and his entry, "Sovereignty," in *The Stanford Encyclopedia of Philosophy*, available online at http://plato.stanford.edu/archives/fall1999/entries/sovereignty.

64. This quote marks Arendt's book as a *livre de circonstance* of the 1960s, and the reference will, I am quite sure, mystify contemporary readers—just continue, for the major point stands without this reference.

65. Hannah Arendt, *On Violence* (New York: Harvest/HBJ Book, 1969), p. 5.

66. Arendt also insists in one of her texts that the United States Constitution knows nothing of sovereignty, but, as we shall see, in this she is mistaken.

67. We no longer speak of husbands as sovereign in relation to their wives although at one point this was common usage, demonstrating yet again the compulsion to create a homology of structures—a series of interpenetrating "ones" rather than the possibility of a plural "many," which might function under different modalities of internal governance: What is apt for families doesn't suit corporations, and so on. See Michael Walzer, *Spheres of Justice* (New York: Basic Books, 1983).

68. Carl Schmitt, trans. George Schwab, *Political Theology: Four Chapters on the Concept of Sovereignty* (Cambridge: MIT Press, 1985). See also David Cumin, *Carl Schmitt: Biographie politique et intellectuelle* (Paris: Les Editions Du Cerf, 2005). Giorgio Agamben, *State of Exception,* trans. Kevin Attell (Chicago: University of Chicago Press, 2005), is described in glowing terms by a "blurber" as "the first book to theorize the state of exception in historical and philosophical context." A professor of aesthetics, Agamben approaches the subject in a deconstructive spirit, and there are useful insights scattered here and there, but his overall thesis is extreme and unpersuasive, radically ahistorical. For his argument that post 9/11 America has forsaken law in favor of force to be convincing, both domestically and externally, the U.S. would have to be under martial law,

the Bill of Rights would have to be suspended, the courts denuded of any authority to checkmate legislative or executive excess, etc., none of which is true.

69. Schmitt, *Political Theology*, p. 5.

70. *Ibid.*, p. 7.

71. *Ibid.*, p. 13.

72. Dietrich Bonhoeffer, *Ethics* (New York: Simon and Schuster/Touchstone Books, 1995), p. 235.

73. Locke's dates are 1632–1704.

CHAPTER 6

1. Locke's dates are 1632–1704.

2. See, for example, Oakley, "Locke, Natural Law, and God: Again," in his *Politics and Eternity*, pp. 217–248. Oakley also offers a considerable bibliography that notes texts endorsing and opposing this position, although the burden of scholarship, at present, tilts towards it.

3. This is, to put it mildly, an almost impossible task for a single chapter, but, given the sweeping nature of what I am doing here, it helps us at least to get some sense of the movement of things.

4. For more on this issue see my *Just War Against Terror: The Burden of American Power in a Violent World* (New York: Basic Books, 2003).

5. Michael Zuckert, *Launching Liberalism* (Lawrence, Kansas: University of Kansas Press, 2002); Jeremy Waldron, *God, Locke, and Equality: Christian Foundations of John Locke's Political Thought* (Cambridge: Cambridge University Press, 2002); Ruth Weissbound Grant, *John Locke's Liberalism* (Chicago: University of Chicago Press, 1987); Peter Josephson, *The Great Art of Government: Locke's Use of Consent* (Lawrence: University of Kansas Press, 2002); Alex Scott Tuckness, *Locke and the Legislative Point of View: Toleration, Contested Principles and the Law* (Princeton: Princeton University Press, 2002); Gillian Brown, *The Consent of the Governed* (Cambridge, Mass.: Harvard University Press, 2001); Bernard Gilson, *L'apport de Locke à la philosophie générale et politique* (Paris: J. Vrin, 2000); Mark Goldie, ed., *The Reception of Locke's Politics* (London: Pickering & Chatto, 1999); J. R. Milton, ed. *Locke's Moral, Political, and Legal Philosophy* (Brookfield, Vt.: Ashgate, 1999); Eldon Eisenach, *Narrative Power and Liberal Truth: Hobbes, Locke, Bentham, and Mill* (Lanham, Md.: Rowman & Littlefield, 2002); Ross Harrison, *Hobbes, Locke, and Confusion's Masterpiece: An Examination of Seventeenth-Century Political Philosophy* (Cambridge: Cambridge University Press, 2003); Peter C. Myers, *Our Only Star and Compass: Locke and the Struggle for Political Rationality* (Lanham, Md.: Rowman & Littlefield, 1998); Joshua Foa Dienstag, *"Dancing in Chains": Narrative and Memory in Political Theory* (Stanford: Stanford University Press, 1997); Kristie Morna McClure, *Judging Rights: Lockean Politics and the Limits of Consent*

(Ithaca: Cornell University Press, 1996); Zbigniew Rau, *Contractarianism Versus Holism: Reinterpreting Locke's Two Treatises of Government* (Lanham, Md.: University Press of America, 1995); Ian Harris, *The Mind of John Locke: A Study of Political Theory in Its Intellectual Setting* (Cambridge: Cambridge University Press, 1994); Joshua Mitchell, *Not by Reason Alone: Religion, History, and Identity in Early Modern Political Thought* (Chicago: University of Chicago Press, 1993); John A. Simmons, *On the Edge of Anarchy: Locke, Consent, and the Limits of Society* (Princeton: Princeton University Press, 1993); James Tully, *An Approach to Political Philosophy: Locke in Context* (Cambridge: Cambridge University Press, 1993); Edward J. Harpham , ed. *John Locke's Two Treatises of Government: New Intepretations*, ed. (Lawrence: University of Kansas Press, 1992); Uday Singh Mehta, *The Anxiety of Freedom: Imagination and Individuality in Locke's Political Thought* (Ithaca: Cornell University Press, 1992); Thomas Pangle, *The Spirit of Modern Republicanism: The Moral Vision of the American Founders and the Philosophy of John Locke* (Chicago: University of Chicago Press, 1988); Ramon Lemos, *Hobbes and Locke: Power and Consent* (Athens: University of Georgia Press, 1978); Merwyn Johnson, *Locke on Freedom: An Incisive Study of the Thought of John Locke* (Austin: Best Print Co., 1977); John Yolton, ed., *John Locke: Problems and Perspectives* (Cambridge: Cambridge University Press, 1969).

6. Though some are certainly making amends. Often the most important contributions along these lines have come from the ranks of those identified as "historians," like Oakley, rather than "official" political theorists. An exception is Jeremy Waldron's brilliant *God, Locke, and Equality: Christian Foundations of John Locke's Political Thought* (Cambridge: Cambridge University Press, 2002).

7. I can perhaps here make amends for my discussion of Locke in my first book, *Public Man, Private Woman,* which I now view as inadequate, overly influenced by the no-longer-persuasive arguments of Roberto Unger.

8. (New York: Mentor Books, 1965). He writes frequently of magistracy, and magistracy is the expression of the sovereignty of the people, as we shall see. Here is a brief accounting of the historic backdrop: The Glorious Revolution, 1688–1689. James II fled to France when William of Orange, a Dutch prince, and his consort Mary, the Protestant daughter of James, entered England with an army. William and Mary accepted an invitation from Parliament to rule as joint sovereigns. The Declaration of Rights and the Bill of Rights (1689) redefined the relationship between monarch and subjects and barred future Catholic succession; actual power shifted from the monarch to Parliament and an Act of Toleration offered limited religious freedom. Locke published his famous *Two Treatises of Government* in 1690. In the backdrop to these events was the execution of Charles I; the Puritan Revolution, a.k.a. English Civil Wars, and the Cromwell Protectorate that initiated a military government. In addition, London was struck

by the bubonic plague (Black Death) in 1665 and an estimated 70,000 people died, quickly followed by the Great Fire of London in 1666 that burned most of the city to the ground. Not a very settled backdrop. (Thanks to Erik Owens, who was at the time a teaching intern for me, for this chronology).

9. Just how shaky we will assess below as I make the argument that Locke's version of religious toleration can push in the direction of monism in public life given his subjectivizing of religious belief.

10. See Locke's *A Letter Concerning Toleration* (Indianapolis, Indiana: Hackett Publishing, 1983), ed. James Tully, p. 50. For example, p. 46 from the *Complete Works of John Locke,* Volume 6 (12th edition): "Again: That Church can have no right to be tolerated by the magistrate which is constituted upon such a bottom that all those who enter into it do thereby ipso facto deliver themselves up to the protection and service of another prince. For by this means the magistrate would give way to the settling of a foreign jurisdiction in his own country and suffer his own people to be listed, as it were, for soldiers against his own Government." On Locke as apologist for the English Revolution, see Garnet Vere Portus, *The Concept of Sovereignty* (Melbourne: Melbourne University Press, 1948), p. 9. Also see Kantorowicz, *The King's Two Bodies*, where he writes: "The idea of Rome's sovereignty passed on to national monarchies and with it the idea of loyalty to Rome and to the universal empire. In other words, the loyalty to a new limited territorial *patria*, the common fatherland of all subjects of the Crown, replaced the supranational bonds of a fictitious universal Empire" (p. 247).

11. The idea of the prince as the living law is beautifully summed up in the address to Emperor Frederick Barbarossa by four doctors (of law) from the famous law school at Bologna (this at the Diet of Roncaglia in 1158) in these words: "You, being the living Law, can give, loosen, and proclaim law; dukes stand and fall, and kings rule while you are the judge; anything you wish, you carry on as the animate Law" (Kantorowicz, *The King's Two Bodies*, p. 129). The difference between the grandiosity of this claim is that parliament, in Locke's vision of things, cannot just give, loosen, and proclaim as it wishes—for it, too, is bound by the prior existence of natural law.

12. (Indianapolis, Ind.: Hackett Publishing, 1983).

13. Oakley, for example, insists that today "few . . . would be inclined to challenge the claim that it is . . . the voluntarist strand that figures most prominently and most persistently in his texts taken as a whole." See "Locke, Natural Law, and God" in *Politics and Eternity: Studies in the History of Medieval and Early Modern Political Thought* (Boston: Brill, 1999), p. 224.

14. Oakley, "Locke, Natural Law, and God," notes the acerbic comments of one Ralph Cudworth, a "Cambridge Platonist," to this effect (p. 231). The rejoinder to this criticism from the "Locke school" of voluntarism is that God

cannot contradict himself; others, however, insisted that God could contravene what he had already ordained if one assumes that his *potentia absoluta* remains active. God must bind his omnipotence, and only omnipotence can bind itself (p. 235). Ockham went so far as to suggest that what we now call vice could be turned into virtue by God given the simple fact that God "wishes it" (p. 236). In this way God could even make it meritorious "to hate God, since he can do anything that does not involve a contradiction, and since acts are good and just or bad and unjust not of their own intrinsic nature or essence but simply because God has enjoined or forbidden them (p. 238). If all this sounds familiar, it is, because the notion that good and evil are just "names" we more or less arbitrarily apply to certain acts as part and parcel of that contemporary form of nominalism known as postmodernism. Oakley identifies the two main strands of medieval natural law as intellectualism and voluntarism and insists that Locke comes down on the voluntarist side. At first blush, of course, it would seem that God's omnipotence and the world of covenant are miles apart; but, in fact, the one appears to engender or make necessary the other. See Oakley's essay on Locke in *Politics and Eternity: Studies in the History of Medieval and Early-Modern Political Thought* (Boston: Brill, 1999). Indeed, at one point in this essay Oakley cites James Tully discussing Oakley—something that helps us to see the scholarly "consensus" that began to emerge surrounding some of the Locke controversies (see p. 223).

15. See John Locke, *The Reasonableness of Christiantiy,* in Vol. VI of *The Works of John Locke in Nine Volumes,* 12th Edition (London: Rivington, 1824). Oakley writes that the covenantal reading of Locke's "natural law thinking draws sustenance . . . not only from our contemporary understanding of . . . late-medieval thinkers . . . but also from the current inclination of some Locke scholars to take more seriously than heretofore the need to probe his unexpected indebtedness to the scholastic past, to stress accordingly the connectedness among his theological, ontological, and epistemological commitments, and, as a result, between his natural and moral philosophizing" (p. 245, "Locke, Natural Law, and God").

16. Locke, *Two Treatises,* p. 426.

17. Locke is not a patriarchalist, though some feminists have claimed so. See his discussion of parental/paternal power in chapter 6 of *Two Treatises.* See also my discussion of Locke in *Public Man, Private Woman.*

18. All of this is drawn from chapter 2 of Locke's *Two Treatises.*

19. Once again we see the privileging of the first person of the Trinity—God the Father—for the second person—Jesus the Christ—came in the form of a servant, sometimes called a slave.

20. The Kansas-Missouri debates dominated politics in 1853–1854. Lincoln challenged Douglas on this issue in the famous Lincoln-Douglas debates of 1858.

21. See chapter V of Locke's *Two Treatises.*

22. Thanks to Dan Maloney who reminded me of this and offered the formulation I am indebted to.

23. *Second Treatise of Government,* book II, chapter 18, section 200 (Laslett edition, 1988).

24. On this, and more, see Glenn Burgess, *The Politics of the Ancient Constitution: An Introduction to English Political Thought, 1600–1642* (Houndmills Hampshire: MacMillan, 1992).

25. As James Tully points out in his introduction to the Letter, Locke wrote a number of essays and tracts on toleration. There is the Letter under consideration; then a *Third Letter for Toleration to the Author of the Third Letter Concerning Toleration*—a response to Jonas Proust—and *A Fourth Letter for Toleration,* "cut short," Tully writes, "by his [Locke's] death in 1704" (p. 2, Letter). Backdrop also includes the Toleration Act of 1689, which denied freedom of worship to unorthodox dissenters, like Locke, who denied the Trinity. His Letter can be construed as in opposition to the state church, Anglicanism. Interestingly, it was the Catholic, Charles II, who, against Parliament, pushed for greater religious tolerance (1660–1685). Locke had begun his involvement in the "religious question" with a plea for absolutism, presumably in order to guarantee civic peace—a peace Charles II could impose. Then Locke changed and endorsed limited constitutionalism and popular sovereignty, although, as Tully points out, he never much trusted Parliament. Locke removes some of the sovereignty he had given the monarch and places it, not in the hands of Parliament, but in the hands of "the people." Tully's splendid introduction covers all of this.

26. Fasolt makes this point in *The Limits of History*, noting that our blinkers surrounding this entire subject are securely "on," with the medieval period seen as messy, even lawless, the Holy Roman Empire as a "joke," the popes as venal, etc. See p. 90.

27. Fasolt, *The Limits of History,* pp. 203–228.

28. A little light bulb flicked on as I reread Locke's argument. One recognizes that a contemporary pragmatic postmodern like late philosopher Richard Rorty promotes his own sharp version of privatization. Rorty reduces all truth claims to matters of subjective opinion. It follows for Rorty that this privatized world is one of irony—an argument Locke could never have gone along with as religious belief was far too important to thus reduce it.

29. Locke, *Letter,* p. 26.

30. On this see p. 33 especially in Locke, *Letter.* All of my extrapolations are drawn, of course, from this letter.

31. Locke, *Letter,* p. 42. Following the Thomistic distinction Locke also launches into a discourse that refuses to conflate sins and crimes. Some sins are also crimes under civil law . . . but not all.

32. See p. 44, Locke, *Letter.*

33. *Ibid.,* p. 50. I cite this to register Locke's views and *not* to offer up his claims as the final word on Islam and politics.

34. Cited in Jean Bethke Elshtain, "Freedom of Religion and the Rule of Law" by Beverly MacLachlin in *Recognizing Religion in a Secular Society,* ed. Douglas Farrow (Montreal: McGill-Queen's University Press, 2004), p. 37.

35. See, for example, Jean Bethke Elshtain, "Toleration, Proselytizing, and the Politics of Recognition: The Self Contested," in Ruth Abbey, ed., *Charles Taylor* (Cambridge: Cambridge University Press, 2004), pp. 127–139.

36. For Rousseau on public-private re: gender questions, see my *Public Man, Private Woman,* pp. 148–170, for a long discussion of a particular thinker in this particular book. See also my *Meditations on Modern Political Thought,* "Rousseau Redux: Bodies Social and Political," pp. 37–54. I give Rousseau a good report in these two works, in part because I was countering the negative interpretations of Rousseau going on at the time in much feminist political theory. Because I am essentially a counterpuncher I often find myself slugging things out in the context of the debates of the moment. In my discussion of Rousseau in *Women and War* matters take a negative turn as I associate Rousseau with "armed civic virtue," see pp. 56–73. I draw variously on some of these previous works in my treatment here.

37. On nature and the natural in Rousseau, see my discussion in *Public Man, Private Woman* and the chapter criticizing Allan Bloom's *The Closing of the American Mind* in one of my collection of essays, *Power Trips and Other Journeys.* And, although I will not discuss it in this chapter because it doesn't focus on sovereignty, Rousseau's "second discourse," *The Discourse on Inequality,* has entirely to do with nature and bodies, beginning with the rather insipid, stupid isolates meandering through forests and eating berries that comprise his vision of "natural man." My discussion in *Meditations on Modern Political Thought* concentrates almost entirely on this work. It is my own favorite among Rousseau's works—the second discourse is highly evocative and interesting, incorporating Rousseau's own version of the Fall—a fall out of nature and into culture.

38. See the previous note. Rousseau turns Hobbes upside down by construing Hobbes's infamous state of nature as a "war of all against all" as, in fact, the sort of condition human beings arrive at in culture and with the denigration of culture over time given that it comes to sever itself completely from the innocence, guilelessness, and transparency of natural man.

39. Jacques Maritain, *Three Reformers: Luther Descartes, Rousseau.* (New York: Thomas Crowell, 1970), p. 96.

40. Maritain, *Ibid.*, sees in this a direct perversion of the Gospel (p. 142).

41. Although ignored by political theorists, throughout France in the centuries following the upheavals of the French Revolution emerged a radical laicism, a spiritualized, feminized Catholicism that challenged the highly masculinist sway of French sovereignty. On this masculinism see my discussion of the French Revolution and the "republic" in *Women and War.* See also historian Ruth Harris's wonderful book, *Lourdes: Body and Spirit in the Secular Age* (London: Allen Lane, Penguin Press, 1999), a book that I would make required reading for all political theorists could I but wave a magic wand and make it so. Harris demonstrates the depth and extent of Catholic-feminine opposition to the demands of strong republicanism. Why this phenomenon has been ignored no doubt has to do with the fact that it was spearheaded by women . . . and sponsored, so to speak, by Catholicism, the religion that remains politically incorrect to many liberal academics.

42. Jean-Jacques Rousseau, *On the Social Contract with Geneva Manuscript and Political Economy*, ed. Roger D. Masters (New York: St. Martin's Press, 1978), p. 53.

43. *Ibid.,* p. 55.

44. *Ibid.,* pp. 61–62.

45. Here it seems as if Rousseau is leaving a good bit to the "private realm" but as he doesn't spell out what all this might be and how it can be sustained through institutional forms, one remains uneasy if one believes in both a strong version of tolerance and in institutional pluralities. *Ibid.*, p. 63.

46. *Ibid.,* p. 65. See also his draconian measures in *The Government of Poland* where he is severe in punishing dissent, trans.Willmoore Kendall (Indianapolis: Bobbs-Merrill, 1972).

47. Rousseau, *Ibid.,* p. 67. Rousseau adds that the founding of a people requires changing human nature and transforming everyone from an individual into a part of the whole (see pp. 68–69).

48. Rousseau, *Ibid.,* p. 99. Rousseau is trafficking in body politic imagery, drawn from medieval corporatism, to his own purposes of course.

49. Rousseau, *Ibid.,* p. 128.

50. Rousseau, *Ibid,* p. 129.

51. Rousseau, *Ibid.,* p. 126.

52. George Orwell, *1984* (New York: Plume, 2003). I can hear the howls of disbelief from Rousseauophiles now. Minimally, I express a worry and a tendency in Rousseau's work.

CHAPTER 7

1. Edmund Burke, *Reflections on the Revolution in France*, ed. Conor Cruise O'Brien (New York: Penguin Classics, 1982).

2. New York: Penguin Books, 1962

3. Arendt, *On Revolution*, p. 76.

4. *Ibid.*, p. 79.

5. *Ibid.*, p. 94.

6. *Ibid.*, p. 106.

7. A significant work that unpacks a politics of absolute willfulness by contrast to "limited will" is Bertrand de Jouvenel's *Sovereignty: An Inquiry into Political Good* (Chicago: University of Chicago Press, 1957).

8. The director, Mr. Wajda, stated in an interview in *Le Monde*, January 6, 1983: "I have always asked myself why the leaders of the Bolshevik Revolution have been interested in these two personalities [Danton and Robespierre]. In a certain sense, the film responds to this question." Cited in Mieczyslaw Szporer, "Andrzej Wajda's Reign of Terror: *Danton*'s Polish Ambience," in *Film Quarterly* 37.2 (1983) 27–33. One reason the film works so brilliantly are the extraordinary performances by Gerard Depardieu as Danton and the Polish actor, Wojciech Pszoniak as Robespierre.

9. Cited in Ruth Scurr, *Fatal Purity: Robespierre and the French Revolution* (New York: Metropolitan Books, 2006), p. 328. Scurr and others note that Robespierre was driven mad by his inability to discern with absolute certainty who was or was not concealing anything, who was or was not a hypocrite. Better not to take a chance and to behead anyone about whom one harbored suspicions (see p. 344). Of course, Robespierre believed that he himself was the embodiment of the revolution as a whole.

10. It is difficult to underestimate the sheer brutality of the Revolution. "In Lyon and elsewhere there were plenty of terrible examples: horrific mass executions . . . and group drownings in the Vendée—crimes against humanity that the revolutionaries would today be called to answer for under the European human rights legislation they themselves pioneered. Robespierre had argued consistently since 1789 that in a time of revolution the end justified the means, and even his advocates have to acknowledge that he did not flinch from the bloodiest implications of his position" (Scurr, pp. 282–283). See also Michael Burleigh, *Earthly Powers: The Clash of Religion and Politics in Europe, from the French Revolution to the Great War* (New York: Harper Collins, 2006).

11. Like Ataturk, the revolutionizing modernist of the Turkish Revolution in 1922 abolished the office of the Sultan, abolished the remnants of traditional society that were part of Turkey, abolished canon law, set up a secular law to govern Turkey, and imposed harsh modernizing economic policies from 1924–1937.

Ataturk modeled his revolution on radical French laicism. Turkish political and religious debates of the present moment revolve around Ataturk's legacy.

12. There have been many brilliant treatments of the depradations of the French Revolution, none more brilliant than Camus' essay, *The Rebel*. I refer to it here and I will take it up again in my discussions of the "sovereign self."

13. Camus was trashed by Jean-Paul Sartre and his minions for even writing *The Rebel*—something that very much counts in Camus' favor.

14. I'm having a bit of fun, okay?

15. It is for these reasons, and others, that Camus opposes the beheading of Louis XVI. Michael Walzer, however, endorses the move. See his arguments in *Regicide and Revolution: Speeches at the Trial of Louis XVI* (New York: Columbia University Press, 1993).

16. Albert Camus, *The Rebel* (New York: Vintage Books, 1956), p. 105.

17. *Ibid.*, p. 106.

18. *Ibid.*, p. 119.

19. *Ibid.*, p. 117.

20. *Ibid.*, p. 122.

21. At this point I'm simply going to assume that the reader understands all the necessary caveats so I need no longer spell them out explicitly. Of course, one cannot deal adequately with a fellow as wordy as Hegel in a few pages. But one can treat him interestingly by locating him as part of certain trends and tendencies that are with us yet, and that is my purpose.

22. *Ibid.*, p. 142.

23. All of this is very convoluted, very dense, and cast in language that makes one's head spin and isn't that intelligible to nonexperts and not even to many experts. Gillespie writes: "Nihilism taken to extreme in Hegel's view rebounds upon itself and reconstitutes itself as the most comprehensive order. . . . Absolute negation . . . must be self-negation, therefore, the negation of negation, and consequently the source of being. . . . The self-negation of nothingness is thus freedom's self-limitation and consequently the establishment of a system of rational necessity." Gillespie, *Nihilism Before Nietzsche*, p. 117.

24. *Ibid.*, pp. 116, 118.

25. G.W.F. Hegel, *The Phenomenology of Mind*, trans. J.B.Baille (New York: Harper and Row, 1967), p. 468.

26. *Ibid.*, p. 474.

27. *Ibid.*, p. 476. Cf. par. 166 of Hegel's *Philosophy of Right*, trans. T.M. Knox (London: Oxford University Press, 1976), pp. 114–115. "Women," Hegel insists, "are not made for activities which demand a universal faculty such as the more advanced sciences, philosophy, and certain forms of artistic production. Women may have happy ideas, taste, and elegance, but they cannot attain to the

ideal." Hegel goes on to compare men to animals and women to plants. The men-as-animals analogy is very troubling in the context of subsequent German history, for Nazi ideology held that Nazism was comprised of "beasts" enacting their necessary task of survival of the fittest, and the beast kills without guilt.

28. Charles Taylor, *Hegel* (Cambridge: Cambridge University Press, 1975), p. 379.

29. Hegel, *Philosophy of Right*, p. 210.

30. I have drawn here and there from my discussions of Hegel in *Public Man, Private Woman*, pp. 170–183, and *Women and War*, pp. 73–75. As well, in *Women and War*, I deploy Hegel's notion of the "beautiful soul" as a name for womanhood as a collective being throughout history, she who embodies certain verities and virtues but they are sealed off into a privatized sentimentalism.

31. Some see a straight line from Luther to Hegel; without Luther, no Hegel. Their reasoning holds that Luther's nominalism does away with the Church as necessary to salvation and moves him in a subjectivist direction. This is the task Gillespie takes up, e.g. I do not believe Luther is guilty as charged—he is far too complex and grace plays far too vital a role in his theology for that.

32. See Ratzinger (Pope Benedict XVI), in his *Introduction to Christianity*, where he writes that Hegel's project historicizes the logos "and with the comprehension of God, also wants to abolish mystery and comprehend the unity of God, to construct it itself according to its own logic. . . . [It] leads us back to a mythology of history, to the myth of a God who brings himself to birth historically" (p. 170). But, contra Hegel, according to Ratzinger, the highest unity is not monistic; God "stands above singular and plural. He bursts both categories" (p. 170). The concrete and particular is of ineffable value as one is speaking of the person made in God's image. Hegel is flat-out wrong that the highest value is located in the universal. Not so, for the concrete and the particular is lifted up and blessed by Christian theology and Christ himself. For the person is irreducible (p. 158). It is a mistake to see the "universal" as somehow more "godlike."

33. Dietrich Bonhoeffer, *Ethics* (New York: Touchstone Books, 1995), p. 98.

34. *Ibid.*, p. 103.

35. *Ibid.*, p. 103. I spell out some of the implications of this deification in *Who Are We? Critical Reflections and Hopeful Possibilities* (Grand Rapids, Mich.: Eerdmans, 2000).

36. I have written of this extensively in other works. See, most recently, *Just War Against Terror: The Burden of American Power in a Violent World* (New York: Basic Books, 2003.)

37. Grotius's dates are 1583–1645. Grotius comes out of the Arminian tradition. Arminians rejected the Calvinist doctrine that grace alone effects human salvation even in the absence of good works to attain salvation. Arminians sought

a working-out of this free will–good works conundrum. They were given to underwriting human acts as either works of God or works of the devil.

38. Edwin Rabbie, ed. (Amsterdam: Grotius Institute, 1990). Chapter 2 of this work is titled "How God should be considered . . . as a ruler." Arguing against the Socinianist/Unitarian strain, Grotius declares that God is a ruler and, contra Socinus, that God did need to become incarnate in order to save men. Socinus mistakenly assumes that a sin against God is just a tort, when in fact it is a sin against the ruler who is responsible for perfect order. Grotius says all sorts of interesting things about the mutual obligations of rulers. Grotius, Locke, and Kant all wrote discussions on atonement, which included a theory of punishment, and argued that in their theories of the state, punishment plays a major role.

39. International politics scholar Martin Wight describes Grotius as one who seeks a Golden Mean. He was a "reconciler and synthesizer." As such, he "was deeply sensitive to human suffering and equally did not imagine that it would ever disappear." So one must distinguish just from unjust wars and strive to contain war's brutality. This is made possible, in part, because of human sociability—our very natures lead us to mutual relations. The law of nature to which we have access is unchangeable, even by God. See Martin Wight, *Four Seminal Thinkers in International Theory,* eds. Gabriele Wight and Brian Porter (Oxford: Oxford University Press, 2005), pp. 39–41.

40. See David L. Gilsinn, *The Theory of Consent: A Study of Sovereignty* (master's thesis in political science, June 2, 1941, Georgetown University), p. 27. As in medieval law, a social compact must be faithfully abided by and executed, and the failure of one party to fulfill obligations releases the other from any obligation. People are not mere aggregates but form a "corporate personality," a "juristic personality" (p. 46).

41. I don't wish to caricature Clausewitz here, for much of what he says makes enormous good sense, including his insistence that political ends must be dominant over military means in time of war; unfortunately, some of those political ends may take on a kind of limitlessness that is very dangerous. Clausewitz's insight that combat is as much a psychological as a political phenomenon; that war fighting itself stirs up hostile feelings even assuming there were few hostile feelings before the war started; his insistence that many emotions get "linked with fighting . . . ambition, love of power, enthusiasms of all kinds" and his recognition that "courage" outweighs what one is tempted to call the "normal" reaction to danger—namely, flight—all remain salient to contemporary discussions of men and battle, men in battle, and the role of civilian sentiment and will in war fighting. See Bernard Brodie, "A Guide to Reading *On War,*" in Carl von Clausewitz, *On War* (Princeton, N.J.: Princeton University Press, 1984), pp. 641–711. See especially *On War*, pp. 137–138. For these thoughts on Clausewitz, I draw a few paragraphs from my book *Women and War.*

42. See Isabel Hull, *Absolute Destruction. Military Culture and the Practices of War in Imperial Germany* (Ithaca, N.Y.: Cornell University Press, 2005). I chaired the committee of Phi Beta Kappa that honored Hull's book with the Ralph Waldo Emerson Award in 2005—richly deserved.

43. See Marshall, *Swords and Symbols*, p. 172.

44. See Daniel Philpott's work on the religious themes in international relations, "The Religious Roots of Modern International Relations," *World Politics* 52 (January 2000), pp. 206–245; "Usurping the Sovereignty of the Sovereign," *World Politics* 53 (January 2001), pp. 297–324. And check out his book *Revolutions in Sovereignty: How Ideas Shaped Modern International Relations* (Princeton: Princeton University Press, 2001).

45. Unfortunately, today's options are presented either as a new form of universalism not glued together by natural law or shared beliefs, or hard-core *realpolitik*. Strong states who themselves protect rights internally are prepared to join others in promoting them externally—certainly the United States is—but this doesn't satisfy contemporary universalists. They embrace international human rights absent an effective enforcement mechanism. People appeal to those rights but are slaughtered with impunity nonetheless. One winds up with a thin, evanescent universalism that is more or less arbitrarily evoked by states who claim some universal jurisdiction, rather than acting *qua* state, e.g., the Spanish courts have been busy in recent years indicting various people. It is certainly reasonable to ask why this is happening and whether a better strategy might be to try to insure that the internal statutory law of each and every state protects rights and provides for punishment should they be violated. It is clear that a "thin" international order cannot do this and a "thick" order is not in the cards for a number of reasons. Despite this, the "universal" is always taken up nowadays as morally, legally, and ethically superior to "the particular." There is an automatic "yes" to the claims of the supposed moral superiority of international institutions over sovereign states. This "Olympianism," as Kenneth Minogue puts it, generates the idea that nationalism lies at the root of all conflicts in the world—despite the fact that both National Socialism and Stalinist communism were universal ideologies based on race and class respectively. See Kenneth Minogue, "Olympianism and the Denigration of Nationality," in *The Worth of Nations*, ed. Claudio Veliz (Boston: Boston University Professors Program, 1993, pp. 71–81), quote from p. 81.

46. Hannah Arendt, "On Violence," in *Crises of the Republic* (New York: Harcourt and Brace, 1972), pp. 107–108.

47. Paul E. Sigmund, *Natural Law in Political Thought* (Cambridge, Mass.: Winthrop Publishing, 1971), p. 99. The colonists were also familiar with the writings of Sir Edward Coke's *Institutes*.

48. 2 Dallas 419, 454. The "one place" Wilson has in mind is, of course, the Preamble to the Constitution. The question before the Court in *Chisholm* was: May a citizen of one state sue another state in the federal courts? The answer: sure. The result: Amendment XI to the constitution to reverse this decision. Amendment XI reads: "The Judicial power of the United States shall not be construed to extend to any suit in law or equity, commenced or prosecuted against one of the United States by Citizens of another State, or by Citizens or Subjects of any Foreign State." Curiously, the Court had declared in 1792 that the "United States are sovereign as to the powers of government actually surrendered. Each State in the Union is sovereign as to all the powers conferred."

49. This address was published as a pamphlet in New York City in 1890.

50. *Ibid.*, pp. 17–18, 23.

51. The genealogy of sovereignty that Phelps assumes begins with the sovereignty of Kings, eventually found intolerable by barons who struck the earliest blow for freedom but then began to abuse their power via the instrument of oligarchy. At this point Parliamentarian sovereignty takes over but it, too, becomes oppressive, so the only way to guarantee a nonoppressive sovereignty is through a constitutional judiciary (p. 16). See also Hymen Ezra Cohen, *Recent Theories of Sovereignty* (Chicago: University of Chicago Press, 1937).

52. *Cohens v. Virginia*, 19 U.S. 264 (1821).

53. 11 U.S. (7 Cranch), pp. 116, 136.

54. 299 U.S. 304. See the cases in Louis Fisher, *American Constitutional Law*, 5th edition, chapter 7, "Separation of Powers" (Durham, N.C.: Carolina Academic Press, 2003).

55. See Abraham Lincoln, "First Inaugural," The Avalon Project of Yale Law School, http://www.yale.edu/lawweb/avalon/presiden/inaug/lincoln1.htm.

56. See, for example, Marshall, *Swords and Symbols*, p. 70.

57. Those wishing to pursue this matter will find a case study in Tim Alan Garrison, *The Legal Ideology of Removal: The Southern Judiciary and the Sovereignty of Native American Nations* (Athens: University of Georgia Press, 2002). Garrison shows the ways in which the word *sovereignty* evoked "different connotations to Indians under the threat of removal than it did for the European political theorists who devised the concept" (pp. 34–35). By the nineteenth century, he continues, American lawyers and political philosophers used the term to mean that some final and absolute political authority existed somewhere in a political community: that a sovereign nation had final say (p. 35). Lawyers for the Cherokee Indian nation, who were all men trained in English common law, used sovereignty in more than a legalistic way but, also, as a spiritual concept connoting "a deep spiritual connection to an ancestral homeland. . . . Sovereignty was a function of historical memory for many Cherokees" (p. 35). Cherokees used *sovereignty* to mean a particular right that could not be arbitrar-

ily overtaken by a higher power. It followed that the legal dealings between the constitutional government of the United States and the particularistic Indian tribes should take the form of treaties—and, for the most part, this is what happened. The Cherokee lawyers could also bring to bear Pope Innocent IV's thirteenth-century insistence that non-Christians possessed the same rights under natural law as Christians. So even though people possessed such sovereign rights, those could be encroached upon under certain circumstances. I have already noted the way in which the doctrine of *terra nullius* was brought to bear against the autonomy of native tribes. Wars of conquest were always a feature of international law and could also be legitimate given certain circumstances (p. 71). This entire doctrine was ambiguous and riddled with tensions and could be brought to bear in behalf of the sovereign encroachment of a superior or, by contrast, the protection of a particular and "lesser" body. So the question in the case of the removal of the Cherokees had to do with whether the Cherokee nation constituted a sovereign power of some sort and, if so, of what sort. Indian lawyers repaired to received doctrines of natural law and natural right to make their case in behalf of the Cherokee. Ultimately, in the case of *Cherokee Nation v. Georgia*, the Court concluded that the Cherokee nation lacked standing as a sovereign power under Article 3 of the Constitution (p. 134). The Cherokee could remain self-governing in certain important respects but they were in the final analysis entirely dependent upon the sovereign power of the United States government. *Cherokee Nation v. State of Ga.*, 30 U.S. 1 (1831). See also Francis A. Brooks, *An Arraignment of President McKinley's Policy Extending by Force the Sovereign of the United States Over the Philippine Islands* (Boston: Alfred Mudge and Sons, 1899).

58. See *Korematsu v. U.S.*, 323 USS 214 (1944). The Court later thought differently about its holding in this particular case, without overturning the notion of the exception altogether.

CHAPTER 8

1. It is not at all clear how a sovereign state in the classical sense and a multiplicity of sovereign selves can happily coexist.

2. Peter Brown, *Augustine of Hippo* (Berkeley: University of California Press, 1967), p. 181. I draw upon some sections of my book *Augustine and the Limits of Politics* (Notre Dame, Ind.: Notre Dame University Press, 1995) here.

3. Augustine, *The Confessions* (New York: Penguin Books, 1961). On the ways in which some contemporary observers fail to make contact with Augustine's complexity and go on to maul his discussion, see chapter 1 of my *Augustine and the Limits of Politics*. This failure of self-understanding stems, I suspect, from the inability of observers to imagine a self that confesses to a greater-than-self. They can only interpret this as a kind of "sick" self-absorption.

4. Augustine, *The City of God*, trans. H. Bettenson (Baltimore, Md.: Penguin Books, 1972), p. 565.

5. I will not take this up here but simply note that, for Augustine, there are warranted beliefs—despite his epistemological skepticism. But we are not able to verify these beliefs all on our own. We cannot be everywhere, see everything, experience everything ourselves. Trust plays a huge role in positing truths. We all rely on others for what we have come to know, and this should inspire a certain humility.

6. Augustine, *The City of God*, p. 623.

7. *Ibid.,* p. 625.

8. Here the famous passage *Ibid.,* pp. 981–982. Augustine imagines someone meeting another person who cannot speak his tongue and then opines that fellowship comes easier with a dog because our language differences alienate us from one another and make it more difficult to see our commonalities.

9. See Augustine, *On the Trinity* (Washington, D.C.: Catholic University of America Press, 1992.) The quote is from Charles Norris Cochrane's classic, *Christianity and Classical Culture* (New York: Galaxy Books, 1959), p. 384. Cochrane defends Augustine against the charge by some liberal theologians that he—Augustine—is trafficking in obscurantisms, leaps into the darkness, etc., and that his work has no bearing on the modern self or modern belief save as what one should not do.

10. See also Augustine, *Select Letters*: *The Letters of St. Augustine,* Fathers of the Church series, 20 (Washington, D.C.: Catholic University of America Press, 1953), no. 41, p. 317. As is always the case with Augustine, he is intent on preserving a complex tension between works and grace, and he chastens those who go too far in one direction or the other, including strong anti-Pelagians who insist that it is grace alone we must rely on, for this leads to a denial of the freedom of the human will. It is a delicate balancing act. See *Select Letters*, no. 50, p. 350.

11. Augustine, *Answer to the Pelagians,* Vol. I (Hyde Park, N.Y.: New City Press, 1997); Vol. II (1998); Vol. III (1999); Vol. IV (1999). Just dipping into these volumes reminds one of the observation of many of Augustine's contemporaries, as well as current scholars, that it is not possible for one person to read everything Augustine wrote—which makes it unbelievable that he wrote as much as he did—before typewriters, before computers. This reminds one that there are a few persons who pop up on this earth who are clearly gifted, nigh miraculous, against even the highest expectations of what human beings might accomplish. Mozart would be another example.

12. *Ibid.,* Vol. IV, p. 99.

13. James Wetzel, *Augustine and the Limits of Virtue* (Cambridge: Cambridge University Pres, 1992), pp. 8, 10.

14. Augustine, *Select Letters*, no. 46, p. 351, and see this point made throughout *On the Trinity*.

15. For a more thorough unpacking see my *Augustine and the Limits of Politics,* chapter 3, "Against the Pridefulness of Philosophy." Augustine himself had to get used to "the style in which God's word is spoken." As a member of a very elite circle of trained rhetors (although he was a boy from the provinces, the Romans tapped unusually capable people for advancement and training), he had memorized the great texts. A rhetor had to be prepared to recite for six or seven hours nonstop. The beauty of language enchanted him. When he first encountered Scripture, he was put off. It seemed rustic, the language of rubes and bumpkins. But then he realized that God humbled himself so that we, all of us, might rise to him. One should not disdain the truth because of the "lowliness" in which it is garbed. Christ himself was humble and humbled to the end. This "is displeasing to the proud."

16. Pope Benedict XVI, *Introduction to Christianity*, p. 249.

17. *Bound to Sin: Abuse, Holocaust, and the Christian Doctrine of Sin* (Cambridge: Cambridge University Press, 2000).

18. *Ibid.*, p. 4. He writes that contemporary Western culture is embarrassed by the doctrine of original sin and sees it as entirely anachronistic. But we have paid the price—a loss of understanding. Original sin, he argues, helps us to understand that all generations of human beings inherit the consequences of the first sin and all subsequent sins and, further, that sin effects a fundamental distortion in our understanding of our own sociality (pp. 14–15).

19. *Ibid.*, p. 30.

20. *Ibid.*, pp. 167–169.

21. *Ibid.*, p. 172.

22. *Ibid.*, pp. 172–173. See also my discussion of Augustine on the self in *Augustine and the Limits of Politics*.

23. *Ibid.*, p. 185.

24. Dialogue drawn from the text of Harper Lee, *To Kill a Mockingbird* (Harper Collins, 1999; published originally in 1960), pp. 317–318.

25. Some ethicists have argued that liberal societies will not be able to sustain their policies for aiding and providing access for the handicapped because the tension between that and the view that no one should be handicapped, that, in a sense, one is culpable for one's inabilities, will at one point become too much. If you are not a full-fledged person, it is much easier to denigrate or destroy you. See, for example, Hans Reinders, *The Future of the Disabled in Liberal Society* (Notre Dame: University of Notre Dame Press, 2000). It is interesting to note that social contract theories also had difficulties with these categories, although

children were easier to deal with than the mentally handicapped. For children will one day grow out of their nonage, but the mentally handicapped never will.

26. My purposes here are critical and constructive. I do not claim that I have by any means exhausted these four thinkers; instead, I want to identify the ways in which each feeds into the creation of sovereign selves.

27. Clemence is a "judge-penitent," once a successful attorney in Paris who judged swiftly and certainly. That world collapsed and he is now a judge-penitent. He embodies, in a sense, both faces of the Janus-faced sovereign self: both strong and soft sovereignty.

28. *The Fall* (New York: Vintage Books, 1991), p. 116.

29. The famous "I think therefore I am" can be found in the 4th section of Descartes' 1637 *Discourse on Method*. Descartes' dates are 1596–1650.

30. Michael Gillespie, unpublished manuscript, "Sovereign State." See also his *Nihilism Before Nietzsche* (Chicago: University of Chicago Press, 1995), pp. 33–63.

31. See "To More, Replies to Objections" (February 5, 1649), pp. 292–296 and *Meditations on First Philosophy*, Meditations Two & Six. Both of these are in René Descartes, *Philosophical Essays and Correspondence*, ed. Roger Ariew (Indianapolis: Hackett, 2000).

32. Benedict XVI, *Introduction to Christianity*, p. 147. Benedict continues that the philosophical God is "pure thought" for "thought alone is divine" (p. 148). Here again we see the wild over-exaggeration of rationalism over love. We are cerebral, not soulful, and "I" is never a "we."

33. J. B. Schneewind, *The Invention of Autonomy* (Cambridge: Cambridge University Press, 1998), p. 187.

34. René Descartes, *The Philosophical Writings of Descartes, Vol. III: The Correspondence* (Cambridge: Cambridge University Press, 1991), p. 245.

35. Hormones course through the brain, e.g., and how much they influence behavior is debated but there is no doubt whatsoever that they influence the brain. This is just one tiny piece of evidence against the Cartesian dualistic view of mind in relation to body. Indeed, the "mind" and "body" categorization is profoundly misleading.

36. Antonio R. Damasio, *Descartes' Error: Emotion, Reasoning, and the Human Brain* (New York: G. P. Putnam's Sons, 1994), p. 247.

37. Jennifer Michael Hecht, *The End of the Soul: Scientific Modernity, Atheism and Anthropology in France* (New York: Columbia University Press, 2003), p. 9.

38. *Ibid.*, pp. 40, 315. Unfortunately, there is a direct connection between these efforts that invited a crude biological reductionism and nineteenth-century racialist theories. Hecht's book is brilliant on this and other cultural as well as scientific issues.

39. Colin Gunton, *The One, the Three and the Many* (Cambridge: Cambridge University Press, 1993), p. 117.

40. Obviously, there is no way to explore his philosophy exhaustively, but I want to display the ways in which "Kantianism" traffics in a strong notion of moral autonomy tantamount to self-sovereignty.

41. Kant advances this argument in *Perpetual Peace and Other Essays* (Indianapolis, Ind.: Hackett, 1983), p. 126. The "maxims" of philosophers must be consulted by nations concerning all questions of war and peace, he insists, for as a class they are "by nature" incapable of forming cliques or intrigue. Anyone who has inhabited the academy for any length of time can only chuckle at this risible presumption. Philosophy departments are no more immune from academic politics and intrigue than any other.

42. Immanuel Kant, *Critique of Pure Reason* (New York: The Modern Library, 1958), p. 195. Kant's dates are 1724–1804.

43. *Ibid.,* pp. 257, 259. Kant holds the emotions at a distance as a dangerous force not bound up with reason. For a compelling critique see Karol Wojtyla, Pope John Paul II, *The Acting Person* (Holland: D. Reidel, 1979). "The fact that with the emergence of an emotion or passion man is prompted to seek some sort of integration and that this becomes a special task for him, does not signify in any way that they are in themselves a cause of disintegration. The view about their disintegrating role appeared in the philosophy of the Stoic school and in modern times was to some extent revived by Kant. If the position advocating in various ways a rejection of emotions so as to act solely according to reason (Kant's idea of the categorical imperative) were to be maintained, then it would be necessary to accept the whole emotive capacity as being itself a source of disintegration in the acting person. The broadly conceived experience of man, with due attention paid to morality, prevents us, however, from accepting this. . . . The view that conceived of human emotivity—and in particular human emotionality—as a source of disintegration is a manifestation of a special sort of ethical and anthropological a priorism, and the essence of any a priorism is to disregard the evidence of experience." (See pp. 243–244.)

44. Martin Wight, *Four Thinkers in International Relations* (Oxford: Oxford University Press, 2005), p. 43.

45. Immanuel Kant, *Groundwork of the Metaphysic of Morals* (New York: Harper Torchbooks, 1964), p. 39.

46. William A. Galston, *Kant and the Problem of History* (Chicago: University of Chicago Press, 1975), p. 201. See also my "Kant, Politics and Persons: The Implications of His Moral Philosophy," *Polity* (Vol. XIV, No. 2, Winter 1981), pp. 205–221.

47. See Schneewind, *Invention of Autonomy*, p. 508.

48. This essay appears in *Between Past and Future* (Baltimore, Md.: Penguin Books, 1968), p. 125.

49. See my discussion of "Kant and Rational Politics," in *Meditations on Modern Political Thought*, pp. 21–35. Feminist critiques have taken Kant to task on a number of grounds, disembodiment being one. Also the role of emotion and sentiment epistemologically speaking. Especially incurring ire is Kant's claim that dependent persons, like women, lack a "civic personality."

50. I do not mean to denigrate a search for the truth but instead to raise questions about a relentless rigorism that cannot live with moral ambiguity. See Bonhoeffer's essay in his *Ethics* (New York: Simon and Schuster, 1995).

51. *Ibid.,* p. 363, note l.

52. *Ibid.*

53. Bonhoeffer goes on to argue that Christianity is not primarily a moralistic system. Those who moralize Christianity treat God as a metaphysical first principle rather than the living trinitarian God who is an agent in history. "Neo-Protestant motive-ethics," Bonhoeffer calls it, with Kant in mind. A strictly moralistic system kills faith and makes it more difficult for us to respond largeheartedly to the neighbor before us. Kant seeks the unity of the ego in conformity with an abstract universal principle.

54. Alexander McCall Smith, *The Sunday Philosophy Club* (New York: Pantheon, 2004), pp. 60–61.

CHAPTER 9

1. Having written about Mill previously, I see no need to precisely repeat myself here. See especially my discussion of Mill in *Public Man, Private Woman,* pp. 132–146. I was examining Mill through the prism of public and private in that work and I especially took him to task for what he has to say in *The Subjection of Women,* arguing that this "feminist" text is, in fact, quite problematic for a number of reasons, not least among these his extraordinarily bleak view of male motivation throughout history, avatars of the "law of force" with only an "odious source" for anything that has to do with traditional relations between men and women. As with most self-sovereigntists, he refuses to see human beings as located under the weight of history and tradition and working, therefore, to carve out some space for human agency in light of this fact. Concerning female motivation, he offers a "cleansed" and beneficent account, unless women attempt to find dominance in the private realm, having been denied it in the public realm, in which case "power" takes over and, according to Mill "power" and "liberty" are eternally antagonistic. This odd blanking-out of power, as if politics could go forward in any meaningful way without the use of power, is part and parcel of Mill's moralistic approach to male and female relations.

2. (New York: Penguin Books, 1983). *On Liberty* was first published in 1859 and has been in continuous publication ever since. It was answered on certain critical points quite persuasively by James Fitzjames Stephens in his *Liberty, Equality, Fraternity*, first published in 1873, although neither Stephens's witty response nor that of any other critic achieved anything remotely approaching the canonical status of Mill's tract. All quotes from *On Liberty* are from the 1983 Penguin edition. I use quotation marks only for long passages. It should also be noted here that liberalism is a many splendored thing. There is an abstract liberalism, shorn from historic shaping, trafficking in sovereign selves. But there is another sort of liberalism, one aware of the ironies of history, the inescapability of moral conflict, and our inability to perfect either the human person or human societies but our responsibility, minimally, to see to it that the least harm is done to persons and to communities. Because American liberalism has gone the way of sovereign selves, offering a criticism is automatically taken to mean that one is illiberal in today's climate, of course.

3. Hannah Arendt, "What Is Authority?" in *Between Past and Future*, offers a provocative discussion of the loss of authority in the modern world.

4. James Eli Adams, "Philosophical Forgetfulness: John Stuart Mill's 'Nature,'" *Journal of the History of Ideas* (1992, pp. 437–454), is instructive on these matters.

5. See my full essay "Mill's Liberty and the Problem of Authority," in David Bromwich and George Kateb, eds., *On Liberty: John Stuart Mill* (New Haven: Yale University Press, 2003), pp. 208–223.

6. See my discussion in *Public Man, Private Woman*. The quote is cited on p. 230 of that work.

7. See my discussion in *Meditations on Modern Political Thought*, pp. 63–68. The cited material is on p. 64.

8. This address is published as a pamphlet (Kailua, Hawaii: published privately by Doris M. Ladd and Jane Wilkins Pultz, 1979). The citation is from p. 1 and all subsequent cites are from the essay. I draw here upon *Meditations*, p. 66. See also the discussion in Beth M. Waggenspack, *The Search for Self-Sovereignty: The Oratory of Elizabeth Cady Stanton* (New York: Greenwood Press, 1989). Waggenspack specifically focuses on Stanton's oratory in this published dissertation. I don't know if anyone has done this, but it would be interesting to compare the novels of Ayn Rand that extol self-capitalization, so to speak. They are paeans to laissez-faire in all things, all of this driven by a relentless rationalism. For Rand human beings are self-made "souls," not embodied creatures. Anything that smacks of weakness, she scorns. For our compassionate outbursts drain away self-sovereignty. Her major novel is *The Fountainhead* (New York: New American Library, 1971). Rand has something of a cult following, people dedicated to burnishing her memory.

9. A caveat: I draw almost exclusively upon *Being and Nothingness* because the presumptions of his early espousal of existentialism have seeped so thoroughly into some radical feminist theories of liberation. In the R. D. Laing and David Cooper translation and précis of *La Critique de la raison dialectique*, Sartre blesses the effort as a faithful account. To ignore the impact of *Being and Nothingness* because Sartre later took on more Marxist baggage ignores much of what remains constant in his work. My reading of Sartre's *Search for a New Method* (New York: Vintage Books, 1968) convinces me that Sartre never succeeded in "synthesizing" Marxism and existentialism tied to the phenomenological tradition. The edition of *Being and Nothingness* I rely on is the Hazel Barnes translation (New York: Philosophical Library, 1956). All quotes, unless otherwise noted, are drawn from this work. One must also note his bloody-minded introduction to Franz Fanon's *The Wretched of the Earth.*

10. *Ibid.,* p. 485.

11. Germaine Bree, *Camus and Sartre*, p. 91.

12. For philosopher Mary Midgely, the "really monstrous thing about Existentialism . . . is its proceeding as if the world contained only dead matter . . . on the one hand and fully rational, educated, adult human beings on the other—as if there were no other life-forms." See her *Beast and Man* (Ithaca: Cornell University Press, 1978).

13. Simone de Beauvoir, *The Second Sex* (New York: Bantam Books, 1968), here quoting someone else, p. xxxix. All other citations are from this text unless otherwise noted.

14. With friends like this, a woman probably doesn't need enemies. See my discussion of Beauvoir in *Public Man, Private Woman*, pp. 306–311. See also my essay "Liberalism and Repressive Feminism," in *Liberalism and the Modern Polity*, ed. Michael J. Gargas McGrath (New York: Dekker, 1978), pp. 33–61.

15. I recount this story in Jean Bethke Elshtain, *Jane Addams and the Dream of American Democracy* (New York: Basic Books, 2002).

16. There is a "feminist" version of Transcendentalism in the work of the redoubtable Margaret Fuller, particularly her book *Woman in the Nineteenth Century in the Writings of Margaret Fuller*, ed. Mason Wade (New York: Viking Press, 1941). Written in 1844, her essay on nineteenth-century women argued that women must express their unique qualities, their "especial genius." Women were the "electrical, magnetic element" in human life—a romantic celebration of nature in general, female nature in particular.

17. For the full story, see my *Jane Addams and the Dream of American Democracy*.

18. All citations are from the American Scholar address available online at www.emersoncentral.com/amscholar.htm. Emerson lived from 1803 to 1882.

19. This, too, is available online at www.emersoncentral.com/divaddr.htm.

20. This sort of thing prompted theologian H. Richard Niebuhr, scoring liberal theology in general, to write, apropos of that theology: "A God without wrath brought men without sin into a kingdom without judgment through the ministrations of a Christ without a cross." Quoted in Alec R. Widler, *The Church in an Age of Reformation* (Harmondsworth: Penguin, 1968), p. 213.

21. Nathaniel Hawthorne, *The Scarlet Letter* (New York: Penguin Books, 1999).

22. All quotations are from "Ethan Brand," an 1850 short story, in Nathaniel Hawthorne, *Selected Tales and Sketches* (New York: Penguin, 1987), pp. 336–357.

23. "The Celestial Railroad," pp. 316–335, in Hawthorne, *Selected Tales*.

24. In *Ibid.*, pp. 259–278.

25. There are no serious students of Christianity who find credible Nietsche's narrative of the origins and establishment of Christianity in the West, any more than students of music find credible his forays into musicology. But Nietzsche did limn brilliantly a certain distortion of the mind or personality called *ressentiment*—spite, envy, and its eruption into politics. Self-sovereignty is here implicated. Suffice to say for now that if you probe deeply into his analysis of Christianity as the "slave religion," inviting a slavish self that envies and desires what oppresses it, you will find traces of the *potentia Dei absoluta* and *potentia Dei ordinata* struggle. For it is only an absolute willful God that generates the creation of a slavish opposite, or might do so.

26. Friedrich Nietzsche, *On the Genealogy of Morals* (New York: Vintage Books, 1989). Nietzsche's dates are 1844–1900.

27. *Ibid.*, p. 33.

28. Again, it would be unreasonable to say Nietzsche hasn't put his finger on something, namely, a tendency in a sickly version of Christianity to celebrate weakness as a positive virtue and to see in any display of strength the sin of pride. This is a distorted version of Christianity but one, alas, that Nietzsche mistakes for the whole.

29. See, for example, *Ibid.*, p. 93. Christianity is a "woman's religion," sneers Nietzsche.

30. The secondary literature on Nietzsche is by now altogether out of control. No human being, even someone dedicating himself or herself full-time to nothing but Nietzschean scholarship could possibly get through it all.

31. Friedrich Nietzsche, *The Will to Power* (New York: Vintage Books, 1968), pp. 10–11.

32. *Ibid.*, p. 25.

33. *Ibid.,* p. 30. Slipping into language he has rejected, Nietzsche tells us that unfortunately man is no longer a beast of prey, he is no longer evil enough. He has become tender and moralized and this is a curse (p. 61).

34. *Ibid.,* p. 267.

35. *Ibid.,* p. 96. The "Jew Paul" is to blame for much of this, according to Nietzsche. Paul, of course, also came and comes in for a whipping in many strains of liberal theology.

36. *Ibid.,* p. 116.

37. *Ibid.,* p. 142.

38. *Ibid.,* p. 149.

39. *Ibid.,* p. 200.

40. *Ibid.,* p. 389.

41. Albert Camus, *The Rebel* (New York: Vintage Books, 1956), pp. 65–80, *passim.*

CHAPTER 10

1. Cormac McCarthy, *No Country for Old Men* (New York: Vintage Books, 2006), pp. 196–197. Thanks to Randall Newman for drawing this passage to my attention. And special thanks to my friend and colleague William Schweiker for his analysis and critique of my categories of hard and soft self-sovereignty.

2. This is the issue of *Time* dated December 25, 2007–January 1, 2007.

3. Robin W. Lovin, in *Reinhold Niebuhr and Christian Realism* (New York: Cambridge University Press, 1995), offers a compelling discussion on the ways in which Niebuhr attempted to walk a fine line between over- and underidentification with his culture.

4. There are many books on this issue. I am personally aware of efforts by feminists to sanitize Sanger's project because she promoted "freedom." I always want to say, "Tell that to the women who were part of the group she consigned to a lesser category, who are to be either inhibited or prohibited from giving birth. Tell that to the young mentally deficient woman," and so on. It is freedom for the robust and healthy.

5. Angela Franks, *Margaret Sanger's Eugenic Legacy: The Control of Female Fertility* (London: McFarland and Co., 2005), pp. 10–11.

6. *Buck v. Bell,* 274 U.S. 200, 207 (1927).

7. See Franks, p. 187.

8. Nor was the United States alone in this. On August 29, 1997, as Franks recounts the tale, Sweden discovered that thousands of "useless" citizens had been sterilized for decades. A eugenics law sanctioned sterilization of some 62,000 persons between 1934 and 1974. "The victims included a woman whose poor vision prevented her from reading the blackboard and caused her to be labeled mentally retarded" (p. 179). Clearly an "ethics of social control" is involved in all this.

9. At times the animus against unsovereign selves became positively vicious. Ian Dowbiggin recounts one meeting of the National Conference on Charities and Corrections, held in 1888, during which the question of what to do with the "feeble-minded" among us came up. A Harvard-trained physician and teacher replied, "I would stamp out and kill the whole brood." Infanticide was endorsed for those who could "never become useful members of society." In 1935 the same sorts of arguments were being mounted, despite what was happening in Germany and despite the fact that scientists themselves were increasingly dubious about the eugenics project. At one Unitarian meeting the conclusion was reached that the incurably insane and mentally retarded ought to be "mercifully executed by the lethal chamber. It is simply social cowardice that keeps imbeciles, and idiot infants and monsters alive," for their deaths would be "socially desirable." See Ian Dowbiggin, *A Merciful End: The Euthanasia Movement in Modern America* (Oxford: Oxford University Press, 2003), pp. 17, 44.

10. *Ibid.* This, of course, was identical to the argument made by National Socialist proponents of eugenics and euthanasia.

11. Christine Rosen, *Preaching Eugenics: American Religions Leaders and the Eugenics Movement* (Oxford: Oxford University Press, 2004), p. 5. Subsequent citations are from this text unless otherwise noted.

12. One interesting feature of all this is that as geneticists grew more dubious about the presuppositions of the enterprise, social reformers became ever more dedicated, lodging their hopes for a brave new world in an increasingly outmoded science.

13. Cited by Roger Shattuck, *Forbidden Knowledge* (New York: Harcourt and Brace, 1996), p. 173. Shattuck, for those who don't know, is—or was, as he died recently—no right-wing crackpot but a National Book Award–winning author. One needs to point this out, alas, as so many are quick to judge naysayers as hopeless bumpkins and troglodytes.

14. Interestingly, in the run-up to World War II it was the neoorthodox, led by Reinhold Niebuhr, who opposed Nazism most vehemently and believed the United States had to fight to stop its spread. The liberal theological swath of the American clergy tended to argue the other direction. It is all rather striking. See Joseph Laconte, ed., *The End of Illusions* (Lanham, Md.,: Rowman and Littlefield, 2004).

15. For this history see Rosen's discussion, pp. 116–117.

16. *Ibid.*, p. 123.

17. *Ibid.*, p. 129.

18. *Ibid.*, p. 185.

19. When I visited the U.K. last year, there was a case in the headlines involving the aborting of a child with cleft palate. One of my own grandsons, indeed the grandson my husband and I are raising as our own child, was in danger of being born

blind, my daughter and I were told during a sonogram. Had we seriously paid attention to that, there would be no precious Bobby in the world. And even if the child had been born with sight impairment, he would still be the precious Bobby.

20. She went on to say had she and her husband followed the advocacy of medical providers they would never have known "the joyous privilege of parenting a child with Down syndrome. . . . Tommy's [not his real name] birth truly transformed our lives in ways we will cherish forever. But how could we have known in advance that we would indeed possess the fortitude to parent a child with special needs? And who would have told us of the rich rewards?"

21. See *Who Are We?* chapter 3, in which I also point out some cases in which genetic alteration, to prevent egregious harm and not on a quest for perfection, seems defensible. So I am not simply a naysayer about all these developments.

22. For the next few paragraphs, I draw from my book *Who Are We?* So the reader seeking full footnote information can turn to the footnotes in chapter 3 of that work.

23. This particular advertisement appeared in the spring of 1999, but one can troll for similar ads today and needn't look far. This is pretty much par for the course. See the *Commonweal* editorial, March 26, 1999, p. 5, in which this liberal lay Catholic journal editorialized that advertisements of this sort suggest that "we are fast returning to a world where persons carry a price tag, and where the cash value of some persons . . . is far greater than that of others." Soberer views from the scientific community also challenge some of these movements, noting that there is a difference between preventing some terminal illness, say, and the genetic "equivalent of cosmetic surgery," for the aim is to make people "taller, thinner, more athletic or more attractive." Scientist Dorris T. Zallen lists potential harms, including reinforcement of "irrational societal prejudices. For example, what would happen to short people if genetic enhancement were available to increase one's height? On this score the historical record is not encouraging." See Dorris T. Zallen, "We Need a Moratorium on 'Genetic Enhancement,'" *The Chronicle of Higher Education* (March 27, 1998), p. A4. When I was on a panel that testified before a subcommittee of the House Judiciary Committee, arguing in favor of a bill to ban human cloning, it was clear to me that the Democrats had lined up to oppose the bill because they viewed everything through the lens of abortion politics. This struck me as very sad, given that the Democratic party was once the party that stuck up for the weak and didn't see anything good in bolstering social prejudices.

24. Some of the most enthusiastic proponents of cloning now, as they did earlier, bring in "theology" or some warped version of it. One aggressive advocate of human cloning, for example, opined that Christians are supposed to be just like God, and God gave us the power to clone, so even God wants this done.

25. Alison M. Jaggar, *Feminist Politics and Human Nature* (Totowa, N.J.: Rowman and Allanheld, 1983), p. 132.

26. Philip Abbott, *The Family on Trial* (University Park: Pennsylvania State University Press, 1981), p. 138.

27. Michael Tooley, "Abortion and Infanticide," *The Rights and Wrongs of Abortion,* Marshall Cohen, Thomas Nagel, and Thomas Scanlon, eds. (Princeton: Princeton University Press, 1974), pp. 54–55.

28. I should note the suppression of discourse on this issue. Women are ridden out of the feminist town on the proverbial rail in the United States if they speak against abortion, or even issue some warnings about an unlimited abortion right, so strong is this orthodoxy. Even women who criticize feminists in other areas conform in this one, although they would never abort their own children. To take up this theme is—or at least at one point was—to be hissed off the stage, or at least steps were taken in that direction!

29. I have written a number of essays on this theme. The most recent, devoted exclusively to abortion, appeared in *Great Cases in Constitutional Law,* Robert George, ed. (Princeton: Princeton University Press, 2000), pp. 175–191. In this particular essay I use a dialogue form between an abortion advocate and myself, a troubled opponent who understands that there will always be abortions in the world and who wishes not to criminalize the activity but to undermine its current normative status as a singular right.

30. This citation is drawn from my piece "Reflections on Abortion, Values, and the Family," in *Abortion: Understanding Differences,* Sidney and Daniel Callahan, eds. (New York: Plenum Press, 1984), pp. 47–145, p. 58.

31. This is the view of Garrett Hardin endorsed by Lawrence Lader, *Abortion* (Indianapolis: Bobbs-Merrill, 1966), p. 156. Lader was a president of Planned Parenthood, a spin-off of Margaret Sanger's earlier operation. He, too, reflected a eugenics urge in his view of the "unwanted" and where they were most likely to come from. He is no "marginal" figure but an important spokesman and player in public discourse and public policy. One thing pro-abortion advocates tend to do, when they engage in polemics, is to argue that the people a critic is citing are somehow marginal figures, of little account.

32. *Ibid.,* p. 156.

33. Peter Singer, *Rethinking Life and Death* (New York: St. Martin's Press, 1994), pp. 132–158, and *Practical Ethics* (New York: Cambridge University Press, 1999). See also Mary Anne Warren, "On the Moral and Legal Status of Abortion," in Marshall Cohen, Thomas Nagel, and Thomas Scanlon, eds., *The Rights and Wrongs of Abortion* (Princeton: Princeton University Press, 1980). See also Mary Anne Warren, *Moral Status: Obligations to Persons and Other Living Things* (Oxford: Clarendon Press, 1997), pp. 201–234.

34. Jonathan Swift, *A Modest Proposal* (Needham, Mass.: Dover, 1996).

Notes to Pages 216–220

35. What is interesting about much of this—coming from nonphilosophers, from legalists or medically trained people—is that they have not examined, certainly not laid out and looked critically at, the theoretical perspective they have embraced.

36. See, for example, Susan Brownmiller, *Against Our Will to Power: Men, Women and Rape* (New York: Simon and Schuster, 1975), p. 131. See my critical review "Against Our Will to Power," in *Telos*, No. 39 (Winter 1976–1977), pp. 327–334.

37. See the feminist classic of that era, Shulamith Firestone, *The Dialectic of Sex* (New York: Bantam Books, 1972). I recall just how brave I felt when I criticized this book in a class I was teaching, Feminist Politics and Theory, some years ago. This led several students to appear in my office in tears because they couldn't bear having feminism criticized. When I pointed out to them that they couldn't consistently endorse radical, liberal, Marxist, and utopian feminism simultaneously, they seemed rather surprised. See the discussion under the "Radical Feminist" rubric in *Public Man, Private Woman* and in the essay I have cited on "The New Feminist Scholarship." Before this day of the feminist apocalypse arrived, some feminists of this sort recommended selective aborting of male fetuses. Critics called this stupendously sexist—which it was.

38. Sally Miller Gearhart, "The Future—If There Is One—Is Female," *Reweaving the Web of Life*, McAllister, ed. (Philadelphia, Penn.: New Society Publishers), pp. 244–284.

39. Barbara Love and Elizabeth Shanklin, "The Answer Is Matriarchy," in Joyce Trebilcot, ed., *Mothering: Essays in Feminist Theory* (Totowa, N.J.: Rowman and Allanheld, 1983), pp. 275–283. The nurturant model for all relationships conveniently forgets that children are not grown-ups; if that model is to hold throughout, someone must always remain a child.

40. See the section on radical feminism in *Public Man, Private Woman*. Also in the essay "The New Feminist Scholarship," *Salmagundi*, No. 70–71, pp. 3–26. It is in this essay that I first used the sex polarist categorization.

41. See my discussion in "The New Feminist Scholarship."

42. Michael Burleigh, *Death and Deliverance* (Cambridge: Cambridge University Press, 1994). The famous essay, published in 1920, "Permission for the Destruction of Life Unworthy of Life," added a scientific imprimatur to a developing prejudice. See p. 15.

43. See Robert N. Proctor's fascinating work, *The Nazi War on Cancer* (Princeton: Princeton University Press, 1999).

44. Dietrich Bonhoeffer, *Ethics* (New York: Simon and Schuster, 1995), p. 147. Bonhoeffer's discussion of nature and "the natural" appears on pp. 142–164.

45. Karla Poewe, *New Religions and the Nazis* (New York: Routledge, 2006), see pp. 10–11, p. 12, p. 24, p. 73, p. 120. Poewe writes that famous figures, including

Jakob Wilhelm Hauer of the German Faith Movement turned back to paganism and drew on elements of Eastern religion; somehow Hinduism and Buddhism were compatible with Nazism, where Judaism and Christianity were not. Since the Nazis regarded Christianity as being "Jewish," the church struggle was a core element of the "Nazi offensive to remove all traces of Jewish life from German society at the time"(p. 24). The church struggle refers to the struggle within German Protestant Christianity that pitted Bonhoeffer and members of the "confessing church" who remained faithful to orthodox Christian theology against the so-called Deutsche Christen, who succumbed to the lure of a purely Germanic Christianity.

46. One Ernst Bergmann, cited in Poewe, *Ibid.,* p. 73.

47. *Ibid.,* p. 74.

48. To this end, if Christianity was to be a part of the new Nazi dispensation, it had to be entirely Germanized, stripped of all Jewishness, and preach a German kingdom of God, a special German knowledge of God. This German faith had to combat the "nonsense" of Christ, which was scarcely a virile image.

49. Perhaps some of the mass killings and genocides and cleansings of the twentieth century have left a horrible imprint on us, so much so that we have internalized a view that human life is cheap and easily dispensed with. I don't know what all is driving this animus against the dead.

50. Cited in Elshtain, pp. 317–318.

51. Thucydides, *The Peloponnesian War,* especially his description of the horrors of the Sicilian campaign.

52. See P. D. James, *The Children of Men* (New York: Knopf, 1992).

CHAPTER 11

1. Camus, *The Rebel*, pp. 282–283.

2. *Auto-nomy*, literally "self-law, self-naming," a law unto oneself.

3. Albert Camus, *The First Man* (New York: Alfred A. Knopf, 1995), p. 195.

4. *Ibid.,* p. 195. This is not the way atheistic existentialists write. This is not the way they think—and that's why Camus insisted he was neither. To be a doubter or unbeliever does not make one an atheist, and Camus' insistence that he was not an existentialist tells us that he did, indeed, believe human beings have a nature—they don't just invent one.

5. Once again, I want to acknowledge the fact that the term *excarnation* is one I heard first from my friend, the philosopher Charles Taylor.

6. Roger Shattuck, *Forbidden Knowledge* (New York: Harcourt Brace, Vintage Books, 1996), p. 99.

7. Pope Benedict XVI, *Jesus of Nazareth* (New York: Doubleday, 2007), p. 228.

8. Primo Levi, *Survival in Auschwitz* (New York: Touchstone, 1996).

9. *Ibid.,* p. 17.

10. *Ibid.,* pp. 26, 37, 51.

11. *Ibid.,* p. 71.

12. *Ibid.,* p. 87.

13. Pope Benedict XVI tells us that the God of faith is, after all, defined by relationship—a God who is neither utterly transcendent nor reductively immanent. This in his masterful *Introduction to Christianity* (San Francisco: Ignatius Press, 1990).

14. Czeslaw Milosz, *The Captive Mind* (New York: Penguin Modern Classics, 2001).

15. Czeslaw Milosz, *The Witness of Poetry* (Harvard: Harvard University Press, 1984).

16. Marilynne Robinson, *Gilead* (New York: Farrar, Strauss, Giroux, 2004), p. 66.

17. *Ibid.,* p. 69.

18. McFadyen, *Bound to Sin* (Cambridge: Cambridge University Press, 2000), p. 61.

19. *Ibid.,* p. 83.

20. Bonhoeffer, *Ethics.* See pp. 142–164 for Bonhoeffer's full treatment of natural life and the body.

21. *Ibid.*

22. Dietrich Bonhoeffer, *Creation and Fall* (New York: MacMillan, 1959), p. 37.

23. Pope Benedict XVI, *Introduction to Christianity*, p. 160.

24. Vaclav Havel, "The Post-Communist Nightmare," *The New York Review of Books* (May 27, 1993), p. 8. 25. Camus, *The Rebel*, p. 5.

26. *Ibid.,* p. 11. This observation links Camus to St. Augustine's systematic unpacking of pride, *superbia.*

27. *Ibid.,* p. 14.

28. *Ibid.,* p. 22.

29. *Ibid.,* p. 42.

30. *Ibid.,* p. 130.

31. *Ibid.,* p. 209.

32. *Ibid.,* p. 250.

33. *Ibid.,* p. 277.

34. Albert Camus, *The Plague* (New York: Vintage International, 1975), p. 308.

AFTERWORD

1. This short reflection appeared originally in the December 1992 issue of *New Oxford Review*, pp. 16–17. It came back to me in a dream as belonging with this book, a premonitory little essay but also, it seems, a postscript.

INDEX